FAITHBOOK FOR CHRISTIAN COUNSELORS

By

Andrew V. Barber, PhD, LPCC, NCC

2016

Dedicated to Jesus Christ

Faithbook for Christian Counselors
© Copyright 2016 Andrew V. Barber

Published by Special Delivery Press
7121 Tierra Alta Ave.
El Paso, TX 79912
(915) 581-7303
werdna_rebrab@yahoo.com

LCCN: 2016903842

ISBN: 978-0-9669702-4-1

Author, Illustrator, and Cover Design: Andrew V. Barber

Subjects: 1. Counseling Methods
               2. Therapeutic Interventions
               3. Positive Change
               4. Faith and Hope
               5. Spirituality
               6. Christianity
               7. Holy Bible

TABLE OF CONTENTS

LIST OF FIGURES AND TABLES viii

INTRODUCTION ix

ABOUT THE AUTHOR xi

BOOKS OF THE BIBLE AND ABBREVIATIONS xii

EVIDENCE BASED PRACTICE 1
    Theoretical and Empirical Foundations 1
    Case Studies 4
    Multicultural Foundations 5
    Conclusions 6
    References 7

SPIRITUAL GROWTH IN COUNSELING 12
    Biblical Perspectives 12
    Christ Inspired Change 13
    Clinical Overview 15

CHRISTIAN COUNSELING PHILOSOPHY 19
    The Basics 19
    Helping Models 25
    Integrated Helping Model 27
    Spiritual Application 28

ASSESSMENT 31
    Clinical Diagnosis 31
    Spiritual Assessment 33
    Assessment Tools 34

DEVELOPMENT 40
    Goals Development 40
    Developmental Stages 42
    Conclusions 52
    Activity 53

TOOLS FOR CHANGE 57
    Spiritual Tools 57
    Staying Connected 62
    Activity 67
    Environmental Modifications 70
    More Changes 73
    Activity 79

TABLE OF CONTENTS

SELF- ESTEEM 83

    Ups and Downs 83
    Higher Powers 84
    Purposeful Living 86
    Activity 89

SELF- CONTROL MECHANISMS 92

    Managing Stress 92
    Activity 97
    Managing Anger 98
    Managing Pain 100
    Relaxation, Breathing and Imagery 106
    Overview of Self-Control 111

MOTIVATION 114

    Theoretical Framework 115
    Hierarchy of Needs 118
    God Meets Our Needs 122
    Conclusions 126
    Activity 128

ASSERTIVENESS 131

    Assertiveness Criteria 131
    Your Rights 133
    Assertiveness Techniques 138
    Activity 140
    Creative Thinking 142
    Activity 148

MAXIMIZING YOUR POTENTIAL 149

    Dreams and Visions 150
    Awareness of Unrealized Potential 151
    Making Connections 152
    Planning for Success 153
    Activity 156
    Creating a Vision 157
    Activity 160

IRRATIONAL THINKING 164

    Errors in Thinking 165
    Decision Making 174
    Activity 178
    Reality Testing 181
    Applications 183
    One Final Note 185

TABLE OF CONTENTS

EFFECTIVE COMMUNICATION 187

    Verbal Communication 187
    Nonverbal Communication 189
    Conclusions 193
    References 195
    Activity 196

OVERCOMING ADVERSITY 198

    Conquering Sin 200
    The Armor of God 204
    Activity 209

RESISTING TEMPTATION 212

    Lust 213
    Greed 215
    Pride 217
    Deceit 219
    Laziness 220
    Idolatry 221
    Activity 224

RESOLVING GUILT 227

    Healthy Guilt 227
    Response to Guilt 229
    Unhealthy Guilt 230
    Activity 233

RESENTMENT AND FORGIVENESS 234

    The Process of Resentment 234
    The Process of Forgiveness 240
    Conclusions 243
    Activity 245

BUILDING RELATIONSHIPS 247

    Friendship 247
    Marriage 248
    Parenthood 253
    Relationship with God 257
    The Household of Saints 259
    Activity 263
    The Impact of Relationships 264
    The Systems Model 265
    Activity 266

TABLE OF CONTENTS

CONFLICT RESOLUTION 269
    Internal Conflict 269
    Conflict with Others 271
    Activity 280

SUPPORT TEAMS 282
    Requirements of Members 284
    Obstacles to Success 287
    Definitions 289
    Process 290
    Activity 292

BEREAVEMENT 293
    Loss 293
    Stages of Grieving 294
    Activity 298

DUMPING THE EMOTIONAL BAGGAGE 299
    Physical Outlets 305
    Mental Outlets 306
    Spiritual Outlets 308
    Conclusions 310
    Activity 312

TRAUMA TREATMENT 314
    Conclusions 320

BAD HABITS 322
    Overindulgence 322
    Slippery Slope 324
    Choices 327
    Activity 330

ADDICTION 332
    Characteristics of Addicts 332
    Treating Addicts 334
    References 337
    Activity 338

SUICIDE PREVENTION 340
    Contributing Factors 341
    Therapeutic Interventions 342
    The Dilemma 343
    Suicide Risk Assessment 347
    Activity 349

TABLE OF CONTENTS

CURBING VIOLENCE 351
    Treatment 354
    References 355

ABUSE AND NEGLECT 356
    Definitions 356
    Warning Signs 357
    Contributing Factors and Consequences 359
    Prevention 361

MORALITY 364
    Activity 370
    The Four Pillars of Fate 371
    References 375
    Suffering 375

CARING AND DOING 380
    References 385
    Final Activity 386

INDEX 388

LIST OF FIGURES AND TABLES

THEORETICAL AND EMPIRICAL FOUNDATIONS	11
FAITH INSPIRED CHANGE	11
CREATED IN THE IMAGE OF GOD	18
ASSESSMENT	39
SAMPLE GANTT CHART	55
DEVELOPMENTAL STAGES	56
TOOLS FOR CHANGE	69
THE PROCESS OF CHANGE	82
UPS & DOWNS	91
SELF CONTROL	113
HIERARCHY OF NEEDS	130
YOUR RIGHTS	141
VISION OF HOPE	163
IRRATIONAL THINKING	180
COMMUNICATION SKILLS	197
THE ARMOR OF GOD	211
THE TEN COMMANDMENTS	226
PROCESS OF RESENTMENT	239
PROCESS OF FORGIVENESS	246
BUILDING RELATIONSHIPS	268
STRATEGIES FOR AVOIDING CONFLICT	281
HOLISTIC EXPRESSION	304
DUMPING EMOTIONAL BAGGAGE	313
SIGNS OF ADDICTION	339
SUICIDE RISK FACTORS	350
FRUIT OF THE SPIRIT	387

INTRODUCTION

Blessings to you from God our Father and our Lord Jesus Christ:

I have worked in the field of psychology, to include research, academia, and counseling, for 35 years. In my experience I have not seen a more powerful healing tool than faith. Certainly love is more powerful, and faith cannot exist without love; for if a person doesn't care he or she never will believe. But until a person believes, nothing will change. That's because they have no reason to try; faith is the best motivator.

I feel fortunate to have been raised in a Christian home, and to have kept the faith all the while, as I enjoy the autumn of my years. In working with students, clients, and patients I have witnessed the power of faith to overcome, change, move on, and achieve. The same is true for my own life. I expect God had a hand in my success, so I give him the credit that I was able to excel in a variety of professional arenas.

After completing 24 years of education, my thirst for knowledge remained unquenched. I had read and studied the Holy Bible but didn't know it as well I as thought I ought. So I turned to God's Word to continue my quest for wisdom and understanding. I've lost count how many times I've read the Bible, but rest assured there's more to come. My knowledge has grown exponentially; each time I am amazed at the learning. I have determined that one can never cease to gain from the insight of Biblical truth. You will expand your horizons further with each reading, even if you read the Bible 1000 times. Being a scientist by trade, I am not the least bit conflicted; rather astonished by the unmistakable accuracy, reliability, and truth of God's Word. But then again, only faith can allow the message to be so crystal clear. Such faith is bestowed by the Holy Spirit.

The change and growth provided by faith is a gift and a power of the spirit. To access this power one can look into the heart, the gate to the spiritual domain, and discover a love connection with God Almighty. He will speak; and if you listen you will know what is right and what is true. God's truth is absolute; it is the light of life which illuminates the path of righteousness. Anyone can plainly see the correct direction if focused on Christ; and God's Word will provide the roadmap. Those who believe will receive the limitless potential for becoming and overcoming.

I began to incorporate spirituality and principles of the Christian faith into my counseling approach about 20 years ago. While my own faith may have been evident, I did not share this with clients prior to that, as I had yet to realize how instrumental it can be to enhance the therapeutic experience. Research studies were coming to light demonstrating the power of faith and prayer, and it dawned on me the obvious connection. I began to incorporate spirituality judiciously, since it is considered politically incorrect in many circles. But employing faith in counseling has gained considerable momentum in the past five to ten years. Now we are seeing sound research proving faith based counseling to be an effective intervention – every bit as good if not better than conventional methods alone.

In recent years, faith and spirituality workshops, counseling workbooks, and associated certification and licensure programs have proliferated. I have studied a lot of these programs and materials, but have not found them to meet my needs. This is largely because they are too complicated or too simplified; they are not quite on target or they miss the point entirely; or they simply are not complete, particularly with respect to Biblical truth.

I have been developing and utilizing my own materials for years. The feedback from clients and practitioners has helped me to expand and refine these materials, to hone in on the essential truths, and to provide the tools that clients want and need. I also have taught licensed practitioners in the helping professions in the use of these tools during continuing education classes. It was the encouragement, feedback, and enthusiasm from professionals and clients that prompted me to publish this material. In fact, it was kind of their idea. I was content using a model that worked, that complimented my personal style, and that received a favorable response from clients and patients.

The success I have achieved using these techniques, exercises, and scriptures has been extraordinary. The degree and speed of change is far greater than any I ever achieved with alternative approaches. It seems unfair not to share this material with the rest of the world; hopefully you will find the methods useful and will obtain the kind of results I have. It all boils down to this: whatever works is worth trying. Not to discount the utility of some of the other models out there; I just didn't find any that worked for me. Of course, God always works. That's why I use a lot of scripture, as long as the audience is amenable to that. It's pretty hard to challenge the Word of God because the wisdom is profound and faultless. So whenever possible I use his words, because they are stronger than mine and can drive the point home much more deeply so it will take root.

It is my hope that the mainstream will acknowledge the efficacy of spiritually based programs and techniques; that they will be viewed as conventional, possibly even preferred, at least for people of faith. Certainly, the research and practical evidence bear witness that faith heals: body, mind, and spirit. Everybody can benefit from that. Even if the client is not interested in a faith based program, the concepts in this text can be understood generically and the activities applied without the scriptural component. If open to the idea, understanding could spark a spiritual awakening, given the difficulty to dismiss or argue with truth.

I would love to receive feedback from anyone that has incorporated my ideas into their practice. I welcome all comments, critiques, and criticisms. I do not pretend to have found the Holy Grail here as there is always room for improvement. Besides, I haven't fully quenched my thirst for knowledge. That's one reason I remain in this field: I learn from everyone, including the clients. So you counselors, teachers, and pastors out there – I'd like to learn from you too; do drop a line and let me know what you think.

Yours in Christ,

Andrew Barber, PhD, LPCC, NCC

ABOUT THE AUTHOR

Andrew Barber has a Doctorate in Psychology, Masters in Guidance and Counseling, and Bachelors in Art. He has had successful and prosperous careers as a Research Psychologist, Counselor/Therapist, and Academician. He has extensive skill in several disciplines to include Counseling (every age from 4 to 84), Teaching (every level from first grade through graduate school), Scientific Research (basic, clinical, and applied), Test and Evaluation (military systems), Human Factors Engineering, Defense Industry Consulting, Counselor Supervision, Program Management, and Executive Administration. He has numerous technical publications to his credit (over 30), has conducted high level briefings, and has presented research papers at professional conferences. Some of his works include the following reference books: *Fundamentals of Christianity: A Bible Study and Guide*, and *Research and Statistics for the Social Sciences*.

After honorably completing his military service as an Airborne Infantryman, he enrolled in college as an art student, earning his Bachelor of Arts Degree and becoming a Certified Teacher. Then he worked as a Caseworker and Counselor finishing his Master Degree in the field of Educational Psychology. His knowledge of experimental design and statistics, and his investigations with adolescent runaways, landed him into the field of psychological research. While working as a Military Scientist and Statistician, he completed his Doctorate Degree in Psychology, progressing to the level of Senior Research Psychologist. Eventually he became a Consultant to the Defense Industry, providing expertise in the areas of human behavior and performance, test and evaluation, ergonomics, man-machine systems, research methodology and experimentation, and technical proposal writing. He held security clearances up to Top Secret/NATO Secret.

Then Dr. Barber returned to academia and counseling, setting up his own clinical practice. He became a Professor of Counseling, Psychology, Religion, and other subjects and eventually was recruited to serve as the Campus Chair for the College of Social and Behavioral Sciences at a major university. After two years he was promoted to Director of Academic Affairs where he oversaw two major campuses. Next he was the Director of Clinical Support Services at a Community Health Center, where he served as resident Psychotherapist and Director of Mental Health and Health Education operations for three clinics. He later served as Lead Therapist, Program Manager, and Department Director at a regional Psychiatric Hospital (160 beds). Dr. Barber has continuously maintained a private practice in Counseling and Consulting for 25 years. He has accumulated over 500 Continuing Education Units (CEU) in Counseling and Psychology and has taught a number of CEU courses over the years. He previously served several years as a Clinical Consultant with the American Society of Clinical Hypnosis (ASCH). He has been an active member of the American Association of Christian Counselors (AACC) almost since its inception.

You may contact Andrew Barber using the following email address.
werdna_rebrab@yahoo.com

BOOKS OF THE BIBLE AND ABBREVIATIONS

Old Testament

BOOK	ABBREV.	BOOK	ABBREV.
Genesis	GEN	Ecclesiastes	ECC
Exodus	EXO	Song of Solomon	SOS
Leviticus	LEV	Isaiah	ISA
Numbers	NUM	Jeremiah	JER
Deuteronomy	DEU	Lamentations	LAM
Joshua	JOS	Ezekiel	EZE
Judges	JDG	Daniel	DAN
Ruth	RUT	Hosea	HOS
1 Samuel	1 SA	Joel	JOE
2 Samuel	2 SA	Amos	AMO
1 Kings	1 KI	Obadiah	OBA
2 Kings	2 KI	Jonah	JON
1 Chronicles	1 CH	Micah	MIC
2 Chronicles	2 CH	Nahum	NAH
Ezra	EZR	Habakkuk	HAB
Nehemiah	NEH	Zephaniah	ZEP
Esther	EST	Haggai	HAG
Job	JOB	Zechariah	ZEC
Psalms	PSA	Malachi	MAL
Proverbs	PRO		

New Testament

BOOK	ABBREV.	BOOK	ABBREV.
Matthew	MAT	1 Timothy	1 TI
Mark	MAR	2 Timothy	2 TI
Luke	LUK	Titus	TIT
John	JOH	Philemon	PHM
Acts	ACT	Hebrews	HEB
Romans	ROM	James	JAM
1 Corinthians	1 CO	1 Peter	1 PE
2 Corinthians	2 CO	2 Peter	2 PE
Galatians	GAL	1 John	1 JO
Ephesians	EPH	2 John	2 JO
Philippians	PHP	3 John	3 JO
Colossians	COL	Jude	JDE
1 Thessalonians	1 TH	Revelation	REV
2 Thessalonians	2 TH		

EVIDENCE BASED PRACTICE

Theoretical and Empirical Foundations

Faith based approaches have increased in popularity among clinicians and their clients in recent years (Buckholtz, 2005; Smith, 1996). More people are seeking practitioners with experience and knowledge of spirituality in general and the Holy Bible in particular (Paul & Asnin, 2005). This has resulted in a marked increase in faith-trained professionals. In fact, many reputable medical schools are incorporating spirituality training into their curriculum (Gunderson, 2000; Moore, 1996). A recent survey showed that 90% of medical schools in the USA incorporate spiritualty in some fashion into their curricula (Koenig, et al, 2010). As a result, networking has by necessity begun to include faith teachers, clergymen/women, churches, and associated spiritual communities and support groups (SAMSHA, 2005).

Fundamental to this philosophy is the holistic health perspective: to be completely (wholly) healthy, one must be well in body, mind, and spirit. Research has proven time and again the great healing potential of spirituality, faith and prayer (Astin, et al., 2000; Schlitz & Braud, 1997). The driving force is faith, without which change, growth and healing are much slower and less apparent. Religious people tend to be healthier overall (Ellison & Levin, 1998). Religiosity and spirituality provide a positive influence on our lives in many respects (Koenig, 2012). They help us to cope, to be moral, to render aid to others, to care about people and ourselves, to be prosocial and altruistic, and to stay out of trouble. They provide courage to face challenges, illnesses, and setbacks, and they promote long and happy lives.

Given that 80% of Americans have a worldview based on the traditional Judeo-Christian foundation (see Pew, 2007), and 65% of Americans consider religion to be an integral part of their life (see Gallop, 2009) it seems intuitively obvious the value of spiritual and faith based approaches in dealing with mental health, physical wellness, and social problems in this country. This would be true especially for people of faith, who prefer and respond better when religious/spiritual discussions and interventions are introduced during the course of counseling (Harris, et.al, 2015; Propst, et. al, 1992).

Let us begin with the connection between spirituality and mental health. The facts bear out that people of faith have fewer psychological problems. Numerous studies have shown that suicide risk is lowest among people with religious convictions: up to four times lower (see Gartner, et. al, 1991). Those who frequently pray are less likely to become stressed, depressed, or suffer anxiety, even after a stressful event (Koenig, McCulloch & Larson, 2001; Larson, Swyers, & McCollough, 1997). Four dimensions of spiritual wellness were negatively correlated with depression in older adolescents and midlife adults, with meaning and purpose in life being the underlying theme for wellness (Briggs & Shoffner, 2006). In a Canadian study (Moritz, et al., 2006), improvement in patients with mood disturbance was significantly greater ($p < .05$) for the home study spirituality group (46%) than a classroom meditation group (26%); this difference was far more powerful when comparing the spirituality group with the control (no intervention) group ($p < .001$). In another study, 71% of mental health patients reported spiritual life as having been significant to their recovery (Bussema &

Bussema, 2007). Research conducted by Francis and Kaldor (2002), found high positive correlations between psychological well-being and church attendance, belief in God, and personal prayer ($p < .001$).

Spiritual intervention in combination with Cognitive-Behavioral Therapy (CBT) has been well established as a valid treatment for depression and anxiety, as good if not better than CBT alone (Hodge, 2006; Hook, et. al, 2010; Worthington, et. al, 2011). In a study by Propst and her colleagues (1992), treatment outcomes were significantly better for depressed, religious patients that received religion based counseling ($p < .001$). Both pastoral counseling (PCT) and CBT with a religious component (RCT) yielded significantly lower depression scores than the waiting list control group (WLC) at posttest ($p < .05$); but the CBT regimen without a religious component (NRCT) did not. A surprising finding was that this effect was particularly true when the RCT group was administered by therapists who themselves were not religious; in fact, the non-religious therapists performed better in the RCT condition than they did in the NRCT condition as measured by lower depression scores ($p < .02$). To repeat, not only do people of faith prefer counseling with a religious slant, they also appear to benefit more from such an approach, even if the practitioners are not faith oriented.

Faith and spirituality are central to the success of Alcoholics Anonymous (AA) and other Twelve Step programs. AA involvement is the most prevalent indicator of continued sobriety (Oakes, et al., 2000; Project Match, 1998); spiritual support, openness, and religious faith practice were found to be key indicators of abstinence and AA attendance. In the context of working the steps, a spiritual awakening seems the catalyst for change and recovery (Zemore, 2007). Staton and associates (2003) found spirituality and worship to be negatively correlated with alcohol and drug abuse among male prison inmates. Applied to substance abuse, prayer was influential in helping people cope, reducing behavior that could lead to relapse, and increasing self-esteem (Larson, et al., 1997).

The research on the beneficial effects of prayer is not limited to mental health; physical health also shows improvement with contemplative prayer. Several researchers have demonstrated the power of prayer to cure physical ailments (Becker, 2000; Janet, 1998; Benson, 1996). Further, the power of prayer is exhibited, not only in personal meditation, but also in prayers conducted by those interceding on behalf of others. Patients who were admitted to a coronary care unit (CCU) showed improvements in patient medical outcomes as a result of intercessory prayer (Harris, 1999). In an earlier study of CCU patients (Byrd, 1997), intercessory prayer was associated with less congestive heart failure, fewer diuretic and antibiotic administrations, fewer episodes of pneumonia, fewer cardiac arrests, and less frequent intubations and ventilations. Interestingly, prayer even showed significant differences ($p < .05$) when the subjects were bush babies with self-inflicted wounds (Lesniak, 2006). In that study, animals in the prayer group showed significant reduction in wound size, increase in red blood cells, and reduction in wound grooming over that of non-prayer group animals. These results suggest that health improvements influenced by intercessory prayer do not require the object of the prayers be human beings. In a comprehensive study sponsored by the American Cancer Society (Gansler, et al., 2008), cancer survivors were inclined to employ the following complementary methods in their recovery: prayer/spiritual practice (61%), relaxation (44%), faith healing (42%), nutritional supplements (40%), meditation (15%), religious counseling (11%), massage therapy (11%), and support groups (10%).

Kliewer's review of the literature (2004) revealed ample studies that demonstrated improvement in physical and mental health as a function of the spirituality of the patients. Improvements in disease outcomes, reductions in hypertension, better lipid profiles, lower cholesterol levels, and improved immune functioning were among the physiological benefits revealed. Psychological benefits included less stress and depression, lower suicide rates, and longer lives for those who were faith oriented. Thus, spirituality appears to be a common denominator for achieving well-being in both mind and body, not to mention spirit.

Possibly the most comprehensive meta-analysis ever undertaken is that of Koenig and associates who examined empirical, peer-reviewed research conducted over the course of the past 150 years and comprising some 3300+ studies looking at the effect of religion/spirituality (R/S) on heath (physical and mental), personality, and social issues. Out of 454 total studies dealing with physical heath, an "overwhelming majority" showed a significant positive relationship between R/S and healing, coping with illness, and dealing with the effects of aging, dementia, and other maladies. Of those studies occurring prior to the year 2000 focusing on mental health, roughly two thirds (476/724) showed a significant positive relationship with R/S (see Koenig, 2009). Noteworthy highlights of this massive undertaking are described below (Koenig, 2012).

With respect to overall wellbeing and happiness the following results were reported. Of 256 studies, R/S was significantly associated with wellbeing in 79% of the studies; only 1% found a significant negative relationship. Related subjects such as hope (73%), optimism (81%), meaning/purpose (93%), self-esteem (63%), and character (70%), also were positively correlated with R/S. Very few of these studies showed a negative association (3% or less). Koenig also examined personality traits and found the following relationships. Risk taking (irresponsibility) was inversely related to R/S 84% of the time; conscientiousness was positively related to R/S 63% of the time; and agreeableness 87% of the time.

Concerning depression, 61% showed R/S to be negatively correlated (6% reported the opposite finding). Cohort studies of R/S predicted lower levels of depression or faster recovery 56% of the time; 10% reported greater depression, and 10% were mixed (inconclusive). In clinical trial studies of depression, 63% showed better treatment outcomes with R/S interventions than both standard treatment methods and control groups; two studies showed standard treatment as superior (7%) and one study had conflicting findings. Looking at the rigorous studies (most sound experimental approaches) 55% showed a negative relationship between R/S and anxiety; 10% showed the opposite result. And regarding psychosis or schizophrenia, 33% reported a negative relationship with R/S, and 23% a positive relationship. While these results seem mixed, psychotic reactions often have religious content (such as delusions of grandeur or auditory/command hallucinations) which would confound the findings and their interpretation.

Social problems also were investigated. Not surprisingly, 240/278 studies of alcohol abuse/dependency (86%) showed a negative association with R/S (only 1% showed a positive association). Similar findings were reported for drug abuse: 84% versus 1%, respectively. With respect to crime, 79% reported negative relationships with R/S (3% reported positive relationships). For social support, 82% of the studies showed a positive association with R/S. For marital instability, 86% reported negative associations with R/S.

With respect to physical health issues the prevailing trend was that R/S promotes health and healing as seen in the lion share of the literature. The following results were gleaned from those studies with the most rigorous methodologies, proving that R/S promotes sound mind and body: heart disease (69%), hypertension (62%), cognitive functioning among sufferers of Alzheimer's/Dementia (57%), immune function (71%), cancer (60%), and pain management (50%). Furthermore, longevity was positively associated with R/S in 75% of rigorous studies (5% showed the opposite trend). Similarly, suicide risk measures were significantly lower as a function of R/S; 75% of the studies reported a negative correlation and 3% a positive one. Understandably, results were commensurate across variables such as suicide, depression, hope, and self-esteem, revealing the positive effect of R/S.

Case Studies

In the paragraphs that follow, a few examples are provided illustrating the success I have achieved in the lives of thousands of clients over two decades, using the integrated holistic approach proposed herein. An objective examination of cases occurring between October, 2005 and March, 2006 revealed very encouraging findings. The clientele being studied consisted of mostly low income Hispanic individuals, of primarily Catholic orientation (including kids, adults, and the elderly).

During that timeframe I had 53 patients exhibiting major depression; the mean (self-reported) level of depression at intake was 7.8 out of 10 (78%). After an average of 4 hours of therapy, the mean depression level was 3.2 (32%). This represents a reduction in depression (as perceived by the clients) of 59% (78-32=46; 46/78=59%). There were 59 patients demonstrating high anxiety; the mean (self-reported) level of anxiety was 8.1 out of 10 (81%). After an average of 4 hours of therapy, the mean anxiety level was 3.7 (37%). This represents a reduction in anxiety (as perceived by the clients) of 54% (81-37=44; 44/81=54%).

Thus, after four sessions, client symptoms for this sample had been lessened by over half. Keep in mind that treatment continued for most of these clients, so there was further reduction, if not elimination of symptoms by the conclusion of therapy. Note that the holistic approach being employed involved integration of services with Primary Care Providers, such that spiritual, mental, and physical health interventions were coordinated. This study provides direct evidence of the utility of the integrated method. Evidence from the literature clearly indicates the efficacy of incorporating spirituality into therapy, and this has been my experience as well.

The first case study that exemplifies the success of this strategy involved a 34 year old woman presenting severe anxiety and panic attacks. Contributing to her stress level were anger, fear, and guilt. The anxiety also caused disturbance in her sleeping. Cognitive-

Behavioral Therapy was employed to help her identify the negative self-thoughts that were consuming her, and to help her refocus on things that were positive and true (much of the negative thinking consisted of lies she was telling herself). Her once great faith in God and her desire to reconnect spiritually with the Lord helped her find the inner strength to move forward with her life and to dispose of the emotional baggage that hindered forward progress. She immediately began attending church more frequently, prayed continuously, and began helping at an outreach ministry for the poor and needy. Her spirit was so uplifted that after only three sessions she was exhibiting zero symptoms (for example, her self-reported anxiety level had fallen from 9/10 to 0/10). Periodic phone follow-ups at two week intervals confirmed that she was still doing great and her anxiety had remained in check. This case is a prime example of the combination of the healing power of faith in God, mental health counseling, and the success that can be achieved with brief psychotherapy. Note that these changes occurred without medication.

The second case involved a 32 year old male, who was seeking to curb what he viewed as an addiction to sex, which he had agonized over many years. He exhibited high levels of depression and anxiety brought on by guilt, anger, and fear. His self-esteem was in the gutter. This was the result of physical, sexual, and emotional abuse experienced as a child, his association with gangs as a teen, and his exposure to repeated violence. These emotions manifested themselves in aggressive acting-out behavior and sexual promiscuity. He felt consumed with lust, which resulted in contracting a venereal disease. These experiences and emotions contributed to suicidal ideations. However, his desire for education and rehabilitation led him to seek individual therapy and he also joined a sex addiction support group. His newfound faith was a source of strength for him as he fought to prevent himself from acting on his sexual thoughts. Thus, the craving was still there but he subdued the compulsion. Through Cognitive-Behavioral Therapy he managed to restructure his thinking and he developed more adaptive behaviors. This was reinforced through positive imagery, spiritual growth, and deliberate changes in his environment. After a few sessions, the therapy took on a more interpersonal slant, as we continued to explore his needs, motivation, goals, and purpose in life. His progress continued to increase in a very positive manner, as he significantly raised his standards of morality and responsibility. After six sessions, he was well on his way, but he desired to continue the therapy because he found it enlightening and inspirational. The most fundamental changes were his ability to resist temptation, to control his thoughts, and to maintain fidelity with his significant other, as well as developing an active church life. It was apparent that he had no intention of falling back to his old ways because a new path was being presented before him.

Multicultural Foundations

Spiritual counseling is not for everyone. During the initial interview, the client's religious or spiritual orientation should be determined. The degree to which religion/faith plays a role in his or her life is of vital importance. If the person is interested in exploring spiritual growth during the course of therapy, then faith-oriented goals and related alternative behaviors may be added to the treatment plan. If the client declines such interventions, or a desire to avoid spirituality is communicated, that perspective must be respected.

Some people do not have and do not desire a religious or spiritual foundation and therefore are uninterested in spiritual growth as a goal of therapy. That is why a person's religious orientation must be identified during the assessment process, and why addressing faith issues should be optional. Clients also have the freedom of changing their minds and introducing or discontinuing a technique or treatment later in therapy. Remember, it's all about choice and free will, rights given to us by God.

Counseling certification programs require coursework in Multicultural Foundations. Since many patients would choose to incorporate spirituality into their counseling, this dimension becomes an essential part of the training. Counselor competency and effectiveness are reflected in a comprehensive assessment of the gender, culture, and spirituality of each client (Passalacqua & Cervantes, 2008). Examination of the person's cultural background usually will indicate their religious orientation, which is often a significant element of their lives. Spiritual well-being and psychological well-being were significantly correlated in a Texas study of Mexican-American Catholics conducted by Ramirez and his colleagues (2007). In a study of inner city psychiatric patients (Wong-McDonald, 2007), 100% of those attending a weekly spirituality group as part of their treatment achieved their life skill goals, compared to 57% who attended a different group during that hour ($p < .0001$). Clearly, some cultural aspects are reflected in faith preferences.

Our forefathers died standing for and protecting such freedoms as speech, assembly, and religion. These liberties are fundamental to our Constitution, Bill of Rights, and Declaration of Independence. We are required by law to refrain from discriminating against anyone on the basis of their ethnicity, religion, sex, or handicap. The Civil Rights Act of 1964 protects all Americans from being prevented to vote, work, or use public facilities. This law also applies to access to mental and physical healthcare. Thus, we are bound to recognize and accommodate such differences, and this necessitates Multicultural Foundations instruction. It follows that we should not only respect and understand culture and religion, but also address it in practice. However, if the client declines such intervention as an intrusion into his or her privacy, that right would take precedence.

Conclusions

A review of the research by Larimore and colleagues (2002) concluded the following: A positive relationship between spirituality and mental and physical health is plainly evident in the literature. Worthington and associates (2011) confirmed that faith based counseling is every bit as effective as traditional approaches, with the added benefit of spiritual growth. Clients generally prefer the option of including spirituality in their treatment, and may avoid professionals that do not provide that option. While clinicians acknowledge the importance of spirituality they lack training in this area. Education programs are beginning to incorporate spirituality as a means to facilitate therapy. Practitioners receiving such training find it an invaluable asset and apply it regularly. While there is a plethora of research indicating the benefits of infusing spirituality into counseling, there is scant evidence suggesting that this treatment approach is harmful in any way. Of course it is not recommended for people who decline this option.

A great number of agencies and institutions are requiring evidence-based practices (see Chorpita, 2000; Drake, et al., 2001; Hoagwood, et al., 2001; Torrey, et al., 2001; Weissman, et. al., 2000). This is especially true of organizations funded by private or government entities, which provide support only if the techniques used have been proven effective empirically. For example, the effectiveness of Cognitive-Behavioral Therapy (CBT) in treating anxiety and depression has been well researched and established (NIMH, 1999a; 1999b). Adding spirituality to the treatment regimen has been proven to enhance the therapeutic experience, with equal or better results than conventional methods such as CBT (Propst, et. al, 1992), and for a variety of mental illnesses as well (Hook, et. al, 2010). Additionally, faith based techniques are quite compatible with traditional counseling practices, because spiritual soundness is an essential component of holistic health.

Professional organizations have advocated the training, and even licensure, of faith based counseling professionals. This movement is warranted given the proven utility of spirituality as a catalyst for growth and change. Spiritually focused approaches have gained considerable momentum and found their way into diverse applications. In fact, spiritual growth may become the preferred method for attaining particular goals, as is the case with reorientation approaches to assist homosexuals who long to leave that lifestyle (Medinger, 2000; Shaw, 2005; Spitzer, 2003; Yarwood, 1998). Many of these individuals actually become heterosexual, or otherwise choose celibacy.

Some organizations and practitioners reject such intervention, arguing that homosexuals are normal and should not be encouraged to change. But who are we to dictate to the client what changes are moral or not? Clients can articulate what they value and what troubles them. Our job is to facilitate goal setting, healing and growth, not to judge clients. If what they are doing is wrong in their minds, it is not our place to persuade them it is not. We can help them determine what is right and lawful in accordance with their belief system, without imposing ours. Spiritual focus seems to facilitate change more than anything, especially when the client desires a revision in his or her moral compass.

References

Astin, J., Harkness, E., Ernst, E., & Krucoff, M. (2000). The efficacy of distant healing: A systematic review of randomized trials. *Alternative Therapies in Health & Medicine, 6*(5).

Becker, N. B. (2000) Study shows prayer is powerful medicine. *Alternative Therapies in Health and Medicine, 6*(1), 28.

Benson, H. (1996). Should you consult God? *Prevention, 48*(12), 60-67.

Bussema, E. F., & Bussema, K. E. (2007). Gilead revisited: Faith and recovery. *Psychiatric Rehabilitation Journal, 30*(4), 301-305.

Briggs, M. K., & Shoffner, M. F. (2006). Spiritual wellness and depression: Testing a theoretical model with older adolescents and midlife adults. *Counseling and Values, 51*(1), 5-20.

Byrd, R. C. (1997). Positive therapeutic effects of intercessory prayer in a CCU population. *Alternative Therapies in Health and Medicine, 3*(6), 87-90.

Buckholtz, A. (2005). Help from above in times of trouble: Growing numbers of people take comfort in faith based therapy. *The Washington Post*, December 06, 2005.

Chorpita, B. (2000). The frontier of evidence-based practice. In A. Kazdin and J. Weisz (Eds.) *Evidence-based psychotherapies for children and adolescents*. NY: Guilford Press.

Drake, R. E., Goldman, H. H., Leff, H. S., et al. (2001). Implementing evidence-based practices in routine mental health service settings. *Psychiatric Services, 52*, 179-182.

Ellison, C. G., & Levin, J. S. (1998). The religion-health connection: Evidence, theory, and future directions. *Health Education and Behavior. 25(6)*, 700-720.

Francis, L. J., & Kaldor, P. (2002). The relationship between psychological well-being and Christian faith and practice in an Australian population. *Journal for the Scientific Study of Religion, 41*(1), 179-184.

Gallup Poll. (2009). *State of the States: Importance of Religion.*
http://www.gallup.com/poll/114022/State-States-Importance-Religion.aspx.

Gansler, T., Kaw, C., Crammer, C., & Smith, T. (2007). A population-based study of prevalence of complementary method use by cancer survivors. *Cancer, 113*(5), 1048-1057.

Gartner, J., Lawson, D., & Allen, G. (1991). Religious commitment and mental health: A review of the empirical literature. *Journal of Psychology and Theology. 19*(1). 6-25.

Gunderson, L. (2000). Faith and healing. *Annals of Internal Medicine. 132*(2), 169-172.

Harris, J., Nienow, T., Choi, A., Engdahl, B., Nguyen, X., & Thomas, P. (2015). Client report of spirituality in recovery from serious mental illness. *Psychology of Religion and Spirituality, 7*(2), 142-149.

Harris, W. S. (1999). A randomized controlled trial of the effects of remote intercessory prayer on outcomes in patients admitted to the coronary care unit. *Archives of Internal Medicine. 159*, 2273-2278.

Hoagwood, K. Burns, B., Kiser, L., Ringeisen, H., & Schoenwald, S. (2001). Evidenced-based practice in child and adolescent mental health services. *Psychiatric Services. 52(9)*, 1179-1189.

Hodge, D. R. (2006). Spiritually modified cognitive therapy: A review of the literature. *Social Work, 51*(2), 157-166.

Hook, J. N., Worthington, E., Davis, D., Jennings, D., Gartner, A., & Hook, J. P. (2010). Empirically supported religious and spiritual therapies. *Journal of Clinical Psychology*, 66(1), 46-72.

Janet, P. (1998). Can prayer heal? *Health, 12*(2), 12(2), 48-54.

Kliewer, S. (2004). <u>Allowing spirituality into the healing process</u>. *Journal of Family Practice, 53*(8), 616-624.

Koenig, H. G. (2009). Research on Religion, Spirituality, and Health: A Review. *Canadian Journal of Psychiatry, 54* (5), 283-291.

Koenig, H. G. (2012). *Religion, Spirituality, and Health: The Research and Clinical Implications.* New York: ISRN Psychiatry.

Koenig, H., Hooten, E., Lindsay-Calkins, E., & Meador, K. (2010). Spirituality in medical school curricula: Findings from a national survey. *International Journal of Psychiatry in Medicine, 40* (4), 391-398.

Koenig, H., McCollough, M., & Larson, D. (2001). *Handbook of Religion and Health.* New York: Oxford University Press.

Larimore, W., Parker, M., & Crowther, M. (2002). Should clinicians incorporate positive spirituality into their practices? What does the evidence say? *Annals of Behavioral Medicine, 24*(1), 69-73

Larson, J. S., Swyers, J. P., & McCollough, M. E. (1997). *Scientific research on spirituality and health: A consensus report.* Radnor, PA: Templeton Press.

Lesniak, K. T. (2006). <u>The effect of intercessory prayer on wound healing in nonhuman primates</u>. *Alternative Therapies in Health & Medicine. 12*(6), 42-48.

Medinger, A. (2000). *Growth into manhood: Resuming the journey.* Colorado Springs, CO: Harold Shaw Publishers.

Moore, N. G. (1996). Spirituality in medicine. *Alternative Therapies in Health and Medicine. 2*(6), 24-29.

Moritz, S., Quan, H., Rickhi, B., Mingfu, L., Angen, M., Vintila, R., Sawa, R., Soriano, J., & Toews, J. (2006). A home study-based spirituality education program decreases emotional distress and increases quality of life – A randomized controlled trial. *Alternative Therapies in Health and Medicine, 12*(6), 26-35.

National Institute of Mental Health (1999). Anxiety Disorders Research at the NIMH. http://www.nimh.nih.gov/publicat/anxresfact.cfm.

National Institute of Mental Health (1999). Depression Research at the NIMH. http://www.nimh.nih.gov/publicat/depresfact.cfm.

Oakes, K. E., Allen, J. P., & Ciarrocchi, J. W. (2000). Spirituality, religious problem-solving, and sobriety in Alcoholics Anonymous. *Alcoholism Treatment Quarterly, 18*(2), 37-50.

Passalacqua, S., & Cervantes, J. (2008). Understanding gender and culture within the context of spirituality: Implications for counselors. *Counseling and Values, 52*(3), 224-239.

Paul, P., & Asnin, M. (2005). With God as my shrink. *Psychology Today, 38*(3), 62.

Pew Research Forum: Religion and Public Life Project (2007). U.S. Religious Landscape Survey. http://religions.pewforum.org/reports.

Project Match Research Project (1998). Matching alcoholism treatments to client herogeneity: Project Match three-year drinking outcomes. *Alcoholism: Clinical and Experimental Research, 22,* 1300-1311.

Propst, L., Ostrom, R., Watkins, P., Dean, T., & Mashburn, D. (1992). Comparative efficacy of religious and nonreligious cognitive-behavioral therapy for the treatment of clinical depression in religious individuals. *Journal of Consulting and Clinical Psychology, 60*(1), 94-103.

Ramirez, A., Lumadue, C., & Wooten, H. (2007). Spiritual well-being and psychological well-being in Mexican-American Catholics. *Journal of Professional Counseling: Practice, Theory and Research, 35*(2), 46-61.

SAMSHA National Mental Health Information Center (2005). Alternative Approaches to Mental Health Care. http://www.mentalhealth.samhsa.gov/publications/allpubs/ken98-0044.

Schlitz, M., & Braud, W. (1997). Distant intentionality and healing: Assessing the evidence. *Alternative Therapies in Health & Medicine, 3*(6).

Shaw, J. A. (2005). A pathway to spirituality. *Psychiatry, 68*(4), 350-362.

Smith, L. (1996). Faith based therapy gaining adherents. *Baltimore Sun,* 10-22-96.

Spitzer, R. L. (2003). Can some gay men and lesbians change their sexual orientation? 200 participants reporting a change from homosexual to heterosexual orientation. *Archives of Sexual Behavior, 32*(5). 403-417.

Staton, M., Webster, J., Hitler, M., Rostosky, S., & Leukefeld, C. (2003). An exploratory examination of spiritual well-being, religiosity, and drug use among incarcerated men. *Journal of Social Work Practice in the Addictions, 3*(3), 87-103.

Torrey, W. C., Drake, R. E., Dixon, L., et al. (2001). Implementing evidence-based practices for persons with severe mental illnesses. *Psychiatric Services, 52,* 45-50.

Weissman, M. M., Markowitz, J. C., Klerman, G. L. (2000). *Comprehensive guide to interpersonal psychotherapy.* New York: Basic Books.

Wong-McDonald, A. (2007). Spirituality and psychosocial rehabilitation: Empowering persons with serious psychiatric disabilities at an inner-city community program. *Psychiatric Rehabilitation Journal, 32*(4), 295-300.

Worthington, E., Hook, J., Davis, D., & McDaniel, M. (2011). Religion and spirituality. *Journal of Clinical Psychology: In Session, 67*(2), 204-214.

Yarwood, M. A. (1998). When clients seek treatment for same-sex attraction: Ethical issues in the 'Right to Choose' debate. *Psychotherapy, 35,* 248-259.

Zemore, S. E. (2007). A role for spiritual change in the benefits of 12-step involvement. *Alcoholism: Clinical and Experimental Research, 31*(S3), 76-79.

THEORETICAL AND EMPIRICAL FOUNDATIONS

- Demand for Faith Based Approaches
- Studies on Faith and Prayer:
  Physical Health, Mental Health
- Biblical Concepts of Faith and Healing
- Holistic Health Perspective:
  Body, Mind, Spirit

FAITH INSPIRED CHANGE

- Change of Heart
- Acting on Faith
- Holistic Expression
- Positive Thinking
- Looking Ahead
- Power of Love
- Spiritual Guidance

SPIRITUAL GROWTH IN COUNSELING

Biblical Perspectives

The healing power of faith is found repeatedly in the Holy Bible. Those to whom Christ and the apostles ministered were healed because they had faith (MAT 14:35-36; ACT 3:16). The very fact that a person seeks help is because they believe they can get better (JAM 5:13-16; ROM 8:26-28; MAR 9:17-27). This belief could be in God, oneself, the therapeutic process, the skill of a professional, or something else; but the underlying force behind their hope of getting better is faith (HEB 11:1). If a person doesn't believe he or she can get better, there is no incentive to try. It comes as no surprise that a spiritually based approach would be especially valuable for a person of faith.

Patients often arrive with medical problems as well as mental health issues. Many of these people have lost their spiritual focus; they are seeking comfort that only can come from God (MAT 11:28; 2 CO 12:9-10; JOH 15:26). Oftentimes, what they need is to reconnect with their spiritual identity and become more hopeful and purposeful (ROM 5:5). A spiritual weakness or emptiness can adversely affect a person's mental and physical health, whereas spiritual strengthening would have an equally positive effect (MAT 9:22; MAR 10:52; LUK 17:19; ACT 3:16).

Great success has been achieved by integrating faith based counseling with traditional approaches, regardless of the person's religion. While several counseling sessions are usually required for measurable change (say around 10), I have seen such change occur in only a few sessions (3-4). That is because change is the goal, and the person believes they can change, and they believe God can help them achieve their goals. And, although you cannot change anyone but yourself, the love of God can change anybody (1 JO 4:9). Such change is immediate, extensive, and lasting (2 CO 3:18; 2 CO 5:17).

Holistic health defines the individual as possessing three components: physical, mental, spiritual. So also, the treatment or cure should integrate all three. We are created in the image of God, who manifests himself to us in three eternal personifications: Father, Son, and Holy Spirit (ISA 48:16; JOH 1:1; 1 JO 5:7-8; MAT 28:19-20). We are like God in many ways. We have a spiritual presence: God the Holy Spirit gives us life (JOH 6:63). Growth is enabled if we stay connected to God spiritually (JOH 15:5). We have a physical presence: God the Son is a perfect human example of obedience and righteousness (1 PE 2:21-22). Wonderful things happen when we follow his example (JOH 13:15-17). We have a mental component: God the Father gives us the Law and a discerning mind that can distinguish good and evil (GEN 3:22; JOH 8:32). Obedience to God makes us more like Christ (EPH 5:1-2).

We have free will to obey or disobey God (DEU 30:19). That is, we make our own choices; and we can choose to change and we can choose the right path (MAT 6:33). We have an inherent ability to know the difference between truth and untruth, and to discern right from wrong. This is our connection to God: call it the conscience, the heart of hearts, the spirit, or whatever you want, but you know what I am talking about. It is a greater power that all humans possess, and it is our connection to the highest power (ROM 8:16; 1 JO 3:24).

Christ Inspired Change

Change begins with a change of heart, because when the Lord enters the heart everything becomes new (2 CO 5:17). God is love and the love of God changes everything. This enables a change in belief. For example, "I can do this, with the help of the Lord" (PHP 4:13; JOH 15:5). Facilitating a change in belief, which is a fundamental CBT technique, enables a change in thinking, and this produces a change in behavior over time. Once the person feels new inside, the old ways rapidly fade; because with each new day the adaptive individual becomes more distant from the maladaptive one. And that is positive growth. And it is achieved more rapidly and with greater fidelity when the individual believes in Christ. So, if God changes my heart, it will change my mind, and a corresponding change in actions will follow. This will ultimately lead to a change in lifestyle.

People need to be active physically, mentally, and spiritually to be completely healthy. Faith without corresponding action is worthless because inaction produces nothing (PRO 10:4; JAM 2:17). Perseverance in the faith enables us to remain connected to the power and wisdom of God's Spirit (ECC 7:25; MAT 22:37). If we live under the umbrella of the Holy Spirit we become conformed to the image of God's Son through the process of sanctification (JOB 32:8; 2 CO 3:18; GAL 5:5; HEB 10:10). Those who follow Christ will realize their full potential because God will reward them with abundant, purposeful, and fulfilling life (MAT 6:33; JOH 14:6; GAL 5:22-23). The Lord will lead you where you need to be. To achieve greater health, willpower, and direction, invite the Holy Spirit to live in you; Baptism, Holy Communion, weekly worship, prayer, and Bible study are examples of such an invitation (PRO 2:10-12; JOH 8:31-32).

If you desire to connect with God, you can do so the same way people connect with one another: speak to him and listen to him. Through meditation, prayer, and calling upon the Lord, we bring our thoughts, desires, and problems to the Throne of Grace (ISA 65:24; MAR 11:23; ROM 8:26). Through worship, Bible study, and daily devotions, God speaks to those who will listen (PSA 119:105; ISA 55:10-11; 1 CO 2:13; 2 TI 3:16). Through witnessing and ministering, God speaks through us to others (MAT 28:19-20; 1 PE 3:15; 1 JO 5:9-10). The bottom line is this: seek God for he is there with you, always (MAT 7:7; REV 3:20).

Exercising the mind, body, and spirit facilitates the expression of feelings and the expenditure of emotional energy. That's right, emotions create energy (negative and positive); this energy can be used to build or to destroy. Destructive ways of releasing emotional energy include hitting, throwing things, yelling, stomping the floor, and battering your self-esteem (PRO 6:16-19; PRO 14:17; PRO 15:1,18; PRO 19:11; PRO 26:24-28). Constructive ways of using this energy include creating a masterpiece, building something in someone's honor or memory, physical fitness, playing, doing chores, and assisting others (ROM 14:5-8,22-23). There are many ways to get emotional material out: express it, expend it, and give it to God.

Our capacity to reason enables positive thinking (true, uplifting, praiseworthy thoughts). When we don't take time to think we are prone to negative thinking (putting ourselves down, internalizing defeating messages from others, reacting on impulse). Our capacity to contemplate enables positive imagery (the cross of Christ, a favorite peaceful place, heaven). Our capacity to hope enables forward looking (the big picture, the finish line with the Lord in heaven, the attractive possibilities that lie ahead). Negative thoughts are contrary, usually untrue, and at the very least, unlikely. Positive thoughts are those which are truthful, uplifting, and pure; and these are healthy for you (PHP 4:8). If you tell yourself you are worthless, ugly, and stupid, but God tells you that you are precious, important (so important he would make the ultimate sacrifice for you), and beautiful (since Christ lives in you) – who is right? Well, Satan is the father of lies (JOH 8:44) and God is the father of truth (1 JO 5:6), so the answer is obvious. When a person begins to tell themselves the truth and believes it, their self-esteem rises immediately.

You must look forward and not backward. Setbacks are not failures; they are stepping stones to success. If you take a step back for every two steps forward, you are still making positive progress. If Christ is in the picture, you are on the right path. Leave the emotional baggage behind; it will only slow you down as it impedes forward progress. Usually, this requires forgiveness: yourself and others. Remember, the love of God can change anyone. If you radiate that love it might change those around you (ROM 12:20-21). Love can exist without faith, but faith cannot exist without love; and it is by faith that we cling to the hope of living with God forever (GAL 5:5-6; ROM 8:24). Let the Lord be your confidence and hope and you will not be disappointed with the outcome (PSA 23:1-6; MAT 6:31-33).

The most powerful force in the world is love, because God is love (1 JO 4:8,16-18). The power of evil is fear (terrorism, hatefulness, torment), which the wicked use to erode hope and obscure love. Do not confuse disparaging fear with righteous fear, which is the reverence and veneration of our awesome God. The two definitions are quite different; the latter is productive, the former, destructive. Love and fear are incompatible, just like light and darkness are incompatible. Light can consume darkness but darkness cannot consume light; love can conquer fear but fear cannot conquer love (PRO 29:25; 1 JO 4:18; 2 TI 1:7). God gives us the power of his love and his light to overcome the evil and darkness that plague our souls, to win the good fight of faith, to dispatch the monster inside, and to prevail over death. You cannot be defeated when you are defended by the Lord; you will win the battle and overcome the opposition if God is on your side (EPH 6:10-18; HEB 4:12). With God, anything is possible; without him, nothing is (LUK 18:27; PHP 4:13).

Harmony among mind, body, and spirit is a reasonable goal of therapy. But the spirit and the flesh are often in conflict (ROM 7:23; GAL 5:17-18). And what are they fighting over? Which one will control the mind and the thoughts (1 CO 2:10-12; GAL 6:8; EPH 4:23)? If the flesh is winning that battle, the person is out of control. If God is in control, the spirit will prevail and abundant life will result (JOH 10:10).

All too often, a troubled person is trying to satisfy an emptiness of the spirit; but one can never fill such a void via worldly things (ROM 8:1-6; 1 JO 2:15). The flesh cannot be satisfied, for it will get tired, hungry, and thirsty again. But God's love satisfies fully (PSA 37:4; PSA 145:14-16; JOH 3:16; 1 CO 13:2-13). Occasionally, conflict involves personal demons (spiritual or mental) which can be dismissed using fruit of the spirit (GAL 5:22-23). If a person is guided by the spirit, he or she will win this war and receive a crown of life (2 TI 4:7-8; JAM 1:12). If the counselor is guided by the spirit, he or she can provide sound guidance to the client who will follow that example. This calls for awakening, edification, and education in the ways of righteousness.

Clinical Overview

Conscientious practitioners gather as much information as possible about the client in order to better serve him or her. Pertinent information could include medical, psychological, familial, social, behavioral, historical, and the list goes on. Many intake processes fail to consider the significance of cultural and religious orientations, however. Since these form the foundation of the family's values and the individual's personal beliefs, they are often the most important, not just to the client but also to the therapist. Spirituality deals with the client's views toward religion, God, and his/her own soul and spirit. Included are ideas about where life comes from, where the person fits into the hierarchy of living creatures, life after death, heaven and hell, sin, guilt, and healing.

Mental health counseling necessitates a relationship between the client and therapist. This relationship is the foundation, and requires communication, trust, rapport, caring, and willingness on the part of the client to change and to grow. If Christ is the foundation of the relationship, these characteristics will come naturally. Thus, therapy involves a partnership between client and therapist, where both provide input; God should be part of that partnership. The client ultimately chooses goals, courses of action, directions to take, and issues to address. The therapist acts as facilitator to this process, helping it to move in the desired direction by uncovering obstacles to forward progress, encouraging disclosure and analysis, and providing objective discussion and summarization.

Thus, the client always has the choice to participate, to change, and to continue. The therapist may provide suggestions, alternatives, and guidance, but it is the client who is responsible for taking ownership of his/her progress. If clients are not involved in the decision making process during therapy, they will be unable to make decisions on their own upon termination of the therapeutic relationship. Those guided by the spirit tend to make proper decisions, in accordance with God's will.

The immediate family may be asked to become involved in treatment planning and therapy; this is always the case when the patient is a child. Training and education are provided to patients and their families about mental and physical health disorders and available treatments and foundation, including faith based. This helps to empower them and to dispel stigmatizing beliefs; it also helps them to ask appropriate and informed questions of a physician or psychotherapist.

The expanded clinical model proposed is comprised of several therapeutic techniques which can be tailored to meet the special needs of the client. It is largely an eclectic approach, founded primarily upon Cognitive-Behavioral, Existential, Client Centered, and Interpersonal paradigms. The approach utilized will depend upon the states and traits exhibited by the client, as well as the client's level of functioning, personality, and intelligence. For example, a behavioral emphasis might be more effective with a child, whereas a cognitive emphasis might be more suitable for an adult. Some people respond well to indirect methods, but for others, a more direct approach works best. Further, symptoms may indicate proven methods, as revealed in evidence-based research. As reviewed earlier, CBT has been shown to be effective in reducing anxiety and depression, especially in combination with spirituality. Regardless of the methods employed, people of all ages can relate to and will respond to God's love, mercy, and strength.

CBT group techniques, Family Focused Therapy, and Family Systems Therapy are good choices for families. Consider that some family members may be having difficulty coping or may be presenting extreme diagnoses as well. Given that many clients and their families are in need of crisis intervention, directive and instructional techniques are commonly utilized, and blend nicely with faith oriented interventions.

A combination of individual, family, and spiritually based applications should be employed in a way that most effectively addresses the client's needs and goals. While the enhanced model proposes brief psychotherapy, the term brief is relative. Therapy is intended to continue for as long as it takes, until such time as the relationship is terminated by either the client or the counselor (or both). Ideally, this will take place when the client's behavioral goals, attitude changes, self-actualization, and/or holistic health have been achieved. For some, satisfaction is attained after only a few sessions, for others, it may take years. By and large, spirituality will accelerate this process.

The therapist should take advantage of every opportunity to consult with other professionals treating the client. Of course, proper written consent forms should be provided to allow for the sharing of information. If the client seeks to attain holistic health, it is important that the therapist understand the person's physical/medical status, his/her mental/emotional status, and his/her spiritual status. This may require consultation with the client's physician or psychiatrist, and possibly his/her minister or priest. In fact, in some cultures, ministers and certain members of the parish or spiritual community play an integral role in the family constellation.

One final note on your commission as a Christian Counselor: your service handbook is God's own Word. It is the only perfectly reliable source for absolute truth and spiritual guidance. If you are to provide such guidance you must receive it as well. It is essential that you know the Bible backwards and forwards. Scrutinize everything you see and hear, to include this textbook. Is it in harmony with God's Word? Everyone has equal potential for understanding, if only they would diligently study, annotate, research, and cherish the Bible.

Our founding fathers were well aware of the significance of the Holy Bible; they fashioned their new republic, politics, and religion after it. Let us likewise fashion ourselves, our lives, our intentions, our aspirations, and our purposes on God's Word. And let us present that example to those we serve. The framers, writers, and signers of our founding documents were very much inspired by the Bible, and believed God to be the author of life and Christianity to be the cornerstone of true faith and our free society. The quotes below exemplify these facts and should be an inspiration to all who enjoy the freedoms and democracy that are held in high esteem in this great land.

"To the distinguished character of Patriot, it should be our highest glory to add the more distinguished character of Christian." – George Washington

"Let us pray that the religion of our Lord and Savior Jesus Christ be known, understood, and practiced among all the inhabitants of the earth." – John Hancock

"I am a real Christian, that is to say, a disciple of the doctrines of Jesus Christ." – Thomas Jefferson

"The Bible is worth more than all the other books that were ever printed." – Patrick Henry

"The Christian religion is, above all the religions that ever prevailed or existed in ancient or modern times, the religion of wisdom, virtue, equity, and humanity." – John Adams

"The Bible is the best of all books, for it is the word of God and teaches us the way to be happy in this world and the next. Continue therefore to read it and to regulate your life by its precepts." – John Jay

"The only means of establishing and perpetuating our republican forms of government is the universal education of our youth in the principles of Christianity by means of the Bible." – Benjamin Rush

"The Bible teaches man his own individual responsibility, his own dignity, and his equality with his fellow man." – Daniel Webster

"I do believe in one God, the Creator and Governor of the Universe, the Rewarder of the good and Punisher of the wicked, and I do acknowledge the Scriptures of the Old and New Testaments to be given by Divine Inspiration." – Benjamin Franklin

HOLY BIBLE

CREATED IN THE
IMAGE OF GOD

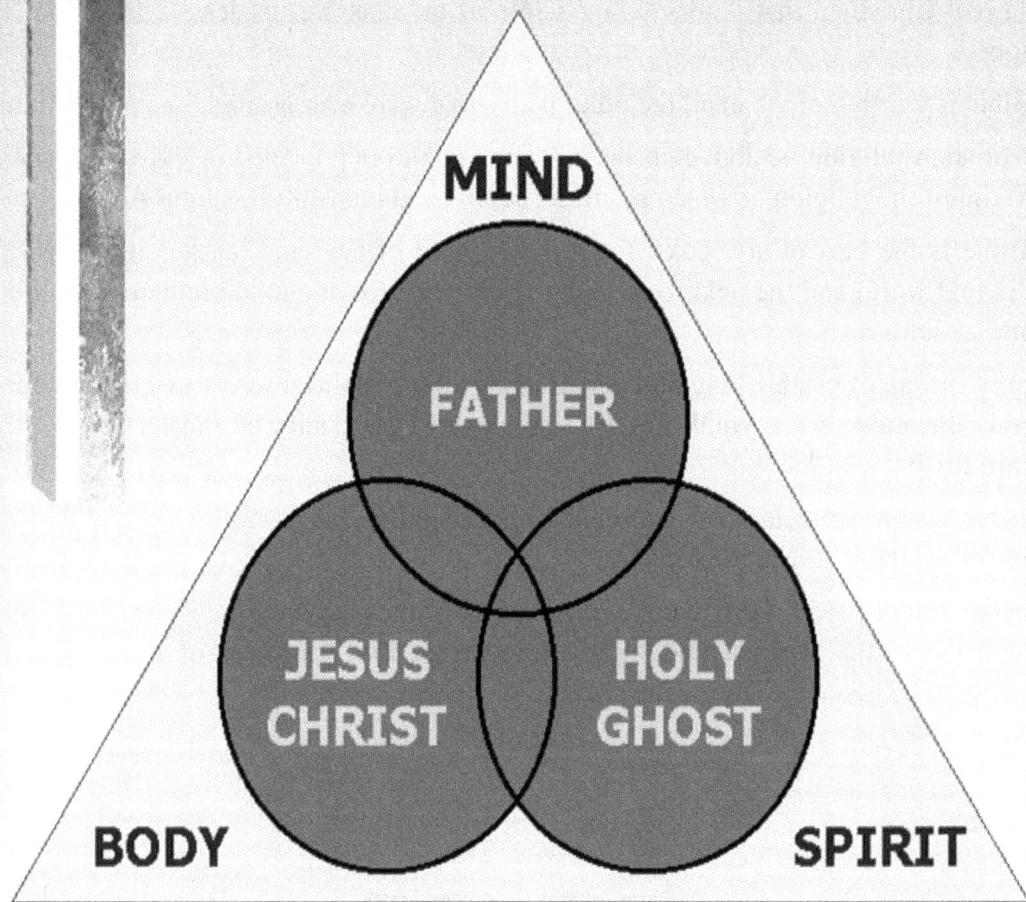

MIND

FATHER

JESUS
CHRIST

HOLY
GHOST

BODY

SPIRIT

CHRISTIAN COUNSELING PHILOSOPHY

The Basics

Christianity, whether of a Protestant or Catholic orientation, is based upon some essential doctrines of faith. Whatever the particular denominational traditions, there should be no compromise when it comes to these tenets. You will find them in the Holy Bible – the foundation of our faith and the final arbiter of truth. If it cannot be found in God's Word, it is not necessary for your salvation. Everyone should be instructed in God's Word and should read the Bible regularly to equip themselves with the means to live a godly life and to refute false teachings.

First and foremost, one must accept and seek God, who exists in three persons. The doctrine of the Holy Trinity is not to be compromised. There are numerous references to the three persons of God in the Bible. Do not let anyone dissuade you with the argument that the term "trinity" does not occur in the Bible; neither does the word "dinosaur" or a lot of other words. But the concept of trinity is spelled out precisely. The following scriptures establish this crucial fact; note that both testaments of the Bible record the triune God.

- ISA 11:1-2 ~ A descendant of Jesse, a Branch, will be born. The Spirit of the Lord shall rest upon the Messiah – the Spirit of wisdom, understanding, counsel, and might, the Spirit of knowledge and the fear of God.

- ISA 48:16 ~ Come and listen. I have not spoken in secret since the beginning. I (Christ) was there all along, and now, the Lord God and His Spirit have sent me. (see JOH 1:1-14)

- MAT 3:16-17 (also MAR 1:10-11) ~ Jesus, after he was baptized, emerged from the water, and the heavens were opened, and He saw the Spirit of God descending like a dove and resting upon Him. And a voice from heaven said, "This is my beloved Son who pleases me very much."

- MAT 28:18-20 ~ Jesus said, "All authority in heaven and earth is given to me. Go and teach everyone what I have taught you; baptize them in the name of the Father, Son, and Holy Spirit."

- JOH 1:1-4,14 ~ In the beginning was the Word, and the Word was with God, and the Word was God. All things were made by Him. In Him was life, and His life was the light of mankind. This Word became flesh and lived among us; and we saw His glory, the glory of the only begotten of the Father, full of grace and truth. (see ISA 48:16)

- JOH 14:26; JOH 15:26 ~ Jesus informed the apostles, "The Comforter, the Holy Spirit, who the Father will send in my name..." and, "I will send the Comforter, the Holy Spirit."

- 2 CO 13:14 ~ Paul's benediction: May the grace of Jesus Christ, the love of God, and the communion of the Holy Spirit be with you.

- PHP 2:5-11 ~ Jesus Christ, though equal with God, took upon Himself the nature of man, and became a humble servant. He was obedient unto death, even a humiliating death on a cross. God has therefore exalted the name of Christ above all others; so everyone should bow before His name, and everyone should confess that He is Lord, to the glory of God the Father.

- COL 2:2,9 ~ My hope is that their hearts will be comforted, being bound together in love, and that they receive the riches of understanding and acknowledgment of the mystery of God, and of the Heavenly Father, and of Jesus Christ. In Jesus Christ the whole deity of God lives.

- 1 PE 1:2,18-22 ~ Peter preached: You have been chosen in advance by God the Father, and sanctified by His Holy Spirit, through the shedding of the blood of His Son Jesus Christ, to whom you have become obedient. May God bless you with His abundant grace and peace. You are not redeemed with corruptible things like gold or silver, you are redeemed with the precious blood of Christ, who was like a lamb without blemish or spots. He, who was ordained before the foundation of the world, was made manifest in these past days just for you. Believe in Him who God raised from the dead and gave glory, so that your faith and hope can remain in God. Your souls will be purified by obeying the truth that the Holy Spirit has shown you; so fervently love your brothers with a pure heart.

- 1 JO 5:7-8,20 ~ There are three that are recorded in heaven: the Father, the Word, and the Holy Spirit. These three are one. The same three bear witness: the Spirit, the Water, and the Blood. The Spirit is The Witness, because the Spirit bears the Truth. We know Jesus Christ who is true so that we may know God who is true. We live in Him who has shown us His Son, the source of eternal life. (see JOH 1:1-14)

Our Heavenly Father gives us the Law, the Holy Spirit imparts the truth, and Jesus Christ provides the atonement. The Law tells us what to do and not to do and is a blueprint for pleasing God; Jesus Christ led the perfect life as an example of obedience to the Father. The truth is found in God's Word and the Word made flesh which is Christ the Lord; it provides the knowledge of salvation and of the gift of eternal life that includes an inheritance in God's kingdom. The sacrifice of Christ paid the debt of our sin, reconciling us to God our Father with the righteousness that he bestowed upon us at his death. His resurrection opened the gates of heaven for all who would believe these important truths. Thus, through his life he conquered the Law, through his death he conquered sin, and through his resurrection he conquered death. This he did for you and me, so that we could be forgiven, receive his righteousness, and live with him as equal heirs in God's kingdom.

- ISA 53:4-12 ~ Surely he has borne our griefs and carried our sorrows; yet we esteemed him stricken, smitten by God, and afflicted. But he was pierced for our transgressions; he was crushed for our iniquities; upon him was the chastisement that brought us peace, and with his wounds we are healed. All we like sheep have gone astray; we have turned – every one – to his own way; and the LORD has laid on him the iniquity of us all. He was oppressed, and he was afflicted, yet he opened not his mouth; like a lamb that is led to the slaughter, and like a sheep that before its shearers is silent, so he opened not his mouth. By oppression and judgment he was taken away; and as for his generation, who considered that he was cut off out of the land of the living, stricken for the transgression of my people? And they made his grave with the wicked and with a rich man in his death, although he had done no violence, and there was no deceit in his mouth. Yet it was the will of the LORD to crush him; he has put him to grief; when his soul makes an offering for guilt, he shall see his offspring; he shall prolong his days; the will of the LORD shall prosper in his hand. Out of the anguish of his soul he shall see and be satisfied; by his knowledge shall the righteous one, my servant, make many to be accounted righteous, and he shall bear their iniquities. Therefore I will divide him a portion with the many, and he shall divide the spoil with the strong, because he poured out his soul to death and was numbered with the transgressors; yet he bore the sin of many, and makes intercession for the transgressors.

- ISA 61:1-2 ~ The Spirit of the Lord GOD is upon me, because the LORD has anointed me to bring good news to the poor; he has sent me to bind up the brokenhearted, to proclaim liberty to the captives, and the opening of the prison to those who are bound; to proclaim the year of the LORD's favor, and the day of vengeance of our God; to comfort all who mourn. (Jesus quoted this scripture when his ministry began: see LUK 4:16-20).

- ZEC 13:7 ~ "Awake, O sword, against my shepherd, against the man who stands next to me," declares the LORD of hosts. "Strike the shepherd, and the sheep will be scattered; I will turn my hand against the little ones.

- JOH 3:16-17 ~ Jesus said, "For God so loved the world, that he gave his only Son, that whoever believes in him should not perish but have eternal life. For God did not send his Son into the world to condemn the world, but in order that the world might be saved through him."

- JOH 11:25-26 ~ Jesus said to Martha, "I am the resurrection and the life. Whoever believes in me, though he die, yet shall he live, and everyone who lives and believes in me shall never die. Do you believe this?" She said to him, "Yes, Lord; I believe that you are the Christ, the Son of God, who is coming into the world."

- ACT 13:38 ~ Let it be known to you therefore, brothers, that through this man forgiveness of sins is proclaimed to you.

- 2 CO 5:21 ~ For our sake he made him to be sin who knew no sin, so that in him we might become the righteousness of God.

- COL 1:19-23 ~ For in him all the fullness of God was pleased to dwell, and through him to reconcile to himself all things, whether on earth or in heaven, making peace by the blood of his cross. And you, who once were alienated and hostile in mind, doing evil deeds, he has now reconciled in his body of flesh by his death, in order to present you holy and blameless and above reproach before him, if indeed you continue in the faith, stable and steadfast, not shifting from the hope of the gospel that you heard, which has been proclaimed in all creation under heaven, and of which I, Paul, became a minister.

- HEB 10:1-10,18 ~ For since the law has but a shadow of the good things to come instead of the true form of these realities, it can never, by the same sacrifices that are continually offered every year, make perfect those who draw near. Otherwise, would they not have ceased to be offered, since the worshipers, having once been cleansed, would no longer have any consciousness of sins? But in these sacrifices there is a reminder of sins every year. For it is impossible for the blood of bulls and goats to take away sins. Consequently, when Christ came into the world, he said, "Sacrifices and offerings you have not desired, but a body have you prepared for me; in burnt offerings and sin offerings you have taken no pleasure. Then I said, 'Behold, I have come to do your will, O God, as it is written of me in the scroll of the book.'" When he said above, "You have neither desired nor taken pleasure in sacrifices and offerings and burnt offerings and sin offerings" (these are offered according to the law), then he added, "Behold, I have come to do your will." He does away with the first in order to establish the second. And by that will we have been sanctified through the offering of the body of Jesus Christ once for all... Where there is forgiveness of these, there is no longer any offering for sin.

The doctrine of salvation is paramount, established on the notion that we are saved by the grace of God simply because we believe. Our acts are an extension of that faith, not a substitute for it. You cannot be saved on the merit of your works. If that were possible you wouldn't need a savior. There is nothing you can do to earn or buy your way into heaven as it is freely given by our merciful Father to all who trust his words and cling to his promises. However, true faith is backed by actions, such as a change in behavior, attitude, or lifestyle. Most religions emphasize works; Christianity alone requires faith in the atonement of Christ.

- PSA 31:23 ~ Love the LORD, all you his saints! The LORD preserves the faithful but abundantly repays the one who acts in pride.

- HAB 2:4 ~ Behold, his soul is puffed up; it is not upright within him, but the righteous shall live by his faith.

- ROM 3:20-22 ~ For by works of the law no human being will be justified in his sight, since through the law comes knowledge of sin. But now the righteousness of God has been manifested apart from the law, although the Law and the Prophets bear witness to it – the righteousness of God through faith in Jesus Christ for all who believe. For there is no distinction: for all have sinned and fall short of the glory of God...

- GAL 2:16,20 ~ Yet we know that a person is not justified by works of the law but through faith in Jesus Christ, so we also have believed in Christ Jesus, in order to be justified by faith in Christ and not by works of the law, because by works of the law no one will be justified. I have been crucified with Christ. It is no longer I who live, but Christ who lives in me. And the life I now live in the flesh I live by faith in the Son of God, who loved me and gave himself for me.

- GAL 3:8-13,21-24 ~ And the Scripture, foreseeing that God would justify the Gentiles by faith, preached the gospel beforehand to Abraham, saying, "In you shall all the nations be blessed." So then, those who are of faith are blessed along with Abraham, the man of faith. For all who rely on works of the law are under a curse; for it is written, "Cursed be everyone who does not abide by all things written in the Book of the Law, and do them." Now it is evident that no one is justified before God by the law, for "The righteous shall live by faith." But the law is not of faith, rather "The one who does them shall live by them." Christ redeemed us from the curse of the law by becoming a curse for us – for it is written, "Cursed is everyone who is hanged on a tree." Is the law then contrary to the promises of God? Certainly not! For if a law had been given that could give life, then righteousness would indeed be by the law. But the Scripture imprisoned everything under sin, so that the promise by faith in Jesus Christ might be given to those who believe. Now before faith came, we were held captive under the law, imprisoned until the coming faith would be revealed. So then, the law was our guardian until Christ came, in order that we might be justified by faith.

- EPH 2:8-9 ~ For by grace you have been saved through faith. And this is not your own doing; it is the gift of God, not a result of works, so that no one may boast.

- 2 TI 1:9 ~ He saved us and called us to a holy calling, not because of our works but because of his own purpose and grace, which he gave us in Christ Jesus before the ages began,

- TIT 3:5-8 ~ He saved us, not because of works done by us in righteousness, but according to his own mercy, by the washing of regeneration and renewal of the Holy Spirit, whom he poured out on us richly through Jesus Christ our Savior, so that being justified by his grace we might become heirs according to the hope of eternal life. The saying is trustworthy, and I want you to insist on these things, so that those who have believed in God may be careful to devote themselves to good works. These things are excellent and profitable for people.

- HEB 12:1-2 ~ Therefore, since we are surrounded by so great a cloud of witnesses, let us also lay aside every weight, and sin which clings so closely, and let us run with endurance the race that is set before us, looking to Jesus, the founder and perfecter of our faith, who for the joy that was set before him endured the cross, despising the shame, and is seated at the right hand of the throne of God.

- JAM 2:17-26 ~ So also faith by itself, if it does not have works, is dead. But someone will say, "You have faith and I have works." Show me your faith apart from your works, and I will show you my faith by my works. You believe that God is one; you do well. Even the demons believe – and shudder! Do you want to be shown, you foolish person, that faith apart from works is useless? Was not Abraham our father justified by works when he offered up his son Isaac on the altar? You see that faith was active along with his works, and faith was completed by his works; and the Scripture was fulfilled that says, "Abraham believed God, and it was counted to him as righteousness" – and he was called a friend of God. You see that a person is justified by works and not by faith alone. And in the same way was not also Rahab the prostitute justified by works when she received the messengers and sent them out by another way? For as the body apart from the spirit is dead, so also faith apart from works is dead.

- 1 PE 1:3-5,8-9 ~ Blessed be the God and Father of our Lord Jesus Christ! According to his great mercy, he has caused us to be born again to a living hope through the resurrection of Jesus Christ from the dead, to an inheritance that is imperishable, undefiled, and unfading, kept in heaven for you, who by God's power are being guarded through faith for a salvation ready to be revealed in the last time... Though you have not seen him, you love him. Though you do not now see him, you believe in him and rejoice with joy that is inexpressible and filled with glory, obtaining the outcome of your faith, the salvation of your souls.

People of faith have an outlook that they are here for a reason. God is generally the one with the reason, or at least people want God's will to be fulfilled in their lives. If they feel that God is with them and guiding them, they enjoy life a lot more and are more purposeful. But people often they feel as if God has abandoned them. What they need most is to reconnect with God and stay connected. This is true for any faith that is founded on a merciful creator.

The foundation for the holistic health view can be found in the Bible. Remember, God exists in three persons: Father, Son, and Holy Spirit. He is not three deities but one God. Each personification of God plays an important role in our salvation. There are a number of scriptures that declare this important truth as reviewed above.

God created us in his image. One way we are similar to God is we possess a mental, physical, and spiritual component. Unlike God, these three are separable in humans. The Holy Spirit gives us life, and communicates God's love and truth through the Holy Bible and the Lord Jesus. God gave us a discerning mind to comprehend that truth so we could acquire the knowledge of obedience, forgiveness, and deliverance. The greatest gift next to life itself is freedom. Without free will we could not please God, because we would not be able to choose him. How could we possibly love God back if we were simply programmed to do so? The most important choices you will ever make are to believe in Jesus Christ and to love him.

- GEN 1:26; GEN 3:22-23 ~ Then God said, "Let us make man in our image, after our likeness. And let them have dominion over the fish of the sea and over the birds of the heavens and over the livestock and over all the earth and over every creeping thing that creeps on the earth." Then the LORD God said, "Behold, the man has become like one of us in knowing good and evil. Now, lest he reach out his hand and take also of the tree of life and eat, and live forever" – the LORD God sent him out from the garden of Eden…

- DEU 6:5 ~ You shall love the LORD your God with all your heart and with all your soul and with all your might.

- MAT 22:37 ~ And Jesus said to him, "You shall love the Lord your God with all your heart and with all your soul and with all your mind."

- 1 TH 5:23 ~ Now may the God of peace himself sanctify you completely, and may your whole spirit and soul and body be kept blameless at the coming of our Lord Jesus Christ.

To be completely healthy, we must nurture our bodies, minds, and spirits. Oftentimes, it is the spirit that gets the least attention. Faith counseling is the means of integrating spiritual health with mental and physical. If your spirit is healthy, the other two will be replenished. God will see to it, to ensure that you bear fruit worthy of repentance (LUK 3:8).

Question: What is the primary reason that people seek counseling? Answer: To feel like a complete person; to become whole again; to be renewed. Spiritual regeneration is the key.

- PSA 51:10-12 ~ Create in me a clean heart, O God, and renew a right spirit within me. Cast me not away from your presence, and take not your Holy Spirit from me. Restore to me the joy of your salvation, and uphold me with a willing spirit.

- ISA 40:31 ~ But they who wait for the LORD shall renew their strength; they shall mount up with wings like eagles; they shall run and not be weary; they shall walk and not faint.

- ROM 12:2 ~ Do not be conformed to this world, but be transformed by the renewal of your mind, that by testing you may discern what is the will of God, what is good and acceptable and perfect.

- 2 CO 4:16 ~ So we do not lose heart. Though our outer self is wasting away, our inner self is being renewed day by day.

- EPH 4:22-24 ~ Put off your old self, which belongs to your former manner of life and is corrupt through deceitful desires, and to be renewed in the spirit of your minds, and to put on the new self, created after the likeness of God in true righteousness and holiness.

- COL 3:10 ~ Put on the new self, which is being renewed in knowledge after the image of its creator.

- TIT 3:5-7 ~ He saved us, not because of works done by us in righteousness, but according to his own mercy, by the washing of regeneration and renewal of the Holy Spirit, whom he poured out on us richly through Jesus Christ our Savior, so that being justified by his grace we might become heirs according to the hope of eternal life.

Helping Models

Every psychological theory, treatment technique, and system of delivery has its applications. But no particular helping model is universally applicable. Some approaches work better than others depending on the client's diagnosis, the circumstances, and the preferences of the client and the therapist. A seasoned therapist will possess a unique helping style, which develops over time from a combination of education, experience, and practice. The more flexible the methodology, the more versatile and the better equipped the practitioner to handle a diversity of clientele. A brief synopsis of the various helping models has been provided to establish a general theoretical framework.

Psychoanalytic – This movement was spearheaded by the likes of Freud and Jung. Much of the impetus was on the unconscious mind, and its influence on behavior and mental health. The focus progressed from anxiety, neurotic defenses, unconscious motivation, and libido, to needs, thought processes, and ego strength. Unconscious material was explored using methods such as the examination of transference and resistance, dream analysis, hypnosis, and projective techniques like free association. Interest in psychology took a giant leap, and many theorists branched out from this philosophy, with the idea that external factors were just as influential as internal. The Interpersonal paradigm, for example, drew attention to relationships, significant others, and how these affect the self. Horney and Sullivan were among those who opened that door.

Existential – Concentration on what was going on inside the person had clearly turned to what was going on outside the person and the interaction of the two. Theorists like Adler and Lewin emphasized that behavior was influenced by family, society, and situational or environmental conditions. These were all part of the person's existence, which was divided into layers of environments, or strata of existence. Concepts such as freedom, choice, relationships, responsibility, experience, and reality were being defined and studied by such notables as Fromm, Laing, and May. Since people did not exist independently, then behavior was necessarily determined by the presence of others, or the lack thereof. Behavior was further explained with respect to groups, society and culture by the renowned social psychologists Bandura, Miller, and Walster.

Behavioral – A great repository of information existed regarding what affects behavior, so theorists began to examine the behavior itself, and how people become conditioned to exhibit predictable patterns of behavior. With Pavlov, Hull, Thorndike, and Skinner leading the way, the world gained an understanding of stimulus-response, drives, classical conditioning, and instrumental conditioning. Behavior could be shaped by introducing reinforcement and extinguished with punishment. Given that the behavior appeared to be a learned response which develops over time, the path was paved for the learning and developmental movements. Enter such theorists as Piaget, Gagne, and Erikson. That we are driven by our needs sparked a renewal of interest in motivation and self-esteem. Thus, personal development was largely directed towards reaching our full potential, our ideal self, and we have Maslow to thank for coining the term self-actualization.

Humanistic – The progression logically advanced towards gaining an understanding of individuality, states, traits, and personality as revealed in the work of Allport, Eysenck, and Williamson. People possessed some characteristics that were intrinsic, some consistent, and some transient. In order to be a helper to unique individuals it was necessary to understand what made them tick. The helping profession had broken out of its shell and the focus on the client and the therapeutic relationship became of utmost importance. Rogers' client-centered approach was groundbreaking in shaping the future of counseling. The process and the experience of therapy became the catalyst for growth, change, becoming. This was elaborated quite well in the writings of Egan. The here-and-now aspect had clear existential ramifications, and the importance of the relationship clearly interpersonal. We also should recognize Wertheimer, Kohler, Glasser, and others for introducing us to Gestalt and Reality therapies, which opened the gates for the upcoming surge of cognitive theorists.

Cognitive – Kelly's idea that individuals can scientifically observe the world and test hypotheses via trial and error was significant. The implication was that people make conscious decisions based on their perception of reality, causality, probability, consensus, and generalization. But people were biased, unreasonable, and illogical; they were not objective about it. This prompted Beck, Ellis, and Festinger to surmise that maladaptive behavior was the result of irrational beliefs and cognitive distortions. Sometimes, all that was necessary was for the person to alter beliefs to modify unwanted behavior or maladaptive responses. Better results could be obtained by making decisions based on rationality over emotionality. Since behavior developed over time due to repetition, one could reprogram that behavior by repeating the adaptive response enough until it became automatic. Thus, bad habits could be unlearned, and new, good habits learned through rehearsal, practice, and reinforcement. If one could tap into these internal processes, one could possibly facilitate this restructuring. So there was a resurgence of interest in internal and unconscious processes. We learned techniques like Neurolinguistic Programming (NLP) from Bandler and Grinder, and Eye Movement Desensitization and Reprocessing (EMDR) from Shapiro, and rediscovered the applicability of hypnosis and visual imagery. It seems the theoretical foundation had come full circle.

Integrated Helping Model

Notice how each expansion built upon previous paradigms, and propelled the field of psychology forward. The discipline gained a more solid grasp of human nature, thinking, behavior, personality, and individual differences. We studied these theories and we learned to practically apply them. And we practiced them while we grew as professionals and discovered what worked for us. This became integrated with our personalities and beliefs into our personal helping model, and ultimately became our service style. Being people of faith, we would be remiss in neglecting the most important aspect of who we are. The faith based model is compatible with any model or style; some of the popular techniques are provided below to exemplify this fact.

Cognitive-Behavioral Therapy – Primarily influenced by the Cognitive and Behavior theorists, CBT is quite agreeable with the spiritual growth model. What we think and how we act are very closely tied to how accurately we interpret truth. Cognitive approaches are primarily based on the client's belief system and how it measures up to reality. The therapist acts as teacher and challenges irrationality, while the client learns cogent thinking and adaptive behaviors. Compatibility with a person's faith system is essential for holistic health; and it aids in deconstructing cognitive dissonance. Helping focuses on change and growth, which is assisted with spirituality since one's motivation for change depends largely on what they believe to be possible and true. Faith provides strong reinforcement; and remorse from sin is a strong motivator to change. If the client wishes to alter how they think, feel, and behave it will be facilitated greatly via spiritual guidance and getting control over thinking.

Client Centered Counseling – Humanistic in orientation is the client-centered approach. People skills are a must for faith based practitioners since relationships are valued by people of faith, especially a relationship with God. Certainly, the fundamental attributes of the skilled helper will come into play, and are not unlike that of Christ himself: accurate empathy, positive regard, respect, genuineness; concreteness, immediacy, confrontation, disclosure; exploration of alternatives, supportiveness, flexibility, realism. These interpersonal skills are necessary for relationship building, and help us to understand the client's relationships with significant others, family, church, God, and the therapist. Conflict resolution, mending bridges, and coping are fundamental goals for most any client. The client adopts the humanistic attributes of the therapist which are a reflection of Christ. This improves relationships and communication; and the hope that faith brings becomes an effective enabler and coping mechanism.

Imagery and Hypnosis – One technique with a Psychoanalytic bent is visual imagery, which is being employed by more and more practitioners. It is one of the principal tools used in relaxation, hypnosis, NLP, and EMDR. There are an unlimited amount of positive images the client can produce that are ego strengthening, uplifting, and provide peace, security, and hope. Therapists will discover faith-inspiring images to be particularly useful in this regard. Note that many religious people, including therapists, have a misconception that hypnosis is incompatible with spirituality; this is based in part on the belief that hypnosis is a form of mind control (which it is not). Hypnosis is actually a means of connecting with one's inner self, via introspection and exploration. It is a magnificent way of helping the client locate and modify internal programming, and reinforce this at multiple levels of consciousness. Before employing methods like hypnosis, EMDR, or NLP a considerable amount of training is necessary. If you can establish a mind-body connection, you will realize the spirit is not far away. And the spirit, my friends, is the key to inner power and strength.

Systems Theory – Here we see the influence of Existentialism. Individuals are better understood in the context of their environment, relationships, and existence. It is especially important to explore interactions, motivations, and influences among family members. Of course, other relationships within the inner circle are very important and worth examining. But the family has more impact on a person than any other entity, so symptoms are often an indication of family dysfunction. The family can learn maladaptive patterns of thinking and behavior and these can be modified just like those of individuals. If unconditional love is generated within the family, many problems disappear, and more of their time together will be of high quality. Family prayer, worship, and Bible study tend to be viewed as quality time.

It is necessary to study the other strata in the environment as well. Notice that each stratum affects how people believe; and how we believe affects how we behave. Alterations in one part of the living system can cause repercussions or reverberations in other areas. Certainly an institution like church should have a positive influence; it definitely did in my upbringing. Religion in general typically elevates moral character and family unity. But the one layer that encompasses the others is the universe which only God can command; and he exists outside of the universe, as well as inside of us. He is all and in all (COL 3:11). Those who believe in Christ will surrender control to the highest power and follow his lead. While each layer influences the individual, the greatest and most necessary influence is God himself.

> ➤ Personal, Interpersonal (Parents, Family and Friends)
> ➤ Institutional, Organizational, Community (Church, Work, and School)
> ➤ Society, Government, Culture (Religion)
> ➤ Heaven, Universe, Eternity (God)

Spiritual Application

Professionally, we are first children of God, and second ministers of his grace and mercy. He has called us into the helping profession to mend, to encourage, to challenge, to liberate, to love, and to reflect Christ. What is our mission as Christian Counselors? This answer and many more are found in God's Word. See how many attributes and objectives apply to you as a faithful servant of the Lord as you review the following passages.

- ISA 61:1-2 ~ The Spirit of the Lord GOD is upon me, because the LORD has anointed me to bring good news to the poor; he has sent me to bind up the brokenhearted, to proclaim liberty to the captives, and the opening of the prison to those who are bound; to proclaim the year of the LORD's favor, and the day of vengeance of our God; to comfort all who mourn.

- ROM 15:1-7 ~ We who are strong have an obligation to bear with the failings of the weak, and not to please ourselves. Let each of us please his neighbor for his good, to build him up. For Christ did not please himself, but as it is written, "The reproaches of those who reproached you fell on me." For whatever was written in former days was written for our instruction, that through endurance and through the encouragement of the Scriptures we might have hope. May the God of endurance and encouragement grant you to live in such harmony with one another, in accord with Christ Jesus, that together you may with one voice glorify the God and Father of our Lord Jesus Christ. Therefore welcome one another as Christ has welcomed you, for the glory of God.

- 2 CO 1:3-7 ~ Blessed be the God and Father of our Lord Jesus Christ, the Father of mercies and God of all comfort, who comforts us in all our affliction, so that we may be able to comfort those who are in any affliction, with the comfort with which we ourselves are comforted by God. For as we share abundantly in Christ's sufferings, so through Christ we share abundantly in comfort too. If we are afflicted, it is for your comfort and salvation; and if we are comforted, it is for your comfort, which you experience when you patiently endure the same sufferings that we suffer.

- 1 TH 5:14 ~ And we urge you, brothers, admonish the idle, encourage the fainthearted, help the weak, be patient with them all.

How is spiritual helping administered? As a Christian counselor, I combine relevant scripture, religious imagery, restructuring of beliefs, and reframing of the worldview, with traditional therapeutic interventions. On occasion, the client may request or respond to praying together; of course, I always pray for them in my heart. It all fits within a Biblical framework and the individual's faith system. I have found that such an approach yields far better results and in much less time than conventional methods alone. Obviously, it depends on the client. If they are not a Christian, or otherwise are not interested in matters of faith and spirituality, they will resist this form of treatment and it simply will not produce any results. We are not in the business to proselytize, so be cautious as to how forceful you appear by refraining from imposing personal beliefs.

The methods described in this manual are designed for use in all settings: individual, family, couples, and group therapy. Given the germane nature of the subject matter, the lessons are applicable to virtually all diagnoses. Spirituality can be blended into any kind of therapy, will apply to any type of mental illness, and can be utilized with any demographic. It is effective employing these techniques in cohesive groups, and also when participants have varying diagnoses, demographics, and/or religious foundations. By the way, these lessons are effective for counseling in non-Christian settings: simply administer them in the generic sense and remove scriptural references. The message and content are globally relevant, whether the audience believes in God or doesn't.

I generally conduct education and process interventions with each topic, for a total of 1-2 hours of therapy per lesson, depending on the degree of discussion. Lessons can be tailored to fit many applications and different time requirements. Activities, figures, and tables provided in this text can be employed as talking points, group discussion topics, face-to-face consultation issues, individual or group study, and homework. Scriptural references also can be used as teaching points and discussion topics, and are provided to reinforce the focus of the lesson, support the premise, and strengthen the client's faith. As you begin the process, share the following sampling of the countless Biblical passages that provide encouragement.

- PSA 27:13 ~ I believe that I shall look upon the goodness of the LORD in the land of the living!

- JER 29:11-13 ~ For I know the plans I have for you, declares the LORD, plans for welfare and not for evil, to give you a future and a hope. Then you will call upon me and come and pray to me, and I will hear you. You will seek me and find me, when you seek me with all your heart.

- JOH 10:10 ~ Jesus said, "The thief comes only to steal and kill and destroy. I came that they may have life and have it abundantly."

- PHP 1:6 ~ And I am sure of this, that he who began a good work in you will bring it to completion at the day of Jesus Christ.

- HEB 12:28-29 ~ Therefore let us be grateful for receiving a kingdom that cannot be shaken, and thus let us offer to God acceptable worship, with reverence and awe, for our God is a consuming fire.

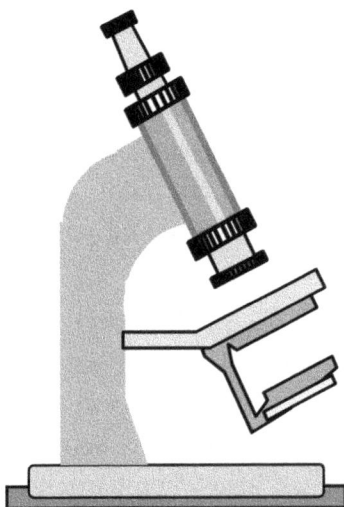

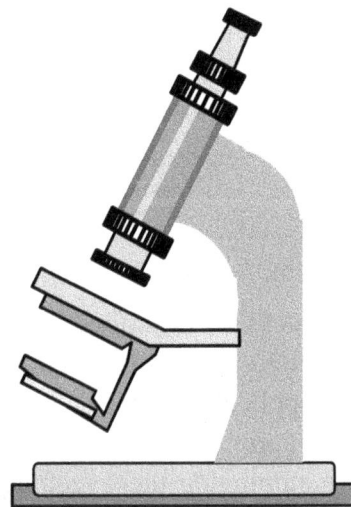

ASSESSMENT

Clinical Diagnosis

The most reliable source of information about the client will undoubtedly be the client. Certainly the family can provide useful information, as well as others who have close contact, and other professionals treating the client. It is often a good practice to get corroboration from these additional sources. Obtain a release of information for every reliable source, if possible. But the clients are the customers and they come to you for a reason. They have inside knowledge of why they are there, what they hope to accomplish, and when they are ready to leave. That's why we must let them choose what to work on, what methods to employ, and how long it should take. That doesn't mean you shouldn't make suggestions or recommendations, or even steer them towards the preferred approach based upon their symptoms and goals. But let them take ownership of the decisions, and they will feel more responsible about achieving results.

In addition to the usual stuff (symptoms, thoughts, feelings, etc.), you also may ask about things that interest your clients, what influences them, what their expectations are, what they fear or worry about, their talents and habits, their abilities, knowledge and skills, their sensitivities, superstitions, imaginations, cultural influences, history, and prior treatment. Some information you can glean from the client via observation, to include personality attributes, communication skills, temperament, processing modalities, and intelligence. Note that the client might not be a reliable source about some of these things.

Instruct clients on the process of assessment and diagnosis and involve them. Allow them to report what their concerns are using the assessment tools provided. Clients will need to identify their symptoms, thoughts, feelings, behaviors, and stressors. Examples are provided in the tables below but there are dozens more that could be included. Do not hesitate to add to the templates: whatever the client feels is important.

Teach clients about the symptoms, behaviors, etc. that he or she reports and how they collectively point to a diagnosis. Discuss the criteria that they meet as you clarify what the diagnosis represents; they should be able to understand the Diagnostic and Statistical Manual (DSM) criteria associated with the diagnosis if carefully explained. Clients can learn the following definitions; most of your clients will exhibit one or more of these conditions.

Affective Disorder: A severe disturbance in mood or emotional state. Anxiety and depression are affective, or emotional, in nature.

Anxiety: A state of extreme worry, fear, nervousness, or uneasiness that is usually unrepresentative of the actual threat or likelihood of a dreaded event occurring. Additional symptoms include increased heart rate and respiration, muscular tension, and a desire to escape; it is different from a normal reaction to danger. Anxiety is reflected in the following disorders: Phobia, Obsessive-Compulsive Disorder, Posttraumatic Stress Disorder, Panic Disorder, Acute Stress Disorder, Generalized Anxiety Disorder.

Bipolar Disorder: A disturbance in mood, also known as manic-depression; alternating and/or unpredictable periods of high and low emotional states of lengthy duration.

Delusion: A false belief. For example, the unsubstantiated belief that people are out to get you is a paranoid delusion; believing to be God is a grandiose delusion.

Dementia: This is characterized by significant cognitive deficit, memory impairment, and confusion; its onset is typically gradual, with steady deterioration, and is often irreversible. Alzheimer's, Huntington's, and Parkinson's represent examples. Dementia also can occur more rapidly with substance abuse and brain injury/trauma.

Depression: Prolonged state of sadness, lethargy, despair, despondency, and/or gloom; characterized by inability to enjoy or find interest in anything, self-defeating messages, isolation and withdrawal, and low self-esteem. It is often accompanied by lack of hygiene, nutrition and sleep, learned helplessness, feelings of guilt and melancholia. Depressive disorders include Major Depressive Disorder and Dysthymic Disorder.

Hallucination: A false sensation or perception. Hallucinations are usually visual (like seeing shadow people), auditory (hearing voices from the dead), or tactile (sensation of bugs crawling all over).

Manic: A feeling of being up, aroused, or on top of your game; characterized by extreme excitement, elation, exhilaration, talkativeness, aggression, and/or hyperactivity. It may involve feeling less sleepy, engaging in risky behavior, flight of ideas, impulsiveness, and irrational plans.

Mood: A repetitive or consistent emotional state. A mood swing represents abrupt changes in mood characterized by extreme ups or downs. Bipolar Disorder is a mood disorder with extreme ups and downs.

Personality Disorder: This is a person with inflexible, maladaptive personality traits that are ingrained and difficult to modify or treat. These traits can interfere with cognitive and social functioning.

Phobia: Intense fear of an object, situation, or event, characterized by significant anxiety. Additional symptoms include faintness, fatigue, palpitations, perspiration, nausea, tremor, panic. Phobia is an avoidance behavior reinforced by the relief response. For example, agoraphobia is the fear of being in an inescapable or embarrassing situation; the avoidance response is to stay home providing temporary relief from the anxiety, thereby reinforcing the avoidance behavior.

Psychosis: A state of mind that is characterized by intrusions of false thoughts, beliefs, or perceptions which appear indistinguishable from reality. Examples are hallucinations and delusions. Psychotic disorders include Schizophrenia, Schizoaffective Disorder, and Substance Induced Psychosis.

Sociopathic: Characterized by antisocial, impulsive, hedonistic (self-indulgent, pleasure seeking), irresponsible, criminal, and/or aggressive behavior; the individual feels guiltless (no remorse), has a warped capacity for love, and often exhibits inadequate adjustment or attachment. Aspects of psychopathology are evident, though some distinguish the two syndromes as differing along social and intellectual lines, respectively.

Spiritual Assessment

With respect to spiritual connections, the more clients are involved in faith activities, the healthier they are. This is the central element of a wholesome support system. You will find that many clients claiming to be Christian are engaged in few if any of the following activities. That is, they do not have an active faith. God wants us to be on fire with respect to our faith, not lukewarm (REV 3:15-16). Try to determine how dedicated and active they are in their Christian walk. If they are not engaged, they need to be.

If you intend to employ spiritual interventions, you first must understand the client's belief system. Well, you should anyway to avoid erroneous assumptions and disagreements. Ask them what their views are concerning the virgin birth, the miracles of Christ, his crucifixion, the sacraments, and salvation; the blood atonement, the resurrection, afterlife, paradise, and eternity. Determine where they stand on the ideas of heaven and hell, creation and evolution, angels and demons, sin and death. See if they adhere to and understand the principal tenets of Christianity: the concept of Holy Trinity, the difference between Law and Grace, justification by faith instead of works, forgiveness of sins, the Sacrificial Lamb, inheritance in the Kingdom of God.

You may notice considerable variation among people of a given faith with respect to what they believe. Islam is a perfect example. While their beliefs mirror many traditional Judeo-Christian notions as revealed in the Koran, some aspects can be interpreted a variety of ways. This is why there are mild mannered Moslems on the one hand and radical jihadists on the other. Of course, you have extreme factions in any religion. But you won't get much flak from people of a particular faith if you quote directly from their holy books. That's why I use a lot of scripture. But even people that purport to be Christians disagree about what the Bible says, how accurate it is, and whether it is the true Word of God.

Find out the degree to which clients esteem the Bible, whether they believe it in its entirety, and if they even read it. I often hear, "I don't read the Bible because there are too many inconsistencies, or it has lost accuracy and meaning over the years, or it is too complicated." None of those assumptions are true (PRO 30:5-6; 2 TI 3:16); but it does take effort and time to get into the Bible. The more the Bible is read, however, the more it is absorbed and the greater the wisdom imparted (2 TI 3:15).

The Christian therapist must be more than a counselor; he or she is also a teacher, and a mentor. That means becoming deeply entrenched in the Bible so as to defend it and explain it (apologetics). This is knowledge that is available to anyone who studies, digests, and practices what it says. Most people believe that God is all knowing, all powerful, and ever present. They will not dispute that he is the source of absolute truth, cannot lie, and keeps his promises. However, they do not always revere the Bible as being inspired by God, unaltered, inerrant, and essential. But the more they hear it and read it, the more it will make sense.

Do your clients have a routine for prayer, do they give to charity, and do they witness and proclaim the faith? They may say, "I pray before I go to bed." Or, "I pray when I'm in a jam." The Bible teaches us to pray constantly (1 TH 5:17). Or, "I help others whenever I can." Or, "I put a little into the offering plate now and then." The Bible teaches that our lives should be a living sacrifice (ROM 12:1); we should tithe (give 10%) of our wealth to the ministry and/or the needy (MAL 3:10); and we should go forth and make disciples (MAT 28:18-20).

Determine if they have a church life, and if so, how extensive is it. You may hear excuses like, "I don't go to church because the people there are fake, or hypocrites." Well, I have encountered different kinds of sinners in church, myself included. Who else goes to church but sinners? Where else should they be going? As the Lord said: Only the sick need a physician (MAT 9:12). Or you may hear, "Sure, we go to church on Christmas and Easter." Or, "Church is too boring." If that is what they think, they either haven't been to church in a long time, or they haven't shopped around for a church that suits them. If they don't like the traditional, formal approach, they should seek a church with a more contemporary format. Fellowship and worship with other Christians is a command of God (HEB 10:25).

Assessment Tools

After gathering essential client information, educate the individual what it all means in a summarization. Give him or her time to process the information; then get them to describe their understanding or insights into the matter. This will guide the direction of treatment and the establishment of a treatment plan and associated goals. Include spiritual growth as a goal if the client is willing. The interventions presented in this book are designed to challenge clients to restructure their belief systems and be reoriented towards truth and righteousness. This creates more adaptive and thoughtful cognitive operations resulting in positive, virtuous actions. Practicing the modified behavior leads to a better attitude, more constructive outcomes, and greater self-esteem. A crucial component to assessment is spiritual assessment as indicated above.

I have attached tools that I developed to perform assessment and diagnosis. I have found them to be very useful. Use them to teach clients the process; and they can learn to use them to perform self-assessments. Both therapist and client can discuss the self-assessment tool to track progress. Establish goals of therapy based upon which issues are rated high, which ones the client wishes to address, and what degree of change he or she will accept.

Have clients complete the diagnostic tool periodically during treatment to see how effective the treatment has been and how much progress has been made. This revised tool is similar to the one I used to conduct performance improvement research. I was able to demonstrate to the administrators, the clients, and the funding sources that our holistic approach was yielding very positive outcomes, as reported in the introductory review of evidence-based practice. Patients also want to see proof that they are getting better, which facilitates further growth and improvement.

Issues that are pertinent to what is bothering me or why I am seeking help.

Circle those items that apply and add others to the list that are of concern to you.

Unpleasant Symptoms – Identify your symptoms. You may choose from among these examples: stress/anxiety, sadness/depression, extreme mood swings, disorientation, cannot concentrate or focus, insomnia, hearing strange sounds or voices, seeing things that aren't there, having weird body sensations, experiencing repetitive body movements, paranoia, amnesia. Include anything you think is important even if they are not in the above list.

_____   _____

_____   _____

_____   _____

_____   _____

_____   _____

Disturbing Thoughts – Identify things that you are thinking that are bothersome or disturbing to you. Here are some possible examples: desire to hurt yourself, wanting to die, desire to hurt others, unpleasant memories keep coming back, cannot remember important things, cannot concentrate, immoral desires, really bad dreams, not interested in doing anything, cannot enjoy anything, disorganized, forgetful, racing thoughts.

_____   _____

_____   _____

_____   _____

_____   _____

_____   _____

Negative Feelings – Identify the negative feelings and emotions that you are having. Here are some examples but you may think of others: angry, afraid, frustrated, hopeless, helpless, worthless, withdrawn, guilty, shameful, lonely, empty, bored, lazy, obsessed, grieving, panicky, irritable, inflexible, vulnerable, stupid.

_____   _____

_____   _____

_____   _____

_____   _____

_____   _____

Destructive Behaviors – Identify behaviors or activities that you are engaged in that are destructive or high risk. Examples include cutting yourself, violent outbursts, alcohol/drug use, gambling, sexual promiscuity, excessive spending, overeating, not eating, not sleeping, oversleeping, poor hygiene, procrastinating, reckless driving, hanging around bad people, going places that are hazardous, unsafe actions, risk or sensation seeking, criminal activity.

_____ _____

_____ _____

_____ _____

_____ _____

_____ _____

Medical Issues – Identify any medical problems you are experiencing. Again, here are some examples but you can add others that are not on this list: illness, disease, infection, injury, bleeding, chronic pain, migraines/headaches, nausea, dizziness, numbness, shaking, chills, chronic fatigue, seizures, hot flashes, life changes (such as menopause).

_____ _____

_____ _____

_____ _____

_____ _____

_____ _____

Environmental Stressors: Identify the situational conditions in your environment or world that are stressing you out. Use examples from the following list and feel free to add others: school, work, marriage, family, peers, crisis, conflict, loss, divorce, neglect, abuse, needs not being met, debt, cannot make ends meet, health problems, legal problems.

_____ _____

_____ _____

_____ _____

_____ _____

_____ _____

Healthy and Unhealthy Relationships: List those relationships that you value or which have been a positive influence in your life. Next list those relationships that you regret or which have been a negative influence in your life. Include all pertinent relationships such as family, friends (or ex-friends), people in your school or work environment, and anyone else that impacts your life, whether alive or dead.

Healthy	Unhealthy

Assets/Strengths: Identify the things that are going your way or are positive for you. Examples may include the following: companionship/intimacy, family, friends, support system, social life, healthy, employed, religious, smart, educated, sense of humor, hobbies, recreation.

Spiritual Connections: Identify the spiritual activities that you currently or have recently engaged in: daily private prayer, daily family prayer, regular church attendance, home Bible study, church Bible study or Sunday school, church teacher or Vacation Bible School teacher, witnessing/evangelism in your community, tithing, financially contributing to your church or the needy, church social events and engagements, church office holder, attending a church support group, going on a church related retreat.

Self Assessment Form

Name _____   **Age** _____   **Date** _____

Rate each symptom or condition from 1 (very low) to 10 (very high).
Leave blank if it does not apply.

___ Abuse (disturbed by current or previous physical, emotional, or sexual abuse)
___ Addiction (hooked on alcohol, drugs, sex, pornography, or gambling)
___ Adjustment Problems (having difficulty adjusting to a new situation or people)
___ Aggression (feeling hostile, violent, or pushy)
___ Anger (feeling mad much of the time)
___ Anxiety/Stress (feeling worried, stressed, or anxious a lot)
___ Antisocial Behavior (wanting to perform terrible things or do something against the law)
___ Attention Deficit/Hyperactivity (cannot concentrate, pay attention, or stay focused)
___ Codependency (depending on others for everything)
___ Communication Issues (cannot get the message across and/or cannot understand others)
___ Conduct/Behavioral Issues (misbehaving all the time; inappropriate conduct)
___ Delusions (believing things that are not true)
___ Depression (feeling sad and blue all the time)
___ Dissociation (feeling detached from body/mind)
___ Eating Issues (eating too much or too little)
___ Elimination Problems (having trouble going to the bathroom)
___ Environmental Issues (problems at home, work, or school)
___ Grief (having a hard time dealing with a loss)
___ Guilt (blaming self for something, or everything)
___ Hallucinations (seeing, hearing, or feeling things that are not real)
___ Impulse Control Issues (uncontrolled desire to do something over and over)
___ Learning Disability (unable to learn things; easily confused)
___ Mania (feeling hyper, with racing thoughts, high energy, talking fast, lots to do)
___ Medical Problems (having a serious or debilitating medical condition)
___ Memory/Cognitive Impairment (not able to remember things or think clearly)
___ Mood Swings (rapid changes in mood; up and down feelings)
___ Neglect (not getting needs met; no help from others)
___ Obsessive-Compulsive Behavior (uncontrollable desire to avoid something, like germs)
___ Panic (feeling frightened, alarmed, or really nervous; breathing hard; heart racing)
___ Personality/Identity Issues (peculiarity in behavior or demeanor; different from others)
___ Phobic/Fearful (irrational and extreme fear or dread of something)
___ Repression (hiding disturbing memories from awareness)
___ Self-esteem Issues (not liking self very much)
___ Sexual Deviancy (doing sexual things that are abnormal and indecent)
___ Sexual Dysfunction/Pain (not being able to perform or have sex)
___ Sleeping Issues (not getting enough sleep or sleeping too much)
___ Suicidal Ideation (death wishes; desire to die)
___ Violence (having been a recent victim or observer of terrible violence)

Rate these issues again after treatment, or after some time passes.
Compare the results with the previous assessment to see how much progress has been made.

ASSESSMENT

- Individual Differences
- Attributes, Abilities
- Personality, Intelligence
- History and Culture
- Unpleasant Symptoms
- Disturbing Thoughts
- Negative Feelings
- Destructive Behaviors
- Medical Issues
- Environmental Stressors
- Relationships
- Assets, Strengths
- Beliefs, Values
- Spiritual Connections

DEVELOPMENT

OBJECTIVE	Learn to develop appropriate goals for a particular age or level of functioning that will expedite forward movement towards fulfilling hopes and dreams.
INTERVENTION	Discuss the various stages of development as applicable. Define the criteria for establishing smart goals relative to one's developmental status.
PLAN	Identify reasonable goals and break them down into objectives, steps, and schedule. Integrate goals into a realistic action plan.

"I'm looking for a lot of men who have an infinite capacity to not know what can't be done."
– Henry Ford

"It is for us to pray, not for tasks equal to our powers, but for powers equal to our tasks." – Phillips Brooks

Goals Development

Every client you serve will be interested in positive growth. It is important to determine what stage of development they are experiencing and what their growth goals entail, ensuring that their aspirations are applicable to their level of functioning and ability. I utilize a variation of the SMART goals technique (originated by Doran, 1981). My goal as a therapist is helping clients establish their own goals, and coming up with sensible ways of tracking their progress. There may be several goals that the individual can pursue at any given time. Goals are designed to propel the person forward in a positive direction, and towards an ultimate, though yet undefined, destination. Here are five components of SMART goals.

S = Simplicity: Make it simple and concise. Complex goals are too difficult to measure and to break down into components. State the target clearly and include only one intended result. Separate goals are needed if you have more than one desired outcome. Otherwise they become too multifaceted to track, to time, and/or to determine which result is associated with which action being implemented.

M = Measurable: There has to be a way to objectively measure progress. A quantitative approach is preferred, but a qualitative measurement can be used if it is directly observable. For example, a goal might be to achieve a 50% reduction in calorie intake; that would be a quantitative goal. Or another might be to submit five job applications in one week. A qualitative goal might be to enroll in school, create a plan, or generate a list of possibilities worth exploring further. There should be an expected product, outcome, or desired performance, such as getting a promotion, making an A in the class, or earning the money for a new car.

A = Achievable: Goals should be realistic and attainable. Don't raise the bar so high that it is unlikely to be achieved. For example, the goal should not be to finish your four-year degree in two years; or to land a job for which you have insufficient education and experience. Start small and work your way up. Instead of shooting for CEO, aim for a promotion to middle management first. Goals are stepping stones towards an ultimate purpose or destination; they are not the ultimate destination.

R = Relevant: The goal should have a specified conclusion that is results-oriented, and which is relevant to the route you wish to take. You need to be sure where you want to go and how you intend to get there. That is, the goal and associated steps must point you in the right direction in a way that is likely to produce the desired outcome. It would be ridiculous to have a goal of getting a commercial driver license if your endgame is to become a teacher. Or, why would a manager require the employee to clean the bathroom if the goal is to coach him on managing time?

T = Timed: There must be a finite amount of time in which to complete the goal. The timeframe should be realistic; not too short not too long. If you make it too short you're setting yourself up for failure; too long and you tend to lose interest or you procrastinate. The timing will vary depending on the goal and the underlying objectives. You can add up the time for each separate task and get a good idea of the total time needed to complete the goal.

Once you have established the criteria for the goal, it is necessary to determine the objectives. The goal is the end, the objectives are the means. Let's say the goal is for an alcoholic to develop a support system to help him or her stay in recovery. Objectives might be to join an Alcoholics Anonymous (AA) group, find a sponsor, move in with the parents, start going to church, and so forth. Each objective may have subordinate steps. For the first objective of joining an AA group, the steps might be first to phone the local AA office and identify clubs near the person's residence; second to select two clubs from the list and attend each one three times; third to decide if either one of these clubs meets the individual's needs, and begin attending that club regularly; or if not, try out some other clubs that may be a little farther from home, until the person feels comfortable with the environment and the people; then start attending there regularly.

Objectives are specific tasks that contribute to the goal. Tasks are of equal importance and do not imply a hierarchy or a sequence. The task delineates a particular action with a direct object, such as attend a support group like AA. Each task has certain steps that must be completed to finish the task. These steps usually follow a particular order. They are like elements of a task, such as make a phone call and obtain a list of AA clubs in the area. Help the client develop a flowchart; this is a useful way of mapping out the goal, objectives, and steps, as well as contingency plans if the process has more than one possible path to the goal.

Goals should be chosen on the basis of where the person is in their growth. This depends largely on their developmental stage. There are a number of great theories from the archives of developmental psychology (as follows) from which to glean goals.

- ➢ Freud: Sexual development
- ➢ Piaget, Gange, Gesell: Cognitive development
- ➢ Erikson, Sullivan, Levinson: Social development
- ➢ Kohlberg: Moral development

"Aim for the stars and maybe you'll reach the sky." – Reinhold Niebuhr

"We aim above the mark to hit the mark." – Ralph Waldo Emerson

Reference

Doran, G. T. (1981). There's a SMART way to write management's goals and objectives. *Management Review*, 70(11), 35-36.

Developmental Stages

It just so happens that I have my own developmental model, which is kind of a consensus, gleaned from the theories I have studied as well as my own experience. It is presented below. Choose treatment goals that are appropriate for the age group represented, but do not put constraints on the possibilities. Models are useful but are mere representations of the likely trends; clearly there will be overlap among the stages. Let us examine each stage of development independently and suggest possible goals for each of them.

STAGE	AGE
Orientation	0-3
Preparation	3-6
Imagination	6-12
Exploration	12-16
Identification	16-21
Occupation	21-35
Specialization	35-50
Resolution	50-65
Retrospection	65-80
Stagnation	80-95
Termination	final year

"Life is a series of natural and spontaneous changes. Don't resist them; that only creates sorrow. Let things flow naturally forward in whatever way they like." – Lao-Tzu

"If we did all the things we are capable of, we would astound ourselves." – Thomas Edison

Orientation (0-3). The child is getting familiar with himself/herself, the surroundings, and individual capabilities. Kids are learning by observing, imitating, and touching while interacting and at play with objects and people. They can organize their experiences, imagine things that are no longer present, and recognize that their actions have consequences. But they have a short attention span for most things and a poorly developed long term memory. They begin talking, but still understand better through physical contact. Caregiving, supervising, bonding, and nurturing are critically important. What goals might a child in this group have? Here are some suggestions; you are encouraged to come up with more.

➢ Establish attachments
➢ Potty training
➢ Recite the alphabet
➢ Learn words and their meanings
➢ Identify who to trust or not trust
➢ Memorize a simple prayer

Preparation (3-6). Life experiences are egocentric, meaning is symbolic, and understanding is more intuitive. The child is being readied to enter the education system; parents often prepare the kid with certain academic and social skills. The child can comprehend permanence and conservation concepts, can anticipate events, and can begin to relate verbal concepts with visual ones. Memory is becoming more reliable, eye-hand coordination is improving, and language skills are advancing significantly. The kid also learns a great deal from playtime with other kids, particularly social skills and self-control.

➢ Learn to apply imagination
➢ Classify objects into categories
➢ Develop responsible behaviors
➢ Obey rules
➢ Take the initiative
➢ Practice sharing
➢ Make new friends
➢ Create something artistic
➢ Recite a personal Bible passage

• PSA 51:10-12 ~ Create in me a clean heart, O God, and renew a right spirit within me. Cast me not away from your presence, and take not your Holy Spirit from me. Restore to me the joy of your salvation, and uphold me with a willing spirit.

• MAT 6:9-13 ~ Jesus taught us to pray like this: "Our Father in heaven, hallowed be your name. Your kingdom come, your will be done, on earth as it is in heaven. Give us this day our daily bread, and forgive us our debts, as we also have forgiven our debtors. And lead us not into temptation, but deliver us from evil."

• ROM 8:26 ~ Likewise the Spirit helps us in our weakness. For we do not know what to pray for as we ought, but the Spirit himself intercedes for us with groanings too deep for words.

Imagination (6-12). The child is in elementary school and being bombarded with the basics. He or she can understand transformation concepts, think abstractly, arrive at generalizations, and consider hypothetical possibilities. These kids learn things rapidly and easily just by doing them. Their minds are very receptive and flexible; they can consider multiple alternatives, and they can correct their behavior. They have a sense of morality, caring, and justice. They are building peer groups with others who are like them or in close proximity, and they are compelled to conform. All of this is building creative faculties and fueling fantasies.

> ➤ Explore personal interests
> ➤ Acquire specific, desired skills
> ➤ Identify consequences for certain actions
> ➤ Learn to cooperate
> ➤ Learn to compromise
> ➤ Identify the relationships between objects
> ➤ Get involved in team building such as sports
> ➤ Visit museums and science fairs
> ➤ Work puzzles
> ➤ Develop a hobby
> ➤ Learn about and discuss Bible stories

• HEB 11:1-40 (paraphrased) ~ Faith is the assurance of things we hope for; it is the proof of good things ahead that we cannot see. Through faith we understand that the universe was framed by the Word of God, that things we see were made from things we cannot see. Because of faith, Abel gave a more worthy offering than his brother Cain. Enoch went straight to heaven without dying. Noah, being unafraid, obeyed God and built the ark. Abraham left his home and country to a foreign land at the direction of God; and his wife Sarah bore their child in her old age. And when Abraham was tried, he was ready to sacrifice his only son Isaac, who later became the father of Jacob the father of Joseph. What great faith was exhibited by Moses who gave up a position of royalty to lead the Israelites to freedom; many miracles he performed with the power of the Holy Spirit proving to Israel that God alone was in charge. Consider also his deputy Joshua, who took command and led the Israelites, conquering Jericho without raising a sword; and how Rahab protected the spies and was spared. What more can I say about the powers of faith? I could tell you about great judges like Gideon, Barrack, Samson, and Japhtheh, and about great kings like David and Solomon, and about the prophets (such as Elijah, Isaiah, Jeremiah, Daniel). Through faith, these people subdued kingdoms, administered justice, enforced treaties, shut the mouth of lions, quenched fires, and escaped certain death. They were weak but were made strong, and they fought valiantly in battle, routing even the greatest of armies. They even raised the dead. They endured torture, refusing to renounce God as a condition for release. They were mocked, beaten, chained, imprisoned, stoned, and beheaded. They wandered the wilderness in shabby clothes, destitute, tormented, and afflicted. Although their life on earth was full of strife, they awaited their deliverance, as we also must do, until God makes us perfect before him.

Exploration (12-16). The individual can formulate and test hypotheses, has developed the ability to logically arrive at solutions, and comprehends basic cause and effect. A change of life is well underway as the young adolescent's hormones are going wild; growth spurts are common both physically and intellectually. Individuals are forming intimate relationships, exploring opportunities, and discovering new things about themselves, not the least of which is their sexuality. They are very concerned about their body image and its effect on connecting with others. While the body begins to resemble that of an adult, emotionally they are still children. There is a considerable amount of social or peer pressure.

> ➢ Explain the concept of law and order
> ➢ Learn proper opposite sex interactions
> ➢ Solve problems, especially social ones
> ➢ Make informed decisions
> ➢ Create plans
> ➢ Take on more roles
> ➢ Try new things
> ➢ Join clubs (like the boy/girl scouts or church group)
> ➢ Articulate beliefs
> ➢ Define spirituality

- DEU 6:1-7 ~ Now this is the commandment – the statutes and the rules – that the LORD your God commanded me (Moses) to teach you, that you may do them in the land to which you are going over, to possess it, that you may fear the LORD your God, you and your son and your son's son, by keeping all his statutes and his commandments, which I command you, all the days of your life, and that your days may be long. Hear therefore, O Israel, and be careful to do them, that it may go well with you, and that you may multiply greatly, as the LORD, the God of your fathers, has promised you, in a land flowing with milk and honey. Hear, O Israel: The LORD our God, the LORD is one. You shall love the LORD your God with all your heart and with all your soul and with all your might. And these words that I command you today shall be on your heart. You shall teach them diligently to your children, and shall talk of them when you sit in your house, and when you walk by the way, and when you lie down, and when you rise.

- 2 TI 3:14-17 ~ But as for you, continue in what you have learned and have firmly believed, knowing from whom you learned it and how from childhood you have been acquainted with the sacred writings, which are able to make you wise for salvation through faith in Christ Jesus. All Scripture is breathed out by God and profitable for teaching, for reproof, for correction, and for training in righteousness, that the man of God may be complete, equipped for every good work.

Identification (16-21). The young adults are beginning to establish an identity that will stick with them throughout life. They are trying things on for size to see what fits and discarding the rest. They need the freedom to explore these things; but within realistic boundaries as the desire for independence is poorly founded, and the tendency to take risks somewhat arbitrary.

That is, they desire the privileges of adulthood but are not fully prepared for the responsibilities, and usually remain financially and emotionally dependent upon their parents. They are fully developed physically, but not psychologically; and not quite integrated into society. It's like being in-between, a very precarious position to be in.

> Take on additional responsibilities
> Pursue academic interests
> Practice inductive reasoning
> Solve complex problems
> Develop a plan for higher education
> Explore different occupational interests
> Master specific tasks
> Define proper rules for intimacy
> Make informed life choices
> Read the entire Bible
> Define God

- PRO 3:5-6 ~ Trust in the LORD with all your heart, and do not lean on your own understanding. In all your ways acknowledge him, and he will make straight your paths.

- MAT 7:13-14 ~ Enter by the narrow gate. For the gate is wide and the way is easy that leads to destruction, and those who enter by it are many. For the gate is narrow and the way is hard that leads to life, and those who find it are few.

- 1 TH 5:21-22 ~ Test everything; hold fast what is good. Abstain from every form of evil.

- JAM 1:25 ~ But the one who looks into the perfect law, the law of liberty, and perseveres, being no hearer who forgets but a doer who acts, he will be blessed in his doing.

Occupation (21-35). The adult is very busy, balancing a number of responsibilities simultaneously, and distributing the available time accordingly. He or she is occupied in several different arenas, to include college, work, social life, marriage, children, and personal interests. They strive for individual competency, accomplishment, recognition, and promotion, while keeping family and relationships a priority. They are basically full grown and at their physical peak: strength, endurance, health, sexuality, and homeostasis. They have developed a set of moral standards and performance standards and try to live up to them. Intimacy is a very important part of life in terms of validation, connection, and release. Friendships also are vital to their need to be needed.

> Get a graduate degree
> Shoot for a promotion
> Explore new forms of intellectual stimulation
> Enter honest and lasting relationships
> Develop a vision for the future
> Establish career goals
> Take reasonable risks

- Perform contingency planning
- Break a bad habit
- Become an officer in a club or church
- Become a Bible school teacher, coach sports, or mentor kids
- Explore personal spirituality more deeply

- ECC 2:22-26 ~ What has a man from all the toil and striving of heart with which he toils beneath the sun? For all his days are full of sorrow, and his work is a vexation. Even in the night his heart does not rest. This also is vanity. There is nothing better for a person than that he should eat and drink and find enjoyment in his toil. This also, I saw, is from the hand of God, for apart from him who can eat or who can have enjoyment? For to the one who pleases him God has given wisdom and knowledge and joy, but to the sinner he has given the business of gathering and collecting, only to give to one who pleases God. This also is vanity and a striving after wind.

- JOB 36:11 ~ If they listen and serve him, they complete their days in prosperity, and their years in pleasantness.

- COL 1:10 ~ Walk in a manner worthy of the Lord, fully pleasing to him, bearing fruit in every good work and increasing in the knowledge of God.

- HEB 10:23 ~ Let us hold fast the confession of our hope without wavering, for he who promised is faithful.

Specialization (35-50). By now the individual is middle-aged, taking on new challenges and setting more lofty goals. There is a sense of urgency to achieve greatness, maximize potential, and attain financial stability and sufficiency. There will be new crises as well as opportunities. Physical changes are occurring such as graying, wrinkles, and weight gain, not to mention female menopause. Women worry about their attractiveness and men their sexual prowess. Men and women both have become firmly established in a career, role, or discipline. It is a good time to branch out, become educated in other fields, take on a leadership role, become a consultant, or start a private business. Entertainment and the cost of living are getting more expensive; financial responsibilities are increasing as well. There is pressure from the generations before you and after you.

- Consider expanding
- Learn special skills
- Do some moonlighting (like teaching a college course)
- Pursue an executive leadership position
- Carve a niche using your unique skills
- Go on a second honeymoon
- Apply crisis management techniques
- Establish a regular exercise routine
- Find enjoyment in outdoor activities
- Keep in touch with family and friends
- Be a pillar of society

> Chair a church committee

- PRO 9:9 ~ Give instruction to a wise man, and he will be still wiser; teach a righteous man, and he will increase in learning.

- 1 CO 12:4-12,26 ~ Now there are varieties of gifts, but the same Spirit; and there are varieties of service, but the same Lord; and there are varieties of activities, but it is the same God who empowers them all in everyone. To each is given the manifestation of the Spirit for the common good. For to one is given through the Spirit the utterance of wisdom, and to another the utterance of knowledge according to the same Spirit, to another faith by the same Spirit, to another gifts of healing by the one Spirit, to another the working of miracles, to another prophecy, to another the ability to distinguish between spirits, to another various kinds of tongues, to another the interpretation of tongues. All these are empowered by one and the same Spirit, who apportions to each one individually as he wills. For just as the body is one and has many members, and all the members of the body, though many, are one body, so it is with Christ… If one member suffers, all suffer together; if one member is honored, all rejoice together.

Resolution (50-65). The kids have flown the coop, the parents are fading away (or gone), and you have a little more time on your hands. You are mellowing and less desperate about succeeding, but there also is the proverbial midlife crisis. There will be a normal fear of making any big changes or taking risks, but don't let that dissuade you. This is largely due to the fact that you have less energy, resilience, endurance, memory, and willpower; you are getting slower, sicker, and more tired. Remember, you need to exercise and you need to relax. As the career winds down the individual or the couple starts looking towards second careers and/or retirement. Decisions are being made on what to do, where to settle, and how to spend the golden years, not to mention how to afford it.

> Identify ways of staying engaged cognitively
> Create a regular social schedule
> Explore new, inexpensive ways of having fun
> Romance your spouse, partner
> Make time for recreation, travel, exercise
> Visit loved ones regularly
> Take care of the grandkids
> Develop different channels to express emotions
> Create or revise a last will and testament
> Become a church elder

- DEU 4:9-10 ~ Only take care, and keep your soul diligently, lest you forget the things that your eyes have seen, and lest they depart from your heart all the days of your life. Make them known to your children and your children's children – how on the day that you stood before the LORD your God at Horeb, the LORD said to me, 'Gather the people to me, that I may let them hear my words, so that they may learn to fear me all the days that they live on the earth, and that they may teach their children so.'

- ROM 12:1-21 (paraphrased) ~ Let your body be a living sacrifice, totally acceptable to God; this is your spiritual act of worship. Do not conform to this world but be transformed by the renewing of your mind. Test and approve what is God's perfect will. Do not think highly of yourself but use sober judgment in accordance with the amount of faith God has given you. Just as our body has many members, each with a separate purpose, so we, being part of the body of Christ, have different responsibilities. We all have special gifts which God in his grace has given us: Some can minister, teach, or provide guidance and counseling. If you have the gift of prophecy, do so in proportion to your faith. If you have the gift of giving, give generously. If you have the gift of leadership, lead with diligence. If you have the gift of mercy, show it cheerfully. Let your love shine, do not hide it. Hate the evil, and hold onto the good. Love one another with brotherly love and honor. Don't be lazy in business matters. Serve the Lord with a glowing spirit. Rejoice in your hope. Be patient in times of trouble. Be consistent in prayer. Help fellow Christians in need. Be hospitable. Bless others, even those who persecute you; don't curse anyone. Rejoice with those who are rejoicing and mourn with those who are mourning. Try to get along. Don't be proud or conceited; humble yourself even before the lowliest of characters. Don't reward evil with evil. Always be honest. Promote peace. Do not seek revenge; God has said that all vengeance belongs to him alone. If your enemy is hungry or thirsty, give him food and drink. Don't let evil get the better of you, but overcome evil with goodness.

Retrospection (65-80). Retirement should be enjoyable; make the most of it. You have a lot of good memories to keep you going; most of the unpleasant memories have faded. But don't forget to look forward, as it isn't over yet. And take precautions, such as regular checkups, memory challenges, and spiritual renewal; and practice moderation in all things. Stay active, socialize, have fun, have sex, but don't overdo it. Your body cannot take much abuse and it will break down easily. Though the body is not as durable the brain still works. But short- and long-term memory will begin fading continuously, as will physical functioning. So keep using it as much as you can or you will lose it faster. Adjustment to losing a spouse will be particularly difficult during this period.

> - It's all right to have a part-time job
> - Continue to develop knowledge base
> - Provide guidance and wisdom to youth
> - Don't stop exercising
> - Find ways to laugh
> - Try new hobbies (painting, crafts, collectibles)
> - Do everything with your spouse
> - Continue being intimate with your spouse
> - If you have lost your spouse, start dating
> - Continue grand-parenting
> - Join a senior citizen center
> - Ponder fond memories by looking through photo albums and memorabilia
> - Volunteer at your church or civic organization

- 1 CO 1:19-25; 1 CO 2:4-5; 1 CO 3:19-20 (paraphrased) ~ It is written: I will destroy the wisdom of the wise, and I will bring to nothing the understanding of the prudent. Where is the wise person? Where is the scholar? Where is the philosopher of this world? Hasn't God made foolish the wisdom of this world? The world through its wisdom did not know God, but through simple preaching, God enabled people who would believe to be saved. The Jews required signs and miracles and the Greeks searched for wisdom and truth. We preach about the crucified Christ, which to the Jews is an obstacle and to the Gentiles is foolishness. But to those whom God has called, both Jews and non-Jews, Christ is the power of God and the wisdom of God. For the foolishness of God is wiser than the wisdom of mankind, and the weaknesses of God are stronger than the might of men. My message and my preaching were not with wise and persuasive words but with the power of the Spirit, so that your faith would be based, not on the wisdom of the world, but in the power of God. The wisdom of this world is foolishness to God. As it is written, God catches the wise in their own craftiness, for the thoughts of the wise are futile.

- 1 CO 15:58 ~ Therefore, my beloved brothers, be steadfast, immovable, always abounding in the work of the Lord, knowing that in the Lord your labor is not in vain.

Stagnation (80-95). Faculties are seriously deteriorating. The body parts are not functioning right if at all; neither is the brain for that matter. It will take much effort just to maintain what you have mentally and physically. One may experience significant issues with sleep disturbance, pain, disability, and/or eating disorders. The person is probably taking a variety of medications. Regular follow-ups with doctors become part of the routine. A retirement home, assisted living, and/or hospice care can be good ideas if there are no relatives or friends nearby or if the old folks cannot fend for themselves. There isn't much new under the sun, but that doesn't mean there cannot be growth or change. Don't allow yourselves to get too disengaged or withdrawn; it is best to keep people around you and be around them.

> - Work crossword or other kinds of puzzles
> - Read a lot (especially inspirational works and comedy)
> - Go for walks
> - Go for scenic rides
> - Develop a regular routine
> - Explore many types of recreation (wading in the pool, shuffleboard, etc.)
> - Call people on the phone
> - Organize things
> - Move into an assisted living or group home
> - Prepare a living trust or advanced directive
> - Have conversations with doctors
> - Eat small meals regularly
> - Practice daily devotions
> - Pray constantly

- DEU 26:7 ~ Then we cried to the LORD, the God of our fathers, and the LORD heard our voice and saw our affliction, our toil, and our oppression.

- PSA 50:15 ~ Call on me in the day of trouble; I will deliver you, and you shall glorify me.

- JAM 5:13-16 ~ Is anyone among you suffering? Let him pray. Is anyone cheerful? Let him sing praise. Is anyone among you sick? Let him call for the elders of the church, and let them pray over him, anointing him with oil in the name of the Lord. And the prayer of faith will save the one who is sick, and the Lord will raise him up. And if he has committed sins, he will be forgiven. Therefore, confess your sins to one another and pray for one another, that you may be healed. The prayer of a righteous person has great power as it is working.

- REV 21:4 ~ He will wipe away every tear from their eyes, and death shall be no more, neither shall there be mourning, nor crying, nor pain anymore, for the former things have passed away.

Termination (final year). Old people usually know when death is near; they have a sense about that. But there is constant uncertainty, because they could cash in at any time due to an illness, disease, stroke, or heart attack. Some people are at peace with the inevitable end, some are not. Certainly, those who lived a life of faith in Christ are less afraid and more prepared. Faith and hope are extremely edifying and stimulating; it is a time to engage in prayer, Bible readings, and visits with the pastor. It is a time to speak with loved ones about the unending loving kindness of our Savior, and the ultimate destination which is our heavenly home.

> - Share your experiences with others
> - Keep in touch with those who matter
> - Have serious conversations about faith and death
> - Talk about the resurrection
> - Say goodbye to family
> - Plan to die with dignity

- PSA 23:4 ~ Even though I walk through the valley of the shadow of death, I will fear no evil for you are with me…

- ECC 7:1 ~ A good name is better than precious ointment, and the day of death is better than the day of birth.

- JOH 5:24 ~ Jesus said, "Truly, truly, I say to you, whoever hears my word and believes him who sent me has eternal life. He does not come into judgment, but has passed from death into life."

- JOH 11:25-26 ~ Jesus said to her, "I am the resurrection and the life. Whoever believes in me, though he die, yet shall he live, and everyone who lives and believes in me shall never die…"

Conclusions

Employ SMART techniques to help clients establish performance goals, identify objectives, and break down tasks into steps. Work through each goal to make it operationally sound, measurable, and doable. Make sure your clients document each component of their action plan, to include timetable, and have them track progress frequently. Evaluate progress together on a regular basis so clients can see the proof of their becoming and changing. This will give them a sense of accomplishment, motivation to persevere, and positive rewards. Once they get a taste of success, they will want more, and will become self-encouraging.

Review the developmental information with clients to identify where they are in their maturation, and where they might be stuck. Discuss the associated generic goals and narrow them down to a few of interest to him or her. This will provide a point of departure, direction, and purpose. The intention is to put the onus on them to choose a realistic course, be optimistic about progress, measure success, and take action that leads to constructive and notable growth. The ultimate goal of therapy is to hand the reins over to clients and let them continue the race with confidence, gain their own momentum, and take pride in their accomplishments, giving thanks to God.

As a therapist, you will have your own goals for therapy. The following are general categories which can be reduced to specific goals. These examples relate to any developmental stage, clinical diagnosis, and therapeutic method. Use the SMART technique to formulate your treatment plan, as it also requires observable and measurable goals.

- ➤ Emotional Healing
- ➤ Rational Thinking
- ➤ Reality Testing
- ➤ Improved Communications
- ➤ Support Systems
- ➤ Teamwork
- ➤ Developing a Plan
- ➤ Direction Finding

- ➤ Coping with Setbacks
- ➤ Ego Strengthening
- ➤ Gaining Self-Control
- ➤ Identity Construction
- ➤ Positive Actions
- ➤ Behavioral Outcomes
- ➤ Overcoming the Sinful Nature
- ➤ Spiritual Growth

"Ever since I was a child I have had this instinctive urge for expansion and growth. To me, the function and duty of a quality human being is the sincere and honest development of one's potential." – Bruce Lee

Activity

Define a problem or a vision that you as an individual, or you as a couple, or you as a family would like to analyze. Your counselor can help you perform this exercise if you need assistance.

_____

_____

_____

Explore (individually or collectively) alternative solutions or strategies.

_____

_____

_____

Select one or two goals that will help you to execute your strategy or plan.

Goal 1 _____

Goal 2 _____

Describe the goal(s) in terms of what, how, when – what you hope to achieve, how you plan to do it, and when you expect to complete it. Define the goal in a way that you can observe and measure progress (percent completed, time expended, etc.).

Goal 1 _____

_____

Goal 2 _____

_____

Identify the tasks that need to be completed to successfully accomplish the goal(s).

Goal 1, Task A _____ Goal 1, Task B _____

Goal 1, Task C _____ Goal 1, Task D _____

Goal 2, Task A _____ Goal 2, Task B _____

Goal 2, Task C _____ Goal 2, Task D _____

Break down the tasks (objectives) into steps required to complete the tasks.

Goal 1, Task A, Step 1 _____ Goal 1, Task A, Step 2 _____

Goal 1, Task A, Step 3 _____ Goal 1, Task A, Step 4 _____

Goal 1, Task B, Step 1 _____ Goal 1, Task B, Step 2 _____

Goal 1, Task B, Step 3 _____ Goal 1, Task B, Step 4 _____

Goal 1, Task C, Step 1 _____ Goal 1, Task C, Step 2 _____

Goal 1, Task C, Step 3 _____ Goal 1, Task C, Step 4 _____

Goal 1, Task D, Step 1 _____ Goal 1, Task D, Step 2 _____

Goal 1, Task D, Step 3 _____ Goal 1, Task D, Step 4 _____

Goal 2, Task A, Step 1 _____ Goal 2, Task A, Step 2 _____

Goal 2, Task A, Step 3 _____ Goal 2, Task A, Step 4 _____

Goal 2, Task B, Step 1 _____ Goal 2, Task B, Step 2 _____

Goal 2, Task B, Step 3 _____ Goal 2, Task B, Step 4 _____

Goal 2, Task C, Step 1 _____ Goal 2, Task C, Step 2 _____

Goal 2, Task C, Step 3 _____ Goal 2, Task C, Step 4 _____

Goal 2, Task D, Step 1 _____ Goal 2, Task D, Step 2 _____

Goal 2, Task D, Step 3 _____ Goal 2, Task D, Step 4 _____

Make a schedule including the timeframe to complete the goal, certain milestones, and projected dates for completing each task/step. List tasks and their steps along the vertical axis, and time along the horizontal axis, and indicate when each task/step begins and when it ends (try the Gantt chart method, which the counselor can explain to you). This makes it easy to check your schedule against your progress.

Track your progress regularly. If necessary revise the plan as it is only a guideline, because things can happen that necessitate an adjustment to your timetable.

← Statement of Goal #1 →

```
Calendar          Week 1        Week 2        Week 3        Week 4        Week 5
----------------  S M T W T F S| S M T W T F S| S M T W T F S| S M T W T F S| S M T W T F S
ACTION ||
------------------------------------------------------------------------------------------------
Task A            ^------------------|
Step 1            ^----|
Step 2                ^------|
Step 3                   ^----|
Step 4                      ^---|

Task B                        ^------------------|
Step 1                        ^----|
Step 2                            ^----------|
Step 3                                  ^------|

Task C                        ^----------------------------------|
Step 1                        ^------|
Step 2                            ^----------------------|
Step 3                                       ^------|

Task D                                    ^--------------------------------|
Step 1                                    ^-----------|
Step 2                                          ^-------|
Step 3                                              ^----|
Step 4                                                 ^---|
Step 5                                                    ^--------|
```

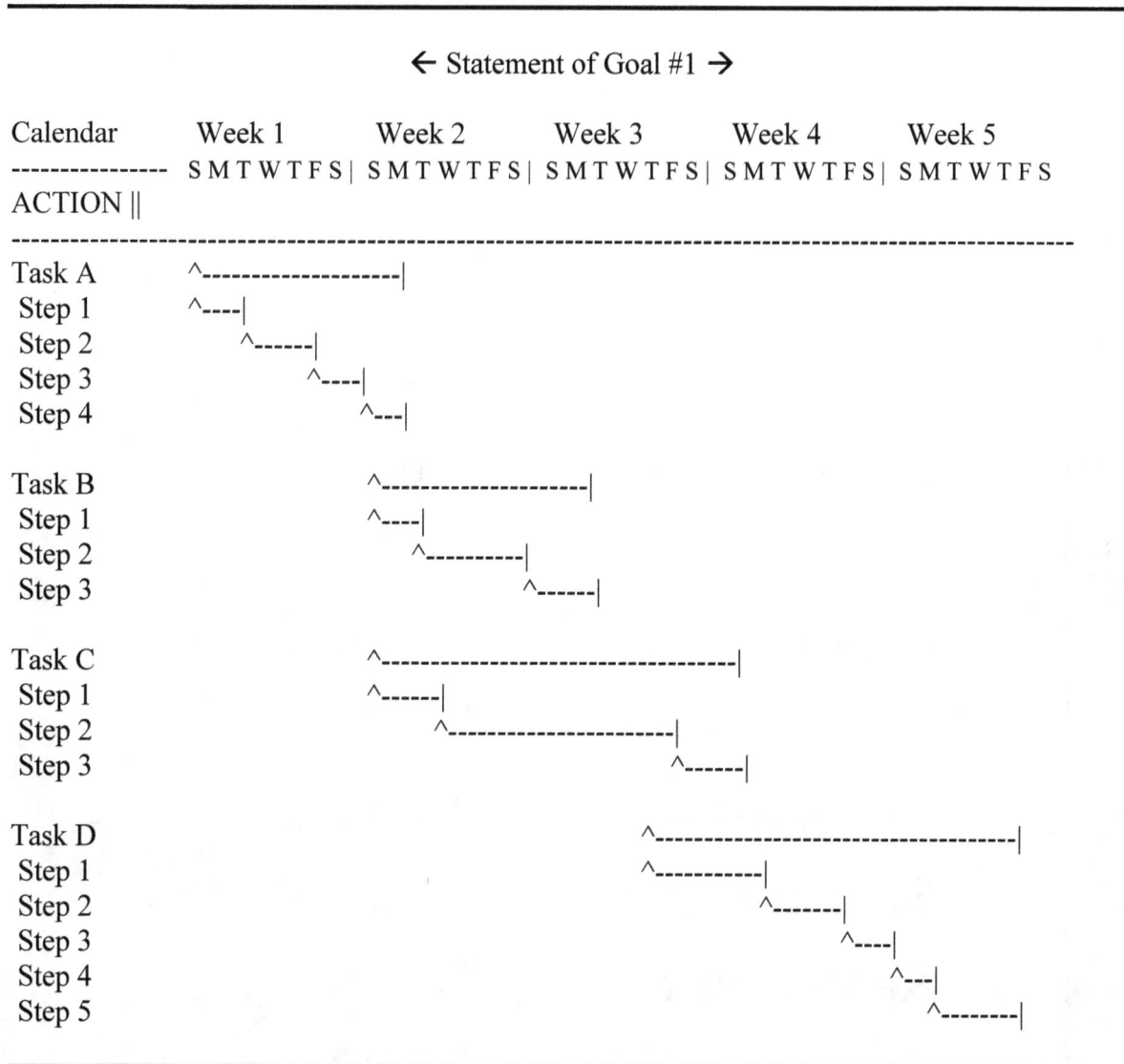

Each task and each step have a projected start time (^), stop time (|), and likely duration (---). Notice that tasks can overlap in that you may be working on more than one task at a time. The steps do not overlap because one step begins when the prior step is finished. When all steps have been performed the task is completed. When all tasks have been performed the goal should be attained.

Track progress in terms of the projected schedule and see if you are ahead of or behind schedule. Remember, the plan is a living document and can be revised as needed, including the schedule. A practical example using a Gantt chart can be found in the Activity for Creating a Vision.

DEVELOPMENTAL STAGES

STAGE	AGE
Orientation	0-3
Preparation	3-6
Imagination	6-12
Exploration	12-16
Identification	16-21
Occupation	21-35
Specialization	35-50
Resolution	50-65
Retrospection	65-80
Stagnation	80-95
Termination	final yr.

TOOLS FOR CHANGE

OBJECTIVE	Learn how a change of heart can change the mind, and ultimately lead to a change in behavior and attitude. Understand how love changes the heart, and faith changes the mind, opening up the gate of hope that reveals the way to glory.
INTERVENTION	Discuss spiritual tools for positive change to include love, faith, hope and patience and how they can dismantle obstacles such as fear, doubt, despair and exasperation, respectively.
PLAN	Face your internal obstacles and overcome them by tapping into higher powers of the spirit; remain connected to that power. Look beyond the hurdles at the possibilities that lie ahead, stay on the right path, and you will realize your dreams.

"When we are no longer able to change a situation, we are challenged to change ourselves." – Victor Frankl

"All misfortune is but a stepping stone to fortune." – Henry David Thoreau

In order to change behavior, direction, or lifestyle a person must change his or her thinking. In order to change thoughts, that person must reexamine beliefs. Before one can modify beliefs, he or she must experience a change of heart. You've probably heard it said: "You can't change anybody but yourself, and you have to want to change." It's true isn't it? Wanting to change requires caring about you, and caring requires love. And the love of God can change anybody. His love will change your heart.

- PRO 3:5-6 ~ Trust in the LORD with all your heart, and do not lean on your own understanding. In all your ways acknowledge him, and he will make straight your paths.

- COL 3:15 ~ Let the peace of Christ rule in your hearts, to which indeed you were called in one body. And be thankful.

Spiritual Tools

God is the source of all love; in fact, God *is* love. The Lord Jesus said that the most important commandment is to love God first, and the second most important commandment is to love others as yourself (MAT 22:35-40). Notice that the second part includes you and implies that you also should love yourself as you do others. All too often, people neglect themselves when it comes to distributing their love; they become too wrapped up trying to satisfy everyone else and end up neglecting their own needs. God comes first, and everyone is next, including you.

- 1 CO 13:2-8,13 ~ If I have prophetic powers, and understand all mysteries and all knowledge, and if I have all faith, so as to remove mountains, but have not love, I am nothing. If I give away all I have, and if I deliver up my body to be burned, but have not love, I gain nothing. Love is patient and kind; love does not envy or boast; it is not arrogant or rude. It does not insist on its own way; it is not irritable or resentful; it does not rejoice at wrongdoing, but rejoices with the truth. Love bears all things, believes all things, hopes all things, endures all things. Love never ends. As for prophecies, they will pass away; as for tongues, they will cease; as for knowledge, it will pass away. So now faith, hope, and love abide, these three; but the greatest of these is love.

- ROM 13:10 ~ Love does no wrong to a neighbor; therefore love is the fulfilling of the law.

"Love is the emblem of eternity; it confounds all notion of time; effaces all memory of a beginning, all fear of an end." – Madame de Stael

One of the chief roadblocks to change is fear (being afraid of failing, or of the past coming back to haunt you, or of what you have become, or that nothing will change, or that it will be too hard). People worry endlessly about unimportant or trivial matters; they seem preoccupied dwelling on life's stumbling blocks. If they expended as much energy working the problem as they did worrying about it, it wouldn't be a problem anymore.

Love conquers the fear that torments our minds. Since the power of love comes from God, it follows that fear must be the power of evil, because the two cannot coexist. Love consumes fear just as light consumes darkness. Love is the greatest power known to mankind. Where do you look when you want to find love? Look into your own heart.

- 1 JO 4:7-12,16-19 ~ Beloved, let us love one another, for love is from God, and whoever loves has been born of God and knows God. Anyone who does not love does not know God, because God is love. In this the love of God was made manifest among us, that God sent his only Son into the world, so that we might live through him. In this is love, not that we have loved God but that he loved us and sent his Son to be the propitiation for our sins. Beloved, if God so loved us, we also ought to love one another. No one has ever seen God; if we love one another, God abides in us and his love is perfected in us... So we have come to know and to believe the love that God has for us. God is love, and whoever abides in love abides in God, and God abides in him. By this is love perfected with us, so that we may have confidence for the day of judgment, because as he is so also are we in this world. There is no fear in love, but perfect love casts out fear. For fear has to do with punishment, and whoever fears has not been perfected in love. We love because he first loved us.

- 2 TI 1:7 ~ God gave us a spirit not of fear but of power and love and self-control.

Fear causes us to have a tormented mind, but love enables us to have a sound mind. If you want to think clearly, and stay focused on the positive, I recommend you invite God's love into your heart. Otherwise, fear will block your path and you may go astray. Thus, the first and most important tool for change in your toolbox is love, which will overcome the obstacle of fear that the devil will throw into your path. Love also overcomes a number of other obstacles such as anger, impatience, and mistrust (1 CO 13:2-8).

Once the person cares enough to amend his or her life, they begin to believe that such change is possible. But you can be sure that Satan will try to destroy your faith by bombarding you with doubt. When it comes to God, we don't doubt him because he never goes back on his Word. But when we place our faith in ourselves or others, there is a chance that we will be disappointed. Therefore, your faith and confidence should be placed in God, who changes everything in your life once you have experienced a new heart within you (PSA 51:10-12). You cannot succeed without God; indeed, without him you will fail. Faith is an important tool in the toolbox, because it helps us overcome doubt, disbelief, and uncertainty, which constantly tries to dominate our thoughts. Doubt comes from the weakness of our flesh, but faith comes by the Holy Spirit; and it is by that faith that you are saved (EPH 2:8-9).

- 2 CO 5:17 ~ Therefore, if anyone is in Christ, he is a new creation. The old has passed away; behold, the new has come.

- HEB 12:2 ~ Look to Jesus, the founder and perfecter of our faith, who for the joy that was set before him endured the cross, despising the shame, and is seated at the right hand of the throne of God.

"Faith makes things possible, not easy." – Author Unknown

"Reason is your soul's left hand, Faith her right." – John Donne

God promises to give us everything we need including the kingdom. That is our hope, and because we have faith, we should not doubt God. If you cling to his promises, you will succeed in achieving the changes you desire, without depending on your own strength, but by allowing the Lord to be your strength and guide. If you follow in the path of righteousness, you will always be heading in the right direction: towards him. God will illuminate the way for you, for his light is ever-present. If you do not see the light, you are off the beaten track or going the wrong way.

- PSA 119:105 ~ Your word is a lamp to my feet and a light to my path.

- PSA 145:14-16 ~ The LORD upholds all who are falling and raises up all who are bowed down. The eyes of all look to you, and you give them their food in due season. You open your hand; you satisfy the desire of every living thing.

- MAT 6:25-34 ~ Jesus said, "Therefore I tell you, do not be anxious about your life, what you will eat or what you will drink, nor about your body, what you will put on. Is not life more than food, and the body more than clothing? Look at the birds of the air: they neither sow nor reap nor gather into barns, and yet your heavenly Father feeds them. Are you not of more value than they? And which of you by being anxious can add a single hour to his span of life? And why are you anxious about clothing? Consider the lilies of the field, how they grow: they neither toil nor spin, yet I tell you, even Solomon in all his glory was not arrayed like one of these. But if God so clothes the grass of the field, which today is alive and tomorrow is thrown into the oven, will he not much more clothe you, O you of little faith? Therefore do not be anxious, saying, 'What shall we eat?' or 'What shall we drink?' or 'What shall we wear?' For the Gentiles seek after all these things, and your heavenly Father knows that you need them. Seek first the kingdom of God and his righteousness, and all these things will be added to you. Therefore do not be anxious about tomorrow, for tomorrow will be anxious for itself. Sufficient for the day is its own trouble."

- HEB 11:1,3,6 ~ Now faith is the assurance of things hoped for, the conviction of things not seen… By faith we understand that the universe was created by the word of God, so that what is seen was not made out of things that are visible… And without faith it is impossible to please him, for whoever would draw near to God must believe that he exists and that he rewards those who seek him.

Looking forward to the possibilities that lie ahead gives us purpose, courage, and direction. If you keep focused on the big picture, you will see the Lord there waiting at the finish line. And he will meet your needs and you will prosper, because that's what he said would happen if you remain connected to him. However, we don't know exactly what his plan is or when it will happen, because if we did, we could anticipate everything and life would be awfully boring. So, we must never give up hope, and that hope leads to glory.

When one feels hopeless, they become desperate, behave irrationally, and they take unnecessary risks. Hope is a powerful tool because it enables us to conquer despair, another one of those obstacles that the evil one uses to distract us from seeing the big picture. Hope becomes the model of change, whereby we can envision what lies ahead, the opportunities available to us, and what positive growth might look like.

- PSA 130:5 ~ I wait for the Lord, my soul waits, and in His Word I hope.

- ECC 8:6-7 ~ For there is a time and a way for everything, although man's trouble lies heavy on him. For he does not know what is to be, for who can tell him how it will be?

- ROM 5:1-5 ~ Therefore, since we have been justified by faith, we have peace with God through our Lord Jesus Christ. Through him we have also obtained access by faith into this grace in which we stand, and we rejoice in hope of the glory of God. Not only that, but we rejoice in our sufferings, knowing that suffering produces endurance, and endurance produces character, and character produces hope, and hope does not put us to shame, because God's love has been poured into our hearts through the Holy Spirit who has been given to us.

- ROM 8:24-25,28 ~ For in this hope we were saved. Now hope that is seen is not hope. For who hopes for what he sees? But if we hope for what we do not see, we wait for it with patience… And we know that for those who love God all things work together for good, for those who are called according to his purpose.

- 2 CO 4:16-18 ~ So we do not lose heart. Though our outer self is wasting away, our inner self is being renewed day by day. For this light momentary affliction is preparing for us an eternal weight of glory beyond all comparison, as we look not to the things that are seen but to the things that are unseen. For the things that are seen are transient, but the things that are unseen are eternal.

"Hope is putting faith to work when doubting would be easier." – Author Unknown

"Hope is the last thing ever lost." – Italian proverb

Clearly, it follows that patience is another valuable tool; this tool proceeds from hope. Never give up, quit, or refuse to try because that is the only way to guarantee failure. Even if we do not succeed the first, second, or tenth time, this does not constitute failure, because once you do succeed in a given challenge then failure is no longer possible, and you will be ready to move onto the next challenge. Unfortunately, it takes time; but our timeframe is usually not in concert with God's. If you trust in the Lord, you know that good things will come your way; you just aren't sure what or when.

Patience overcomes exasperation, giving up, quitting. The more you try the better you get. And when you triumph, you'll have a new skill that you can bring with you as you take a giant step forward. If God is on your side you cannot fail, because he is fighting with you. But you must be prepared to wait until his time without doubting or trying to beat the clock. For he may lead you to a destination well beyond where you thought you were going.

- 1 SA 17:47 (paraphrased) ~ Just before David defeated Goliath in battle, he told Goliath that he and his army would fall because the battle belonged to the Lord.

- PRO 19:21 ~ Many are the plans in the mind of a man, but it is the purpose of the LORD that will stand.

- LUK 21:19 (KJV) ~ Jesus said, "The result of your patience is to possess your soul."

- ROM 12:12 ~ Rejoice in hope, be patient in tribulation, be constant in prayer.

- GAL 5:5-6 ~ For through the Spirit, by faith, we ourselves eagerly wait for the hope of righteousness. For in Christ Jesus neither circumcision nor uncircumcision counts for anything, but only faith working through love.

- JAM 1:2-4 ~ Count it all joy, my brothers, when you meet trials of various kinds, for you know that the testing of your faith produces steadfastness. And let steadfastness have its full effect, that you may be perfect and complete, lacking in nothing.

"Patience and perseverance have a magical effect before which difficulties disappear and obstacles vanish." – John Quincy Adams

"Patience is also a form of action." – Francois Rodin

Like a skilled Olympic athlete, you can run this race and win the crown. It is best to stay focused on the road ahead and never lose sight of the goal. While the finish line is not yet in view, it is still clear in your mind. You will notice the hurdles that you must breach, but they will not mask your vision of what lies beyond. And you will leap over them with ease, because you have trained hard for the event and in the process developed the patience and ability to persevere. Before, you considered the hurdles as obstacles that often obscured your sight of the goal. But they were not obstacles at all, just challenges that you faced head-on and eventually overcame, thereby apprehending additional knowledge and skill. In fact, these challenges became opportunities for further success, each of which got you closer to the objective, which strengthened your resolve, confidence, and character.

"Obstacles are those frightful things you see when you take your eyes off your goal." – Henry Ford

Legend has it that a journalist once asked Thomas Edison to explain the countless attempts to construct a light bulb in which he failed. Allegedly, Edison replied that he simply discovered 10,000 ways that it wouldn't work. But none of these can be considered failures by virtue of the fact that he eventually succeeded. While there is ambiguity as to when and if this conversation took place, it is definitely consistent with the inventor's style. And the message is quite clear: a lack of success does not constitute failure, because once you get it you have succeeded. There are not 10,000 failures in one column, and one success in the other column. The only way Edison would have failed is if he had totally given up. But he persevered; and his success is still evident today. The incandescent light bulb continued to be the prevalent form of lighting for close to a century. Thus, it wasn't about overcoming a myriad of mistakes, because the invention was a smashing success.

"If at first you don't succeed, try, try again." – Thomas Palmer (attributed)

The gifts of love, faith, hope, and patience – they are freely given and form the basis of your connection to God. Love provides the desire, faith the belief, and hope the opportunity; all that is left is to wait for the right timing. Notice how each spiritual tool builds upon the previous. Love enables us to care, to have desire; and Christ is our desire. Once you experience a change of heart, you can change your mind: you can begin to believe. Until you do, nothing will change because you do not think it possible. Faith is the evidence for which we hope, giving us the incentive to act on that faith. But we must wait until the right time, as results will not arrive until we are ready, and that takes considerable patience, and work. God alone knows the right time. If he let us do it our way or on our time we would never succeed. But his plan will prevail no matter how badly we mess it up, as long as we don't give up.

These spiritual gifts provide the inner strength that enables you to overcome adversity and periodic setbacks. The key to employing these tools effectively is staying united with God in spirit. We connect with God the same way we connect with others: communication. Speak to him often in prayer; listen to him as you read and meditate on his Word, and when the Holy Spirit speaks to you through ministers of the Word.

Staying Connected

The apostle John was very close to the Lord Jesus, and probably knew him as well or better than anybody. John defines God most succinctly through his personal interactions with Christ. How would you fill in the blank, God is _____? John reports that God/Christ is the way, life, love, light, truth, word, and spirit. This is how we can stay close to Christ like John did: follow his light, stay on the path (the way of righteousness), walk in his truth, meditate on his word, radiate his love, dedicate your life to him, and abide in his spirit forever.

- JOH 3:33 ~ Whoever receives his testimony sets his seal to this, that God is true.

- JOH 4:24 ~ Jesus said, "God is spirit, and those who worship him must worship in spirit and truth."

- JOH 8:12 ~ Jesus said, "I am the light of the world. Whoever follows me will never be in darkness, but will have the light of life."

- JOH 11:25 ~ Jesus said, "I am the resurrection and the life. Whoever believes in me, though he die, yet shall he live."

- JOH 14:6 ~ Jesus said, "I am the way, and the truth, and the life. No one comes to the Father except through me."

- 1 JO 1:5 ~ This is the message we have heard from him and proclaim to you, that God is light, and in him is no darkness at all.

- 1 JO 4:8,16 ~ Anyone who does not love does not know God, because God is love. So we have come to know and to believe the love that God has for us. God is love, and whoever abides in love abides in God, and God abides in him.

- 1 JO 5:6,20 ~ This is he who came by water and blood – Jesus Christ; not by the water only but by the water and the blood. And the Spirit is the one who testifies, because the Spirit is the truth. Let Christ live in you and his light will show you the way. And we know that the Son of God has come and has given us understanding, so that we may know him who is true; and we are in him who is true, in his Son Jesus Christ. He is the true God and eternal life.

Let Christ live in you and his light will show you the way. Always look forward, not backwards, expecting only that God's purpose in your life will be revealed in due time and the timing will be impeccable. Stay on the highway that takes you to the ultimate destination, which is heaven, where the gift of eternal life with the Lord awaits you. Meanwhile, enjoy the journey as you explore all the possibilities, because you will discover meaning in your life, purpose to everything that happens, and direction at every crossroads (MAT 6:31-34).

- MAT 22:35-40 ~ And one of them, a lawyer, asked him a question to test him, "Teacher, which is the great commandment in the Law?" And he said to him, "You shall love the Lord your God with all your heart and with all your soul and with all your mind. This is the great and first commandment. And a second is like it: You shall love your neighbor as yourself. On these two commandments depend all the Law and the Prophets."

- JOH 14:2-3 ~ Jesus said, "In my Father's house are many rooms. If it were not so, would I have told you that I go to prepare a place for you? And if I go and prepare a place for you, I will come again and will take you to myself, that where I am you may be also."

- JOH 15:3-5 ~ Jesus said, "Already you are clean because of the word that I have spoken to you. Abide in me, and I in you. As the branch cannot bear fruit by itself, unless it abides in the vine, neither can you, unless you abide in me. I am the vine; you are the branches. Whoever abides in me and I in him, he bears much fruit, but apart from me you can do nothing."

- 1 CO 2:9 ~ But, as it is written, "No eye has seen, nor ear heard, nor the heart of man imagined, what God has prepared for those who love him." (see ISA 64:4)

- GAL 5:22-23 ~ But the fruit of the Spirit is love, joy, peace, patience, kindness, goodness, faithfulness, gentleness, self-control; against such things there is no law.

- PHP 4:8 ~ Finally, brothers, whatever is true, whatever is honorable, whatever is just, whatever is pure, whatever is lovely, whatever is commendable, if there is any excellence, if there is anything worthy of praise, think about these things.

Staying connected to God means to have Christ living in your heart. God is love; and his love lives in you if you invite him in. So if you seek him, look inward; tap into the love by digging deep into your heart. Staying connected to God means thinking in your mind, "What would Jesus do?" We must always be mindful of him in order to steer clear of the stumbling blocks that Satan uses to distract us. Staying connected requires spiritual focus, listening to your conscience, and heeding God's Word. Let the Holy Spirit guide you into all truth.

- LUK 17:20-21 ~ Being asked by the Pharisees when the kingdom of God would come, Jesus answered them, "The kingdom of God is not coming in ways that can be observed, nor will they say, 'Look, here it is!' or 'There!' for behold, the kingdom of God is in the midst of you."

- JOH 16:13,15 ~ Jesus said, "When the Spirit of truth comes, he will guide you into all the truth, for he will not speak on his own authority, but whatever he hears he will speak, and he will declare to you the things that are to come… All that the Father has is mine; therefore I said that he will take what is mine and declare it to you."

- ROM 8:16 ~ The Spirit himself bears witness with our spirit that we are children of God.

- 1 CO 2:16 ~ For who has understood the mind of the Lord so as to instruct him? But we have the mind of Christ.

- 2 TI 3:14-15 ~ Continue in what you have learned and have firmly believed, knowing from whom you learned it and how from childhood you have been acquainted with the sacred writings, which are able to make you wise for salvation through faith in Christ.

Remain positive and truthful in your outlook. Don't let the negativity rule your mind; such thoughts will bring you down, and usually have no semblance of truth. No challenge is too menacing or temptation too great that you cannot overcome with the Lord beside you. Bring your troubles to him and he will give you peace, assurance, and conviction. Your dreams will come true and you will become the person you strive to be, and were meant to be.

- MAT 11:28 ~ Jesus said, "Come to me, all who labor and are heavy laden, and I will give you rest." (He will carry it for you.)

- LUK 1:37 ~ For nothing will be impossible with God.

- PHP 4:13 ~ I can do all things through him (Christ) who strengthens me.

- JAM 4:7 ~ Submit yourselves to God. Resist the devil, and he will flee from you.

- 1 PE 1:3-6 ~ Blessed be the God and Father of our Lord Jesus Christ! According to his great mercy, he has caused us to be born again to a living hope through the resurrection of Jesus Christ from the dead, to an inheritance that is imperishable, undefiled, and unfading, kept in heaven for you, who by God's power are being guarded through faith for a salvation ready to be revealed in the last time. In this you rejoice, though now for a little while, if necessary, you have been grieved by various trials.

- 1 JO 4:4 ~ Little children, you are from God and have overcome them, for he who is in you (Christ) is greater than he who is in the world (Satan).

The new you begins now! Everything is changing and it will continue. There is nothing from the past that you need to bring with you except wisdom. Even some of your past relationships will be history. You will be gaining momentum and they will be losing it, especially if you are on the right path and they have wandered into darkness. To be connected to God often means separating yourself from the world. You can show people the truth, and lead them to glory if they will follow. If they are not interested, you may lose them in your rearview mirror. But it will be they that have separated from you.

- MAT 10:14 ~ And if anyone will not receive you or listen to your words, shake off the dust from your feet when you leave that house or town.

- 2 CO 5:17 ~ Therefore, if anyone is in Christ, he is a new creation. The old has passed away; behold, the new has come.

- 2 CO 6:14,17 ~ Do not be unequally yoked with unbelievers. For what partnership has righteousness with lawlessness? Or what fellowship has light with darkness? What accord has Christ with Belial? Or what portion does a believer share with an unbeliever? Therefore go out from their midst, and be separate from them, says the Lord, and touch no unclean thing; then I will welcome you.

- JDE 1:19 ~ It is these who cause divisions, worldly people, devoid of the Spirit.

The changes that have begun will result in a change of lifestyle. You will want to modify your behavior and forsake your evil ways. Disconnect from people, places, and things that would influence you to return to your old ways or steer you from the right path. Above all, you must stop living a lie and always walk in love, faith, and truth.

- PSA 1:1 ~ Blessed is the man who walks not in the counsel of the wicked, nor stands in the way of sinners, nor sits in the seat of scoffers.

- PRO 1:10 ~ If sinners entice you, do not consent.

- EPH 2:1-5 ~ You were dead in the trespasses and sin in which you once walked, following the course of this world, following the prince of the power of the air, the spirit that is now at work in the sons of disobedience – among whom we all once lived in the passions of our flesh, carrying out the desires of the body and the mind, and were by nature children of wrath, like the rest of mankind. But God, being rich in mercy, because of the great love with which he loved us, even when we were dead in our trespasses, made us alive together with Christ…

- EPH 5:11 ~ Take no part in the unfruitful works of darkness, but instead expose them.

- GAL 5:25 ~ If we live by the Spirit, let us also keep in step with the Spirit.

- 2 JO 1:6 ~ And this is love, that we walk according to God's commandments; this is the commandment, just as you have heard from the beginning, so that you should walk in it.

- 3 JO 1:4 ~ I have no greater joy than to hear that my children are walking in the truth.

Now is the time to turn over a new leaf. Make a commitment to living a clean and healthy life. If you do not, you will be stuck on a road that leads nowhere. The path of righteousness is the way of freedom, the way of the spirit. It is God's Spirit that gives you the power to persevere, and the power to resist those who would block your way or try to drag you down, including the devil himself.

- EZE 33:12 ~ The righteousness of the righteous shall not deliver him who transgresses, and as for the wickedness of the wicked, he shall not fall by it when he turns from his wickedness, and the righteous shall not be able to live by his righteousness when he sins.

- JOH 8:34 ~ Jesus said, "Jesus answered them, "Truly, truly, I say to you, everyone who practices sin is a slave to sin."

- JAM 4:4 ~ Do you not know that friendship with the world is enmity with God? Therefore whoever wishes to be a friend of the world makes himself an enemy of God.

- JAM 4:7,17 ~ Submit yourselves therefore to God. Resist the devil, and he will flee from you. So whoever knows the right thing to do and fails to do it, for him it is sin.

Imagine you are in Las Vegas, and the devil approaches you with a wager. He is willing to pay you one million dollars against the price of your soul, heads you win tails you lose. It is a sucker bet for sure, and you flatly turn him down. Then he ups the odds and says you can spin the wheel of fortune; you only have one chance in four to lose. But even a 75% chance of winning the million is not enough for you to wager your soul. So he ups the ante again and gives you a 95% chance to win. Still you do not give in, so he offers you 99% chance of a win. Only a fool would take that bet, you tell him. There is nothing valuable enough in the entire world that could match the price of your soul (MAT 16:26). Besides, Satan cannot offer you anything that you do cannot attain yourself, through faith in Christ.

The Lord offers you the following proposal, and you have 100% of winning everything, and absolutely nothing to lose. Just seek him, his righteousness and his kingdom, and you receive all of this, as well as everything you need in this life (MAT 6:31-34). Why not put your faith and trust in that proposition rather than gamble on the world? If you're going to bet your life, put it on Christ. It's a sure thing! But nothing else in this universe is.

- HEB 10:39 ~ But we are not of those who shrink back and are destroyed, but of those who have faith and preserve their souls. (also LUK 21:19)

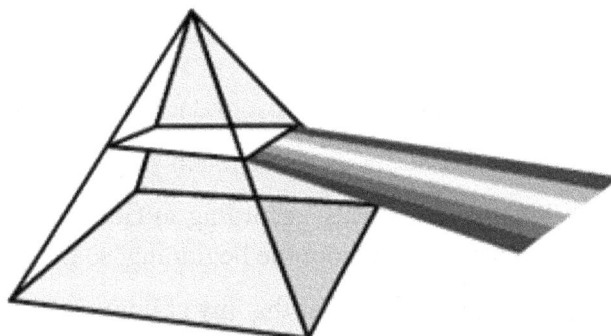

Activity

Define your higher power.

_____

_____

_____

Which obstacles are you facing now? _____

How can you overcome these obstacles? _____

What are your aspirations? What do you hope will happen?

_____

_____

_____

Describe some of your dreams and aspirations.

_____

_____

_____

How can your higher power help you to achieve your hopes and dreams?

_____

_____

_____

_____

How do the following attributes keep you connected to God and his Son Jesus Christ?

Love

_____

_____

_____

Light

_____

_____

_____

Truth

_____

_____

_____

Life

_____

_____

_____

Spirit

_____

_____

_____

Way (staying on the path)

_____

_____

_____

Environmental Modifications

OBJECTIVE	Identify additional changes that must be made to complement the changes being made to beliefs and behaviors. These changes may be internal (inside you) or external (outside you). Whenever changes are identified, adequate substitutes should be considered.
INTERVENTION	Discuss the various factors that contribute to defeatist thinking, that present temptations to fall away, that pressure one to give up, or to discourage one from trying. Recognize those roadblocks impeding upon success, and remove them from the environment.
PLAN	Identify areas in your life where change is needed, and develop an action plan to make necessary modifications. Rethink what is truly important and vital to a complete overhaul in priorities, direction, and lifestyle.

"Progress is impossible without change, and those who cannot change their minds cannot change anything." – George Bernard Shaw

Whenever profound changes are being made to beliefs, attitudes, or behaviors, corresponding changes need to be made in the environment. The changes discussed below imply finding healthy substitutes. If you want to quit drinking, you need to stop going to bars. If you want to be more religious, start going to church. There are external triggers that create the climate or the temptation to fall back into the old ways. Some triggers can be avoided; some will need to be faced. For example, relationships that we value, which are worth salvaging, will need to be faced. Relationships worth abandoning should be avoided.

Thus, the first change that should be addressed is people. Those who are not supportive of the new you and the changes you are undergoing might be part of your problem. I grew up in the era of sex, drugs, and rock-and-roll. When I became older I realized that the sex and drugs part were unhealthy and unrighteous. I decided to leave that lifestyle and convinced a close friend to do the same, or so I thought. He changed his mind. Furthermore, he thought it more important that I respect his decision to continue to use drugs, than for him to respect mine to quit. He was doing drugs in front of me. There ended a long friendship. Looking back, I realized that all we had in common was partying and getting high. Of all people, I thought he would be part of my support; but he was really part of my problem.

- PRO 1:10 ~ If sinners entice you, do not consent.
- 1 CO 5:11,13 ~ Do not associate with anyone who bears the name of brother if he is guilty of sexual immorality or greed, or is an idolater, reviler, drunkard, or swindler – do not even eat with such a one… Purge the evil person from among you.

- COL 3:5 ~ Put to death therefore what is earthly in you: sexual immorality, impurity, passion, evil desire, and covetousness, which is idolatry.

Once change commences, the client will have to reexamine the relationships in his or her life. It will become relatively obvious which people to avoid immediately. For instance, a kid that wants to get out of a gang must stop hanging around gang members. When we associate with negative people it just makes us negative and it brings us down. And we begin to think and feel as they do; and we end up going nowhere in our lives because that is where they are headed.

Even those relationships that are valued need to be placed on hold. The person undertaking change must focus on himself or herself, at least for the time being. As selfish as that may seem, it really is not. As I pointed out earlier, people can get wrapped up ensuring everyone else gets their needs met to the detriment of their own.

We are supposed to love others as much as ourselves; often it is oneself that is being denied the love or attention. You can't fix a relationship if you are still broken. You cannot heal others if you are ill. So if reform is needed in your life, start with yourself and focus on you. I have seen numerous hospitalized patients try to take on someone else's problems to divert attention from their own. I have to take them aside and firmly explain that they are there for their own treatment, and not to interfere with the progress of others.

- MAT 7:3-5 ~ Why do you see the speck that is in your brother's eye, but do not notice the log that is in your own eye? Or how can you say to your brother, "Let me take the speck out of your eye," when there is the log in yours? You hypocrite, first take the log out of your own eye, and then you will see clearly to take the speck out of your brother's eye.

If someone truly cares about you, he or she will understand what you are going through. Your loved ones will not be so selfish as to expect you to attend to their needs when they know full well you are struggling with yours. It may come as a surprise who will be there for you and who will not when you are in a crisis.

I had a client who was suffering from alcoholism and he emphasized this point in a recovery group. His friends, mostly drinking buddies, would tempt him frequently to go out on the town. He stressed that he didn't need that kind of temptation, though they argued vehemently that he didn't have to drink beer to hang out with them. They said he could drink soda pop or something. They completely missed the point didn't they? It wasn't them it was the environment and the lifestyle. He was surprised, however, that a distant cousin came to his rescue to help him conquer the alcohol; and they became the best of friends. In time, one of his old drinking buddies finally came around and joined him in his quest to kick the habit. He learned who his true friends and family were within the first three months of his sobriety.

- ROM 16:17 ~ I appeal to you, brothers, to watch out for those who cause divisions and create obstacles contrary to the doctrine that you have been taught; avoid them.

- 1 TH 5:11 ~ Therefore encourage one another and build one another up, just as you are doing.

- 2 TH 3:14-15 ~ If anyone does not obey what we say in this letter, take note of that person, and have nothing to do with him, that he may be ashamed. Do not regard him as an enemy, but warn him as a brother.

The next modification that must take place is the places that are frequented. Consider again the alcoholic, who would stop by the tavern on his way home from work. He may decide to go a few blocks out of his way just to avoid the place entirely, and not be tempted to stop if he was to see so-and-so's car in the parking lot. Or the drug addict, who must steer clear of certain neighborhoods, street corners, and hangouts. Sometimes, it is prudent to pick up stakes and move altogether: move into your own place, or with your parents, or to another part of town, or even out of the state. If you are trying to avoid certain people, you'll have to avoid the places they are often found. The best way to avoid evil is don't go there.

I had a patient return to the hospital a week after he was discharged. He had a good recovery plan that included relocating. Unfortunately, he relocated only blocks from where he was living before. It wasn't long before he was hanging around the same people. Fortunately, once he saw himself falling back into the same lifestyle, he got back into rehab before getting too far off track.

- PSA 10:2-3,7-8 ~ In arrogance the wicked hotly pursue the poor; let them be caught in the schemes that they have devised. For the wicked boasts of the desires of his soul, and the one greedy for gain curses and renounces the LORD… His mouth is filled with cursing and deceit and oppression; under his tongue are mischief and iniquity. He sits in ambush in the villages; in hiding places he murders the innocent.

- MAT 6:21 ~ For where your treasure is, there your heart will be also.

Another change relates to things. You may need to discard things, like paraphernalia, little black book, pornography, memorabilia, and anything else that could be a trigger, hold you back, or knock you off track. A former patient of mine cleared all the numbers in her cell phone and blocked numbers she didn't want calls from. She moved residences without leaving a forwarding address; only a handful of people were told about it. Her intention was to remove people, places, and things that reminded her of the life she left behind. Another patient had an addiction to pornography. He made it his mission to dispose of his entire collection of porn: magazines, books, videotapes, etc. He placed security measures on his computer to block any risqué websites from being accessed or popping up on his screen. It was a wise decision because his small children were at that inquisitive stage where they would often dig into his belongings; the fact that such things were hidden only increased their curiosity. He removed all reminders and temptations: out of sight and out of mind.

- JOB 31:26-28 ~ If I have looked at the sun when it shone, or the moon moving in splendor, and my heart has been secretly enticed, and my mouth has kissed my hand, this also would be an iniquity to be punished by the judges, for I would have been false to God above.

- MAT 13:41 ~ The Son of Man will send his angels, and they will gather out of his kingdom all causes of sin and all law-breakers.

- 1 JO 2:15-16 ~ Do not love the world or things in the world. If anyone loves the world, the love of the Father is not in him. For all that is in the world – the desires of the flesh and the desires of the eyes and pride of life – is not from the Father but is from the world.

- TIT 3:9 ~ But avoid foolish controversies, genealogies, dissensions, and quarrels about the law, for they are unprofitable and worthless.

We can make changes to our playmates, playgrounds, and playthings. Events can be changed as well, meaning avoid certain gatherings, celebrations, and other occasions where enticements or triggers are known to be present. A recovering alcoholic should go to the wedding and not the reception, and to the funeral and not the wake. Why would you attend a family reunion if persons are abusive towards you or your partner? What good would it do to lend someone money who hasn't paid back the last three loans? I had another friend who became so hooked on drugs he started selling his belongings; his house looked like a rummage sale. I was tempted to buy his oak desk for a fraction of its value; but I had to decline because I knew he would put the money up his nose. Imagine having that desk in my den, as a constant reminder how a one-time friend hit bottom and lost everything.

Substitute healthy events for unhealthy ones. Attend church activities instead of pagan ones. Celebrate Christmas and New Years with your true family and not your so-called friends, and definitely not alone. If something brings you down, do something else, possibly even the opposite thing. Make plans to enjoy yourself and your loved ones where your bad habits are not welcome.

Modifications to time also should be entertained. Yes, you can change time. Change the time you go to bed and the time you get up in the morning. Change when you do things, and how long it takes. Change the amount of time you spend or don't spend. For example, if you are overweight, take more time to eat less food, and eat less often. If you are alienating your family, spend more time with the kids and less on the computer. Take your wife out to dinner instead of making her cook; dine together and not in front of the television.

When changes have resulted in giving up particular behaviors or activities, you will definitely have more time on your hands. This time should be spent on hobbies, exercising, or making improvements to you and your environment. Especially spend more quality time with loved ones and with God. Use the time for uplifting things and you will get a lot more gratification than you did doing the things you are quitting. Make all of your time quality time. Don't waste time, because time is life.

"If you want to truly understand something, try to change it." – Kurt Lewin

More Changes

When we make a radical change in our lives, many things will be different. Usually the goal of change is to think, feel, and/or behave another way. To pull this off, changes in surroundings will be necessary as discussed above. Not only does this involve removing things from the environment, it also involves adding some things. Most importantly, help the client develop a support system of people and places. Our major backing comes from God, so you certainly should add him into the mix, and make time for him. Next, is your inner circle, be it spouse, family, friends: significant and valuable relationships that comprise your moral support. Make time for them.

Also, clients may need professional help. There may be a need for continuity of treatment, or aftercare, complete with psychiatric follow-ups, medication management, and counseling (individual, marital, family). Support groups are very helpful. If your client is an addict, the support system could include groups like alcoholics, narcotics, gamblers, etc. anonymous. There are support groups for just about everything: overeating, divorce, parenting, grief, sexual deviancy, OCD, PTSD, you name it.

A solid church should be a major aspect of the support system. A good church offers a variety of services to include worship and Bible study; social engagements and celebrations; men's, women's, children's, couples groups; and all kinds of activities. Everyone needs a church home. The only requirements are a strong Biblical foundation, a feeling of the presence of the Holy Spirit, Christian fellowship, and a sense of belonging. If these conditions are not met, search for another church. Instead of isolating and confining themselves to their abode, clients need to do things that get them out of the house. That is, a wholesome social life is uplifting, especially if spent with people who are interesting, engaging, and of superior character.

- DEU 31:12 ~ Assemble the people, men, women, and little ones, and the sojourner within your towns, that they may hear and learn to fear the LORD your God, and be careful to do all the words of this law.

- MAT 18:20 ~ Jesus said, "For where two or three are gathered in my name, there am I among them."

- ROM 12:4-5 ~ For as in one body we have many members, and the members do not all have the same function, so we, though many, are one body in Christ, and individually members one of another.

- EPH 2:19-22 ~ So then you are no longer strangers and aliens, but you are fellow citizens with the saints and members of the household of God, built on the foundation of the apostles and prophets, Christ Jesus himself being the cornerstone, in whom the whole structure, being joined together, grows into a holy temple in the Lord. In him you also are being built together into a dwelling place for God by the Spirit.

- EPH 4:3,11-13,16 ~ And he gave the apostles, the prophets, the evangelists, the shepherds and teachers, to equip the saints for the work of ministry, for building up the body of Christ, until we all attain to the unity of the faith and of the knowledge of the Son of God, to mature manhood, to the measure of the stature of the fullness of Christ, from whom the whole body, joined and held together by every joint with which it is equipped, when each part is working properly, makes the body grow so that it builds itself up in love.

- HEB 10:24-25 ~ And let us consider how to stir up one another to love and good works, not neglecting to meet together, as is the habit of some, but encouraging one another, and all the more as you see the Day drawing near.

The primary thing that really has to change is the person's priorities. I often have to remind them that they are important people, so important Christ would die for them. Further, next to God we are to love others as we love ourselves. Clients need to remember that they are included in the latter. In fact, they need to allow themselves to be first priority (after God of course) until they get better. When I ask groups about their priorities, most of them will reply that they either didn't have God first, or they weren't placing themselves among the second group. They're so worried about others they neglect themselves. They forget that they are just as important as everybody else.

Some think themselves unworthy of being loved, or incapable of love. Yet when you ask them if there are people in their lives that they love, there always is. And they have been loved before as well; but maybe there isn't someone in their current lives that loves them. Only that is where they are wrong; eventually they will see there are people who care about them. You should be able to convince them that you care about them, and that God cares. God loves them unconditionally, just like a mother loves her child even when he misbehaves. The objective is to allow your clients to see that they are valued, and deserve to be loved by others, and are perfectly loved by Almighty God.

The problem is this: although they have loved and understand it, they neglect to disseminate any affection to themselves. Oftentimes you are the hardest person to love, and therefore to forgive. Like I've said before, change begins with a change of heart; that requires caring. If you don't care, nothing will ever change. They say, "I don't know how to love myself." But they will agree that they know how to love, and that everyone has a right to be loved. If you are capable of being loved and you know how to love, then you surely can give some of that love to yourself. It takes practice like most everything to get the hang of it.

- ROM 5:8 ~ God shows his love for us in that while we were still sinners, Christ died for us.

- 2 CO 5:17 ~ Therefore, if anyone is in Christ, he is a new creation. The old has passed away; behold, the new has come.

- JOH 3:16 ~ Jesus said, "For God so loved the world, that he gave his only Son, that whoever believes in him should not perish but have eternal life."

Clients must be reminded that with God first in your life, and believing your needs, happiness, and health are just as important as anybody, you can begin to take action that will help you move forward. It doesn't mean you intentionally forget about others, but they need to be further down the priority list until you gain some momentum. The rest of the priorities will fall into place where they ought. Let the client declare what is of greatest importance: spouse, children, family; perhaps job, career, or schooling; and whatever. As long as they get numbers one (God) and two (everybody) right, they're on their way to constructive change. And it all hinges on the greatest gift of all: love (ROM 13:10).

- COL 3:14 ~ Above all these put on love, which binds everything together in perfect harmony.
- 1 PE 4:8 ~ Above all, keep loving one another earnestly, since love covers a multitude of sins.

Clients will need to change what brings them satisfaction. They can find replacements which provide far more gratification than the behavior being extinguished. Consider the addict that was about to have her kids taken away if she didn't clean up her act. She realized just in time that she would much rather spend quality time with her children than with her drugs. (Unfortunately, I've seen an awful lot of parents that lost their children after multiple attempts were made to assist them). Ultimately, change necessitates substituting new, adaptive responses for the old, maladaptive ones. Since the new action will produce positive results, it will be a vast improvement: it will bring a sense of accomplishment, and that will stimulate a desire for more. For more on this, refer to the Ups and Downs lesson.

Help the client to examine their expectations as well. Sometimes they expect results immediately. You can see how this would relate to the matter of gratification, since the current trend in our culture is to want what you want right now. The expectation of immediate gratification is partly the reason people get hung up in the first place. They seldom consider the long-term effects of their behavior.

But change takes a lot of time and a lot of work. The more preconditioned the person the longer it will take to change, because it takes longer to unlearn something than it does to learn it. We're talking a complete rewrite of internal programming. For many, the journey will be lengthy and arduous, but well worth the trip in the end. It will involve a lot of practice and even more patience. The more determined the person the less time it will take. Perseverance is the key. A halfhearted effort will not succeed. The reason it will fail is because a change of heart is a complete change, not a partial, temporary, or convenient one.

The only thing that is certain is this: God will make good on his promises. He promises that he will provide all our needs, he promises that we will have an abundant life, and he promises he will give us unique abilities to utilize in the furtherance of his kingdom. We shouldn't try to anticipate what will happen, or how, or when. Indeed, God makes it clear that we will have to wait for the right time. Inform the client that when that time comes, he or she will be ready. If a person has grandiose expectations that are not met, there will be disappointments. If they take it as it comes they won't be disappointed if the outcome is less than desired; but they might be pleasantly surprised when it exceeds their wildest dreams. Remember this: when we expect something negative, we usually get it.

Not having specific expectations doesn't mean you shouldn't plan and take steps. Obviously, decisions must be made on how to improve your life: school, job, social life, spiritual life, and so forth. Each positive action will move you forward; God will direct your path along the way. There may be some detours, obstacles, and switchbacks but they are all leading to the same destination. Besides, if you could anticipate every turn, the excursion would be uninteresting. So just take it one day at a time and enjoy every moment. All of it, the good times and the bad times, is part of your preparation. One thing is for sure: If you are in a positive state of mind, focused on the truth, following the light, and living in the spirit of love, you will like what you find down the road.

- 1 CO 2:9 ~ But, as it is written (by Isaiah), "No eye has seen, nor ear heard, nor the heart of man imagined, what God has prepared for those who love him."

We also need to train our clients to alter their attributions or assumptions. Attributions are perceptions concerning cause-effect relationships. For example, we may presume that we know the reason someone acted the way they did. Like, she hurt me because of something I said (or maybe she was just having a bad day). We may predict a favorable reaction if we act a certain way towards others. But it doesn't always work out that way does it? So you buy her a box of candy and realize she is on a diet because she thinks she is too fat, thereby adding insult to injury.

People are not very objective in the way they observe the world and are frequently wrong about what causes what. That is, our experience is hardly generalizable to the world, or a population, or even to our own inner circle. We tend to believe that others think like us, or want the things we want. Hint: why don't you just ask them?

Teach your clients to be scientific in the way they collect, examine, and organize information by developing and testing internal models of behavior, experience, and causality. It is a proven fact that knowledge of statistics, critical thinking, and logic improves decision making. I'm not suggesting you send your clients to college to study experimental methodology, but a basic understanding of probability, normal distribution, sampling, and correlation enable us to see trends, identify relationships among variables, and accurately ascribe causality. This topic is covered in greater depth in the Irrational Thinking lesson.

One of the beauties of group therapy is getting different points of view, which helps each participant see how they stand on certain issues relative to the others. They also learn respect for alternate viewpoints, and get a larger picture of the issue as well. They often realize that their experience is not representative of the experience of others because we all see the world through a different set of eyeballs. Even though they are experiencing the same group at the same time each will have a different opinion of me and the other participants. Such revelations create insight; when they get it, encourage them to share it with the group.

Change results in new directions, all of which lead to God's purpose in your life if you keep him first. That purpose lies along the path of righteousness. If you stay on this path you will never get lost, but if you get off the path you may not find your way back. God illuminates the way for you, which is Christ. He leads you down the path and opens doors, equipping you to serve and prospering you in the process.

- ROM 12:3-8 ~ For by the grace given to me I say to everyone among you not to think of himself more highly than he ought to think, but to think with sober judgment, each according to the measure of faith that God has assigned. For as in one body we have many members, and the members do not all have the same function, so we, though many, are one body in Christ, and individually members one of another. Having gifts that differ according to the grace given to us, let us use them: if prophecy, in proportion to our faith; if service, in our serving; the one who teaches, in his teaching; the one who exhorts, in his exhortation; the one who contributes, in generosity; the one who leads, with zeal; the one who does acts of mercy, with cheerfulness.

- 2 CO 5:20 ~ Therefore, we are ambassadors for Christ, God making his appeal through us. We implore you on behalf of Christ, be reconciled to God.

- EPH 5:8-13 ~ At one time you were darkness, but now you are light in the Lord. Walk as children of light (for the fruit of light is found in all that is good and right and true), and try to discern what is pleasing to the Lord. Take no part in the unfruitful works of darkness, but instead expose them. For it is shameful even to speak of the things that they do in secret. But when anything is exposed by the light, it becomes visible.

- 1 PE 2:9 ~ You are a unique, chosen generation, a priesthood and holy nation, because you praise Him who called you from darkness into His marvelous light.

When God is the center of your life he becomes your life. Your entire lifestyle changes, because he forms you into his image. He has given us his example: Christ. He wants you to follow Christ, to act like him, talk like him, see like him, look like him, shine like him, and love like him. He takes your sin and gives you his righteousness so you can be free, saved, and set an example. And others will be able to find their way through you, as you point the way which is through Jesus. No matter what you become you are above all a child of the living God. In your family, your career, your community, you can shine the light of his love. Remember, God is love. As that love has changed you so your love can change others, because love changes everything and everybody.

- PRO 16:3 ~ Commit your work to the LORD, and your plans will be established.

- 2 CO 5:19-21 ~ In Christ, God was reconciling the world to himself, not counting their trespasses against them, and entrusting to us the message of reconciliation. Therefore, we are ambassadors for Christ, God making his appeal through us. We implore you on behalf of Christ, be reconciled to God.

- 1 JO 2:6 ~ Whoever says he abides in him ought to walk in the same way in which he walked.

- 1 TI 4:12 ~ Let no one despise you for your youth, but be for the believers an example in speech, in conduct, in love, in faith, and in purity.

"You must be the change you wish to see in the world." – Mahatma Gandhi

Activity

If you want to change who or what you are, it will require additional changes in your environment. Changes may be necessary regarding the **people** with which you associate, the **places** you go, the **things** that you cherish or use, the **events** that you attend, and the **time** you spend on certain activities or with certain people.

What changes do you think should you make? Ponder this question and indicate the changes you should make, and how you might go about it. Also, consider substitutes; that is, when you remove something, replace it with something better.

Changes in People

_____

_____

Changes in Places

_____

_____

Changes in Things

_____

_____

Changes in Events

_____

_____

Changes in Time

_____

_____

There are other aspects of your life that will change when you change.

Think about how you would make modifications in these areas: **Support**, **Priorities**, **Gratification**, **Expectations**, **Assumptions**, **Direction**, **Lifestyle**.

Who or what should be part of your support system?

_____

_____

_____

How should you change your priorities?

_____

_____

What could give you more gratification?

_____

_____

How should you modify your expectations?

_____

_____

How should you modify your assumptions?

_____

_____

How should your direction change?

_____

_____

How should your lifestyle change?

_____

_____

_____

Describe the new you as you grow in Christ and continue to walk his path.

_____

_____

_____

_____

_____

_____

How is this different from the old you?

_____

_____

_____

_____

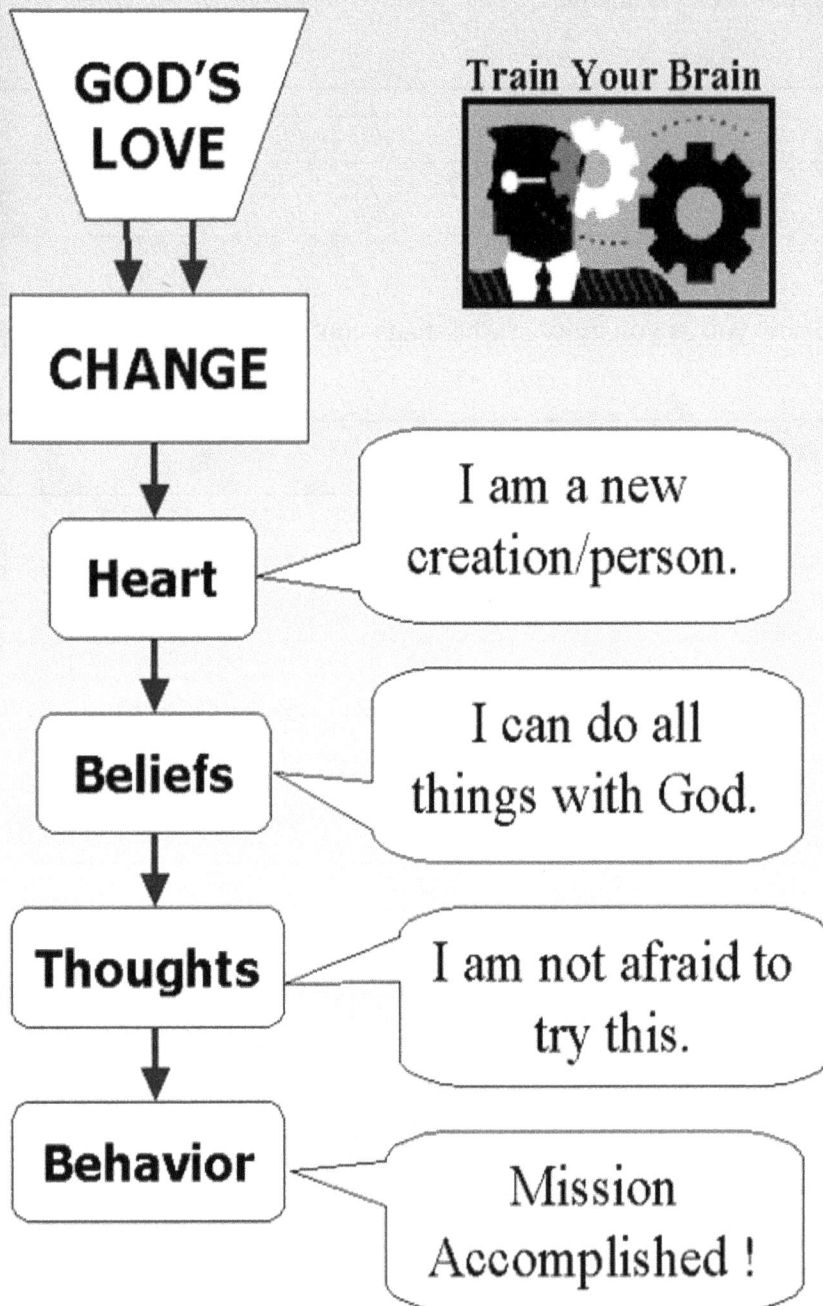

THE PROCESS OF CHANGE

GOD'S LOVE

Train Your Brain

CHANGE

Heart — I am a new creation/person.

Beliefs — I can do all things with God.

Thoughts — I am not afraid to try this.

Behavior — Mission Accomplished !

SELF-ESTEEM

OBJECTIVE	Learn how self-esteem moves up and down with respect to mood. When you are down or in a bad mood, and you act on that, you usually get negative results.
INTERVENTION	Discuss things that bring people down and things that lift them up. Notice that the things that bring us down are negative and the things that lift us up are positive. Recognize that the uplifting things are more powerful and true, and are opposite those that bring us down.
PLAN	Focus on the positive, uplifting things and act on that to achieve positive results. Learn to tap into these higher powers and discover that success is within your grasp.

"It is never too late to become what you might have been." – George Eliot

"A pessimist sees the difficulty in every opportunity; an optimist sees the opportunity in every difficulty." – Winston Churchill

Ups and Downs

Self-esteem is esteem (love) for oneself. If you do not love yourself, why is that? The answer to that question is the very thing that is bringing you down. Self-esteem is associated with the ups and downs in life. For example, depression brings us down; laughter lifts us up. Loneliness brings us down and companionship lifts us up. Disappointment brings us down and excitement lifts us up. An excellent group exercise is to get the participants first to think of things that bring them down. The most common responses are listed in the table below. I write their responses on the board. Then I'll get each participant to examine the final list and pick the top three to five things that bring them down the most. I record that information in their respective progress notes. Patients are remarkably astute at self-examination and usually zero in on real sources of their poor self-esteem.

The next part of the exercise is for participants to think of things that lift them up. As they respond, I list these things on the board across from their opposite (refer to the table below). Eventually, they will catch on and notice that each item on the board has an opposite. Again, every participant will pick the top three or so that lift them up and I will record that in their progress notes. When I provide them feedback, they discover that there is one or two that bring them down which are directly opposite to one or two that lift them up. So, if it is failure that brings someone down, it is achieving something that will lift them up. All it takes is action. If he or she would get something done there would be a sense of accomplishment. But doing nothing yields the same, because the only true form of failure is not to try at all (e.g., to give up). But if they keep trying, eventually they will succeed and they can chalk that one up in the success column.

- LAM 3:19-22 ~ Remember my affliction and my wanderings, the wormwood and the gall! My soul continually remembers it and is bowed down within me. But this I call to mind, and therefore I have hope: The steadfast love of the LORD never ceases; his mercies never come to an end.

Participants quickly understand the obvious result from the table, that the things which bring us down are negative, and untrue. The things that lift us up are positive, true, and more powerful. And the difference in power is like day and night. For example, the cure for despair is hope, which has the power to drive away the despair. When one has hope, hopelessness cannot enter because hope is the greater power.

Higher Powers

So if you want to raise your self-esteem, I tell them, tap into your higher powers. They are fruits of the spirit (or conscience, if they prefer), which always knows the truth, and always knows what is right. Though we know right from wrong, we often choose wrong.

God gave us the gift of discernment; all humans possess that knowledge. Consider the toddler, sitting in a highchair, who tosses his oatmeal on the floor just to get mom's attention as she busily washes the dishes. Mom scolds the child and says no, no, as she waves her finger; then she cleans up the mess. She gives the kid another bowl of oatmeal who promptly tosses it on the floor just as she turns her back. The toddler laughs, knowing it is wrong even when he did it the first time. Someday that child will learn accountability.

- GEN 2:16-17; GEN 3:6,22-24 ~ And the LORD God commanded the man, saying, "You may surely eat of every tree of the garden, but of the tree of the knowledge of good and evil you shall not eat, for in the day that you eat of it you shall surely die." So when the woman saw that the tree was good for food, and that it was a delight to the eyes, and that the tree was to be desired to make one wise, she took of its fruit and ate, and she also gave some to her husband who was with her, and he ate. Then the LORD God said, "Behold, the man has become like one of us in knowing good and evil. Now, lest he reach out his hand and take also of the tree of life and eat, and live forever." Therefore the LORD God sent him out from the garden of Eden to work the ground from which he was taken. He drove out the man, and at the east of the garden of Eden he placed the cherubim and a flaming sword that turned every way to guard the way to the tree of life.

- GAL 5:18,22-23 ~ If you are led by the Spirit, you are not under the law... The fruit of the Spirit is love, joy, peace, patience, kindness, goodness, faithfulness, gentleness, self-control; against such things there is no law.

We know what is right and we know what is true. How do we know these things? We just do, deep in our hearts. Your inner spirit will not lie to you. It will always tell you the truth even as you try to talk yourself out of it. The client may be thinking there is no hope and is ready to give up; or in their despair they do something desperate like take an overdose, attempt suicide, or run away from home. Yet, after thinking about it carefully they discover that the truth is, there is hope, there always has been. But there is none if you don't believe. So a modification in that belief is required to see it.

- PRO 12:19 ~ Truthful lips endure forever, but a lying tongue is but for a moment.
- ISA 45:21 ~ Declare and present your case; let them take counsel together! Who told this long ago? Who declared it of old? Was it not I, the LORD? And there is no other god besides me, a righteous God and a Savior; there is none besides me.

"You yourself, as much as anybody in the entire universe, deserves your love and affection." – Buddha

Every time I teach this lesson, I ask which item in the right hand column is the greatest power of them all; the general consensus is almost always "love." Recall the words of the apostle John: God is light and God is love; and love drives away fear, as light drives away darkness. The magnitude of difference is easily illustrated by a simple demonstration. I turn out the light making the room completely dark, until I flick a lighter. One simple flame will defeat the darkness, but there is no darkness in the world that can destroy light. Obviously, light is the greater power; so much greater that darkness cannot exist where there is light.

Each item that brings one down is far weaker than its opposite that lifts him or her up. And all one has to do is choose, column A or column B. Put this way it seems an easy choice: think about the truth, focus on the positive, let your higher power take control, concentrate on uplifting things. When you are in a positive state of mind, the negative cannot get in; but the positive can drive out the negative. If you act when you are negative, what kind of results can you expect? What if you act on the positive?

It is written: Whatever is true, honest, pure, lovely, virtuous, praiseworthy, and uplifting – think about these things (PHP 4:8). Don't think about all that negative junk that isn't even true and is bringing you down. Of course, this is easier said than done. It takes extensive practice because you have to unlearn some bad habits and erroneous beliefs, and replace them with new programming. It takes considerably more effort to modify a program than to develop one.

- PSA 119:105 ~ God's word is a lamp to my feet, and a light to my path.

To repeat, clients are usually very good at self-assessment. And they see clearly the solutions to what is bringing them down. It surprises them just how simple the mental task is and how profound the answer is. It's all about mindfulness: taking time to think in every situation, and reasonably exploring the facts. The fact is, if you need confidence, start believing in yourself. Better yet, let God be your confidence. If you are bored, do something. Don't just sit there. If you are lonely, go meet some people or call a friend. Strike up a conversation with a stranger and find some common ground. There are plenty of lonely people out there just waiting for someone to visit with them.

Improving one's self-image requires them to believe that they can overcome. But they can't do it alone, they need help. With God on their side they can overcome anything and become anybody. Everyone has equal potential for greatness; that is the truth. How can we know? Because: God has promised it. You can accomplish anything if you are connected to

Christ. So tap into your higher power; it is your connection to the highest power. And you will find it by looking into your own heart. The power has been there all along.

- JOH 15:5 ~ Jesus said, "I am the vine; you are the branches. Whoever abides in me and I in him, he it is that bears much fruit, for apart from me you can do nothing."

- ACT 10:34-35 ~ Peter said, "Truly I understand that God shows no partiality, but in every nation anyone who fears him and does what is right is acceptable to him."

- GAL 3:28 ~ There is neither Jew nor Greek, there is neither slave nor free, there is no male and female, for you are all one in Christ Jesus.

The best way to bring up your self-esteem is to quit sending yourself negative messages that are untrue. Tell yourself you are important, capable, and responsible. Don't let the negativity overtake you and pull you off course. Those things that bring you down can become obstacles, or roadblocks to some which they cannot see beyond. But they are not permanent.

"When you find yourself in a hole, stop digging." – Will Rogers

"It ain't what they call you, it's what you answer to." – W.C. Fields

I had a lady in my group a few years back who was a track star. I asked her, "When you run the hurdles, do you focus on the hurdles?" After a short pause she responded, "Well, no, I focus on the goal. I have the finish line in mind and the path that takes me there in view. I can see the hurdles, but if I dwell on them I'll trip over them." She explained, though she doesn't see the finish line immediately, it is clear in her mind. And after each hurdle and every lap her determination to complete the race is magnified, knowing that she is getting ever nearer to the goal. Soon, the finish line comes into view and she begins to sprint with a second wind that is a product of her willpower and perseverance.

"Self-love, is not so vile a sin as self-neglecting." – William Shakespeare

"The man who acquires the ability to take full possession of his own mind may take possession of anything else to which he is justly entitled." – Andrew Carnegie

Purposeful Living

Such is life. If you dwell on the hurdles or setbacks they get bigger or more difficult to face. You need to keep focused on the goal, which was glory to St. Paul. That was his hope as it is for all Christians. But there is still a ways to go, and a purpose yet to be fulfilled for your life. The fact that you are here proves there is a reason to keep going. You will fulfill one purpose after another until God calls you home. Your destiny was not to be found dead from an overdose, or doing life for murder, or living under a bridge. But God can even use that to glorify his name. If you live your life for the Lord, he will use you in ways that you never imagined. Like the athlete, if you see only the obstacles in your path, you may lose hope, or drop out of the race. You need to keep looking ahead, and beyond the hurdles. And you need to trust God.

There weren't enough obstacles, setbacks, or hurdles in the world that could distract St. Paul from the goal or prevent him from fulfilling God's purpose in his life. In fact, he welcomed the challenges, because each one prepared him for his mission and thrust him forward to the next purpose that God had planned for him. Every challenge made Paul stronger and gave him additional wisdom and experience for the trials to come, until he fulfilled his final purpose of personally bringing the Christian faith to Rome, knowing it would cost him his life. But look at the impact that mission had on the world. The emperor Nero was butchering Christians by the dozens, and Paul would be among them. But the seed was planted, and it grew. In time, Rome would adopt the Christian faith as its official religion and this would result in the Roman Catholic Church. God's Word spread to every corner of the earth, just as Jesus commissioned. Like Paul, when God uses you to plant a seed, he provides the nurturing until that seed grows into a tree of life. And like Paul, you are capable of doing great things for God. And the reward is glory.

- MAT 17:20 & MAR 4:30-32 (paraphrased) ~ Jesus said, "If you had faith the size of a mustard seed you could move mountains; nothing would be impossible." Jesus also said, "To what can you compare the kingdom of God? It is like a grain of mustard seed; when planted it is one of the smallest of seeds. But it grows into a large shrub that is greater than all the herbs; it shoots out great branches so that the birds build their nests under the shadow of it."

- 1 CO 3:7 ~ Neither he who plants nor he who waters is anything, but only God who gives the growth.

God has a greater purpose planned for you. Do you want to discover what it is? Then don't get bogged down by the obstructions in the path ahead, or let the potholes and ruts steer you in the wrong direction. The things that bring us down are of this world, and will get you off track, leading towards darkness and destruction. But as long as you stay in the light you will never get lost or lose your way, for Christ is the way. He will lift you up when you fall, not to mention raising you up on the last day. Let him guide your walk and you will know which direction to take and decision to make, for Jesus' sake.

- PSA 116:8; PSA 145:14 ~ For you have delivered my soul from death, my eyes from tears, my feet from stumbling… The LORD upholds all who are falling and raises up all who are bowed down.

- JOH 14:19 ~ Jesus said, "Yet a little while and the world will see me no more, but you will see me. Because I live, you also will live."

- PHP 1:6 ~ And I am sure of this, that he who began a good work in you will bring it to completion at the day of Jesus Christ.

It takes perseverance. You won't win a medal on your first run. Who among you has ever mastered something the first time you attempted it? It took me years to get the hang of golf. Even if there were things I had natural talent at, it didn't make them easy to master. But like the track star, you never give up. She kept training. She knew how many steps to take and how high to jump; the only thing left was faster. And with each attempt: a small improvement, getting closer and closer, on the way to Olympic gold perhaps. Like Paul said, you have to train to compete, so keep running the race and fighting the good fight. And a great prize will be yours: a Crown of Life.

- 1 CO 9:24-27 ~ Do you not know that in a race all the runners run, but only one receives the prize? So run that you may obtain it. Every athlete exercises self-control in all things. They do it to receive a perishable wreath, but we an imperishable one. So I do not run aimlessly; I do not box as one beating the air. But I discipline my body and keep it under control, lest after preaching to others I myself should be disqualified.

- 2 TI 4:7-8 ~ Paul wrote to Timothy: I have fought the good fight, I have finished the race, I have kept the faith. Henceforth there is laid up for me the crown of righteousness, which the Lord, the righteous judge, will award to me on that Day, and not only to me but also to all who have loved his appearing.

- JAM 1:12 ~ Blessed is the man who remains steadfast under trial, for when he has stood the test he will receive the crown of life, which God has promised to those who love him.

"If we all did the things we are capable of doing, we would literally astound ourselves." – Thomas Edison

"Make the most of yourself, for that is all there is of you." – Ralph Waldo Emerson

"Everybody is a genius. But if you judge a fish by its ability to climb a tree, it will spend its whole life believing that it is stupid." – Albert Einstein

"If you hear a voice within you saying you cannot paint, then by all means paint, and that voice will be silenced." – Vincent Van Gogh

Keep in mind that the things which lift you up are positive, true, and powerful: vastly more powerful than the things that bring you down. These are your higher powers, fruit of the spirit, and blessings from God. If something brings you down, do the opposite. If a negative thought enters your mind, change it to a positive thought. You will find the ability and strength from within you, because the solution is of the spiritual realm, and an extension of your spirit.

One final note: this exercise will point to topics worth focusing on in future groups or therapy sessions. For example, there were several people in a particular process group that selected conflict as one of the things that really brought them down. So for the next session, we did the lesson on Conflict Resolution. Thus, the order of presentation in this text is not concrete but flexible. Each lesson stands alone in providing a focus or a principle. I don't think I have ever presented the material in the exact same sequence suggested in this manual.

Activity

List some things that bring you down.   List some things that lift you up.

_____   _____

_____   _____

_____   _____

_____   _____

_____   _____

_____   _____

Compare the list on the left with the list on the right.

Identify those which have a direct opposite (draw a line to connect them).

You will see the problems on the left and the solutions on the right.

The things you think about will determine what you act upon. If you think negative you ultimately will act negative. Uplifting things are positive so focus on those; they are also the truth. And the positive vibrations will drive away the negative attitude. And the positive actions will produce favorable results.

Comment on how you might remove the things that bring you down and focus on the things that lift you up by taking some positive action. That is, what are you willing to do or to try to raise your self-esteem or get past the hurdles?

_____

_____

_____

_____

_____

Activity

Check each attribute that you possess from both columns. Add up the positives and the negatives separately. In which column do you have the most checkmarks? You can identify ways of raising your self-esteem by examining the negatives and developing a strategy to turn them into positives. Remember, it is your own self-messages that lift your self-esteem or bring it down; and the ones that bring you down are usually untrue.

CHARACTERISTICS OF SELF-ESTEEM	
Positive Self-Image	**Negative Self-Image**
Confident	Doubtful
Motivated	Unmotivated
Involved (Participatory)	Uninvolved
Resourceful (Initiative)	Dysfunctional
Responsible	Blaming, Critical
Trustworthy/Trusting	Mistrusting
Thoughtful	Thoughtless
Decisive	Indecisive
Assertive	Indolent/Listless
Self-Aware	Self-Denigrating/Defeating
Purposive	Misguided
Solutions Oriented	Apathetic
Understanding	Disconnected
Cooperative	Unworthy
Optimistic	Pessimistic
Self-Controlled	Helpless
Non-Judgmental	Uncompassionate
Accepting	Avoiding
Contented	Displeased
Energetic	Despondent
Tenacious	Fearful
Competent	Dependent
Composed	Unreliable
Conscientious	Careless
Honorable (Integrity)	Disreputable
Dependable	Whimsical

"Too many people overvalue what they are not and undervalue what they are." – Malcolm Forbes

UPS & DOWNS

BRINGS YOU DOWN ↓		LIFTS YOU UP ↑
Sadness		Happiness
Deceit		Honesty
Stress, Anxiety		Peace of Mind
Pain, Suffering		Health, Courage
Neglect	Freedom	Empowerment
Rejection		Appreciation
Abuse, Trauma		Nurturing, Caring
Failure		Success, Accomplishment
Doubt	<< False True >>	Faith, Confidence
Confusion		Understanding
Boredom	Modifications	Activity, Enjoyment
Despair	<< Negative Positive >>	Hope
Fear, Worry		Love
Disappointment		Excitement
Taunting, Harassment		Encouragement, Praise
Anger, Frustration		Patience, Satisfaction
Conflict		Reconciliation
Loneliness		Friendship, Intimacy
Betrayal		Trust, Loyalty
Injustice, Unfairness		Justice, Fairness
Guilt, Shame		Justification, Pardon
Loss, Grief		Acceptance, Fellowship
Helplessness		Assertiveness
-- DARKNESS --		-- LIGHT --

SELF-CONTROL MECHANISMS

OBJECTIVE	Learn how to better manage and cope with emotions and feelings, such as stress, anger, and pain (physical and emotional). Recognize that reactions to others are often automatic and irrational.
INTERVENTION	Discuss the effects of stress, anger, passion, and pain on mental, physical, and spiritual health, and learn potential coping mechanisms to maintain control, handle the discomfort, gain peace of mind, and reduce reliance on medication.
PLAN	Develop strategies and methods of managing and expressing feelings, reconstructing thought processes, maintaining composure, and redirecting responses in a more adaptive and productive manner.

"For when the great scorer comes to mark against your name, he writes not that you won or lost but how you played the game." – Grantland Rice

Managing Stress

It is relatively easy to know when you are stressed if you are mindful of your stressors and if you recognize the symptoms: you don't want to eat, you can't sleep or relax, you have no interest in sex; you don't want to do anything and/or you really don't care. Maybe you have no patience, no peace of mind, you can't get what you want, or you cannot enjoy things you used to enjoy. You feel tense, afraid, anxious, and/or angry; or maybe you are simply sick and tired of being sick and tired. Does that sound about right? With too much of that garbage on your plate you begin to develop mental, physical, even spiritual complications.

People know exactly what is causing their stress, be it financial, medical, emotional, relational, legal, social, occupational, educational, or whatever. Take time to analyze associated memories, thoughts, feelings, reactions, and self-messages; be cognizant of your limitations, your boundaries, and your priorities. In short, practice self-awareness. What most people do not realize is there are literally dozens of things they can do to reduce the stress and to enjoy life again. The main thing is to do something about stress, not just let it multiply like bacteria in a Petri dish. Because if stress keeps adding up, it will become overwhelming; and that's when people often do something totally counterproductive, possibly destructive. A maladaptive response is all too common because we tend to overreact to stress or blow it out of proportion when it doesn't seem to ease up or when we can't stop dwelling on it.

In this lesson we will review the myriad of options available to deal effectively with stressors. The more of these techniques you use the greater will be your confidence, self-esteem, and coping ability. As always, a holistic approach is proposed.

"There are more things to alarm us than to harm us, and we suffer more often in apprehension than reality." – Lucius Annaeus Seneca

Physical Wellness: Being healthy in your body enables you to endure more mental stress. First, you need 7-8 hours of restful sleep daily. The best time to sleep is at night, or at least at a regular time that fits your schedule. It is not recommended that you sleep in the daytime except perhaps for the proverbial power nap. Limit yourself to a nap of 15 minutes or so; otherwise you will be cutting into the time you hope to be asleep later. Second is diet and nutrition; eat well balanced meals covering a variety of food groups. Supplement your meals with essential vitamins and minerals. Take medicine only as prescribed or as needed, in accordance with the doctor's recommendation. And remember to drink plenty of fluids, especially water. Avoid certain foods and drinks that create discomfort or make you ill. And never overdo it with anything; moderation in all things is advised (1 CO 6:12; 1 CO 9:25; PHP 4:5). Too much caffeine or alcohol should especially be avoided (PRO 20:1; EPH 5:18). Thirdly, you need a regular fitness routine. Exercise helps build strength, enhance circulation, improve respiration, relieve pain, and reduce fatigue. Join a gym, take an aerobics class; go swimming or running; try yoga; you also might consider martial arts, maybe Tai Chi. Don't forget to stretch before and after you exercise. Team sports is another excellent way to get exercise and lower your stress level; join a softball team, or meet up with other basketball friends; play with the kids or grandkids at home or the park. Experts say you need aerobics, toning, and maintenance elements for a well-rounded fitness program. These three elements could be met with dancing, weight lifting, and walking. Also, you could take up gardening, do some landscaping or yard work, or clean the house. A favorite activity to de-stress includes a hot bath/shower or soaking in a Jacuzzi, followed by a cooling down period. Or try massage therapy, get a facial, or a manicure. Maintain proper hygiene and personal grooming. Definitely, don't smoke. I've heard many people say that they like to smoke a cigarette when stressed; it may provide a temporary feeling of relief, but by no means can you remove stress by doing something unhealthy (nicotine is actually a stimulant, it does not relax you). Finally, a wholesome and passionate sex life does wonders for your mental health; just make sure it is with the one to whom you are married. Sex with your soul mate is very spiritual, not just physical like masturbation or fornication.

"Heavy thoughts bring on physical maladies; when the soul is oppressed so is the body." – Martin Luther

Spiritual Support: Spiritual growth and support are facilitated by going to church, reading the Bible, fellowship with believers, and prayer (PSA 46:1-3; PSA 94:19; MAT 11:28-30). Being around people of faith can be very uplifting; some of the best support groups are found in a solid church home. Remember, your primary home is in heaven if you believe in Jesus Christ. Being close to him is imperative. Give thanks to God frequently, and count your blessings daily. Read scripture and meditate on it. Open your heart to the Lord and let him in. Whatever you do or do not do, do it for the Lord (1 CO 10:31; COL 3:17,23-24). Follow the Golden Rule and help others whenever you can or when you have some free time (LUK 6:31; LUK 10:27; GAL 5:14). Altruism, giving, and love are great stress relievers. Be willing to forgive others and forgive yourself as well (PSA 79:9; MAT 6:14-15; ACT 3:19; COL 3:13).

Love others and love yourself (MAR 28-32; GAL 5:14; JAM 2:8); love cures a multitude of problems (1 CO 13:1-13). Think positive things that are pure, lovely, virtuous, and praiseworthy (PHP 4:6-9). Send these kinds of messages to yourself to replace the destructive self-talk. Also, send encouraging messages to friends and loved ones through letters, cards, and phone calls. Surround yourself with love and loved ones; sometimes it just takes a bear hug to cure your stress (PRO 12:25). Most importantly, bring your troubles, worries, and pain to the Throne of Grace constantly through prayer (JER 29:11-14; PHP 4:6-7; 1 TH 5:16-18). Finally, you may find a nature hike to be a very powerful and uplifting experience. Getting back to nature always helps me to reconnect to God's Holy Spirit as it brings to mind just who is behind all of this beautiful creation that the Lord made for us. Any sort of escape will help, especially if that involves a spiritual journey. Try a change in scenery. Vacations are a good idea; you should schedule a long weekend at least three times a year, and a long vacation at least once per year. It helps to get away every so often and escape into a different world. If you can't leave, escape into your mind. Relaxation, breathing, and imagery exercises are an excellent way to get into the "zone," as they call it in sports psychology. Sometimes you can enhance the mood with soft light, inspirational music, or pleasant aroma. You can tap into your inner power and strength which is why I consider these techniques to be of the spiritual realm. Mediation helps you connect with your heart and feel the love of God. In a way, the experience provides a renewal to your soul (PSA 51:10-12; ISA 40:31; ROM 12:1-2).

"Man is not worried by real problems so much as by his imagined anxieties about real problems." – Epictetus

"As a rule, what is out of sight disturbs men's minds more seriously than what they see." – Julius Caesar

Mental Exercises: Since stress is largely mental, a fantastic way to deal with stress is to be cognitively busy; refocus your mental energy. There are countless ways of keeping your mind challenged, stimulated, and engaged. Everyone gets preoccupied with worry, grief, or emotional pain at times. The best way to avoid it is to be occupied thinking about something productive. This enables a person to focus on the present and not be worrying about the future or dwelling on the past. This is one reason that talk therapy is so effective. It keeps one grounded in the here and now: what *is* happening (MAT 6:34; ROM 8:28; 1 PE 5:7-10). It gets the person concentrating on solutions not problems; and it provides an outlet for expressing the emotional material in a constructive manner. Conversation and communication are the means to that end; therefore, touching base with friends and family also can bring about a modicum of inner peace. Socializing with others, participating in support groups, and being with people in general helps to cure the loneliness and boredom. In other words, dealing with stress is easier when you are not alone; being alone only serves to make stress the focal point. But if you can't be with others at that moment in time, you still can occupy your mind by working on crossword puzzles, jigsaw puzzles, or brain teasers. Or you can do some problem solving or decision analysis. Read books, research topics, learn new things, maybe take an online class. Occupy yourself with hobbies. Draw pictures, paint paintings, do craftwork. Learn to play a musical instrument; sing, or listen to music. Write prose, poetry, letters, or an entry into your journal. Bake a cake or cook a meal. That is: create something.

Sometimes you can conger something in your mind by daydreaming, deep concentration, fantasizing, imagining, and so forth. Or, you can have the fantasy provided for you by going to the movies, reading novels or comic books, or whatever. I find that producing your own imagery, fantasies, or stories is far more gratifying, however.

"I have never known any distress that an hour's reading did not relieve." – Montesquieu

"If you are depressed you are living in the past. If you are anxious you are living in the future. If you are at peace you are living in the present." – Lao Tzu

"The greatest weapon against stress is our ability to choose one thought over another." – William James

Emotional Release: Since stress elicits a lot of negative emotions, it helps to vent those emotions. Clearly, there are many ways of doing this, but it all boils down to letting them out. That is, it is detrimental to your health to hold these feelings inside as they will eventually come out one way or another. Oftentimes, a good cry is what a person needs. At other times, what they need is a good laugh. Both of these outlets can be healthy if controlled. But it is always uplifting if one is able to smile. Have you ever noticed that simply turning a frown upside down will do the trick? Of course, anything that is fun or entertaining will remove a somber mood as long as the person can get into it. Try going to an amusement park; try playing games. You know, play therapy, which is usually associated with children, can benefit people of all ages. Naturally, the games that children and adults play will differ, unless the adults and kids are playing together. Of course, the methods described in previous paragraphs will afford some degree of emotional release as well.

Behavior Modification: A change in behavior is warranted when you are bogged down with stress. Simply put: Get out and do something instead of sitting alone feeling sorry for yourself. Unfortunately, too often the person is stressed out because they have taken on too much. They are overwhelmed with all the responsibilities and duties; they have overextended themselves. It is necessary to mix sufficient pleasure with business to maintain a relative balance. And it is necessary to take breaks once in a while: allow yourself time to ponder and to unwind. You might try just slowing down. It's about placing your mind elsewhere and responding to that. Yes, there will be times when you simply cannot ignore the many tasks set before you, all of which have deadlines, requirements, and specifications. When that is the case, more planning is required. Make a to-do list of all the things you need to get done; then prioritize that list. Start plugging away by beginning with the most important or stressful item, and working your way down the list until all have been checked off. Practice budgeting your time just like you do (or should be doing) with your money. It's about being responsible with time and money. You will find you have enough, with some left over for rest, recreation, and recuperation. And each goal you achieve will give you a sense of accomplishment, motivating you to persevere, and not be distracted by the appearance of a heavy load you wish not to carry. Progressive success will raise anybody's self-esteem. So organize, schedule, and manage the workload and you won't get overwhelmed by it. Another way to avoid stress is to avoid stressors: like certain people, places, and situations. Maybe you can plan ahead so that you will not be there then; otherwise, prepare yourself in advance for anticipated stressful situations. You can develop strategies, tactics, scripts, and role plays so that you do not lose your cool, overreact, or possibly say or do something that you might regret. Sometimes you must stand your ground and not give in. Either way: Do not fail to meet your own needs by focusing on everybody else's needs all the time.

"How beautiful it is to do nothing, and then to rest afterward." – Spanish Proverb

"When I look back on all these worries, I remember the story of the old man who said on his deathbed that he had had a lot of trouble in his life, most of which had never happened." – Winston Churchill

For more information on stress relief, the reader is referred to the lesson on Dumping the Emotional Baggage. And study the approaches reviewed in the Conflict Resolution lesson, especially if the stress you are experiencing is in regards to a relationship that you value.

- PSA 23:1-6 ~ The LORD is my shepherd; I shall not want. He makes me lie down in green pastures. He leads me beside still waters. He restores my soul. He leads me in paths of righteousness for his name's sake. Even though I walk through the valley of the shadow of death, I will fear no evil, for you are with me; your rod and your staff, they comfort me. You prepare a table before me in the presence of my enemies; you anoint my head with oil; my cup overflows. Surely goodness and mercy shall follow me all the days of my life, and I shall dwell in the house of the LORD forever.

- PSA 55:22 ~ Cast your burden on the LORD, and he will sustain you…

- MAT 6:25-34 ~ Jesus said, "I tell you, do not be anxious about your life, what you will eat or what you will drink, nor about your body, what you will put on. Is not life more than food, and the body more than clothing? Look at the birds of the air: they neither sow nor reap nor gather into barns, and yet your heavenly Father feeds them. Are you not of more value than they? And which of you by being anxious can add a single hour to his span of life? And why are you anxious about clothing? Consider the lilies of the field, how they grow: they neither toil nor spin, yet I tell you, even Solomon in all his glory was not arrayed like one of these. But if God so clothes the grass of the field, which today is alive and tomorrow is thrown into the oven, will he not much more clothe you, O you of little faith? Therefore do not be anxious, saying, 'What shall we eat?' or 'What shall we drink?' or 'What shall we wear?' For the Gentiles seek after all these things, and your heavenly Father knows that you need them all. But seek first the kingdom of God and his righteousness, and all these things will be added to you. Therefore do not be anxious about tomorrow, for tomorrow will be anxious for itself. Sufficient for the day is its own trouble."

- ROM 8:32 ~ He who did not spare his own Son but gave him up for us all, how will he not also through him graciously give us all things?

- COL 3:7-10 ~ In these you too once walked, when you were living in them. But now you must put them all away: anger, wrath, malice, slander, and obscene talk. Do not lie to one another, seeing that you have put off the old self with its practices and have put on the new self, which is being renewed in knowledge after the image of its creator.

Activity

Check the items below that might help to manage your stress. Make sure you have several options to choose from within each modality. Discover what works for you and circle those items. Cross out those items that do not work for you or make the stress worse. Repeat the exercise often, until you have tried most if not all of these strategies. Add some ideas to the bottom of the list and try those also. Continue to practice stress relief and improve the quality of your life. Note that some items tap into more than one of the three domains below.

Physical Wellness	Spiritual Support	Mental Exercises
Sleep 7-8 hours at night	Church attendance	Keep mind busy
Limit a nap to 15 minutes	Daily prayer, thanks	Daydream, fantasize
Balanced, nutritious diet	Bible study, devotions	Problem solving
Drink enough water, fluids	Fellowship with believers	Decision making
Take vitamins, minerals	Christian support	Puzzles, brain teasers
Prescribed medicine only	Count your blessings	Quality conversation
Avoid too much caffeine	Follow Golden Rule	Socializing
Avoid too much alcohol	Love others and forgive	Go to the movies
Join a gym or fitness class	Love, forgive yourself	Go to amusement park
Aerobic exercise, dance	Altruism, helping others	Play games
Weight lifting, isometrics	Pure, uplifting thoughts	Write letters, send cards
Swim, run, bike, walk	Encouraging self-talk	Journaling
Yoga; Tai Chi	Encouraging others	Write prose, poetry
Stretching with exercise	Time with loved ones	Read books, do research
Team sports	Bear hugs	Take a class or two
Play with kids, grandkids	Nature hikes	Play a musical instrument
Massage therapy	Vacation escapes	Listen to beautiful music
Hygiene and grooming	Relaxation	Hobbies, arts and crafts
Healthy sex in marriage	Deep breathing	Organize things
Singing	Support groups	Aromatherapy
Slow down	Meditation	Positive imagery
Baking, cooking	Mix business with pleasure	Prioritize, plan, budget
Clean house, yard	Keep your cool	Strategize, role play
_____	_____	_____
_____	_____	_____
_____	_____	_____
_____	_____	_____

Managing Anger

Anger is a normal emotion, in that everyone experiences it from time to time. Anger produces negative energy that can be destructive or constructive depending on how you channel the energy. But it can be dangerous when not kept in check, or when the anger has no outlet for expression. Many forms of sin can be linked to anger, including resentment, hatred, prejudice, slander, abuse, aggression, violence, and assault. When anger leads to hate we become vulnerable to a multitude of serious and devastating sins.

- PRO 14:17 ~ A man of quick temper acts foolishly, and a man of evil devices is hated

- PRO 22:24-25 ~ Make no friendship with a man given to anger, nor go with a wrathful man, lest you learn his ways and entangle yourself in a snare.

- PRO 29:22 ~ A man of wrath stirs up strife, and one given to anger causes transgression.

- EPH 4:26,31 ~ When angry, do not sin; do not let the sun go down on your anger… Let all bitterness, wrath, anger, clamor and slander be put away from you, along with malice.

There are different types of anger, to include the fight or flight preservation response, the reaction to perceived harm or maltreatment from others, and the development of an angry disposition or temperament. The response to anger can range from disappointment or irritability to contempt or unbridled rage. Thus, anger can be expressed passively, aggressively, or a combination of both (passive-aggressive). Passive anger is characterized by indifference, detachment, aggravation, obsessiveness, manipulation, mistrust, blaming (self or others), selfishness, and/or sneakiness. Aggressive anger is characterized by bullying, violence, destructiveness, resentfulness, harming or punishing (self or others), explosiveness, and/or threatening or punitive behavior.

It is best to stop and think before letting anger get the better of you. Most of the time, you will realize that the initial reaction is founded on an irrational belief, as is the case with resentment. Usually, the excuse for anger is attributed to external causes. But we choose how we feel, not others. We must be consistently mindful of the circumstances and rethink the perceived motives of others. This requires one to delay the response and thoughtfully consider alternative explanations, rather than rush into a conclusion that may lead to an angry outburst.

- PRO 15:1,18 ~ A soft answer turns away wrath, but a harsh word stirs up anger... A hot-tempered man stirs up strife, but he who is slow to anger quiets contention.

- ECC 7:9 ~ Be not quick to become angry, for anger lodges in the heart of fools.

- MAT 5:22 ~ Jesus said, "Everyone who is angry with his brother will be liable to judgment; whoever insults his brother will be liable to the council; and whoever says, 'You fool!' will be liable to the hell of fire."

- JAM 1:19-20 ~ Let every person be quick to hear, slow to speak, and slow to anger; for the anger of man does not produce the righteousness of God.

Anger is often a response to frustration, like when we couldn't get the hang of something, or we expected better results, or we thought our performance was below some standard. Thus, frustration can lead to anger directed against oneself. Certainly, we get frustrated with others as well, and get angry with them in the same manner. Regardless, anger is harmful to me just as much as it is when I vent it upon others. It is a communicable disease that can irreparably damage relationships.

Factors that increase susceptibility to anger include depression, stress, worry, fatigue, illness, pain, and intoxication. A simple disagreement can become a heated argument; a passing insult becomes an exchange of progressively more abusive speech; a public slight turns into a pattern of harassment; a rejection turns into cruel and unusual punishment.

Some people simply have control problems; they either don't try or don't care and their anger gets unmanageable. This is clearly unhealthy and self-destructive. Equally destructive is to hold it in. It's like a bottle of champagne that gets shaken every time the person is bothered by something; eventually it will spew all over the place when the lid is blown and the person explodes. Such an event may lead to heart attack, stroke, or mental breakdown. Anger will continue to get worse if not properly vented.

The expression of anger is universal with respect to the facial expression: flushed cheeks, tightened eyebrows, flaring nostrils, clenched teeth/jaw, and fixed stare. You can tell when anger is coming on if you are in tune with your body. It often starts with muscle tension, maybe in the eyes, neck, arms, or belly. Tension builds up and things speed up, like heart rate and respiration. This will result in your body heating up, and you may get sweaty on the palms, armpits, or forehead. This may lead to headache, nausea, or other discomfort. Eventually, the physical symptoms will lead to a negative thought. You want to prevent the negative thought from entering your mind.

It usually takes only twenty minutes or so for the anger to subside. That is, it loses momentum or power over time. Use that time to channel the anger in a way that doesn't hurt anybody including you. It will go away even faster if you practice relaxation, breathing, and/or imagery techniques. These methods enable one to tap into his or her inner power and strength. Anger can be a slippery slope if not properly controlled or channeled.

The lessons at the end of this section provide strategies and techniques to gain control over negative feelings and behavior. I generally combine relaxation, breathing, and imagery into one exercise. I will use anger as an example of how the body can instruct the mind. As stated above, anger usually begins with tension, followed by increase in heart rate and respiration, until the body heats up and the person perspires heavily and/or gets hot headed. Of course, the anger process may differ between persons; but that process can be halted at any stage, prior to the intrusive, negative thought. Remember, that's what you want to prevent: the negative thought. It will get you into a negative mood, and any action you take in that state of mind will be damaging to you and anyone you take it out on.

If the mind is receptive to signals from the body, it will recognize the signs that anger is brewing and it can tell the body to shift into reverse. If the feeling is tension, send commands to the muscles to relax; let that relaxed feeling progress to other areas of the body. If things are going too fast slow it down by taking deeper, longer, and fewer breaths. This will slow the breathing which will slow the rest of the bodily functions, and promote greater relaxation. If the person is getting too hot, send commands to the body to chill out. Once a pleasing state of inner peace is reached, the mind will be receptive to positive imagery, which will block the negative thought from entry.

"Anger will never disappear so long as thoughts of resentment are cherished in the mind. Anger will disappear as soon as thoughts of resentment are forgotten." – Buddha

"Anger, if not restrained, is frequently more hurtful to us than the injury that provokes it." – Lucius Annaeus Seneca

Managing Pain

"Those things that hurt, instruct." – Benjamin Franklin

Pain interferes with overall functioning and quality of life. There are many types of pain. Pain can be constant, intermittent, or periodic. It can be physical: stinging, pinching, pulling, poking, burning, shocking, stabbing, aching, or throbbing. It can be emotional: sad, afraid, anxious, angry, frustrated, hopeless, helpless, or guilty. It can be spiritual: stain of sin, demon possession, lake of fire. It can be a sensation, perception, or emotion. Acute pain from an injury, illness, or physical state will usually subside and eventually disappear after healing has taken place. Chronic pain can continue after healing, or when there is a debilitating, traumatic, or degenerative event or condition that does not pass; and it can get worse.

Pain receptors can detect extreme temperature, uncommon pressure, chemical irritation, or some combination. Nociceptive pain can be either somatic (caused by injury to peripherals, supportive tissue, or structure), visceral (internal organ injury, inflammation, deterioration, or disease), or superficial (skin and surface tissue). Neuropathic pain is lingering pain after the body has healed or due to recurring pain from past trauma or disease. Some pain cannot be linked to any discernable ailment but is just as real to the sufferer. Such pain is referred to as psychogenic (exhibited in somatoform conditions, hypochondriasis, psychosomatic illnesses, and conversion disorders). Phantom pain can occur after an amputation, or when neurological responsiveness has ceased. Breakthrough pain is the kind that occurs suddenly, is transient, and is unaffected by medication; it is most familiar to cancer patients. Incident pain arises from movement of limbs and joints and is common among those with arthritis.

Pain is the most common reason people consult a physician. The best way to diagnose pain is to determine what type of pain is felt, the location of the pain, variations in intensity, and the factors or conditions that cause the pain to elevate. Historical information will help to determine how and when it began, and when it flares up or subsides. Also relevant is what works to relieve the pain or to manage it.

Imagine the pain and agony that Christ endured for you and me. Imagine the pain that his mother Mary and his close friend John endured as they watched Jesus being tortured to death. Imagine the pain that God the Father felt allowing his Son to bear the entire sin of humankind. It makes my pain look insignificant by comparison; it helps diminish my pain.

- ISA 53:4-12 ~ Surely he has borne our griefs and carried our sorrows; yet we esteemed him stricken, smitten by God, and afflicted. But he was pierced for our transgressions; he was crushed for our iniquities; upon him was the chastisement that brought us peace, and with his wounds we are healed. All we like sheep have gone astray; we have turned – every one – to his own way; and the LORD has laid on him the iniquity of us all. He was oppressed, and he was afflicted, yet he opened not his mouth; like a lamb that is led to the slaughter, and like a sheep that before its shearers is silent, so he opened not his mouth. By oppression and judgment he was taken away; and as for his generation, who considered that he was cut off out of the land of the living, stricken for the transgression of my people? And they made his grave with the wicked and with a rich man in his death, although he had done no violence, and there was no deceit in his mouth. Yet it was the will of the LORD to crush him; he has put him to grief; when his soul makes an offering for guilt, he shall see his offspring; he shall prolong his days; the will of the LORD shall prosper in his hand. Out of the anguish of his soul he shall see and be satisfied; by his knowledge shall the righteous one, my servant, make many to be accounted righteous, and he shall bear their iniquities. Therefore I will divide him a portion with the many, and he shall divide the spoil with the strong, because he poured out his soul to death and was numbered with the transgressors; yet he bore the sin of many, and makes intercession for the transgressors.

- MAT 27:46 ~ And about the ninth hour Jesus cried out with a loud voice, saying, "Eli, Eli, lema sabachthani?" that is, "My God, my God, why have you forsaken me?"

"The worst pain a man can suffer: to have insight into much and power over nothing."
– Herodotus

In order to mitigate pain to a manageable level so that one may continue to persevere and function, there are some techniques that may help. The objective of this lesson is to present methods to aid people in dealing with pain and not let pain stop them from achieving their goals. Of course, some pain is so debilitating that it seems insurmountable. Or is it?

Increase Functioning. Health, fitness, and activity are of utmost importance in moving past physical and emotional pain. The stress that pain puts on the psyche is magnified when one is in poor physical, mental, or spiritual health; pain will aggravate poor health in these domains. For example, there is a causal link between depression and pain. If the person does not keep active, they will lose additional functioning. Physical exercise is very important, because it can help one to de-stress, and it releases endorphins into the body that include natural painkillers. Keeping the mind engaged is equally important as physical exercise. In one of my pain groups a lady said she didn't know why she was wasting her time attending the group. But after the second session she made an interesting disclosure. She informed that she found the lesson and discussion interesting and that it grasped her attention, to the degree that she wasn't thinking about her pain the entire session. I explained that diverting attention from the pain works because most of the pain is psychological. Dwelling on the pain worsens it; focusing on something constructive and uplifting lessens the pain precisely because you aren't absorbed in it. It is essential that the individual find things to do and keep working the body, mind, and spirit. If you discover something you enjoy, it will give you the motivation to do it. Try things you haven't tried before. It may surprise you that there are things you like, are good at, or that work in which you were previously unaware. And don't forget – assert yourself. If you do not act, you will easily fall back into a state of isolation and inactivity. That is, to keep functioning at your highest level, you need to keep functioning.

Diet and Nutrition are essentials whether you have pain or not. But pain will be more incapacitating if one eats too much or too little. Oftentimes, the sufferer needs to lose weight; carrying excess weight will make physical pain a lot more agonizing, and can cause strain. Determine what weight is ideal for your height, bone structure, and mass. Calculate the necessary intake of calories beyond which it would prevent necessary weight loss. Then determine how quickly you want to reduce and establish a daily caloric limit. Keep a record and chart your progress; increase or decrease calorie intake accordingly. Distribute the meals to maximize the way your body uses food: either have three square meals or have five moderate snacks throughout the day: whatever works for you. Be sure to eat from the primary food groups and take vitamins and supplements. It might be a good idea to consult a dietitian.

Sleep Planning helps to get the maximum amount of restful sleep; too much or too little sleep is not good. Create a comfort zone; configure the sleep environment to get the most out of your sleep time. Don't stay in bed too long and don't take lengthy or frequent naps during the day. Try to sleep mostly at night, and try to sleep through the night as best you can. Fashion an ambience conducive to comfort and peacefulness. Control the climate to suit you. For example, some people like it cool in the room and then have extra covers to feel snug; others like it better warmer and with fewer covers. You may have soft music or environment sounds echoing in the background. I used to love the sound of waves beating against the rocks by our family cottage at the lake; the resonance would lull me to sleep. At home I prefer dead silence. But that is impossible in the suburbs with teenagers and dogs yelping at all hours. So now I prefer a fan, or some kind of white noise that is not annoying but masks the ambient sounds that are. I also like it pitch dark; any ambient light is intrusive because my brain thinks the dawn is coming. People often wear eye masks or earplugs to veil the interference. Some prefer a nightlight. I know people that leave the television on; some like it loud, some soft. You could have a pleasant scent emanating; try aromatic emitters, candles, or incense. Because of my back pain, I need three fluffy pillows, one each for my head, chest, and legs. I'll sleep on one side for a while, wake up stiff, move the pillows and flip over, and maintain that position for a while. Setup your bed, pillows, and bedroom in a way that makes you want to dive in and sink. Try a gravity bed, or an adjustable bed, or test different mattresses at the local sleep store. You don't want to dread getting into bed with the thought that it will be hard to get up. Find out how you like it and configure the environment that way. Go to bed and get up at a set time. A circadian rhythm arranged around the pain will regulate your body and adjust your brain. It is advisable to develop a routine to unwind before bedtime, say about an hour prior to retiring. Take a hot shower, watch television, read, and/or meditate; whatever helps you to relax or mitigate the pain. Do not engage in activities that get you wired, such as exercise, video games, arguing, or studying something intensely.

Keep Busy and **Take Breaks** throughout the day. You want to be tired when it is bedtime. Stay engaged and stimulated during waking hours to keep your mind occupied, so you won't be preoccupied with the pain. Work your routine around pain episodes. For example, there may be times of the day when you have more pain or less pain. Start a routine of physical exercise working it into the pain schedule. Discover exercises to participate in that do not exacerbate the pain, but rather strengthen the muscles that support the afflicted area. Although I can't play basketball or volleyball anymore, I can still swing a golf club and walk eighteen holes. That works okay for me. Find what works for you. Make sure you schedule periodic breaks. You don't want to overexert yourself or overdo it. For some people breaks are best when the pain is likely to come: by taking the break during the episode of pain it may reduce or eliminate some of the pain. For other people, they want to take the break during a non-pain cycle in order to relax better. Then they can be busy during the peak pain periods so they won't think about it as much. Keep moving your body and engage your brain. I find if I stand or sit too long I get stiff, so I move around periodically to stay loose.

Activity Planning will assist you in filling your calendar. Remember, you need to exercise your body, mind, and spirit. The objective is to increase achievements and decrease avoidance behavior. Physically you can perform chores, organize things; take walks; play with the kids or grandkids, take care of animals, go shopping, or dancing; travel, take short trips in the car. Mentally you can call people on the phone, socialize with friends and family, even converse with strangers. Engage your brain in studies, research, and reading. Make time for recreation, excitement, and entertainment. Laughter really is the best medicine (see PRO 17:22); research confirms it also. It is good for your soul. So exercise your sense of humor as well. Spiritually you can pray, read the Bible, go to church, have family devotions, or meditate. Yoga is a very good way to exercise body, mind, and spirit. Take classes and you may find there are some body positions you can sustain longer. Have activities to fill your quiet time as well. Try journaling, hobbies, arts and crafts, reading books, listening to or playing music, singing, working puzzles or brain teasers. There are a lot of things you could be doing.

Develop your coping mechanisms. There are ways of reducing pain in intensity and frequency. Have a repertoire of many methods and learn which work for you. I can manage pretty well if my pain is around a three out of ten. If I can reduce it from a seven to a three, I practically won't even notice it. If your pain is a ten, wouldn't an eight be an improvement? If an additional technique dropped it to a six, that would be even better. The more techniques you have that work, the greater will be your threshold for pain.

Medication Management: Medicine helps; it's a proven fact. If you suffer with major depression an antidepressant will balance out the mood; this is a medication that needs to stay in your system even when you feel okay. Tranquilizers help to ease anxiety. And if it is physical pain from an injury or degenerative disease, painkillers are necessary. There are different types of painkillers such as over-the-counter analgesics (aspirin and ibuprofen), narcotics (includes opiate based analgesics), anesthetics, anti-inflammatory drugs, muscle relaxers, anticonvulsants, and tricyclic antidepressants. But we want to diminish our dependence on specific drugs by managing the pain in other ways. Medications like benzodiazapines and opiates are highly addictive. Such addictions are very hard to break; in fact, prescription drugs have become the most prevalent addiction of our time. If the pain or anxiety isn't that bad, you don't need to take anything. People have a tendency to take their medicine for relief of other symptoms; for example, if it helps with the physical pain they may start using it for psychological pain. If they already are sleepy they take a sleep aid anyway. Before they know it, they're taking pills for any kind of discomfort. And the more they ingest, the less the medicine works. These medications should be taken only as needed or directed. Besides, the effect is only temporary, and often it doesn't remove the discomfort entirely. More painkillers seldom provide additional relief; it only makes the person feel loopy. So you need other options that will lessen the pain further. Do not depend exclusively on pills.

Progressive Relaxation, Deep Breathing, Positive Imagery: I have met skeptics saying that these processes won't work, especially for their pain; and I have proven many of them wrong. I have conducted countless pain groups and I employ these techniques regularly. I usually introduce them early in the process; and I often open subsequent sessions with a refresher. I always inquire their level of pain or anxiety before and after the exercise. One lady had endured excruciating pain from hydrocephalus and a corresponding botched surgery to correct it. The result was confinement to a wheelchair and a constant pain ranging from eight to ten. The first time we used relaxation, breathing, and imagery this lady was surprised to discover her pain had dropped from a ten to a five. The second time, I asked what her pain level was after the session. She paused, stopped to think, and in wonderment she said "zero." Apparently, she had a natural talent for dissociation and tapping into her inner power – better than I can that's for sure. She was an inspiration to the others, and became the voice of comfort that soothed their pain more than I could. They told her that she should be a counselor, giving her greater hope and purpose to move beyond her handicap and become somebody. Hence, the power of that inner strength which comes from above; it's within everyone, but some will have to work harder to master it. I have repeatedly emphasized in this text the need to think positive; it helps you feel positive. This relates to the power of the mind over the body. If they work in concert one can achieve a great synergy and achieve unbelievable levels of control. That is, getting into a positive, pleasant, and peaceful place where body and mind are integrated enables the spirit to join in and unleash an inner power that will surprise most people when they discover it. Everybody has it; for many it remains untapped. More on this topic is provided at the end of this section.

Cognitive Restructuring: Intrusion by negative, defeating thoughts will stop progress in its tracks. My advice is to change the channel. One pain patient had recurring nightmares and flashbacks from when she was molested by a trusted love one. She kept having the same bad dream for forty years. She would see a shady character approaching her from a void of darkness. Being a woman of faith, I reminded her how any amount of light will break the darkness; I recommended that she imagine herself switching channels to the bright program. The light would expose the evil lurking in the darkness and energize her love. Her response would be to forgive and let go, just as the Lord did for her. She practiced every night; she was comforted by the light and little by little, found the inner peace to forgive the perpetrator. Then the dreams finally stopped. Block negative self-messages that are untrue. It's the same concept as blocking the pain by shutting off the efferent signal from reaching the brain. Enable positive thoughts that are true, elevating, and more powerful, by concentrating on inspiring images, pleasant memories, and faith. Rehearse these thoughts and images often, every time the intrusive thought tries to enter the mind. In time, you can unlearn the old program and replace it with a new one. Reprogramming by means of repetition reconfigures the neural pathways in the brain in same manner that constant bombardment on the psyche alters the chemistry in a negative way. Obviously, one must practice the new program as often as the old one is triggered. It also is wise to rehearse the program at lower levels of consciousness, and this can be accomplished with relaxation and imagery. The objective of cognitive restructuring is to open the program or memory and reexamine the contents; it is much like unpacking emotional baggage and removing each item for a complete overhaul and cleaning. Each piece of information is categorized, organized, and synthesized. When you repack the bags you leave a lot of stuff out that you don't need or doesn't fit. The rest is reconfigured in a way that provides meaning which was otherwise hidden amongst the clutter or debris. In a way, this exercise lightens the load by leaving only the essential data required to reroute the process, so that the activation or trigger engages a new adaptive response sequence. More on cognitive reconstruction can be found in the section on Trauma Treatment.

Support Systems: Remember to build teams, comprised of loved ones, professionals, and groups composed of others that suffer as you do. Your inner circle includes those who are with you through thick and thin. Pets are part of that team as they can love unconditionally as well. Social service, mental health, and medical professionals such as psychotherapists, case workers, nurses, physical therapists, psychiatrists, surgeons, chiropractors, etc. comprise another team. One or more support groups should be added to your list of teams. Go to therapy groups, pain groups, AA/NA meetings, Bible studies, social functions, weight-watchers, or whatever specialty meets your needs. Another support could be related to your physical exercise regimen: trainer, yoga instructor, aerobics class, etc. The bottom line: the more support the better. Refer to the section on Team Building for more information.

Alternative Treatments: The pain patient may benefit from surgery, chiropractic treatment, physical therapy, massage therapy, hydrotherapy, and/or certain topical or herbal therapies. Techniques such as yoga, hypnosis, acupuncture and acupressure have been known to help people. Much of the success in alternative treatments can be attributed to faith. Thus, spirituality (prayer, meditation, worship) would be an effective option for people who believe or who want to believe in the power within.

Because of sin, we suffer. Because of sin, Christ suffered. Therefore, all must suffer and all must endure pain. Pain is a part of life. But it will be temporary.

- GEN 3 (paraphrased) ~ The fall of Adam and Eve brought sorrow, pain, and suffering. That was their reward for sin. And sin became a curse that would affect all human beings.

- ROM 8:18-22 ~ I consider that the sufferings of this present time are not worth comparing with the glory that is to be revealed to us. For the creation waits with eager longing for the revealing of the sons of God. For the creation was subjected to futility, not willingly, but because of him who subjected it, in hope that the creation itself will be set free from its bondage to corruption and obtain the freedom of the glory of the children of God. We know that the whole creation has been groaning together in the pains of childbirth until now.

- 1 PE 3:17-18 ~ For it is better to suffer for doing good, if that should be God's will, than for doing evil. For Christ also suffered once for sins, the righteous for the unrighteous, that he might bring us to God, being put to death in the flesh but made alive in the spirit.

"Pain is inevitable. Suffering is optional." – Buddhist proverb

Relaxation, Breathing, and Imagery

Progressive relaxation calms a person down and relieves the tension. Breathing and counting can be used to slow things down and also will produce greater relaxation and calmness. Uplifting thoughts and positive suggestions help people to cool off and introspect. Imagery allows one to find a comfortable, favorite place where he or she feels content, safe, and at peace. Meditation also can be used to achieve this positive state. The objective is to create a composed and collected place in your mind where the negative thought is uninvited.

The power of the imagination is extraordinary; people have been known to get better merely by imagining it. You also can develop ailments that way, as with psychosomatic illnesses. If you keep thinking negative, that's what you'll get. Think positive. Have your clients imagine role playing, performing, remembering, becoming, finishing, or changing. Remember, thinking provides the impetus for doing. Imagining you can do it enables you to believe it possible. Envisioning the program enables one to fix the bugs in it. Consider the following case exemplifying the power of the imagination.

I once had a five year old client with a serious case of enuresis. His parents were being investigated for neglect due to alcoholism. He and his brother were temporarily removed to ensure the parents followed through with their treatment; that treatment included mandatory counseling for the parents and the children. When the boys returned to their home shortly thereafter, the youngest already had regressed and was wetting his bed every night. The boy had a great imagination and was quite the artist, so we played a visual imagery game. First, I asked him to press on his tummy. "Do you feel that," I asked. He said, "It feels like I have to pee." "That's right," I replied, "You pressed down right where your bladder is." After some relaxation exercises, I had him imagine that his body parts could talk to each other. If he was asleep at night and he felt that sensation, his bladder would tell his brain, "It feels like I have to pee." Then his brain would command the eyes to open. His eyes would open and tell his feet to swing out and touch the floor. Once his feet felt the cold linoleum, they would signal the legs to stand up and walk towards the bathroom. When he arrived, the legs would tell his brain, which would send commands for his hands to lower his trousers and his legs to sit down. Once his butt felt the cool toilet seat it would inform the bladder it was in position and all systems were go. Then the bladder would empty itself, after which he could reverse the process and return to bed. It was a seven stage process that we rehearsed seven times. I helped him write down the steps and instructed him to practice them in his mind seven times every day: when he woke up in the morning, when he ate breakfast, when he arrived at school, during lunchtime, when he returned home from school, at dinnertime, and when he went to bed. He shared this schedule with his parents who helped him rehearse the steps as prescribed. Each week when I came to visit he would report on his progress and recite the procedure from memory. After one week, he only pissed three times; after two weeks, twice. After three weeks he pissed once; and it ceased after that. If a five year old can modify his behavior in this manner, anybody can. He developed a program by visualizing the process, and it became a habit through rehearsal and practice.

Relaxation, breathing, and imagery are skills you definitely want to teach your clients. It usually takes me about 1.5 hours to teach these skills to a group. This also stimulates a good half hour of discussion for a full two hours (one to two sessions). Most participants amaze themselves at their ability to gain self-control in this manner. I usually record how much pain or anxiety they report before the exercise and then after. They are compelled to keep practicing these skills when they realize they can drop their stress or pain level from an eight to a three in just minutes. I have seen persons get a handle on their tension, pain, anger, or fear after only one application or via one particular technique. They discover a natural aptitude that was unrealized until they experienced it. This is the benefit of exploring things you have never tried; you may surprise yourself at what you are capable of.

Such techniques allow a person to get into a positive state of body and mind, thereby preventing the destructive thought that could lead to a regrettable action. The methods also facilitate access to the higher power within. Teach and use them to get control over emotional or physical pain, or any negative state, before it gets control over your thoughts and you lose control. Once a person learns to tap the inner programming, it can be modified accordingly. Some people can shut the gate that transmits pain to the brain, or block the destructive thought with positive imagery, or perform software maintenance on their hard drive.

I generally combine relaxation, breathing, and imagery into one exercise. After progressive relaxation, the suggestion is made to systematically slow the breathing. Then I introduce uplifting imagery. I let the group select if they want to go to the beach or the forest. Participants are welcomed to go to anyplace they wish, in case they do not choose the place that others did. In the example below, I will use the beach scene.

Progressive Relaxation Script

As you sit in your chair adjust your body position until you feel very comfortable. Usually the optimum position is with your legs apart and your feet flat on the floor. You may find that placing your arms along your side with the palms of your hands resting on your lap is a most relaxing position. In a completely relaxed posture you will reduce the tension in your extremities allowing the free flow of blood throughout your body. You may choose to make minor adjustments in your posture, but for the most part, you can remain perfectly still, once you feel cozy.

Allow yourself to drift away, leaving this place behind. Concentrate on what is going on inside of you. As your eyes begin to shut, take a long, deep breath. Exhale slowly, and notice the feeling of relaxation that is coming over you. Your eyes may be closed, but you can still focus; yes you can focus inwardly. Look deeply into your soul to search for that place where your body, mind, and spirit come together. The room around you may have disappeared from view, but you are still aware of many things. You are aware of whom you are, and you are aware of what's going on beneath the surface of your consciousness. You have no desire to attend to the outside world because the inside world is more interesting right now. You may hear my voice in the distance, but everything else is fading out, as you concentrate on what you are experiencing within.

Your mind and body are well connected now. You will find that your body will respond to commands from the brain. You can imagine away tension, pain, or emotional discomfort simply by commanding it to depart. Just send a message to the muscles in your body to relax and they will respond. You may discover a heaviness beginning to spread into your entire body. It feels good doesn't it? It's like a huge pitcher filled with warm, soothing relaxation is being poured into you from an opening at the top of your head. And that feeling of calmness and relaxation is driving away all the tension as it gradually fills your body. The tension around your forehead and eyes is now evaporating into the air as the relaxation seeps in. This feeling is spreading throughout your face. That's right; send commands to those muscles to relax as you feel that calmness continuing to move down from around your eyes, down into your cheeks, your chin, and deeper into your neck. Allow all that tension in the muscles of your neck to flow away, replacing it with a feeling of total relaxation. That feeling is flowing into your shoulders as you command them to likewise relax, giving a sensation of heaviness as your body seems to sink deeper into the chair. Go ahead and shrug off all that tension and discover your body getting heavier, sinking deeper into a state of relaxation, but at the same time feeling lighter, as if floating. Feeling heavy yet floating; isn't it wonderful? The muscles in your back are relaxing now; all that tension is being absorbed by the chair. This sense of relaxation keeps raining in, spreading into your arms, down through your hands; driving all that tension out through your fingertips, and into the air as you command each muscle group to become calm and still. Next, your chest and abdomen are being filled with the sweet calmness that keeps moving down, getting deeper; now entering your hips and your buttocks. All of those muscle groups have been ordered to relax as the mind-body connection is strengthened. The muscular tension you may have felt earlier has dissipated, some being absorbed by the chair and the rest just evaporating into thin air. The flow of relaxation, like clean, crystal water continues to flow into your legs, and down into your ankles, collecting in your feet, where all that tension flows out of your feet and into the floor.

Your entire being has achieved a stable mood of calmness and oneness, and you are gaining new understanding. You are very much aware of the fact that you have achieved a superb state of relaxation and tranquility. Isn't it fascinating how your mind and your body cooperated in this manner? Allow yourself to enjoy this pleasant moment of quietness, calmness, and serenity. It is something you have accomplished on your own, by tapping into your inner strength and power. You can be confident in your ability to control yourself, and the knowledge that you can return to this restful and peaceful state whenever you wish. It is there at your command. You produced the relaxed condition that you are now experiencing, and you can do it again, anytime and anywhere.

We sometimes experience the tensions and stresses of everyday life, and all too often we allow them to affect us in a negative way by getting angry, upset, irritable, nervous, or anxious. Yet all the while, we possessed this capability within our own inner spirit: the power to drive away tension, calm ourselves, relax, and reach an inner state of peace. We do not have to let the external world get to us, or control us; for we can seize control in all that we think and feel by focusing inwardly. After all, the way we feel and behave is not produced from outside of us, but rather from inside of us. The power is within each and every one of us to control our emotions, our thoughts, and our actions. And now you have discovered that power, and you have rewarded yourself with this state of serenity and bliss. You will remember what you have achieved through this simple exercise. You located your inner being, the source of your internal programming. And you can access this potential anytime you like, whenever you feel the need to relax, calm down, and take control.

Deep Breathing and Imagery Script

This exercise begins with a long, smooth, deep cleansing breath. Draw a breath deeply into your lungs. Bring the air in slowly, slowly, hold it, hold it; now let it out slowly, slowly. One more time, take a pure, deep breath, hold it, and slowly exhale. It feels good doesn't it? Amazing how we take for granted such a splendid feeling. But now let us concentrate on that feeling, as we inhale and exhale slowly and deeply. Let all that positive, refreshing, wholesome air enter, and exhale all that tension, pain, and negativity. Begin to count your breaths, deliberately slowing down your respiration. Your breathing will continue to deepen because you will be taking fewer breaths: first breath, feeling calmer and slower, twice as relaxed as before; second breath, feeling twice as relaxed as the first. With each breath feeling more calm and more deeply relaxed. Keep counting until you drift into a very calm and silent state of continuation. You may notice, as your breathing continues to slow, you become even more relaxed; and as you relax further, your breathing slows down even more. Fewer, deeper breaths are making you profoundly settled and serene, free of stress, as you slow down all of your operating systems.

Anytime you feel tense or uneasy, sit down, close your eyes, and take a few deep breaths. Keep slowing it down as you progressively relax each muscle group from your head to your toes. You can use these techniques to reverse the onset of tension, anger, or anxiety; to get your mind off of troubling thoughts, or to subdue the discomfort of pain: emotional and physical. If you feel tense, allow your body to alert the mind, and establish that mind-body connection. The mind will respond accordingly, thanking your body and commanding it to reverse that state, and convert tension into relaxation. If you feel like things are going too fast, have your body notify the mind; the mind will respond in like fashion, modifying the speed by slowing your heartbeat and respiration. In the same manner you can change the temperature from too hot to cool; that's right just chill out a little. Keep thinking calm, slow and cool. Very good; I am impressed. You have made yourself, and me, proud.

As you enjoy this feeling of freedom and control, allow your mind to drift away to the beach. Imagine you are floating in space in the direction of your favorite beach. There, you see it in the distance, slowly coming into view. You can't wait to get there, and then you realize that you are already there. Get the big picture in your mind: the sandy coastline, the palm trees, the endless waves rolling into shore. There you are; standing by the ocean; feeling close to nature, God, and the spirit within you. Enter into your vision with all of your senses, and take a stroll down the curving coastline. Yes, that's excellent.

Feature all the beautiful colors: the deep blue sky above with fluffy white clouds just drifting along; drifting like you are, through the vastness of space and mind. And notice the greenish-blue color of the sea, with its whitecaps splashing into the beige colored sand. Green leaves of the palms are flowing in the breeze, towering above your head; resting on tall, brown trunks that bend with the wind. Isn't it beautiful? Observe the various textures that are present: the grainy texture of the dry sand, the foamy texture of the surf, the wooly texture of the clouds, the slick texture of the wetness surrounding you. You have a fantastic visual of the scenery, but can you hear it? Listen to the roar of the waves as they crash into the shore. Don't you just love that sound? Pay attention to the wind as it whispers through the trees; it is whispering a message to you from your heart, where exists your power to love. Maybe you can hear the seagulls up above, calling to each other as if to say, "Life is magnificent and this view is breathtaking." If you concentrate you will be able to feel the panorama of the landscape, as you continue to amble along the shoreline. Notice how the warm, dry, soft sand squishes between your toes when you press your foot into its fine granules. As you step with the other foot you notice a cool, wet, firm foundation until your foot sinks a little into the moist sand. Warm on one foot, cool on the other, you think to yourself. While wandering further down the line, you detect a cool, gentle breeze coming off the water, caressing your cheek. At the same time you realize a warm feeling as the sun strokes your other cheek. Cool on one cheek, warm on the other, you think to yourself. Your sensation of touch is operating perfectly, and you feel the entire vista deep inside your essence. Check out some of your other sensations. Can you smell the salt in the air? Can you taste the sweet, clean air in your mouth and lungs? Take another clean, cleansing breath of that fresh, exhilarating air and exhale the stale negativity. Once again, breathe in the positivity and exhale the negativity. You have wandered far away from civilization and external pressures, into your private, secret getaway.

Just over the rise there lies a cove, right up ahead. It is surrounded by palm trees and hidden within it, a lagoon. Approaching nearer to the handsome display nature has revealed, you realize that this lagoon appears untouched by human hands and feet. It is your personal escape; nobody else can enter without your permission because it belongs to you. You erect a stake in the sand upon which flies your banner, your colors, as you claim this beach as yours; like dropping an anchor you have etched this location into your memory. As you stand there, upright like the trees around you, gaze at the horizon, where the sun is ever rising into the heavens. Notice how it sheds its golden rays over the water, producing a bridge of light proceeding from the horizon right up to your feet where you are standing. You see your direction ahead, but the purpose lies beyond the horizon. If you keep on that path of light, you will fulfill your purpose, and it will lead you all the way to the glory land. Here is your point of departure into the vastness of your unconscious mind. Take a few steps out into the water. Do not be afraid, because if you begin to sink, the Lord will lift you up. If it gets too uncomfortable, just turn around and you'll be right back where you dropped anchor. Allow yourself to explore the unknown for a moment. Who knows what you will find? Maybe you will see a fish leaping from the water, a piece of driftwood floating by, a seabird passing overhead, a message in a bottle. Have a conversation with the wildlife; explore the lagoon or the water; or stroll along the bridge of light. Enjoy it one more moment before returning from your excursion, and whatever you discover, bring it forward with you. You're doing great. Wherever you are at this moment, drop another anchor; each location represents a steppingstone down into your subconscious mind. Every time you return you can follow the same staircase lower, deeper, and farther, as you approach ever nearer to your soul. And each time you return, drop another anchor and you will add another step to the staircase.

Return now to the shore and gaze again across the bridge of light, remembering everything. It is time to begin the journey back. Heading up the beach you are slowly returning to the here and now. Suddenly, you discover you are about to step on a seashell. Instead, you step aside, reach down, and pick it up. It is a good specimen you surmise, as you place it next to your ear. Instead of hearing the ocean, you receive a message that only you can hear. Carry it with you all the way back home. Log this experience in the archives of your memory. Remember how you eased the tension by relaxing yourself, and how when things were too fast you slowed down, and when things were too hot you cooled off. Remember how you found a private, peaceful place, where you felt safe, tranquil, happy, and in control. When you go there, the negative cannot get in because it is a place of power and of peace. At that special spot you laid a claim, and you can return to your private lagoon anytime you desire. In an instant, you can be there where you dropped anchor the first time. Escape the turmoil and chaos of the external world, into the perfect, quiet, secure, and joyous world within. Discover and remember the wisdom you brought with you when you return.

Practice these skills often. Each time you return to your favorite place, explore further and continue to discover yourself and your higher power. And now, as you gradually return to a state of alertness, you will begin to notice your surroundings again. Little by little, you are becoming more awake, focusing again on the reality taking place outside of your body. You slowly open your eyes, and readjust your body position, realizing how refreshed you feel. In addition, you realize you have renewed faith, and hope, and strength, and direction. Perhaps you feel a sense of confidence in yourself, satisfied with what you have accomplished. Isn't it great to be in control and connected to the power of everlasting love? How do you feel?

Overview of Self-Control

Self-Esteem: To value oneself; which has to come from within, as it is how you see yourself.

Coping: Face setbacks, responsibilities, or challenges in a way that increases the likelihood of remaining positive in your outlook and achieving positive results; coping is a controlled way of dealing with reality. Coping strategies include: exercise/fitness, meditation/prayer, arts/crafts, journaling, music, self-expression, talking to someone, laughter.

Composure: Keep a sense of calmness and serenity during challenges or when completing an arduous task or duty; composure is not letting things get to you. Aspects of composure include: patience, calmness, grace, serenity, sincerity, strength.

"Not being able to govern events, I govern myself." – Michel de Montaigne

Confidence: Being able to believe and trust in yourself or others; faith in one's ability; self-reliance, self-assurance; being reasonably sure. Aspects of confidence include: assurance, assertiveness, trust, courage, thoughtfulness, awareness, understanding, motivation.

"Self-control is the chief element in self-respect, and self-respect is the chief element in courage." – Thucydides

"Many of life's failures are people who did not realize how close they were to success when they gave up." – Thomas Edison

Cooperation: Engage with others to achieve a common goal; having a shared purpose; providing assistance to others when asked; working together. Aspects of cooperation include: acceptance, assistance, communication, teamwork, rehearsal, participation, reliability, accountability.

"Everything that irritates us about others can lead us to an understanding of ourselves." – Carl Jung

"Teamwork is the ability to work together toward a common vision, the ability to direct individual accomplishments toward organizational objectives. It is the fuel that allows common people to achieve uncommon results." – Andrew Carnegie

Restraint: Withhold words or actions in accordance with your better judgment; reserve the right to wait before speaking or acting; restraint is thoughtful hesitation. Aspects of restraint include: reframing, reprogramming, practice, discipline, reflection, rethinking.

"Blessed is the man who, having nothing to say, abstains from giving wordy evidence of the fact." – George Eliot

"Lettin' the cat out of the bag is a whole lot easier than puttin' it back in." – Will Rogers

Character: Traits and attributes that define a person, especially in terms of the standards of behavior he or she exhibits; character encompasses one's personal ethics. Aspects of character include: respect, humility, integrity, dignity, empathy, honesty, morality.

"To handle yourself, use your head; to handle others, use your heart." – Eleanor Roosevelt

Leadership: The ability to provide direction and guidance in a way that generates respect and cooperation; the qualities necessary to lead. Aspects of leadership include: understanding, credit/praise, organization, analysis, coordination, networking, delegating, managing, and encouraging.

"He who controls others may be powerful, but he who has mastered himself is mightier still. He who conquers others is strong; he who conquers himself is mighty." – Lao Tzu

- PRO 25:28 ~ A man without self-control is like a city broken into and left without walls.

112

SELF CONTROL

- **Coping**
- **Composure**
- **Confidence**
- **Cooperation**
- **Restraint**
- **Leadership**
- **Character**

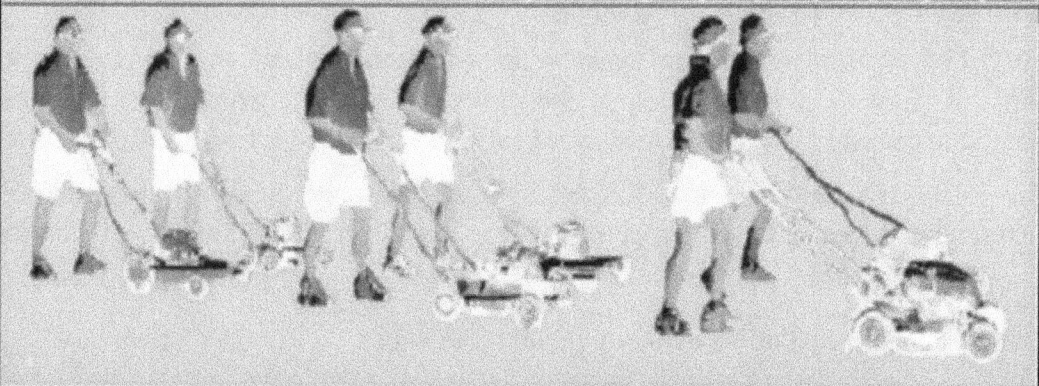

MOTIVATION

OBJECTIVE	Learn to be achievement oriented and strive to maximize your full potential. Discover that anything of value will motivate one to act, especially if it meets their needs in life.
INTERVENTION	Discuss the relationships among self-esteem, getting needs met, and motivation. Identify needs that remain unmet and possible ways of addressing them. Recognize what it means to be self-actualized.
PLAN	Overcome the stumbling blocks that prevent forward progress. Strive to become all you can be and you will realize your ideal self.

"You cannot help men permanently by doing for them what they could and should do for themselves." – Abraham Lincoln

"The rung of a ladder was never meant to rest upon, but only to hold a man's foot long enough to enable him to put the other somewhat higher." – Thomas Huxley

You may have noticed one of the prevailing themes in this text: convincing your clients that they are here for a reason and that a greater purpose awaits them, if only they will believe. Each hurdle, each challenge, each accomplishment is a steppingstone that propels us in the direction God has laid out. If we stay on this path we will discover God's purpose. I often ask my clients, "Don't you want to discover your purpose?" Then keep it going. The will comes from the power of hope, and the esteemed value of becoming, which provide the incentive to keep trying, to move forward, and to apprehend the abundant life God has promised. The best motivator is to identify something of value worth pursuing.

- PSA 36:9 ~ For with you is the fountain of life; in your light do we see light.

- PSA 48:14 ~ This is God, our God forever and ever. He will guide us forever.

- JOH 10:10 ~ Jesus said, "The thief comes only to steal and kill and destroy. I came that they may have life and have it abundantly."

- PHP 3:13-14 ~ Brothers, I do not consider that I have made it (the prize) my own. But one thing I do: forgetting what lies behind and straining forward to what lies ahead, I press on toward the goal for the prize of the upward call of God in Christ Jesus.

- JAM 1:12 ~ Blessed is the man who remains steadfast under trial, for when he has stood the test he will receive the crown of life, which God has promised to those who love him.

"How much pain has cost us the evils which never happened." – Thomas Jefferson

"How soon not now becomes never." – Martin Luther

Theoretical Framework

Let us begin the discussion of motivation by establishing a foundation for self-esteem. The field of psychology had a major growth spurt with the psychoanalytic movement. Freud introduced the phenomenon of self-esteem when defining the ego. His structure of the personality, while probably not intentionally, tracks with the holistic health paradigm. The id, which is governed by the pleasure principle, is akin to the flesh, or physical domain. The ego, which sticks to a mental principle called reality, buffers the lusts of the flesh against the prohibitions established by society. The superego presides over the morality of the individual; it resembles the spiritual side, which follows the perfection principle.

Although we internalize the morality of our parents and our culture, discernment is an inherent ability endowed by God. At some point in time we become accountable for our actions, having fully adopted a proper ethical stance. Theoretically speaking, when we sin, the ego has slipped up and allowed full expression by the id. So the superego steps in and punishes the ego with guilt. Those people who always blame themselves, or drown in guilt and shame, have an overbearing superego. Thus, their ego has been battered into oblivion, and their self-esteem is in the dirt. Those with no sense of remorse or guilt have allowed the conscience or superego to take a backseat. The ego becomes so controlling they think only of their desires and nobody else. Clearly, there is a healthy balance whereby the ego is not overly inflated or deflated. Such a balance would produce a healthy self-image.

- GEN 1:26 ~ Then God said, "Let us make man in our image, after our likeness. And let them have dominion over the fish of the sea and over the birds of the heavens and over the livestock and over all the earth and over every creeping thing that creeps on the earth."

Ego strengthening is a treatment goal designed to raise one's self-esteem. When the ego is hurt, the esteem goes down. Freud proposed defense mechanisms as ways of protecting the ego from disturbing or defeating thoughts, such as the guilt that comes with taking responsibility for being wrong, sinful, or a fool. Memories can be triggered that bring back these unpleasant feelings; in fact, it is the emotional baggage that keeps those memories afloat. So we try to repress the memory because we don't want to think about it; for every time we do it is every bit as troublesome as before, and this brings us down all over again. Some of the more common ego defenses are listed below.

- ➢ Repression: hiding the event or content of the memory from conscious awareness (all ego defense mechanisms are a form of repression) – The traumatized soldier tries to block the memory of a fallen comrade, believing he could have prevented it somehow.

- ➢ Rationalization: self-deceptive approach to explaining something away – An alcoholic in recovery uses a friend's wedding (or his funeral) as an excuse to fall off the wagon.

- ➢ Denial: choosing not to see the obvious truth – The weekend warrior binges on drugs believing he doesn't have a problem because it is perceived as under control.

- ➢ Regression: falling back to an earlier stage of development – The child is jealous of the new arrival in the family and poops his pants to get mom's attention.

> Conversion: a psychological disturbance is converted into physical symptoms – The battered divorcee's emotional pain is converted into hysterical paralysis.

> Projection: attributing one's traits to another – The aggressive and abusive husband tells his wife she has anger management problems.

Unfortunately, the more you try to hide the unpleasant memory the more neurotic you become; and it still seems to find its way back into conscious awareness despite efforts to keep it away. We beat ourselves upside the head with the baggage each time it rears its ugly head, and this drives our self-esteem into the ground. Obviously, it is not healthy to carry the baggage, but only the wisdom of the experience. For more on this topic, the reader is referred to the chapter on Emotional Baggage.

Psychoanalytic theorists paved the way for their successors to explore novel concepts: ego, self-esteem, neurotic needs, and unconscious motivation. One contemporary was Karen Horney, who was developing her interpersonal approach. She surmised that motivation is not exclusively unconscious and that external factors affect it as much as internal factors. She focused on the idea of the self, which is affected by relationships, the desire to get needs met, and how others contribute to that goal; and the self-esteem goes down when things are not going well. Her list of neurotic needs included the following: affection, approval, borders, power, recognition, self-esteem, achievement, independence, and superiority/perfection.

Horney dissected the self into three components. The ideal self is the perfect me (perfection principle). It is the person I want to be; the me who has completely maximized my potential. The real self is what I tell myself I am, the personal me, the perceived me who often falls short of who I want to be (reality principle). The greater the distance between the real and the ideal, the lower is the self-esteem. Then we have the actual me, the interpersonal me, the way others perceive me (or at least the way I view their perception of me). Again, the more distance between the actual and the ideal, the poorer is my self-image. So, if I am internalizing negative messages from others, or sending them to myself, it is driving my self-esteem down because it is damaging to my ego.

But those negative messages are simply untrue. I am not a good-for-nothing, stupid, ignorant moron that will never amount to anything. How do I know that? Because God is telling me I am important, precious, and so valuable that he would die for me. He tells me I can do anything if I stay connected to him (PHP 4:13). So who are you going to believe?

• JOH 15:1-6 ~ Jesus said, "I am the true vine, and my Father is the vinedresser. Every branch in me that does not bear fruit he takes away, and every branch that does bear fruit he prunes, that it may bear more fruit. Already you are clean because of the word that I have spoken to you. Abide in me, and I in you. As the branch cannot bear fruit by itself, unless it abides in the vine, neither can you, unless you abide in me. I am the vine; you are the branches. Whoever abides in me and I in him, he it is that bears much fruit, for apart from me you can do nothing. If anyone does not abide in me he is thrown away like a branch and withers; and the branches are gathered, thrown into the fire, and burned."

Maslow picked up on these ideas which culminated into his famous pyramid. His model was based on the previously cited work, tapping into the insight of needs, becoming, motivation, and self-esteem. In theory, needs have priorities, and one can move up the ladder by getting basic needs met, then moving on to the next level and up and up. Of course, one can be on more than one level at a time, or may move up and down, and up again; it doesn't have to be unidirectional. And getting all subordinate needs met is unnecessary for attaining the more lofty ones. Meeting needs lower in the hierarchy enables upward movement but is not a requirement for it.

Again, I don't know if it was Maslow's intention, but his hierarchy seems to track with the holistic health paradigm. The basic needs, or lower level needs, are largely physical and emotional. The next plateau is mental, such as getting your learning, educational, and cognitive needs met. Then there is the spiritual domain, and another set of needs emerges that is connected to nature, the brotherhood of man, and God. That's where we start becoming the ideal or perfect me (i.e., becoming more like Christ). In the diagram below I have left the top of the pyramid empty because I believe we can transcend self-actualization. That is, we never actualize or realize our full potential until we are like Christ: pure, unblemished, immortal. And that takes place when Christ returns for us.

- JOH 17:22-24 ~ Jesus prayed to God, "The glory that you have given me I have given to them, that they may be one even as we are one, I in them and you in me, that they may become perfectly one, so that the world may know that you sent me and loved them even as you loved me. Father, I desire that they also, whom you have given me, may be with me where I am, to see my glory that you have given me because you loved me before the foundation of the world."

- ROM 8:16-18 ~ The Spirit himself bears witness with our spirit that we are children of God, and if children, then heirs – heirs of God and fellow heirs with Christ, provided we suffer with him in order that we may also be glorified with him. For I consider that the sufferings of this present time are not worth comparing with the glory that is to be revealed to us.

- PHP 3:20-21 ~ But our citizenship is in heaven, and from it we await a Savior, the Lord Jesus Christ, who will transform our lowly body to be like his glorious body, by the power that enables him even to subject all things to himself.

- COL 3:4 ~ When Christ who is your life appears, then you will appear with him in glory.

- 1 PE 1:2-4 ~ According to the foreknowledge of God the Father, in the sanctification of the Spirit, for obedience to Jesus Christ and for sprinkling with his blood: May grace and peace be multiplied to you. Blessed be the God and Father of our Lord Jesus Christ! According to his great mercy, he has caused us to be born again to a living hope through the resurrection of Jesus Christ from the dead, to an inheritance that is imperishable, undefiled, and unfading, kept in heaven for you.

- 1 JO 3:1-2 ~ See what kind of love the Father has given to us, that we should be called children of God; and so we are. The reason why the world does not know us is that it did not know him. Beloved, we are God's children now, and what we will be has not yet appeared; but we know that when he appears we shall be like him, because we shall see him as he is.

Hierarchy of Needs

Beginning at the ground floor, the basic biological needs come first. To be physically healthy we need to get enough to eat and drink, and plenty of sleep; one could argue we also need to maintain the species via procreation. No matter how many needs we have, when the basic needs are not satisfied, it is very difficult to think about the other ones. Consider the boy who is picked up by the police for shoplifting a soda, candy bar, and bag of chips. The cops assume that he is just another juvenile delinquent. But soon they discover that he has never met his father and his mother has spent the welfare check on drugs. There is nothing in the house to eat, and he told his mother he was famished; so his mother suggested he go to the store and pilfer some food. His motivation simply was driven by hunger. This was an actual case I had early in my career. You can see how easy one can misinterpret another's motivation, like the police did in that situation.

Working our way up the hierarchy to the next floor, we find safety and security. Any survivalist will tell you that once you have located food and water sources, you need to find or build a shelter for protection from the elements and the critters. In our next scenario, the police grab some guy who has broken into an abandoned building. They assume that this is another street urchin, a derelict who is looking for something to steal. They find out that the poor man lost his job due to the faltering economy. Months went by until the bank threatened to repossess his house and car. His wife grabbed the kids and left him before he knew they were even gone. He lost everything, became homeless, and had been sleeping in a culvert in the rain and cold. He was looking for shelter and a warm place to sleep for the night. He had no intention of robbing the place; there wasn't anything there of value. People will do whatever it takes to survive, it's natural.

Most of us have never experienced what it's like not to have these lower level needs met. But we can well imagine what it would do to our self-esteem if we did have to face it someday. I remember times when I had to live out of my car, or eat beans and franks for a week as I struggled to support myself through college. And that was bad enough. However, love and belonging, which are next in the hierarchy, are desires that all human beings possess; when unmet, it is very hard to feel good about oneself. I'm sure everyone has experienced that emptiness before.

Loneliness is awful; and nobody wants to be alone their entire life. And having nobody to love or to love you is equally despairing. But with God you are never alone are you? And he loves you unconditionally. I have talked to numerous young men that were once involved in gang activity. Many acknowledged that the primary reason they were in the gang in the first place was to get these needs met. Like the young lad in the first scenario, most didn't have a father in their life, and often the mom had no time for them. So they sought comfort and camaraderie from others that were in the same boat. Some of them were not bad kids, they just needed to belong; and it led them down the wrong path.

After going through a painful divorce, I didn't think I wanted to try marriage again. But God had another plan, and I found someone that meets my needs. I realized that God knew a lot better what I needed than I did. But again, that is precisely what he promises isn't it? I didn't want to be alone; I was just afraid of making a commitment and having it fall apart again. God provided to me a soul mate when I wasn't even looking for one; he provides everything we need if we focus on his righteousness. That doesn't mean you're always going to get what you want, however. But when he gives you what you need you'll discover that you wanted it all along.

Once our physical needs are satisfied it is easier to concentrate on the mental ones. And fundamental to our mental health is a positive self-image. We want to feel like we are important, interesting, capable, and competent. Often, we need recognition and reassurance from others to feel that way. I remember when I was promoted to an executive position at a psychiatric hospital. The CEO asked me if I could pull a department together that was struggling and in need of leadership; the job came with a promotion and a raise. But that is not the only reason I accepted the position; I welcomed the challenge as well. As promised, I learned the operation in a month, and took another month to reorganize the operation. By the third month the department had come together, we were working like a team, morale was better, and department goals were being met or exceeded. After a few months, that CEO was reassigned to another city. His replacement had a lot of changes in mind, including having identified someone else to fill my slot. I started getting a lot of criticism and very little recognition, even though I was attaining the performance goals that had been established. The position was no longer meeting my needs, and I wasn't interested in an offer to direct another department, so I stepped down and resumed my previous position as program manager and lead therapist. Some people thought I was forced out, others thought I couldn't cut it, or that I had screwed up and was being demoted. But the fact of the matter, I simply wasn't content. Being happy is definitely better for your self-esteem than being frustrated. I needed to be recognized and appreciated, and the patients provided that while the corporate leadership did not. Besides, I kept the same pay grade so it was an all-around win for me.

The cognitive needs represent our aspirations for achievement, competency, and approval. In order to succeed, grow, and improve, skill, knowledge, and education are required. That is, if you want to keep becoming, and accomplish greater things, then more study, experience, and training will help you get there. You can turn your weaknesses into strengths, expand your horizons, multiply your options, and open new doors. You also learn more about yourself: your interests, abilities, strengths, and desires. That for me was another reward in the above example.

When I finished my obligation with the Army, I didn't know what I was going to do. I didn't think I was very smart (I barely passed the SAT exam and attained average marks in grade school). I didn't really value education. Oh, I'd heard the arguments that college would provide more opportunities, but I wasn't looking that far ahead. But the government offered the G.I. Bill, without which I never could have afforded college as my parents didn't have the money. So I gave it the old college try. Since I didn't think I had much going for me I majored in Art (I had sold paintings so I figured I had some talent in that field). I continued to make average grades or worse. During the third year into my degree plan I had to take a humanities course as an elective. My friend and I found one that fit both our schedules; that is the only reason I took Abnormal Psychology. It was hard, but I liked it. At that point I began to see the value of education: not that it opened doors of opportunity, but it opened windows in my mind. I had learned something about myself that I never knew: I had an interest in Psychology. Who would've thought that, seeing how I used to hate science (the only class I ever flunked in grade school)? After I got my bachelor degree I still didn't know what I was going to do with an art degree, so I decided to become a teacher. I found out that teachers made more money with an advanced degree so I got my masters in Educational Psychology, majoring in Guidance and Counseling. Like most graduate students, I was scared of Statistics. Everyone said it was the make-or-break course. I didn't have any idea what it was about. Well, I learned another thing about myself that I didn't think possible: I had aptitude for statistics. Now if God had given me a list of natural abilities to choose from I would have bypassed that one; but it's one he gave me. I eventually would become a Research Psychologist, and conduct tests and evaluations for the government; and then I would teach statistics to college students, and coauthor a textbook in statistics. Look how that one event my junior year in college changed my life. Needless to say, I came to value learning in a big way; I developed a thirst for it. That's why I invite new challenges. I encourage all my counselees to seek more learning and discover the value of opening windows as well as doors.

The important lesson here is that it wasn't because I lacked intelligence, talent, or potential; although that was the message I was telling myself. What I lacked was motivation. I didn't have any until I discovered something interesting enough, and valuable enough; then I was willing to do the work. Learning became an incentive, particularly as it led to a greater understanding of me. A sure way to raise one's self-concept is to accomplish something amazing. If you want to motivate clients to do so, it has to be something they value. If they don't recognize its future value or importance, there is no inducement to exert additional effort or persevere when the chips are down. Anybody can see that there are thousands of possibilities worth exploring. The payoff is when you make the discovery that you have interests, abilities, and potential that hadn't before been revealed, much less realized.

Information is the great equalizer. It turns the unknown into known. It creates more comprehension, knowledge, and wisdom. You can be good at anything if you put your mind to it. You may already be good at it. I certainly never dreamed I could be good at something like statistics, especially given the fact that I'd never even heard of it when I was a college freshman. And while I didn't have a natural talent in psychology, I found it appealing so I worked very hard to master it. I was the first in my family line to receive a doctorate degree, and in psychology of all things. I am living proof that anybody can do this; you only have to believe. And faith opens up the highest echelon in the pyramid: spiritual needs.

- 1 TI 6:20-21 ~ O Timothy, guard the deposit entrusted to you. Avoid the irreverent babble and contradictions of what is falsely called "knowledge," for by professing it some have swerved from the faith.

Once we become successful we begin to enjoy the more subtle things in life. We can find beauty in anything: a landscape, a sunset, a tree, even a well designed chair. What's more, we draw the beauty out of people by looking at their gifts and not their faults. Stop to smell the roses, they say. Aestheticism is the pursuit of beauty, the love of nature, the appreciation of all things, and a way of connecting to one another and to God. It creates a sort of mystical relationship to all of God's creation. Spirituality is a way of reaching the higher powers we possess, and the highest power of the Almighty. We learn respect for his will and his commandments. Justice, fairness, law and order are among the loftier needs. They motivate us to do the right thing, care about others, avoid temptation, and quit our evil ways.

At the top of Maslow's hierarchy is self-actualization. Theoretically, with subordinate needs met, we can eventually feel complete. Our full capacity becomes realized; the ideal me is actually me. We are maximizing our potential. So is that it? Absolutely not, because the ability to become, to learn, and to excel is unlimited and unending. There are more possibilities yet ahead, greater discoveries to be made, and another purpose to be fulfilled. Horney theorized that we can achieve a positive self-concept by bringing the ideal, real, and actual self into congruence. If who we want to be is who we believe we are, and who others believe we are, then we have attained the perfect self. Note, that the ideal person exists the moment he or she starts believing, which initiates the process of becoming.

- JAM 1:2-4 ~ Count it all joy, my brothers, when you meet trials of various kinds, for you know that the testing of your faith produces steadfastness. And let steadfastness have its full effect, that you may be perfect and complete, lacking in nothing.

The story of Joshua comes to mind as a model of motivation (see NUM 13, 14, 26; DEU 31). Moses sent Joshua, Caleb, and ten others to perform reconnaissance on the land of Canaan. Only Joshua and Caleb returned confident that they could possess the land. The other ten spies spoke negatively about their chances, claiming that the inhabitants were too strong and virtually invincible, neglecting the obvious that God had directed the Israelites to take the land because he intended for them to have it. The mob rallied behind the pessimistic spies believing their false report, much to the objection of Joshua and Caleb. For mistrusting God, every adult aged 20 and above would die in the wilderness and never see the promised land, save Joshua and Caleb. Moses would turn his command over to Joshua who would lead the Israelites across the Jordan River, and defeat one army after another with God fighting by their side. They sacked Jericho without resistance or casualties. The confidence and trust Joshua and Caleb had for God catapulted them to become leaders and elder statesmen for the nation of Israel. Certain that God would make good on his promises, they became everything God meant for them to be, achieved great victories, and obtained their inheritance.

"It is a most mortifying reflection for a man to consider what he has done, compared to what he might have done." – Samuel Johnson

God Meets Our Needs

Understand this: once you believe in yourself and in God's purpose for your life, the becoming has begun. You are a wonderful person because you are his. Everything has become new. You don't have to wait until you finish your doctorate, or meet your soul mate, or land that dream job. You will fulfill one purpose after another; and each one will be part of your preparation for the next. So let God be your confidence, your direction, and your self-concept. You are his and he lives in you, and he has prepared a place for you, and you are already on your way. Not just on your way to heaven, but on your way to becoming like Christ: perfect in righteousness. You will achieve great things, and become all you were meant to be, and attain true freedom. And it begins now.

- COL 1:19-22 ~ For in him all the fullness of God was pleased to dwell, and through him to reconcile to himself all things, whether on earth or in heaven, making peace by the blood of his cross. And you, who once were alienated and hostile in mind, doing evil deeds, he has now reconciled in his body of flesh by his death, in order to present you holy and blameless and above reproach before him.

- 1 TH 5:23 ~ Now may the God of peace himself sanctify you completely, and may your whole spirit and soul and body be kept blameless at the coming of our Lord Jesus Christ.

Any point in the hierarchy can be a hurdle, or a roadblock that inhibits forward progress. Each individual needs to examine his or her own life and situation, and determine what is blocking the way. As I said, there may be many obstacles. And the movement isn't always up. But if you take a few steps forward for every step backward you are achieving positive results. Start acting like your ideal self and see the positive effect on your self-esteem. This will motivate you to persevere, to achieve, to realize your dreams, and more. The bottom line is this: God will meet all your needs. He should be your motivation.

God will meet your basic biological needs (PSA 23:1-6).

- MAT 6:31-34 ~ Jesus said, "Therefore do not be anxious, saying, 'What shall we eat?' or 'What shall we drink?' or 'What shall we wear?' For the Gentiles seek after all these things, and your heavenly Father knows that you need them all. But seek first the kingdom of God and his righteousness, and all these things will be added to you. Therefore do not be anxious about tomorrow, for tomorrow will be anxious for itself. Sufficient for the day is its own trouble."

- PSA 145:14-16 ~ The LORD upholds all who are falling and raises up all who are bowed down. The eyes of all look to you, and you give them their food in due season. You open your hand; you satisfy the desire of every living thing.

God will provide all your safety and security needs.

- LEV 25:18-19 ~ God decrees: Therefore you shall do my statutes and keep my rules and perform them, and then you will dwell in the land securely. The land will yield its fruit, and you will eat your fill and dwell in it securely.

- JOB 11:18 ~ And you will feel secure, because there is hope; you will look around and take your rest in security.

- PSA 91:11-12 ~ For he will command his angels concerning you to guard you in all your ways. On their hands they will bear you up, lest you strike your foot against a stone.

- PSA 46:1 ~ God is our refuge and strength, a very present help in trouble.

- PRO 29:25 ~ The fear of man lays a snare, but whoever trusts in the LORD is safe.

God is the primary source for meeting your love and belonging needs. God's love preserves us and sustains us. We are his children and we belong to him. And he will never leave us or forsake us. Jesus is our friend and companion; he is always with us in spirit. God will fulfill our needs for love and companionship. Such love is never ending. And radiating that love will attract the right people into our lives.

- JOS 1:9 ~ God said, "Have I not commanded you? Be strong and courageous. Do not be frightened, and do not be dismayed, for the LORD your God is with you wherever you go."

- PSA 145:20 ~ The LORD preserves all who love him, but all the wicked he will destroy.

- JOH 15:14-15 ~ Jesus said, "You are my friends if you do what I command you. No longer do I call you servants, for the servant does not know what his master is doing; but I have called you friends, for all that I have heard from my Father I have made known to you."

- MAT 28:18-20 ~ And Jesus came and said to them, "All authority in heaven and on earth has been given to me. Go therefore and make disciples of all nations, baptizing them in the name of the Father and of the Son and of the Holy Spirit, teaching them to observe all that I have commanded you. And behold, I am with you always, to the end of the age."

- ROM 8:35-39 ~ Who shall separate us from the love of Christ? Shall tribulation, or distress, or persecution, or famine, or nakedness, or danger, or sword? As it is written, "For your sake we are being killed all the day long; we are regarded as sheep to be slaughtered." No, in all these things we are more than conquerors through him who loved us. For I am sure that neither death nor life, nor angels nor rulers, nor things present nor things to come, nor powers, nor height nor depth, nor anything else in all creation, will be able to separate us from the love of God in Christ Jesus our Lord.

- 1 CO 6:19-20 ~ Do you not know that your body is a temple of the Holy Spirit within you, whom you have from God? You are not your own, for you were bought with a price. So glorify God in your body.

If it is recognition and approval that you need, put your trust in God. If we acknowledge Christ in our lives, he will acknowledge us before God and the angels. If you live in Christ, he will lift you up and your self-esteem; he will be your confidence. He pulls all Christians together in unity of spirit. You can find a constant source of strength and edification in Christ and his church.

- 1 SA 2:30 ~ Therefore the LORD, the God of Israel, declares: "I promised that your house and the house of your father should go in and out before me forever," but now the LORD declares: "Far be it from me, for those who honor me I will honor, and those who despise me shall be lightly esteemed."

- JOB 4:6 ~ Is not your fear of God your confidence, and the integrity of your ways your hope?

- LUK 12:8-9 ~ Jesus said, "And I tell you, everyone who acknowledges me before men, the Son of Man also will acknowledge before the angels of God, but the one who denies me before men will be denied before the angels of God."

- 2 CO 13:11 ~ Finally, brothers, rejoice. Aim for restoration, comfort one another, agree with one another, live in peace; and the God of love and peace will be with you.

- PHP 2:2 ~ Complete my joy by being of the same mind, having the same love, being in full accord and of one mind.

- 1 TH 5:11 ~ Encourage one another and build one another up, just as you are doing.

- HEB 3:14 ~ For we have come to share in Christ, if indeed we hold our original confidence firm to the end.

No matter how much education you have, you will always be able to increase your learning. If you desire wisdom, if you desire knowledge and understanding, if you want to be mentally engaged, turn to God's Word. He is the source of all knowledge and truth. Seek his wisdom and he will expand your understanding in ways you cannot yet comprehend.

- PRO 4:7-9 ~ The beginning of wisdom is this: Get wisdom, and whatever you get, get insight. Prize her highly, and she will exalt you; she will honor you if you embrace her. She will place on your head a graceful garland; she will bestow on you a beautiful crown.

- PRO 13:11 ~ Wealth gained hastily will dwindle, but whoever gathers little by little will increase it.

- 1 CO 1:19-25; 1 CO 2:4-5; 1 CO 3:19 ~ It is written: I will destroy the wisdom of the wise, and I will bring to nothing the understanding of the prudent. Where is the wise person? Where is the scholar? Where is the philosopher of this world? Hasn't God made foolish the wisdom of this world? The world through its wisdom did not know God, but through simple preaching, God enabled people who would believe to be saved. The Jews required signs and miracles and the Greeks searched for wisdom and truth. We preach about the crucified Christ, which to the Jews is an obstacle and to the Gentiles is foolishness. But to those whom God has called, both Jews and non-Jews, Christ is the power of God and the wisdom of God. For the foolishness of God is wiser than the wisdom of mankind, and the weaknesses of God are stronger than the might of men. My message and my preaching were not with wise and persuasive words but with the power of the Spirit, so that your faith would be based, not on the wisdom of the world, but in the power of God. For the wisdom of this world is foolishness to God. As it is written, He catches the wise in their own craftiness.

- 1 CO 15:58 ~ Therefore, my beloved brothers, be steadfast, immovable, always abounding in the work of the Lord, knowing that in the Lord your labor is not in vain.

- 2 TI 3:14-16 ~ But as for you, continue in what you have learned and have firmly believed, knowing from whom you learned it and how from childhood you have been acquainted with the sacred writings, which are able to make you wise for salvation through faith in Christ Jesus.

"God gives us dreams a size too big so that we can grow into them." – Author Unknown

To achieve the ideal self, the perfect me, totally self-actualized, one must strive to become like Christ. Little by little, he purifies your spirit through the work of sanctification. And when he returns to take his people home to heaven, you will be among them: faultless and unblemished like him. You will be pure and without sin, to live forever in his kingdom, with a glorified body that will never die. Imagine Christ when you ponder what you can become: his equal with respect to the inheritance and righteousness you will receive as a permanent member of God's household. That is ideal in the hierarchy of God.

- JOH 1:12 ~ But to all who did receive him, who believed in his name, he gave the right to become children of God.

- ROM 8:28-31 ~ We know that for those who love God all things work together for good, for those who are called according to his purpose. For those whom he foreknew he also predestined to be conformed to the image of his Son, in order that he might be the firstborn among many brothers. And those whom he predestined he also called, and those whom he called he also justified, and those whom he justified he also glorified. What then shall we say to these things? If God is for us, who can be against us?

- EPH 4:22-24 ~ Put off your old self, which belongs to your former manner of life and is corrupt through deceitful desires, and to be renewed in the spirit of your minds, and to put on the new self, created after the likeness of God in true righteousness and holiness.

- 2 TH 2:13 ~ But we ought always to give thanks to God for you, brothers beloved by the Lord, because God chose you as the firstfruits to be saved, through sanctification by the Spirit and belief in the truth.

- HEB 12:22-23 ~ But you have come to Mount Zion and to the city of the living God, the heavenly Jerusalem, and to innumerable angels in festal gathering, and to the assembly of the firstborn who are enrolled in heaven, and to God, the judge of all, and to the spirits of the righteous made perfect.

- 2 PE 1:3-4 ~ His divine power has granted to us all things that pertain to life and godliness, through the knowledge of him who called us to his own glory and excellence, by which he has granted to us his precious and very great promises, so that through them you may become partakers of the divine nature, having escaped from the corruption that is in the world because of sinful desire.

"Desire is the key to motivation, but it's determination and commitment to an unrelenting pursuit of your goal – a commitment to excellence – that will enable you to attain the success you seek." – Mario Andretti

Conclusions

"Whether you think you can or whether you think you can't, you're right." – Henry Ford

"Never build your emotional life on the weaknesses of others." – George Santayana

Becoming the ideal you starts right now. Listen to what God is telling you. He has a reason for your life; if that were not true you wouldn't be here. Do not listen to the negative messages others are telling you or that you are telling yourself. They simply are not true. You can do this, and more. There will be trials and setbacks, but they will pass, so don't get hung up on them. Everybody has equal potential for greatness, only not in the same things. You could be President of the United States, the CEO of a big corporation, a psychologist, accountant, architect, physician, attorney, or whatever is your dream. If you can imagine it, God can make it happen. Nothing is impossible with God; and nothing is possible without him. There is no mountain too great that you cannot scale, no valley too wide that you cannot traverse, no challenge so ominous that you cannot handle.

Look at the astrophysicist Stephen Hawking. Despite a debilitating disease (ALS), that struck him in the prime of his youth and turned him into a quadriplegic, he was not deterred. He persisted, earned a doctorate degree, and became one of the most renowned theoretical physicists in the world. He has taught graduate students, and he has authored numerous books on subjects ranging from the enormity of the cosmos to the supremely diminutive particles of quantum mechanics. He does all this with the aid of science and technology, and the love of his wife and kids. Surely, there were skeptics that believed he couldn't possibly achieve anything, especially given that he wasn't expected to live into his thirties. He simply chose not to be one of the skeptics. Are you one of the skeptics?

I had a graduate student in my Multicultural Foundations class several years ago. He was 75 years old. Several students ridiculed him with comments like, "What are you doing here?" Or, "You should be sunbathing on a beach somewhere." He worked hard and was an A student. Finally, after some encouragement, he stood before the class and told them flatly that he was a retired veteran, who served three tours in Vietnam, was wounded twice, traumatized and disabled. He was retired, and raised three beautiful children who had grown up to be honorable and God-fearing citizens. He never lost his love for this country; he felt a debt to the Army and his country, and a desire to give something back. It was his intention to finish his Masters in Counseling, obtain his license to practice, and work with disabled, wounded, and traumatized service members and veterans. And who better? He had experience and knowledge that cannot be taught. He had a purpose and a goal and was not going to let his age or health get in the way. Most of all, he had motivation to continue becoming. His gentle but persuasive speech shut the mouths of those who poked fun at him. They were embarrassed to

126

discover that his quest was loftier than theirs. Who was more qualified than he, having experience the others didn't have? I addressed the class with the following scenario. Assume that all of you obtain your master degree and a license to practice. And let's say I am a wounded warrior returning from Afghanistan or Iraq suffering from PTSD. All things being equal, who do you think I would I prefer among you to be my therapist? All eyes pointed in his direction. It was unanimous: Given that he had unique knowledge of battle trauma, having been wounded and disabled by war, he would understand me better than anyone else in the room, because he had experience the others did not.

Everyone is uniquely qualified for his or her calling. Actually, nobody is more qualified than you because your experience is exceptional. So when God calls, I recommend you respond accordingly. He will find a way to use your talents and knowledge in service to him, his kingdom, and his flock – in a way that only you can. I really like the passage in Isaiah where the prophet has a vision of seraphim (read ISA 6:1-8). He contemplated his mediocrity and the privilege of being privy to witnessing angels and the glory of heaven. Suddenly he heard the voice of the Lord calling, "Who shall I send to be my messenger." Isaiah responded to the call, saying "Here I am, send me!" It is time to answer God's call, don't you think?

I am again reminded of the story of Caleb, the faithful spy who was determined to claim the land of Canaan, despite allegations by others that the inhabitants were invincible. Caleb and Joshua would be the only two adults to cross the Jordan River forty years later and occupy that territory. After receiving his portion of the land Caleb proudly declared in his old age (85 years old) that he was still prepared to fight the Lord's battles and be a soldier of the faith, acknowledging that his strength was, and always would be, in the Lord God (read JOS 14:5-15).

Stay on the highway and focus on the horizon. You will be amazed at what you find beyond that horizon. Have you heard? The sky is the limit, figuratively and literally. Don't be in a big hurry; you'll get there soon enough. Take your time and enjoy the ride. Yeah, there may be a few bumps, curves, and detours; these just make the journey more interesting. But stay on the highway; don't exit, take a hiatus, or look for shortcuts. In the meantime, don't worry; God will guide you in that journey and meet all of your needs along the way.

You do not have to make it to the other side of the river before you can feel self-actualized. You have already begun to become. You'd never build a bridge starting from the far side of the river; just keep adding another span each day. When you make it to the other side you may be surprised what you find there: the land of milk and honey perhaps. After you complete that mission, God will have another one for you. Each one readies you for the next. You do not maximize your full potential when you reach your destination, because there will be another. Your mission is complete and your ideal self realized when God calls you into his glorious presence. And even that represents a new beginning.

"Only those who will risk going too far can possibly find out how far one can go." – T.S. Eliot

Activity

Describe your ideal self. What characteristics would you possess if you were everything you wanted to be?

_____

_____

_____

_____

What are some of the negative messages you are receiving from others or from yourself?

_____

_____

_____

How do these negative messages conflict with your concept of the ideal you?

_____

_____

_____

Examine the pyramid of needs and identify which needs are not being met sufficiently in your life.

_____

_____

_____

_____

What could you do to meet those needs or to create an opportunity to meet them?

_____

_____

_____

Rate your current self-esteem using the following scale (circle a number).

very poor self-esteem → 1 2 3 4 5 6 7 8 9 10 ← very good self-esteem

Where would your self-esteem be if you got all of your unmet needs met?

very poor self-esteem → 1 2 3 4 5 6 7 8 9 10 ← very good self-esteem

What steps will you take to make some progress towards getting those needs met?

_____

_____

_____

_____

List some of your strengths.	List some of your weaknesses.
_____	_____
_____	_____
_____	_____
_____	_____
_____	_____

It is possible to turn those weaknesses into strengths. How might you accomplish this?

_____

_____

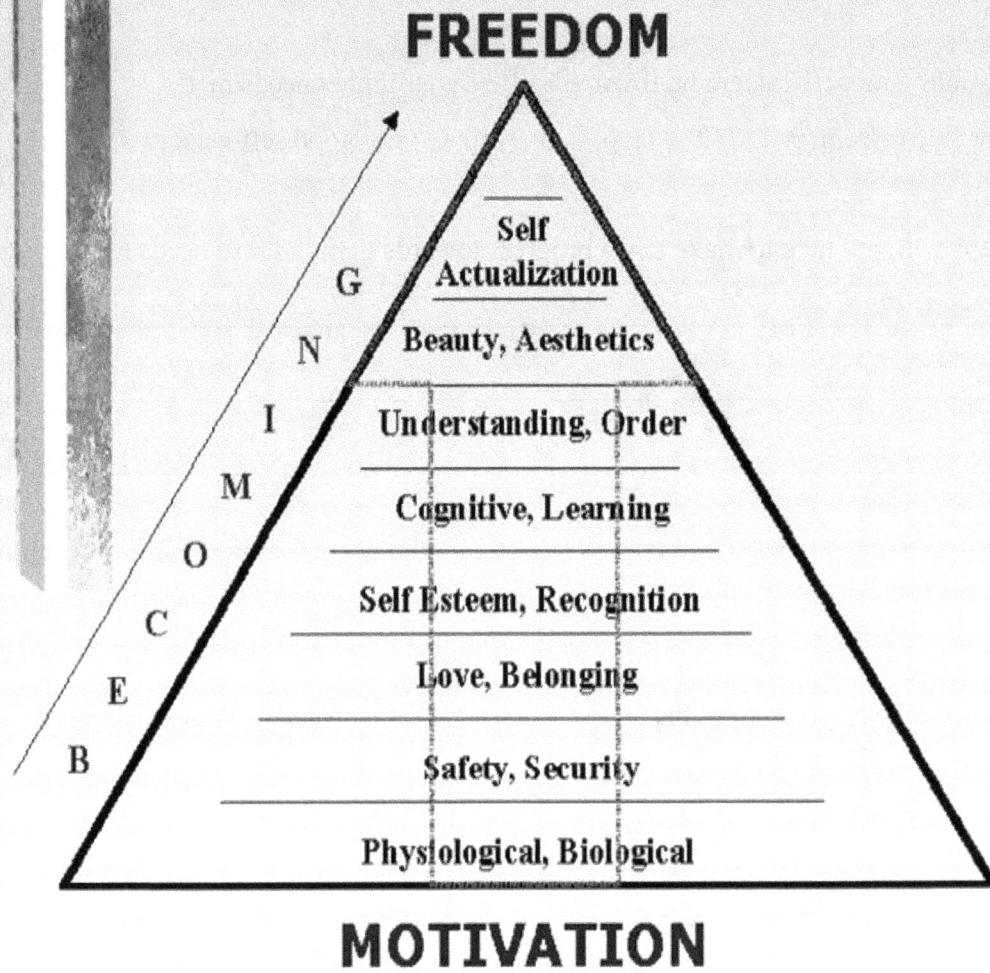

HIERARCHY OF NEEDS

FREEDOM

Self Actualization

Beauty, Aesthetics

Understanding, Order

Cognitive, Learning

Self Esteem, Recognition

Love, Belonging

Safety, Security

Physiological, Biological

G N I M O C E B

MOTIVATION

ASSERTIVENESS

OBJECTIVE	Learn how to express thoughts, opinions, desires, ideas, needs, feelings, values and beliefs in a respectful and positive manner and you will increase positive outcomes.
INTERVENTION	Define assertiveness and discuss how a person asserts oneself by taking affirmative action. Recognize your rights and be prepared to take a stand for them.
PLAN	Practice assertiveness to improve communications, cope with stressors, solicit help, and obtain better results.

"There is nothing noble about being superior to some other man. The true nobility is in being superior to your previous self." – Ernest Hemingway

To assert means to express oneself with confidence and clarity. Assertiveness is a skill whereby the individual speaks his or her mind in a positive and purposive manner, with genuineness, honesty, and respect. It is a diplomatic action that is taken to achieve a specific end. Those that do not take action by asserting themselves are unlikely to achieve many goals. That is, if you want results its up to you to obtain them. But there is a way to do it that presents a positive attitude and yields positive outcomes.

One of the basic privileges extended to all Americans in the Bill of Rights is to speak freely. You have a right to your own needs, desires, aspirations, opinions, ideas, beliefs, values, feelings, and concerns; and you have a right to make them known to others. When we let the beliefs, opinions, and needs of others trump ours, we tend to become frustrated, angry, or even hateful. But there is a method for communicating effectively, without being negative emotionally, attitudinally, or verbally. Simply stated, being assertive is standing up for your rights in a thoughtful, controlled, and humble fashion.

Assertiveness Criteria

➢ Express your thoughts, opinions, ideas, goals, beliefs or feelings;

➢ Use respect, honesty, integrity, humility, and genuineness;

➢ Make it simple, clear, and concise;

➢ Demonstrate confidence and self-control;

➢ Have a positive end result or future goal in mind.

Assertiveness requires some planning and forethought. There should be a clear objective in mind, and a desired result such as landing that promotion. Figure out what you are going to say and how you intend to present yourself. Then, apply Occam's razor to the script; in other words, cut it down to size. Short and sweet as the saying goes. Get to the point as quickly as possible; don't beat around the bush (to coin another cliché). Once you have the script tightened up, rehearse it a few times and find your rhythm. Be ready to convey your message with a smooth, clear, friendly, and modest tone.

Next, you need to dispense with the emotion; you want to present yourself calm and collected. That's what I mean by self-control: keep intense emotions in check. It's okay to show some subtle passion, enthusiasm, and desire as long as you don't overact. Just be yourself; do not pretend to be someone you are not or to exhibit characteristics that are not genuine. Attributes like honesty and reverence come natural to those who practice humility, respect, courtesy, and gentleness; you shouldn't have to pretend to possess them or to put on a show. If this isn't you, you'll need to swallow your pride and learn to be more modest, reasonable, and selfless. I've often said, a little bit of humility will go a long way. If you appear conceited, forceful, nervous, or inflexible, you will not come across as authentic or reverent. And don't forget integrity: you must occupy the moral high ground and ensure your goals are honorable and ethical.

Third, demonstrate confidence, which will follow if you have your facts straight. Do your homework. Research the topic thoroughly so you do not misspeak or make an error. Back up your assertions with real data. Note that confidence also implies boldness, meaning courage and self-assurance, not aggressiveness or haughtiness. Confidence demonstrates that you believe in yourself and enables you to be persuasive and believable. It suggests that you are sure of yourself and therefore, must know what you are talking about.

Would you get the promotion if you slithered into the room, looking frightened as a church mouse, asking in a shaky voice that you desired a raise? Then the boss asked, "Why should I give you a raise?" and you replied that you hadn't had a raise in two years and you thought you were due. Not likely going to cut it is it? What if you came into the room, well dressed, smile on your face, head held high and asked for the raise? After the boss asked why, you replied that you had filled in for the manager in her absence on several occasions; you had studied the personnel manual, was well versed in her job description, understood fully the duties you needed to fulfill for that position, and you were prepared to answer questions in that regard; you had a good working relationship with all the customers/clients and knew them by name; and you also had been doing research on the corporation and had some ideas about new marketing ventures into areas where the company had opportunities and capabilities. Do you think that would work better? If you were the boss, which of those two candidates would you promote?

I remember once after receiving a promotion, I was given some very good advice. The regional director suggested that I could have been less verbose. She said the panel had planned a thirty minute interview and I took forty-five. I was trying to impress them with all my knowledge and experience; but they got the point long before I had completed my answers to their questions. I was trying so hard they were baffled. A few good examples would have convinced them as much as several. I was lucky I got the job. So cut it down to size. People who you would persuade value their time as much as you do. A large part of assertiveness is getting help from others, so get to the point quickly and don't waste their time.

Your Rights

"We hold these truths to be self-evident, that all men are created equal, that they are endowed by their Creator with certain unalienable rights, that among these are life, liberty, and the pursuit of happiness." These are the most commonly quoted words from our Declaration of Independence. Of course, Thomas Jefferson, being a man of God, got this idea from the Holy Bible. He said that the truth is obvious, or self-evident: God made us all equal insofar as we have the same potential for greatness, the same capability of discerning right from wrong, and the same unalienable rights as every other human being on the planet. And among those rights are freedom, choice, and free will.

- JOH 8:31-32,36 ~ As he was saying these things, many believed in him. So Jesus said to the Jews who had believed him, "If you abide in my word, you are truly my disciples, and you will know the truth, and the truth will set you free. So if the Son sets you free, you will be free indeed."

- GAL 3:28 ~ There is neither Jew nor Greek, there is neither slave nor free, there is no male and female, for you are all one in Christ Jesus.

- 1 CO 2:12-13 ~ Now we have received not the spirit of the world, but the Spirit who is from God, that we might understand the things freely given us by God. And we impart this in words not taught by human wisdom but taught by the Spirit, interpreting spiritual truths to those who are spiritual.

- COL 3:4,10-11 ~ When Christ who is your life appears, then you also will appear with him in glory… Put on then, as God's chosen ones, holy and beloved, compassionate hearts, kindness, humility, meekness, and patience, bearing with one another and, if one has a complaint against another, forgiving each other; as the Lord has forgiven you, so you also must forgive.

- JAM 1:25 ~ The one who looks into the perfect law, the law of liberty, and perseveres, being no hearer who forgets but a doer who acts, he will be blessed in his doing.

Any right given to you by God is not to be denied by others because they didn't give you that right in the first place. Such rights are unalienable: they may not be taken from you and you may not be alienated from them. Whenever those rights are denied, it is a violation of God's Law; it also is a violation of the law of our land. You are permitted by law to pursue happiness and liberty in any way you desire as long as it does not violate the law or infringe on another person's right to the same. While there are various penalties depending on the seriousness of the infraction, violating one of God's laws brings the death penalty.

- PRO 8:36 ~ God says, "He who fails to find me injures himself; all who hate me love death."

- ROM 6:23 ~ For the wages of sin is death, but the free gift of God is eternal life in Christ Jesus our Lord.

- JAM 1:14-15 (paraphrased) ~ Everyone is tempted when they are enticed by their sinful desires, which when conceived, brings forth sin; and sin when finished brings forth death.

When governments deny rights to the populace it is tyranny. The result is often a revolt or revolution; such was the case during the American Revolution. Patrick Henry taught us that slavery is not a reasonable price to pay for peace. That is to say, if you start giving up your freedoms, you will end up giving up your happiness as well. Reasonable people take a stand for their rights; that's one of the things that make this country great. Many patriots have given the ultimate sacrifice to protect these freedoms and rights. That's what God calls us to do: dedicate our lives as a living sacrifice (ROM 12:1).

"If liberty means anything at all, it means the right to tell people what they don't want to hear." – George Orwell

If you are not getting your needs met, or nobody is listening to your opinions, or your rights are being infringed, you can do something about it. It requires that you take action. Happiness is not a right; you have to pursue it. It is not going to drop out of the sky into your lap. Don't just sit there; go and get it. However, you cannot depend on others to provide your happiness and peace of mind. But if people you care about can help you get your needs met, or make you happy, tell them and teach them how.

- PSA 34:14 ~ Turn away from evil and do good; seek peace and pursue it.

Freedom of speech is a rare privilege in this world. Not only do you have the right to speak your mind, you have a right to change it. In fact, you probably should, especially if you don't believe in yourself, or you don't think you have anything important to contribute, or you are afraid, embarrassed, or unsure of yourself. People that do not assert themselves or act on their beliefs are usually basing their indecision on erroneous reasoning. If that is the case they are probably lying to themselves.

- DEU 11:16 ~ Take care lest your heart be deceived, and you turn aside and serve other gods and worship them.

- GAL 6:3 ~ For if anyone thinks he is something, when he is nothing, he deceives himself.

- JAM 1:22 ~ But be doers of the word, and not hearers only, deceiving yourselves.

You have the right to make your own choices, including occupational, educational, recreational, social, political, etc. Of course, parents are allowed some control over the choices children make for good reason. But any choice is a personal decision, constrained only by the standards of morality that guides that person. If you are making choices that go against those standards, you know full well it is the wrong decision. If someone compels you to do something that goes against your better judgment, you have the right to say no.

- PRO 16:3 ~ Commit your work to the LORD, and your plans will be established.

- ISA 7:15 ~ He shall eat curds and honey when he knows how to refuse the evil and choose the good.

- 1 CO 10:13 ~ No temptation has overtaken you that is not common to man. God is faithful, and he will not let you be tempted beyond your ability, but with the temptation he will also provide the way of escape, that you may be able to endure it.

- JAM 4:17 ~ So whoever knows the right thing to do and fails to do it, for him it is sin.

You have the right to be sure, and the right to say you don't know. You have the right to care about a cause or position, or not to care about it. You have the right to agree and to disagree, to conform or not conform; to explain yourself or not explain; to start something, finish something, or quit something. There are times you should be serious and there are times when it's okay to be silly. There is a time and a place for everything. There are situations when some things are appropriate and situations when they are not.

- ECC 3:1-8 ~ For everything there is a season, and a time for every matter under heaven: a time to be born, and a time to die; a time to plant, and a time to pluck up what is planted; a time to kill, and a time to heal; a time to break down, and a time to build up; a time to weep, and a time to laugh; a time to mourn, and a time to dance; a time to cast away stones, and a time to gather stones together; a time to embrace, and a time to refrain from embracing; a time to seek, and a time to lose; a time to keep, and a time to cast away; a time to tear, and a time to sew; a time to keep silence, and a time to speak; a time to love, and a time to hate; a time for war, and a time for peace.

You have a right to your privacy. If you don't want to give out personal information then don't. If you feel it is none of their business, it isn't. If you want to talk about it go ahead; if not, remain silent. You have a right to be yourself, and to change that if it will make you a better person. If you don't like yourself, then you need to change. If your self-esteem is low, you have the power to lift yourself up. You have the right to be treated fairly and to receive equal justice under the law.

You have the right to enter relationships that meet your needs and discontinue those that do not. You have a right to be loved and respected; in fact, both should be given unconditionally. Does a person have to earn your respect? No, you give it. Do they always return your love, respect, or thoughtfulness? No, but it will come back to you in other ways. By the way, you should love and respect yourself as well (MAT 22:37-40). Everybody deserves to be loved. God loves all people equally; so should we. And that includes you.

- ROM 13:10 ~ Love does no wrong to a neighbor; therefore, love is the fulfilling of the Law.

- COL 3:14 ~ And above all these put on love, which binds everything together in perfect harmony.

- 1 PE 4:8 ~ Keep loving one another earnestly, since love covers a multitude of sins.

Sometimes it is necessary to take risks to get what you want. Do not shy away from challenges, things you haven't tried before, or facing your fears. It requires courage to take risks; but it is foolish to take unnecessary risks. Take calculated risks. Sometimes, you'll win, sometimes you'll lose. A wise person will learn from their mistakes as well as their successes. You have the right to be imperfect, to make mistakes, to accept the consequences, and to make amends. But never forget that, while you have all the aforementioned rights, so do others; they too have the right to care, believe, act, opine – or not.

A compassionate person will accept the shortcomings of others, forgive them, and give them a second chance. Everyone deserves a second chance, including you. But if someone has no intention of changing, you have the right to deny them another chance. Consider the battered wife who continuously allows her abusive husband to return, believing false promises that he will refrain from beating her. There is a reasonable limit to allowing a mistake to be repeated over and over. Einstein once said that insanity is to keep repeating the same action expecting a different result. If it doesn't work, try something else; don't just give up. Eventually you will figure it out, maybe sooner.

We should follow the example of Christ and forgive our neighbors (MAT 6:14-15), serve others (MAT 25:40-45), and love our enemies (MAT 5:44). But that doesn't mean we have to be their friend, ally, or companion. It just means we treat all people with dignity, respect, and consideration. People will notice that you are a person of character and that will create opportunities. Certainly, God will notice; in fact, he's the one opening the doors.

- PSA 1:1 ~ Blessed is the man who walks not in the counsel of the wicked, nor stands in the way of sinners, nor sits in the seat of scoffers; but his delight is in the law of the LORD, and on his law he meditates day and night.

- EPH 5:11 ~ Take no part in the unfruitful works of darkness, but instead expose them.

Assertiveness is an art; and the more you practice it, the better you get at it. Like sculpture, you mold your attitude and demeanor into a communication machine, that keeps it simple, sets the record straight, and gets the point across. This manner of conveying your message yields positive results a lot more often than any alternative strategy. Assertiveness is never pushy, overbearing, unpleasant, or threatening to the recipients of the message. In a way, it's an invitation for others to get to know you, to be a part of your life, and possibly to have a stake in it as well.

- JOB 9:14 ~ How then can I answer him, choosing my words with him?

Assertiveness is quite different from aggression. Actually, they are practically in direct opposition. Aggression infringes on the rights of others. Assertiveness ensures everyone is treated equally and that nobody's rights are violated. Consider the definition of assertiveness presented at the start of this lesson and contrast that with aggression. Aggressive people push their opinions or beliefs on others; they are loud, bullish, selfish, intimidating, humiliating, and disrespectful. That's not in control, that's out of it. They are seldom genuine or honest, but often phony and deceitful. Their message is uninteresting, irrelevant, and/or erroneous. It's not simple or clear, it's complicated, illogical, or convoluted. Their confidence is unfounded, as they are often overconfident, arrogant, misinformed, or just plain ignorant. That's because they are interested only in themselves, not the needs or opinions of others. They don't have the facts straight. If they were so sure of themselves they wouldn't have to be abrasive to convince or persuade you. A message that is positive and true can be digested without it being forced down your throat.

The other extreme is to be overly passive and let people walk all over you. Such a person may have the attributes of respect and genuineness, but are neither confident nor in control. They let others control them, and become dependent on that simply to avoid conflict. They are very unlikely to speak their minds or express their opinions and beliefs, much less stand up for their rights. They subordinate their opinions or needs to the degree that others will too. Both aggression and passivity lack assertiveness, given our working definition. People tend to avoid or resent aggressive people, and often take advantage of passive people. Either way, such persons are often dissatisfied because they seldom get their needs met.

Note that scripture provides similar guidelines as to how to bring someone to faith. These characteristics should be incorporated into all of your communications. If they are effective in sharing God, they will be effective in any other type of sharing. The reason is this: we are reflecting Christ when we share him in a humble and respectful manner. You can reflect God in all of your interactions by adopting the Biblical formula.

- PRO 11:2 ~ When pride comes, then comes disgrace, but with the humble is wisdom.

- PRO 15:28 ~ The heart of the righteous ponders how to answer, but the mouth of the wicked pours out evil things.

- ROM 12:3,16-18 ~ For by the grace given to me I say to everyone among you not to think of himself more highly than he ought to think, but to think with sober judgment, each according to the measure of faith that God has assigned... Live in harmony with one another. Do not be haughty, but associate with the lowly. Never be wise in your own sight. Repay no one evil for evil, but give thought to do what is honorable in the sight of all. If possible, so far as it depends on you, live peaceably with all.

- 1 CO 8:1-2 ~ Now concerning food offered to idols: we know that "all of us possess knowledge." This "knowledge" puffs up, but love builds up. If anyone imagines that he knows something, he does not yet know as he ought to know.

- 1 PE 3:15 ~ In your hearts honor Christ the Lord as holy, always being prepared to make a defense to anyone who asks you for a reason for the hope that is in you; yet do it with gentleness and respect.

For a great example of assertiveness, read the Old Testament book of Esther, who was raised by her cousin Mordecai after her parents died. Mordecai was a man of integrity, honesty, and respect. He taught Esther to be a lady of such character, and she became the Queen of Persia. The trustworthy and truthful Mordecai brought honor to King Xerxes. This honor was returned to him on several occasions. Mordecai uncovered the evil plot by Haman to eradicate the Jews, of which Esther was one. With the assertiveness and humility that was taught her, Esther apprised her husband of what was afoot. The king became furious with Haman and had him hanged on a gallows which Haman had prepared for Mordecai, who later replaced Haman as the king's second.

"Moral cowardice that keeps us from speaking our minds is as dangerous to this country as irresponsible talk. The right way is not always the popular and easy way. Standing for right when it is unpopular is a true test of moral character." – Margaret Chase Smith

Assertiveness Techniques

Assertiveness improves communications, prevents misunderstandings, and solidifies relationships. It increases satisfaction, raises confidence and self-esteem, and commands respect. It enables one to make decisions, solve problems, cope with setbacks, and achieve goals more effectively. Assertiveness also reduces social anxiety, fear, and depression.

Lack of assertiveness seems to be a prevalent problem among the clients I serve, insofar as they lack many of the necessary characteristics outlined above. They cannot seem to collect the wherewithal to take action, make a decision, or believe in themselves. They yield to others in every situation, they procrastinate, or they are too lazy or apathetic; they have given up totally, or they are just plain tired. These are difficult habits to break as it requires a complete overhaul to one's conditioning. People don't realize that they have the power to get their needs met, to pursue happiness, and to become anybody they want to be. What it takes is faith. The therapist provides the encouragement, but the faith is up to them. Don't forget, those that Christ and the apostles healed became whole because of their own faith. A faith healer doesn't do the healing; God does, for those who believe.

After defining assertiveness and discussing each of the criteria and associated components, use the list of rights for a great group exercise. Ask participants about their rights and see how many they come up with. You can generate a lot of discussion about each item. They will probably think of some things that are not on the list. Every so often I find myself revising the list as it tends to grow longer the more I conduct this exercise.

Sharing opinions in group helps people learn to assert themselves. If there are people in the group that are not participating, prompt them to give an opinion. Keep doing this until they are comfortable speaking up without being asked. Teach participants the importance of respecting others' opinions and the fact that everyone's point of view is valuable. Sharing opinions and insight leads to other kinds of sharing. You will find that groups become like a family, providing support for one another, and lifting members up when they are down. They develop cohesiveness, such that everyone feels comfortable speaking their minds without fear of rebuke. I like to point out such assertiveness when it occurs, to reinforce the behavior. The more they practice these behaviors the greater their aptitude at communicating, edifying, and believing.

The following is a sampling of techniques that you can employ to improve assertiveness.

- ➢ Believe in yourself
- ➢ Think before reacting or responding
- ➢ Plan ahead (have a game plan and a script)
- ➢ Do your homework, research
- ➢ Be specific when you ask or when you state your case (I want, need, think)
- ➢ Ask for and give feedback, clarification

- Give a reason for your opinion, feelings, desires
- Say no or yes only when you mean it
- Show respect to everyone at all times
- Recognize others' sensitivities, discomfort, vulnerabilities
- Advocate for others' rights as well as yours
- Confront others politely and redirect them as necessary
- Defend yourself tactfully and reasonably
- Accept responsibility for your actions, words
- Learn to negotiate, compromise (find common ground)
- Refrain from being judgmental
- Use positive language (not: I don't like, you should not, I can't)
- Be gracious about receiving compliments and criticisms
- Verify the accuracy of stated or implied facts
- Keep records (date, time, activity, results)
- Offer solutions not excuses
- Use body language to reinforce the message
- Turn your weaknesses into strengths
- Be self-aware and self-monitoring
- Don't give in and don't give up
- Always follow through
- Stick to the point, agenda
- Practice, practice, practice

"The best thing you can do is the right thing; the next best thing you can do is the wrong thing; the worst thing you can do is nothing." – Theodore Roosevelt

"Twenty years from now you will be more disappointed by the things you didn't do than by the ones you did. So throw off the bowlines. Sail away from the safe harbor. Catch the trade winds in your sails. Explore. Dream. Discover." – Mark Twain

Activity

How assertive are you? Answer each statement using the following scale:

1 = agree a lot, 2 = agree a little, 3 = not sure, 4 = disagree a little, 5 = disagree a lot.

___ If someone asks for my opinion I am embarrassed to tell them.

___ When I disagree with someone I probably won't speak up.

___ I let my spouse (significant other) make most of the decisions.

___ If a friend asks me to do something I don't want to do, I often give into them.

___ I seldom ask for help, even when I'm not sure what to do.

___ If someone asks for my opinion I might not give a totally honest answer.

___ I would never tell my friends things that I dislike about them.

___ My spouse (significant other) and I seldom talk about our problems.

___ I have a hard time saying no to people.

___ I never vote in political elections.

___ I prefer not to get involved in family planning and decision making.

___ When someone is wrong I am not the one to tell them.

___ I shy away from debates.

___ If everyone else is doing something, I usually go along, even if I don't want to.

___ I'm afraid to ask people for favors, especially if they might say no.

___ People tend to take advantage of me.

___ When I have a falling out with someone, I dwell on things I should have said or done.

___ It is very hard for me to apologize to people.

___ I don't have a whole lot of confidence when trying new things.

___ I deserve a raise but I'm not sure if I should ask my boss.

Add up your scores, and you will have a value between 20 and 100. Work on raising your score to 75 or better. Items rated 1 or 2 indicate areas you should focus on.

- **Speak Your Mind**
- **Life, Liberty, Happiness**
- **Change Your Mind**
- **Needs, Feelings, and Desires**
- **Opinions and Ideas**
- **Beliefs, Values, Religion**
- **Explain Yourself**
- **Not Give an Explanation**
- **Make Choices**
- **Disagree**
- **Say No**
- **Say I Don't Know**
- **Self Esteem**
- **Privacy**
- **Be Yourself**
- **Justice**
- **Be Loved and Respected**
- **Love and Respect Yourself**
- **Seek Relationships**
- **End Relationships**
- **Care About Something**
- **Not Care About Something**
- **Be Serious**
- **Act Silly**
- **Take Risks**
- **Make Mistakes**
- **Another Chance**

YOUR RIGHTS

Creative Thinking

OBJECTIVE	Develop an ability to think outside the box. Expand your horizons by exploring uncharted territory.
INTERVENTION	Explore different ways to stimulate creative thinking by challenging the intellect and the imagination.
PLAN	Practice expanding thought processes by fantasizing, solving puzzles and riddles, deconstructing complex problems, and recording thoughts and ideas. Discover more effective and innovative solutions to problems and dilemmas.

"The biggest problem in the world could have been solved when it was small." – Witter Bynner

"We can't solve problems by using the same thinking we used when we created them." – Albert Einstein

If you want to make a difference, or carve a niche, or excel in a discipline you need to be able to think "outside the box" as they say. That is, you don't want to limit yourself to doing things the same way, every time. Take off the blinders and search for more effective methods, innovative alternatives, and better outcomes. There are a number of exercises and activities that you can perform to enhance your creative instinct. They are designed specifically to get you out of your comfort zone and into a world of novelty, intrigue, diversity, obscurity, and discovery.

Brainstorming: This technique allows a free flow of thought without restrictions. Opinions or ideas just pour out no matter how ridiculous, unlikely, or vague. Set a time limit and see how many things you can add to the possibilities list before the time runs out. Everything is included in the list without scrutiny; the longer the list, the larger the panorama of options. The next step is to organize these ideas into categories according to similarity: attributes in common, conceptual relatedness, comparable requirements, etc. This is easily accomplished when the ideas are written on index cards, the list is cut into pieces, or a computer is used to sort them. You can do this exercise by yourself or get others to help you generate options. Bounce the ideas off of colleagues after you have organized and prioritized them. I often encourage patients to make a list of possible physical, mental, and spiritual activities using this technique; they will have many options to choose from to keep active and healthy upon discharge. Use brainstorming as a group exercise; it is fun and generates a lot of participation.

Journaling: Keep a writing tablet and pen with you so you can write down thoughts, feelings, and ideas. Incorporate illustrations, charts, and figures to further embody the meaning and intent; cut and paste pictures that depict the thought. Not only is journaling therapeutic, it helps you to remember ideas that have potential. Oftentimes, these thoughts come out of nowhere and depart just as quickly, unless you record them for future reference. When you are idle, write down whatever comes to mind. Regularly peruse your journal embellishing thoughts, recognizing patterns, and allowing the ideas to progress, regress, or split into different paths. Keep developing any ideas that have merit. As you continue to revisit old thoughts you may find some worth keeping, rearranging, or enlarging. Whenever you reach an impasse, return to the journal and record new approaches or just read it to see if stimulates more contemplation. Consider the journals of Leonardo da Vinci, where he imagined things like military weapons, civil engineering projects, even helicopters. He described these things and drew diagrams of them. Many of those ideas actually became reality during his life; some became reality long after his death and were astonishingly similar to his original designs.

Incubation: Turn your conscious brain off for a while, after you have been racking it mercilessly. Enable the analytical and inductive compilations to hatch in your subconscious. This is the principle behind the so-called eureka phenomenon. You can study a problem to death and get frustrated, after which further examination just becomes counterproductive. So you take a break: have a snack, take a shower, go for a walk. Then, all of a sudden, the answer is there. It filtered up to awareness after your unconscious had a chance to categorize it, analyze it, synthesize it, and realize it. Research has shown that people should take a short break after every few hours of intense cognitive work to capitalize on this capability, and avoid becoming mentally fatigued. So give your creative brain a chance to play with the information and maybe a light bulb will illuminate in your head: kind of how Edison might have figured it out. I discovered this when I was a young college student. I used to cram for 12 hours or so into the wee hours of the morning for each final exam. I'd be disappointed when I would get a 75%. Eventually, I figured out that I was reaching overload to the extent that some of the information was spilling out (kind of like overfilling a glass with water by 25%). I started using my brain more effectively by organizing the data systematically and configuring it in a way that made it easier to retrieve from memory. I developed mnemonics that would facilitate access to the concepts and details. I began making scores like 95%; and that after only about 8 hours of studying with breaks inserted. I achieved this by reconfiguring the study material, and reducing it to clusters, chunks, pieces, bits, etc. I developed a hierarchy among the data that enabled rapid recall of large amounts of information using keywords and imagery. Note that a simple cue can be used to activate an idea, picture, or explanation when the input data are arranged in a fashion that permits ready retrieval.

Meditation: Configure the environment to maximize thought generation. Devise a place which will stimulate creative thinking by modifying the ambience, climate, and scenery. Incorporate soft, soothing music, a pleasant scent, favorite colors, perhaps soft light: whatever arouses deep concentration, pleasant mood, and inspiration. You also can establish that environment in your head just by imagining it. You may find that you contemplate or meditate the best at certain times of day, in certain locations, or while engaging in particular chores or pastimes. I used to wander into the boondocks to get away from the chaos, interference, and fast pace of civilization, just so I could empty my head of it all. I find nature very inspiring as it reminds me that God is ever present – something I often forget when I'm busy, overwhelmed, or stressed. Next time you go on a road trip, take the scenic route. Take time to ponder deeply about significant events in your life: past, present, or future. And above all, take time to ponder about God and commune with him regularly.

Brain Exercises: There are ways of challenging yourself to use more of your brain. Certainly anything that taps into the capacity afforded by the lower levels of consciousness is great as this activates the multiprocessing capabilities. Pay attention to the workings of your mind, at multiple levels.

➢ Learn – I have never exhausted my yearning for learning: it teaches me about me, as well as expanding my knowledge of the universe. Take classes or read books about stuff you never studied before, until you grasp the material sufficiently to converse about it. Read constantly, ask questions of subject matter experts, debate people, and attend workshops and seminars. Expand your horizons in diverse arenas. I remember picking up a book from the library on astrophysics to peruse while visiting a sick loved one in the hospital. I didn't think it would be that interesting but I was wrong. I ended up reading several such books and discovered an interest I never knew I had.

➢ Investigate – Pour over topics of interest by researching them extensively; gather as much data as you can; classify the information via taxonomy; perform data analysis and reduction; and develop plausible interpretations. Record your results in notebooks cataloged by topic. Practice dissecting problems into smaller and smaller parts. Envision the process, program, or performance from start to finish: prelude, circumstances, activation cues, procedures, behaviors, end results, and associated consequences. Experiment on the process by incorporating new variables, manipulating existing variables, and observing the outcomes scientifically. Deconstruct the attributes, assumptions, predictions, and conclusions. Develop a design for repeating the experiment in order to calibrate the working model. Test and measure alternatives and determine which ones consistently yield benefits. Identify useful trends, metaphors, analogies, products and byproducts. Continue to build upon the expanding knowledge base, and update internal models.

➢ Imagine – Do not allow your imagination to be replaced by a television, video game, or movie. Create your own stories, games, adventures, and dreams. Visualize the entire program, episode, or scenario. Develop a mental map of the interrelationships among related factors, ideas, and thoughts. Identify landmarks, routes, and neural pathways that can be activated, accessed, and retrieved using encoded input patterns. Try looking at the picture from different points of view, angles, or frames of reference. Imagine yourself portraying a variety of roles and predict how each character would examine the idea, data, problem, or dilemma. What types of solutions might you arrive at if you were in someone else's shoes? Ask people of other disciplines about their perspectives to get alternative viewpoints. Evaluate opposing opinions, and prepare to argue them as if they were yours. Imagine yourself fulfilling roles, achieving milestones, and taking on responsibilities as if it were actually happening. When it does you will be prepared, because you had been planning and rehearsing it.

➢ Switch – Establish links between hemispheres of the brain and alternate between them. Employ verbal cues that activate visual representations, and vice-versa. Switch modalities from visual to verbal, and back again. Conceptualize what the verbal explanation would look like pictorially; define the image in terms of how you would explain it verbally. You also can incorporate a kinesthetic component to get the feel of it. Or try to get a taste of it, or smell. Use all five senses to experience the phenomenon. Create a screenplay, storyboard, or comic book representation that incorporates all the senses, the scenario, the dialogue, and the product/conclusion.

➢ Reason – Attend courses in logic, critical thinking, inductive and deductive reasoning, convergent and divergent thinking, and statistics. Identify common fallacies of logic, obstructions to rational thinking, and generate examples of them. Try inverting the problem or reversing it. For example, conceive doing something that would totally defeat the objective for another look; it might point to an added approach or change in tactics. In short, improvise. Find several paths that lead to a single destination; discover how one path can branch off into several that lead to more destinations. Identify more than one solution to a single problem, as some questions have many valid answers. Explain how one answer can be applied to a number of questions.

Get Busy: Fertilize your thoughts, nurturing them like a potted plant, and watch them grow. Try numerous techniques, log your successes and mistakes, and continue to observe, chronicle, and apply. Don't procrastinate, and don't spend too much time; take sufficient time and energy to get the point, or exhaust your prospects, or create an opportunity. Then pursue it. The key word is action. Invent things, construct things, and produce things. Take things apart and rebuild them, or use the parts to build something else. Be like the child playing with blocks; each occasion he or she configures the same blocks in a unique arrangement. I've always said: if you want to change or acquire a behavior, you have to change your mind, meaning acquire the thought. This begins with a change of heart; you have to want to be creative. Then start believing that you are creative, and you will begin to act creative. Allow your creative ideas to evolve into action plans, and watch as your creative talent increases.

Information: Contemplate the developmental aspect of creativity via the examination, manipulation, and compilation of information. Below is my brainstorm on that topic; notice how I delimited the problem grammatically to further challenge my creativity. Also, you may notice how the terms seem to progress in the developmental aspect.

Imitation	Integration	Illumination
Imagination	Investigation	Intuition
Inquisition	Iteration	Ideation
Inspection	Interpretation	Improvisation
Interaction	Interpolation	Implementation
Instruction	Induction	Innovation
Illustration	Introspection	Invention

God is a prime example of how things can be created that have yet to be realized. All that is observable in this universe was produced by the thoughts and command of God. If you can imagine it God can make it happen, and maybe you can too. For all things are possible with God, but without God – well good luck.

- PRO 25:2 ~ It is the glory of God to conceal things, but the glory of kings is to search things out.

- ECC 7:24-25 ~ That which has been is far off, and deep, very deep; who can find it out? I turned my heart to know and to search out and to seek wisdom and the scheme of things, and to know the wickedness of folly and the foolishness that is madness.

- ROM 1:20 ~ For his invisible attributes, namely, his eternal power and divine nature, have been clearly perceived, ever since the creation of the world, in the things that have been made. So they are without excuse.

- HEB 11:3 ~ By faith we understand that the universe was created by the word of God, so that what is seen was not made out of things that are visible.

- JAM 3:17 ~ But the wisdom from above is first pure, then peaceable, gentle, open to reason, full of mercy and good fruits, impartial and sincere.

The straightest route to expanding your horizons, developing your creative gifts, and producing fruit worthy of your calling is to tap into the wisdom of God. He gives this wisdom freely to all those who request it (JAM 1:5). In fact, God invites you to seek his knowledge and truth so that he can impart these gifts to you. This understanding is transferred from his spirit to yours in its purest form. God's Word is an excellent starting point. You will, no doubt, be astounded at the increase in your wisdom, your horizons, and your potential, if you continue to delve into the Bible. I sure was. The Bible is so broad and deep; it will take numerous readings to start grasping the big picture. And if you continue to read the entire text again and again, you will see your knowledge growing exponentially. Each reading of it will increase your horizons further and further.

- JOB 32:8 ~ But it is the spirit in man, the breath of the Almighty, that makes him understand.

- PRO 2:2,4,6,10 ~ Make your ear attentive to wisdom and incline your heart to understanding; seek it like silver and search for it as for hidden treasures... For the LORD gives wisdom; from his mouth come knowledge and understanding; wisdom will come into your heart, and knowledge will be pleasant to your soul.

- 1 CO 1:24 ~ To those who are called, both Jews and Greeks, Christ the power of God and the wisdom of God.

- COL 2:2-4 ~ That your hearts may be encouraged, being knit together in love, to reach all the riches of full assurance of understanding and the knowledge of God's mystery, which is Christ, in whom are hidden all the treasures of wisdom and knowledge.. I say this in order that no one may delude you with plausible arguments.

Give God a try if you want to find true wisdom, direction, and purpose.

- JER 29:13 ~ God says, "You will seek me and find me, when you seek me with all your heart."

- MAT 7:7 ~ Jesus said, "Ask, and it will be given to you; seek, and you will find; knock, and it will be opened to you."

Consider Christopher Columbus, an ordinary man in most respects, and yet a great man in others, especially navigation by sea. He had an idea about a business venture that could open up trade with India, by establishing a shipping route around the globe (note that people of even modest intelligence did not believe the world was flat). Conceive the impact: boatloads of goods arriving in India in a matter of weeks, rather than months of dragging the cargo across land several thousand miles. Columbus had to go to a foreign government to get funding for his idea. I imagine him being at sea for weeks, with a crew contemplating mutiny, ready to throw the man overboard; until some seaman in the crow's nest shouted "Land Ho!" At first, Columbus figured it was India; regardless, he found people, resources, and possibilities and took this message back to Queen Isabella.

Columbus would make the trip five times, setup a colony, and bring back hope. As the legend goes, it finally hit him on his final voyage that he had not discovered a trade route to India, but an uncharted world altogether. Well, he obviously wasn't the first to find the Americas, because there were many that made it there before him (via Iceland-Greenland and down the Atlantic Coast; across the Atlantic Ocean from Africa to Mexico; over the Bearing Strait and down the Pacific Coast, etc.). But when Columbus did it, he returned; it was just the right time. And that event became one of the most momentous in history. Look at the impact on the human race. Suddenly, people came in droves to this new land of opportunity and freedom; and they still do. The moral of the story is this: everyone has the ability to make an impact. It's about cultivating an idea, seizing the moment, and pursuing a dream. You may think you are ordinary, but through Christ you are extraordinary, and capable of doing great things. More on this can be found in the lesson on Maximizing Your Potential.

Get your clients to think about and discuss their creative ideas. Encourage clients to write down their ideas, bounce them against their loved ones, nurture and cultivate them. The following quotes epitomize the unlimited application of creative thinking and will usually stimulate interesting discussions.

"Fantasy, abandoned by reason, produces impossible monsters; united with it, she is the mother of the arts and the origin of marvels." – Francisco de Goya

"The intuitive mind is a sacred gift and the rational mind is a faithful servant. We have created a society that honors the servant and has forgotten the gift." – Albert Einstein

"If the doors of perception were cleansed, everything would appear to man as it is, infinite." – William Blake

"The thoughts that come often unsought, and as it were, drop into the mind, are commonly the most valuable of any we have." – John Locke

Activity

Let's see how well you can think outside the box. Try these exercises to measure your creative thought potential. Compete with other members of the group or with your friends. Time yourself: five or ten minutes for each exercise. Compare your answers with those of others. Whatever works is fair game. Good luck!

List as many ways you can think of to use a screwdriver (other than just turning screws).

_____ _____ _____ _____

_____ _____ _____ _____

_____ _____ _____ _____

_____ _____ _____ _____

_____ _____ _____ _____

_____ _____ _____ _____

List as many ways you can think of to use a coat hanger (other than hanging clothes).

_____ _____ _____ _____

_____ _____ _____ _____

_____ _____ _____ _____

_____ _____ _____ _____

_____ _____ _____ _____

_____ _____ _____ _____

List as many ways you can think of to use bricks (other than constructing a wall).

_____ _____ _____ _____

_____ _____ _____ _____

_____ _____ _____ _____

_____ _____ _____ _____

_____ _____ _____ _____

"There's nothing more dangerous than an idea, when you only have one idea." – Alain

MAXIMIZING YOUR POTENTIAL

OBJECTIVE	Participants will understand they are here for a reason, with unique gifts and responsibilities; and if they explore the possibilities they will discover their purpose in life. This will motivate them to pursue their dreams and reach the pinnacle of their achievement potential.
INTERVENTION	Teach participants to dream big and believe in the possibilities. Discuss the concept of hidden potential and ways of tapping into latent abilities, interests, and talents.
PLAN	Develop a plan to achieve greatness, capitalize on opportunities, and stay active and focused every day. Make the most out of life by remaining engaged, expanding perspectives, and appreciating the value and potential of experience. Recognize that destiny is within one's control.

Have you ever wondered why you are here in this particular location, in this city, and at this particular era in history? You were born into this realm of space-time for a reason; that is, you are not an accident and your presence is required. How do I know this? Because you are here are you not? You are who you're supposed to be. You have uniqueness unlike anybody else: your demeanor, personality, appearance, experience, gifts, pathway, purpose, and destination. Variations among persons' attributes and character are also by design – God's design. Accept who you are, and what you are, and why you are, and you will begin to become all that you were meant to be.

- EST 4:14 ~ Mordecai replied to Esther, "For if you keep silent at this time, relief and deliverance will rise for the Jews from another place, but you and your father's house will perish. And who knows whether you have not come to the kingdom for such a time as this?"

Every experience adds up to a lifetime of becoming. That's why I constantly remind the reader to find the value and meaning of their successes and setbacks, their tragedies and victories. Wake up to the reality that you are in control, insofar as God has given you freedom of choice and the gift of discernment. You are the producer and director of your life story. You can create your future and you can pursue happiness as you define it, as long as you proceed in accordance with God's will and his rules. While the Lord continuously transforms you into the image of his son Jesus Christ, you are allowed to manipulate matter as a sculptor, and convert your world into the image of your dream or vision. All it takes is a pure and heartfelt desire (see PSA 145:16).

- MAT 25:29 ~ Jesus said, "To everyone who has will more be given, and he will have an abundance. But from the one who has not, even what he has will be taken away."

When your desire and convictions are founded on Christ you will have an abundant and fulfilling life (JOH 10:10). Make every second count. Live each day as if it were your last, with no regrets about yesterday or expectations about tomorrow. Enjoy every assignment, situation, and location by appreciating its potential, value, and beauty. Get the most out of what you have and be responsible with what you receive.

Do it now. Stop putting it off. Don't look for excuses but solutions. And always do your best no matter how mundane or monotonous the chore by being conscientious and thorough, both in the huge things and the tiny ones. Life is an adventure, take pleasure in the excursion. Live it for Jesus and each day he will have something new for you (2 CO 5:17).

- PSA 46:1 ~ God is our refuge and strength, a very present help in trouble.

- PRO 18:3 ~ When wickedness comes, contempt comes also, and with dishonor comes disgrace.

- ECC 9:10 (NIV) ~ Whatever your hand finds to do, do it with your might, for in the grave, where you are going, there is neither working nor planning nor knowledge nor wisdom.

Dreams and Visions

I believe that dreams and visions can occur at the conscious level, the unconscious level, or both. Both are an expression of our inner being: an experience of the soul if you will. Everyone has them, but not all listen to them or develop them. Sometimes people share visions or dreams in common; good examples include a husband and wife team; striving for the American Dream; and achieving Dr. Martin Luther King's dream of a nation of mutual respect and equal opportunity. Review the following definitions of a dream and a vision.

➢ Dream: A presentation of thoughts and images joined sequentially to produce an event, scenario, possibility, or slice of life, like a motion picture.
➢ Vision: A message, revelation, or conceptualization of particular clarity in which one apprehends a purpose, outcome, mission, or calling, presented as one big picture.

The current research on dreams occurring during sleep demonstrates their utility in organizing input data, updating our internal models, and preparing us for possible future events. The entire dream, its contents, and its symbolism are all an extension of you, the dreamer. And your dreams, whether happening asleep or awake, might indicate a message, direction, or calling. I encourage everyone to record and analyze these dreams because they can instruct and they can inspire. Similarly, the vision serves the same purpose. The only real difference between the two is the dream is a series of pictures that collectively produce a situation or state of affairs, and the vision is one complete view of it.

Practice thinking big in order to get the big picture. Obviously, one must think outside the box to accomplish this since big won't fit into the box. Get a vision of hope and see what it looks like to you. Write a description and/or draw a picture of it. Fill in the details of how happy you would be to reach your dreams; it will add new and profound meaning to your life.

Remember this: Everyone is created in the image of God and given understanding, rights, talents, and potential. We are great in some way or another and not so great in other ways. Thus, everyone is ordinary yet capable of greatness. We only have to explore, expose, and exploit the potential within us, keeping in mind that our goals and actions must be in accordance with God's will and plans in order to have his guarantee on it. Ask yourself or your clients what historical figures, relatives, or mentors (however ordinary) did great things and had a positive influence on their lives (Lincoln, Columbus, St. Peter, grandparent, etc.).

"Our aspirations are our possibilities." – Robert Browning

"Hope is a waking dream." – Aristotle

Awareness of Unrealized Potential

"The most common commodity in this country is unrealized potential." – Calvin Coolidge

Everyone has abilities and potential; some they are aware of, some not. Most of us know about certain talents that we currently possess or previously possessed. Most of us don't know about all the latent talent which still lingers untapped. Often the prospects go undetected simply because the individual fails to delve into and unmask that potential. The best way of uncovering undiscovered aptitude, interest, and genius is to start exploring the possibilities. This will make you aware of a great many things that you didn't know you were capable of, had aptitude in, or valued enough to be willing to work on it. The following actions will enable you to triumph in becoming aware of and reaching your full potential.

> ➤ Be Observant: Become aware of your environment. This requires that you carefully examine your surroundings, the people, the situational conditions, and how you fit in. You can train yourself to be more observant by sharpening your senses, just as law enforcement officers are trained to have a keen eye for details.
> ➤ Be Attentive: Pay attention to everything you see happen, everything that people say and do, and the associated consequences (whether good or bad). People tend to tune out a large portion of their world and miss the beauty, the point, or the opportunity. Understand that every moment and every situation has potential, so seek it out.
> ➤ Be Insightful: Discover your strengths, abilities, and hidden potential, as well as your shortcomings and weaknesses. Strive to turn the negatives into positives. Endeavor to excel; do not be satisfied with competency, shoot for mastery. For all you know what you thought was a weakness or flaw was actually hidden potential. Recognize the resistance in your heart and reverse its polarity in order to build confidence. That is, take the resistance, convert it into acceptance, and channel that energy into action.
> ➤ Be Purposeful: Seek your purpose, your mission, your calling, and you will find the motivation to persevere. You will be willing to do the work because the outcome is something you value and/or gives meaning to your life. This will keep you focused and committed. Strive for timeliness and accuracy of every response or performance.
> ➤ Be Intuitive: Identify opportunities, milestones, and decision points. Be prepared to seize the moment, choose an alternative, or make up your mind. Listen to what your spirit is telling you and follow your instincts; inside your heart you will know which fork to take, what words to speak, and what decision to make. Reflect on the decision, meditate on it, maybe sleep on it. Then be prepared to take immediate action.

> Be Responsible: Accept your roles and duties and execute them in a conscientious, accurate, and timely manner. Do your best in every undertaking no matter how relevant (or irrelevant) it may seem. Everything you think, do, say, and experience integrates perfectly into God's plan. So put your heart into it.

"When I let go of what I am, I become what I might be." – Lao Tzu

"Alas, for those that never sing, but die with their music in them." – Oliver Wendell Holmes

Making Connections

There are many ways of connecting ourselves to the world so as to achieve greatness, fulfillment, and happiness. These connections range from internal to external, animate to inanimate; they may be individual, collective, worldly, or supernatural. Connect with objects, yourself, other people, institutions, places, times, and most of all God

> Communicating creates connections with other people and strengthens relationships.
> Networking creates connections with experts, professionals, and those who have power to help us succeed, open doors, or provide direction.
> Learning creates fresh connections among the neurons in the brain. Training creates and strengthens programs and pathways, develops skill and precision, calibrates our internal models, and refines our strategies. Ascertain what you know, do not know, and what you need to know. Compare that with what God says (absolute truth).
> Practicing reinforces internal connections in the mind, such as linking the conscious with the unconscious, the serial processes with the parallel, and the verbal memory with the visual (left and right hemispheres of the brain). It enables one to maximize mental resources by automating certain activities, priming appropriate behaviors, and increasing efficiency and effectiveness (timing and accuracy) of certain tasks.
> Reconstructing creates connections between components of objects, concepts, or experiences. Take things apart, inspect each one, and put them back together again. Figure out how things work together to produce a product, idea, machine, or outcome. Understand that the whole is greater than the sum of its parts and how each part contributes to the collective mission, performance, or effect.
> Conceptualizing creates connections between thoughts and ideas, and organizes disparate pieces of information into clusters of meaning which collectively produce greater information, implication, and insight.
> Introspecting creates connections within oneself, helping an individual to tune into inner strength, abilities, inspiration, and undeveloped potential. Locate your God given gifts and open them. Every day is Christmas because your life, faith, and purpose are all gifts from God, and each day is a new beginning.
> Orienting creates connections between the person and the real world. That is, it keeps us grounded in reality. Not that dreaming and fantasizing are unproductive, but goals and destinations must be realistic. You can set the bar as high as you want and still reach plateaus that exceed your expectations. But remember, the path will probably take you to destinations that you did not imagine or plan. So keep an open mind and

stay focused on the here and now during the execution of your plan. Don't spend your time dreaming if it is time to act; don't contemplate when it's time to participate.

➤ Experimenting helps to connect stimuli with responses to determine the possible costs and benefits of a decision or action. Exploring focuses our curiosity and also helps to identify preferred choices from among the possibilities.

➤ Proceeding creates connections between you and your environment, which modifies the time-space continuum in which you exist, and which ultimately shapes the future. It has been theorized that every event has an effect on the entire universe; for example, the batting of the wings of a butterfly is felt by God and affects even the outermost regions. This is part of God's grand design. Since God gives us free will we have a hand in our destiny, regardless of the fact that he knows in advance what we will choose. Yes, you can choose your emotions, thoughts, dreams, and direction. Notice how events in the lives of people have changed the world, from inventors and scientists, to prophets and evangelists, to the resurrection of Jesus Christ.

➤ Believing creates connections to God and is proof that what you wish for or hope for is already yours. Without faith it is impossible to please God, much less receive his blessings. He wants you to succeed and to be happy; and if you focus on God you will, because that's what he promises. Knowing that your strength comes from the Lord gives you confidence in yourself that you can accomplish anything; whereas without God you cannot.

➤ Seeking creates connections to your inner power and potential, to others who would take the journey with you, to the future victories ahead in your path, to your calling, and to your Savior.

"The greatest danger for most of us is not that our aim is too high and we miss it, but that it is too low and we reach it." – Michelangelo

Planning for Success

In other chapters I have discussed developing creative thinking, establishing SMART goals, building support teams, and producing a game plan. Your vision provides the motivation because it has real value. It is up to you to make it happen, never doubting that God is on your side and will help in ways you'll never understand. So get busy and take breaks; budget your time using a phased approach. Focus on God and not the hurdles. Pray to him for guidance, perseverance, and patience.

Expand your vision by breaking it down into its parts. Map it out as if planning a cross country vacation. Then disembark on a mysterious, miraculous, and magnificent voyage. Nurture and cultivate your dream by applying your gifts; and watch the dream grow. Your purpose will evolve into an adventurous and authentic excursion towards total fulfillment, spiritual wealth, and a positive self-image that resembles Christ.

• PRO 23:7 (KJV) ~ As he thinks in his heart, so is he …

• MAT 13:31-32 ~ Jesus put another parable before them, saying, "The kingdom of heaven is like a grain of mustard seed that a man took and sowed in his field. It is the smallest of all seeds, but when it has grown it is larger than all the garden plants and becomes a tree, so that the birds of the air come and make nests in its branches."

- 2 CO 12:10 ~ For the sake of Christ, then, I am content with weaknesses, insults, hardships, persecutions, and calamities. For when I am weak, then I am strong.

The Game Plan

➢ Preparation: The following groundwork should be performed to lay a foundation.
- o Research – Information gathering, experimentation, evaluation, organization, interpretation, application
- o Rethink – Assumptions, beliefs, possibilities
- o Reframe – Perspectives, outlook, opinions, desires
- o Redefine – Your picture or vision, success, yourself
- o Redesign – Game plan, roadmap, operations
- o Restore – Faith, motivation, ambition, determination

➢ Mission Statement: This is a description of the end game or desired destination and the route you plan to take to get there.

➢ Storyboard: This is a depiction of the entire sequence leading from preparation, through execution, all the way to conclusion. Like a comic book, each scenario is mapped out to include scenes, characters, and dialogue. It's good to have a visual representation complete with pictures and notes like a presentation. Use your creative thinking abilities to envision and document the process.

➢ Tactics and Doctrine: This is your strategy to include rules, boundaries, approaches, techniques, and contingency plans. Tactics reflect the operational process and define an approach predicted to bring success. Doctrine represents the principles, guidelines, and policies that delimit what to do or not to do, and how.

➢ Goals and Objectives: This is the breakdown of the tasks and milestones that must be completed to reach the destination and fulfill the mission. They include actions and steps: the means to the end game.

➢ Timeline: This is the schedule and the anticipated timing of steps, tasks, and goals. It gives you a framework in which to pace yourself, and elucidates the milestones that you hope to reach and when.

➢ Resources: This defines the equipment, supplies, people, financial investments, and time required to support the mission.

Keep in mind that you must be flexible with respect to the plan, timeframe, even the destination. Establish a daily objective and follow it through. Try different methods and strategies until you know what works. Successes and failures provide definition regarding how to standardize or update your plan. Rehearse your roles, your lines, and your performance. Get yourself into the zone: your inner control, strength, and power. Visualize what you need to do, how you would do it, and what victory would look like. See yourself completing the mission and experience the corresponding lift to your sense of worth. Execute tasks without distraction or reconsideration. Assess the results and adjust your responses as needed. Give yourself reassuring and encouraging messages so that you never surrender your hope or passion. Give thanks to God each day for opportunities, for progress, and for every outcome. And you will thrive, and God will reward you in astonishing ways.

Character and Attitude

Expand your skills, polish your character, and practice the arts of adaptation, persuasion, and negotiation. Challenge yourself to take on progressively more responsibility and authority. Invest your time, energy, and a lot of hard work and the remunerations and rewards will collect like grains of sand in an hourglass. Produce, promote, and exhibit fruits of the Spirit (GAL 5:22-23; EPH 5:9; 2 PE 1:5-8).

- ➢ Kindness: an attitude of benevolence, compassion, and graciousness
- ➢ Respect: positive regard and esteem for others and yourself
- ➢ Helpfulness: lending a hand whenever you can
- ➢ Generosity: giving of oneself and one's wealth; paying it forward
- ➢ Resoluteness: purposeful and determined
- ➢ Dignity: nobility, character, and honor
- ➢ Integrity: virtue, honesty, truthfulness, trustworthiness
- ➢ Perseverance: never giving up; tenacity

The following quotes make for a great discussion. Get participants' understanding and reaction to the statements below regarding the potential that exists in every situation.

"There will come a time when you believe everything is finished. That will be the beginning." – Louis L'Amour

"What seems to us as bitter trials are often blessings in disguise." – Oscar Wilde

"Be of good cheer. Do not think of today's failures, but of success that may come tomorrow. You have set yourselves a difficult task, but you will succeed if you persevere; and you will have a joy in overcoming obstacles – a delight in climbing rugged paths which you would perhaps never know if you did not sometimes slip backward, if the road were always smooth and pleasant. Remember, no effort that we make to attain something beautiful is ever lost." – Helen Keller

"It's not the critic who counts, not the one who points out how the strong man stumbled or how the doer of deeds might have done them better. The credit belongs to the man who is actually in the arena; whose face is marred with the sweat and dust and blood; who strives valiantly; who errs and comes up short again and again; who knows the great enthusiasms, the great devotions and spends himself in a worthy cause and who, at best knows the triumph of high achievement and who at worst, if he fails, at least fails while daring greatly so that his place shall never be with those cold and timid souls who know neither victory nor defeat." – Theodore Roosevelt

"Life achieves its summit when it does to the uttermost that which it was equipped to do." – Jack London

Activity

Below is a list of some of the top occupational areas in the USA. Circle all of the vocations that you would be willing to investigate, explore, or learn about.

Accountant	Marketing Specialist
Automotive Service	Nurse
Civil Engineer	Paralegal
Computer Analyst	Pharmacist
Database Administrator	Physical Therapist
Dental Hygienist	Physician, Surgeon
Electrical Engineer	Plumber
Employment, Recruitment	Program Management
Environmental Engineer	Public Relations
Financial Adviser	Radiology Technician
Firefighter	Real Estate Agent
Heating, Refrigeration	Retail Sales Representative
Information Technology	Secretary
Law Enforcement	Social Worker
Lawyer	Software Developer
Maintenance, Repair, Carpentry	Teacher

Which of the following fields of study seem interesting, or are worth looking into? Circle all that apply. These are things you should try, learn about, or explore further to see if you have interest or ability. Compare your selections to those above.

Agriculture	Geometry
Architecture	Government
Astronomy	Interior Design
Biology	Journalism
Bookkeeping	Law
Business	Literature
Chemistry	Manufacturing
Communications	Mathematics
Cooking	Mechanics
Computers	Medicine
Criminology	Military Science
Ecology	Nutrition
Economics	Photography
Education	Physics
Electronics	Politics
Engineering	Psychology
Fine Arts	Sociology
Forestry	Theater
Geology	Zoology

Creating a Vision

OBJECTIVE	Create a vision of hope; get a picture of it in your mind. Develop your vision by breaking it down into goals that would move you in the direction of realizing it.
INTERVENTION	Discuss what hope might look like. Identify what would make you happy, successful, or get you going in a positive direction. Develop an action plan that would facilitate making your dream or vision a reality. Identify the roadblocks that you may encounter along the way, especially the negative self-messages that are inhibiting your progress.
PLAN	Everyone's goal is to have a fulfilling, abundant, happy, and prosperous life. Imagine what that would entail and make it happen by establishing actions that could turn the possibilities into reality.

"Vision is the art of seeing the invisible." – Jonathan Swift

Do you dream? I am not talking about when you are asleep or when you daydream. I'm talking about having a dream or vision of the future – your future. How often do you take the time to look forward and envision what you might become or achieve by defining what success, happiness, and fulfillment might look like? What exactly do you wish for? Would you enjoy life better if it was more interesting, fulfilling, productive, challenging, stimulating, entertaining, or what? Figure out the what, and then try to get a picture of it in your mind. Once you can visualize the big picture you have developed a vision.

Everyone should have a vision or two, or more. I mean, who wants to remain where they are at and never move beyond? The status quo, the bare minimum, the everyday routine: it all gets very boring after a while, does it not? So go ahead and break away; move on, up, out, or along. Find a dream worthy of you and you will automatically have hope. Don't forget, however, that it starts with desire: a change of heart. That change will quickly lead to changing your mind; because if you want it bad enough you will believe it possible. As soon as you start believing it possible, you have hope.

"Destiny is not a matter of chance, but of choice. Not something to wish for, but to attain." – William Jennings Bryan

"Dissatisfaction and discouragement are not caused by the absence of things but the absence of vision." – Author Unknown

The first phase of the process to becoming, discovering, changing, or realizing is to create the vision. Get a picture of it in your head; maybe even diagram it on a piece of paper. Annotate the thought with words that describe what your dream looks like, sounds like, and feels like. Ask yourself: What do I value enough that is worth making a concerted effort to achieve? Do you seek education, vocation, intimacy, companionship, wisdom, self-actualization? Use your imagination. Remember, anything of value to you will provide the incentive and motivation to pursue it. But it isn't just going to show up on your doorstep; you have to make the effort; you have to persevere and never give up. It's mostly up to you whether it comes to pass or does not.

Continue to develop the vision by breaking it down into components, goals, steps, milestones, or however you are led in your heart. Embellish the dream by filling in the details. What would it take to pull it off? What goals, needs, or requirements must be met to succeed? How can you get from here to there? How long should it take if you are diligent and committed? Identify the prospects worth exploring and begin. Allow yourself some flexibility, however, because some options may not pan out. But when you discover the ones that fit your identity, personality, interests, and/or abilities – well that is the payoff. Such insight and opportunity is worth more than gold and will move you into action.

"Throughout the centuries there were men who took first steps, down new roads, armed with nothing but their own vision." – Ayn Rand

"Your vision will become clear only when you can look into your own heart. Who looks outside, dreams; who looks inside, awakens." – Carl Jung

"You cannot depend on your eyes when your imagination is out of focus." – Mark Twain

The next thing you need to do is identify and examine the roadblocks in your path to victory, especially the ones you have invented yourself. In particular, what negative messages are you sending to yourself that are sabotaging your own success? Do you think that it is hopeless, you can't cut it, it will be too hard, it's too late, or you don't know how? These self-destructive thoughts are simply untrue. So ask, what lies am I telling myself? Whatever lies you are telling yourself, tell yourself the opposite; after all, that is the real truth anyway. If you don't change your mind and subdue or defeat the negativity, your dream will be the casualty. Send yourself positive, uplifting messages and you will start obtaining a lot better results a lot faster.

Thus, as you are identifying the internal and external obstacles, begin by developing your battle plan to dismantle these barriers and get to work. Each roadblock you tear down, each hurdle you breach, each setback you overcome, each obstacle you dismantle will raise you higher and move you farther at the same time. This will build your confidence, trust, hope, determination, and self-esteem.

"As selfishness and complaint pervert the mind, so love with its joy clears and sharpens the vision." – Helen Keller

God has made it clear that he has a purpose for our lives, a destiny that fits into his plan to give us abundant life. And though he has put into place his grand design, and though you know that you fit into his great plan and he has a role for you to fulfill, still he gives you choices. Just make sure that your vision is consistent with his perfect will. If you are following the path of righteousness, then your vision will not pull you away or change your direction. And because it is in accordance with God's will he will help make it come to pass, but in his own time. So be patient; and everything will fall into place at precisely the correct time.

"It is very dangerous to go into eternity with possibilities which one has oneself prevented from becoming realities. A possibility is a hint from God. One must follow it." – Soren Kierkegaard

- HAB 2:2-3 ~ And the LORD answered me: "Write the vision; make it plain on tablets, so he may run who reads it. For still the vision awaits its appointed time; it hastens to the end – it will not lie. If it seems slow, wait for it; it will surely come; it will not delay."

- JER 29:11 ~ For I know the plans I have for you, declares the LORD, plans for welfare and not for evil, to give you a future and a hope.

- JOH 10:7-10,14-15 ~ Jesus said to them, "Truly, truly, I say to you, I am the door of the sheep. All who came before me are thieves and robbers, but the sheep did not listen to them. I am the door. If anyone enters by me, he will be saved and will go in and out and find pasture. The thief comes only to steal and kill and destroy. I came that they may have life and have it abundantly… I am the good shepherd. I know my own and my own know me, just as the Father knows me and I know the Father; and I lay down my life for the sheep."

Once you have created your prototype vision, start cultivating it. It will grow and evolve. Every time you get an idea or an inspiration, record it in your journal. Continue to enhance and enlarge the vision; watch the big picture come into focus as you put the pieces together. It may change or take a new course, but that's okay as long as it moves you forward and toward the face of God. It will be the most exciting journey of your life, knowing that your dream is in the making and God is leading you to it. If Christ is your partner he will use your abilities, your experience, your spirit, and your vision for the service of his kingdom. And just as he has inspired you, you will become an inspiration to others.

- DEU 30:15,19-20 ~ God sent this message to the Israelites: See, I present to you life and prosperity, or death and destruction. Today I have called heaven and earth as witnesses against you, that I have set before you these choices: life or death, blessings or curses. I recommend that you choose life, love the Lord your God, listen to His voice, and cling to Him; for He is your life. And He will give you many years in the land…
- PRO 3:5-6 ~ Trust the Lord with all your heart and do not lean on your own understanding. In all your ways acknowledge Him and He will make your paths straight.
- 1 CO 12:31 ~ If you eagerly desire the greater gifts, I will show you the most excellent way.
- PHP 4:13 ~ I can do all things through Christ who strengthens me.

"It don't matter where you're at 'cause you ain't there yet." – Andrew Barber

Activity

Begin to design your vision. Take time to meditate on it, and get a picture in your head of what hope, happiness, or success might look like. It helps to make a list of possibilities worth exploring; a list of things that you value, that you might find interesting, and that would motivate you to expend the effort.

_____

_____

_____

_____

_____

Recognize the obstacles in your path, to include those external to you and those that are within you. In particular, listen to the messages you are telling yourself. Are they encouraging or discouraging; positive or negative; getting you moving or getting you stuck? Paul wrote that we should think about things that are true, beautiful, uplifting, virtuous, and praiseworthy. Such things are in accordance with God's will. If you are thinking negative, destructive, or defeating thoughts, they are untrue.

_____

_____

_____

_____

_____

Identify some of the goals you need to attain, or tasks you must complete, or milestones that you must reach to get to your destination. These are stepping stones along the path going forward that point you in the right direction and facilitate your expedition. Allow this list to grow as God illuminates your path and your vision becomes clearer.

_____

_____

_____

_____

_____

A sample Gantt chart for developing the vision of hope is given below using the three stages described in the activity above. An example could be the American Dream: being a successful business person, living in your own home, with your spouse, kids, and pets. Continue to embellish the dream and let it evolve. As you detail each task and step, the dream begins to spring to life. It becomes more believable and possible, especially when you start executing (^) and completing (|) the tasks. The dream becomes even more real as you track your progress and get more of the hurdles behind you. Complete all the goals and the dream is realized. In the example below, the goal should be accomplished in about 3 ½ weeks.

GOAL: VISION OF HOPE

	Week 1	Week 2	Week 3	Week 4	Week 5
Calendar	S M T W T F S|	S M T W T F S|	S M T W T F S|	S M T W T F S|	S M T W T F S

Task 1 – Establish the Vision/Dream.
    ^-------------------|

Step 1 – Get a picture in your mind of what happiness might look like.
      ^----|

Step 2 – Draw a picture of it on paper: use diagrams, photographs, magazine cutouts, etc.
        ^-----|

Step 3 – Annotate the picture with a description of the sounds.
       ^----|

Step 4 – Describe how it feels by imagining yourself in the picture.
        ^---|

Task 2 – Analyze Anticipated Obstacles, Roadblocks, and Problems.
      ^---------------------------|

Step 1 – Identify negative self-messages that are untrue or self-defeating.
       ^----|

Step 2 – Identify internal barriers that must be overcome: fear, doubt, impatience, etc.
        ^----------|

Step 3 – Identify external barriers that may emerge: people, places, things.
         ^------|

Step 4 – Identify methods for removing barriers.
          ^------|

Task 3 – Breakdown the vision into components: goal, tasks, and steps.
       ^---|

Step 1 – Identify the goals or milestones that will keep you moving forward.
       ^------|

Step 2 – Break the milestones down into tasks and steps.
         ^-------------|

Step 3 – Identify tasks and steps for removing barriers (identified in Task 2).
          ^------|

Step 4 – Identify resources needed to accomplish tasks: people, time, finances, equipment.
            ^--------|

Step 5 – Prepare the Gantt Chart and document the overall game plan.
              ^-----|

161

Activity

To establish your vision/dream, draw a map or tree diagram. Begin at the roots and show how the path leads from where you are now all the way to the glory land, your ultimate destination. Include landmarks you wish to pass and milestones you wish to reach along the journey. Include any and all possibilities that are worthy of consideration: job fields, training or college degrees, marriage and family plans, and personal triumphs: past (roots), present (trunk), and future (branches).

ROOTS
Family
Friends
Support

TRUNK
Resources
Spirituality
Direction

BRANCHES
Education
Vocation
Marriage
Children

LEAVES
Growth
Productivity
Health

FRUIT
Prosperity
Becoming
Blossoming

VISION OF HOPE

Imagine Your
- Possibilities
- Opportunities
- Potential
- Destiny

IRRATIONAL THINKING

OBJECTIVE	Learn to stop and think before making choices or decisions. Examine irrational thought processes that lead to poor decisions and negative consequences, and practice mindfulness regularly.
INTERVENTION	Discuss fallacies of logic, distortions in thinking, and false beliefs that cause people to make bad choices, come to erroneous conclusions, and achieve poor outcomes.
PLAN	Identify where thinking is irrational, opinions are biased, and beliefs are false in order to revise them, thereby improving decision making and results. Become more scientific in gathering and interpreting information.

"It is not to be forgotten that what we call rational grounds for our beliefs are often extremely irrational attempts to justify our instincts." – Thomas Huxley

One of the prevailing themes of this text is that clients need to change their thinking about a great many things. Irrational thinking leads to errors in judgment, misunderstandings, and misperceptions. Oftentimes, if the person would take time to reconsider they would realize that they don't have all the facts, or what they thought was factual actually is not. People tend to assume too much. Everyone needs to be thoughtful in their decisions, plans, attributions, and assessments, and not just react. I have pointed out repeatedly to use reason not emotion. A reasonable person will do their research, look at the data objectively, and be careful about drawing inferences when the information is incomplete. This requires one to think first and then decide. Relationship problems, emotional pain, and mental health issues are often the direct result of irrational thought processes.

- ACT 2:1-13 (paraphrased) ~ On Pentecost, the disciples preached the Gospel and everyone present heard the preaching in their native tongue. But scoffers claimed the disciples were drunk, refusing to see the obvious miracle that had transpired before them. That assumption prevented them from listening to the message of salvation.

- ACT 16:22-34 (paraphrased) ~ The crowd attacked and beat Paul and Silas; and they were thrown into prison. But at midnight a great earthquake shook the prison and broke open the doors to the cells. The jail keeper awoke and saw the doors were open, and was about to kill himself, assuming the prisoners had fled and that he was in big trouble. He would have died had Paul not alerted him that they were still present. Not only was the man spared, he and his family became converted and gained the gift of eternal life. The jailer's assumption almost resulted in his death; he could have lost everything, including his soul.

- 1 TI 6:3-7 ~ If anyone teaches a different doctrine and does not agree with the sound words of our Lord Jesus Christ and the teaching that accords with godliness, he is puffed up with conceit and understands nothing. He has an unhealthy craving for controversy and for quarrels about words, which produce envy, dissension, slander, evil suspicions, and constant friction among people who are depraved in mind and deprived of the truth, imagining that godliness is a means of gain. But godliness with contentment is great gain, for we brought nothing into the world, and we cannot take anything out of the world.

Cognitive Behavioral Therapy was largely influenced by the work of Ellis and Beck, who correctly pointed out that distortions in beliefs and cognitions lead to a lot of problems. Their directive styles were designed to challenge clients to rethink how they look at the world, to modify their belief system and make it more reality-based, and develop appropriate cognitive skills with respect to observing their environment and gathering information. Many problems we create ourselves due to bad thinking or reasoning. Remember, we act on what we think. If we are negative in our mind, unproductive actions likely will follow. If we are wrong in our opinion or perception the wrong decision or conclusion ensues. The solution: seek truth and you are likely to change your mind.

An astute therapist will recognize when the client is inaccurate or incongruent in how he or she is responding, reacting, or assessing. A skilled therapist will challenge the client's belief system or thought process without being disrespectful or condescending. A persuasive therapist will help the client to objectively evaluate the alternatives, and will subtly steer the client in the direction of rational choices and attributions. The receptive client will learn to make decisions with mindfulness and confidence, and will take ownership of the decision and whatever consequences arise, positive or negative. These all contribute to responsible behavior. The objective is to capture each thought and maintain rational control over it.

- 2 CO 10:5 ~ Paul wrote: We destroy arguments and every lofty opinion raised against the knowledge of God, and take every thought captive to obey Christ.

Errors in Thinking

This chapter will address common errors in thinking. Many of these concepts overlap since they are all related to the same phenomenon: irrational decisions.

Overgeneralization: This occurs primarily because of poor sampling, which is the number and quality of observations upon which an opinion is based. Since the entire population cannot be observed, a representative subset of that population must suffice. But you wouldn't want to make presumptions about life in the USA by sampling only people on the west coast; that would not be a representative sample. When a scientist conducts an experimental study a reasonable sample size, usually more than thirty, is required; and that sample is drawn randomly so that all possible members of the population have equal chance of selection. And inferences drawn from those data are still viewed with caution. But the average individual bases opinions on his or her limited experience; that experience is seldom demonstrative of others, much less of an entire group or population of people. Just because something happened to a colleague, and your cousin, and your neighbor's friend, it doesn't imply there is a trend. A sample of three doesn't come close to being generalizable to anything. Even if you have experience with something and you have observed it occur 7 out of 10 times, that may not be a reliable trend. Now, 7/7 times, that could be a predictable trend at least for you, but maybe not applicable to someone else.

Your clients need to learn to be more objective in the way they monitor people, the environment, and events. If it happened before that is not evidence it will happen again, even if the circumstances are similar. If Sally won't go out with you, maybe Susie will. Besides, Sally may have a good reason; she may be sick, have another engagement, or may be bombarded with homework. The assumption that she must hate your guts is illogical, especially if she barely knows you (that's the reason you asked her out in the first place, because you wanted to get to know her). Even if she does hate your guts it doesn't mean that other girls do, much less everybody else in your school.

The most common form of overgeneralization is jumping to conclusions. The above example would fit the definition. Maybe you have heard this one. A jealous husband answers the phone and the other line hangs up just as he says hello; he realizes this has happened a few times before. He thinks about his wife coming home late from work last night, and how nice her boss treated her at the office party. Then there was the time her boss called on Saturday and she had to go into the office for a few hours. Immediately he draws the conclusion that she is having an affair with the boss. It all started with a suspicious call that was more easily explained as a prankster, wrong number, or telemarketing machine that already connected another call. He considered this to be supportive evidence of his suspicion when he had absolutely no hard evidence whatsoever.

A set of random events will not predict anything. A number of setbacks or failures do not imply that it's over or pointless. Like the gambler's fallacy suggests: several losses do not increase the probability of an impending win. The odds of a fair coin coming up heads is still 50/50 no matter how many times tails has occurred. Remember, do not assume or have preconceived expectations. For example, we can never know with certainty what another person thinks or feels, but most reasonable people will tell us if we ask them. I often warn clients about having unsupported expectations, especially negative ones where you are sure to create a self-fulfilling prophecy.

A lot of the world's problems are caused by overgeneralization, to include stereotyping, prejudice, and bigotry. Globally labeling a group of people based on limited exposure to them is akin to ignorance. Labeling often takes the form of establishing the identity of others based upon their failings and shortcomings, or any other characteristic deemed undesirable. I dislike labeling because it creates a stigma, like telling a child he or she has ADHD. Maybe the kid has it, maybe not; it's a speculative diagnosis. But it will likely cause him or her some distress and may result in the child becoming discouraged.

Cognitive Conceit: This is when we are too smart for our own good; we think we know it all so we're always right. Because we think we know so much we tend to seek only that information supportive of our opinions. This is known as confirmation bias; we give more credibility or weight to confirming evidence than to disconfirming evidence. Or, I may downright ignore evidence or opinions that do not agree with mine. Consider the source of the information and that will determine its reliability. If I find several reliable sources reporting the exact same thing, that information would be a lot more credible than something I saw on television, read in a tabloid, found on the Internet, or heard in the lunchroom. If a neurologist told you that you required brain surgery would you not seek a second or third opinion, or would you let the doctor commence to cut open your head? Insurance companies require preventative measures and precautions for such costly and risky procedures, and for good reason: reliability reduces risk and uncertainty which increase cost. Research has shown that people will ignore valid statistical evidence in favor of their own judgment or gut feeling. It's analogous to the lady who picked her horse to win because she likes the name, while her husband picked the statistical favorite. Unfortunately, the husband could be embarrassed when she wins simply because some events really do defy the laws of probability.

Another phenomenon called the knew-it-all-along effect is the notion that I knew something would happen that way, after it already happened. If you had asked me beforehand I may not have known with certainty what to expect; but I sure knew it after the fact. Ever heard someone say, I knew they would win the game, or lose the championship, or be the Super Bowl victor, or whatever? If they were that smart they should have bet the farm on their team before the season started. Another example is found in the cliché 20-20 hindsight. We have perfect vision when looking backwards; too bad it doesn't work that great when looking ahead. I should've, would've, could've… Well, since you didn't what are you going to do now?

People can be so wise in their own eyes. I've come across persons that think they are experts in all kinds of stuff. They speak with self-assurance about things they know little or nothing about. You can be discussing quantum physics with a professor and they'll chime in with their opinion on it. It is a sensible strategy to listen to those that are more knowledgeable and you might learn something. Certainly, if you are an expert in the field people can learn from you. But we can learn from anybody, even the fool, if we listen carefully.

Avoidance is a common defense of those exhibiting cognitive conceit. They are so sure of themselves that they refuse to listen to opposing arguments or opinions. They know the facts as they know them and that means people who disagree don't know. They will talk over you, ignore you, leave, change the subject, or insult you. They also use a defense mechanism called distraction. What they won't do is listen. Politicians are notorious at this. It aggravates me when they do it so I am forced to change the channel on them. I prefer to hear all sides of an argument before making up my mind. If I had to decide based on only those two, I would select the one that was respectful, not the one that was aggressive or impolite.

Freud's defense mechanisms represent a form of avoidance. We want to avoid the emotional pain associated with the memory or trauma because it hurts. It especially brings down the self-esteem when we feel responsible, or we think we are to blame due to the guilt we are feeling. That's why we don't want to think about it, so we repress it via rationalization, denial, projection, etc. It is far more therapeutic to process it than to repress it. That is, you must face your fears or you will be forever running from them.

- PRO 26:12 ~ Do you see a man who is wise in his own eyes? There is more hope for a fool than for him.

- ROM 12:3 ~ For by the grace given to me I say to everyone among you not to think of himself more highly than he ought to think, but to think with sober judgment, each according to the measure of faith that God has assigned.

Extreme Reasoning: For some people, everything is black and white; there is no gray area. It's either left or right, up or down, in or out, good or bad. For some, it is all or nothing. If it doesn't come out exactly right, throw it away and start over (or just give up). If I don't succeed I'm a failure. If I don't get my way I don't want to participate. I'm not satisfied with second best, or pretty good. If you're not 100% in agreement with me you might as well be in total disagreement. If I catch you in one lie I'll never be able to believe another word you say. If you get one fact wrong you have nothing more to say that I want to hear.

One of Beck's favorite words was catastrophizing (it's not in my dictionary). It's the end of the world; nothing is ever going to get better; it all adds up to a horrible catastrophe. For example, a client has an argument with his spouse, gets a speeding ticket trying to get to work on time, and then the boss asks him to come to the office. He's convinced he's about to be fired for being late again, but all the boss wants him to do is tackle an important task. But even that is a catastrophe. He thinks why me? Someone else can do the job. Life isn't fair. So he has a terrible day, all day, and everybody gets to hear about it. Your clients might believe their life is a living nightmare, but it is usually just a collection of minor setbacks. Even if there are major setbacks it could be worse. And it can always get better; but probably not overnight.

- 2 CO 4:8-10,16-18 ~ We are afflicted in every way, but not crushed; perplexed, but not driven to despair; persecuted, but not forsaken; struck down, but not destroyed; always carrying in the body the death of Jesus, so that the life of Jesus may also be manifested in our bodies... So we do not lose heart. Though our outer self is wasting away, our inner self is being renewed day by day. For this light momentary affliction is preparing for us an eternal weight of glory beyond all comparison, as we look not to the things that are seen but to the things that are unseen. For the things that are seen are transient, but the things that are unseen are eternal.

When we blow things out of proportion it is referred to as magnification (you're making mountains out of molehills my mother would say). Or maybe we trivialize it; this is minimization (it's a drop in the bucket my father would say). Of course, what is important to me may not be to you, and vice-versa. But if it is important to someone you care about then you ought to make it important to you. Besides, if it is trivial to you but important to your spouse, then it would be a small sacrifice for you to help him or her solve it (seeing how it's a small thing to you). But the payoff is well worth the effort when it is a big deal to your partner (you may get a big reward).

Narrow-mindedness is just as extreme. These people often concentrate on the negative side of things. They can find something wrong with just about anything. If it is 95% perfect they'll gripe about the 5% that isn't. I have seen so many clients constantly worrying about the "what ifs" in life; most of the time the probability of "if" is miniscule. They don't notice the excellent chance that "if" won't happen. Focus on what is, not what if. When you're preoccupied about something that might happen you're oblivious to what's happening right now. People get into such a negative state of mind they dismiss anything that has positive potential. It's as if they want to be miserable. So if you give them a compliment they'll believe you're hiding an ulterior motive. It's like having a one-track mind. To them, there's only one alternative and it's worthless.

Emotional reasoning is extreme. This is when a person bases an observation, decision, or conclusion on what he or she is feeling. Like the other examples in this discussion, such a leap is utterly unfounded. It's a form of jumping to conclusions. "Since I am feeling fearful something bad is about to happen." "I should be feeling better by now so I must be a hopeless case." "I feel guilty so that means I am to blame." "My parents are always fighting and threatening divorce; it must be my fault, there must be something wrong with me." "I think I'll stay in again today because if I go out I'll probably get stuck in traffic." Or one from King Solomon: "I can't go to work today; there could be a lion roaming the streets."

Extreme reasoning is flatly unreasonable, and people who are demanding are extreme. Heaven forbid that they should care about anybody else's feelings or needs. It gets back to the immediate gratification problem. They always come first. It's their way or the highway. Then there are those who are commanding. There is only one way of doing things: their way. They will watch you just to make sure, even if you have a better system that is more effective and/or efficient. These characteristics often surface after a relationship has formed. These people are some of the most difficult clients to work with, because they don't want to change their minds. There is nothing wrong with them. It's everybody else who is screwed up, right?

Reliability Errors: Information seeking must be systematic, organized, and as comprehensive as possible (if time permits). Most people base their decisions on a very narrow perspective and using limited resources. Research has shown that the most available information is seldom the most credible. More recent information will be readily available but not necessarily historically accurate. What makes it available is the fact that it is still fresh in your memory. Salient information which sticks out in your mind is available only because it had a profound impact, positive or negative. Frequently occurring events make information more available simply because the greater number of occurrences. And the primacy effect happens because the first occurrence is memorable. I will examine these factors in a simple example.

Let's say I want to evaluate what type of woman makes the best kisser: the independent variables include hair color, body type, age, and ethnicity. The measure of kissing effectiveness is the pleasure I derived from it. I distinctly remember my first real kiss (primacy) when I was about fifteen years old. I also remember my last kiss (recency) just before I left to work this morning. I recall one or two ladies who were either excellent kissers or terrible kissers (saliency). And I know how my wife kisses because I've kissed her more often than anybody else (frequency). If I base my analysis on these data my results will be skewed, because I am neglecting the dozens that I have kissed through the course of my lifetime. The fact is I can't even remember all the girls I've kissed; some I kissed only once, some I dated a few times, some I went with for months. Fortunately for me, it is an easy decision: my wife wins (or I'm in the doghouse).

The moral of the story is this: don't let your decision, opinion, or idea be constrained by only that information right at hand. It will not be an informed choice or a complete one. Don't confine yourself to one or two sources; seek multiple sources. When I was a graduate student, there were two major libraries available to me to conduct research. The nearest one had about 20% of the literature I sought; the farthest one had about 60% of it. If I had based my research efforts solely on convenience I would have missed out on a lot of good information. But with 80% of the facts I had a much broader understanding of the phenomenon I was investigating; and I produced a superior research paper as a result.

As I said before, you alone will not be a very reliable source. The more sources you look into the more you discover convergence and replication. For example, when studying the Bible you will find a great number of scriptures that deal with a particular topic. When you interpret scripture in light of scripture you get a very good appreciation for what the Bible is teaching; much better than just taking one or two passages out of context. A good example is in trying to understand the book of Revelation. If you read it in isolation you will not get the full extent of the meaning. It makes more sense to combine that reading with the study of the writings of other eschatological (end of times) prophets (such as Isaiah, Jeremiah, Ezekiel, Daniel, Joel, Micah, Zechariah, Paul, and Jesus). Pulling all these writings together you can begin to get a more thorough understanding. More witnesses equates to more reliability. Old Testament law required a minimum of two or three eyewitnesses to sentence someone to death (NUM 35:30; DEU 17:6; DEU 19:15; 2 CO 13:1; HEB 10:28). In the case of Christ, they screened several witnesses until they could find two false witnesses willing to lie so that the church leaders could execute him in accordance with their law (MAT 26:60).

Look at the hundreds of Old Testament prophecies about the coming of Messiah; then compare those to the story of Jesus in the New Testament. There are sources from different times, places, and languages yet all of their testimony comes together like a jigsaw puzzle. It is amazing how these prophets were able to describe the birth, life, ministry, death, and resurrection of Christ so comprehensively hundreds of years in advance. Well, it's not that amazing when you consider the source of that information: God Almighty. The point is, consider the sources of your information. How reliable are they? As for me, if I have God's Word on it – that is always good enough. In the Gospels, there are four that testify to the truth; and their testimony is in agreement.

- MAT 17:1-9 ~ And after six days Jesus took with him Peter and James, and John his brother, and led them up a high mountain by themselves. And he was transfigured before them, and his face shone like the sun, and his clothes became white as light. And behold, there appeared to them Moses and Elijah, talking with him. And Peter said to Jesus, "Lord, it is good that we are here. If you wish, I will make three tents here, one for you and one for Moses and one for Elijah." He was still speaking when, behold, a bright cloud overshadowed them, and a voice from the cloud said, "This is my beloved Son, with whom I am well pleased; listen to him." When the disciples heard this, they fell on their faces and were terrified. But Jesus came and touched them, saying, "Rise, and have no fear." And when they lifted up their eyes, they saw no one but Jesus only. And as they were coming down the mountain, Jesus commanded them, "Tell no one the vision, until the Son of Man is raised from the dead."

- 2 PE 1:16-21 ~ For we did not follow cleverly devised myths when we made known to you the power and coming of our Lord Jesus Christ, but we were eyewitnesses of his majesty. For when he received honor and glory from God the Father, and the voice was borne to him by the Majestic Glory, "This is my beloved Son, with whom I am well pleased," we ourselves heard this very voice borne from heaven, for we were with him on the holy mountain. And we have the prophetic word more fully confirmed, to which you will do well to pay attention as to a lamp shining in a dark place, until the day dawns and the morning star rises in your hearts, knowing this first of all, that no prophecy of Scripture comes from someone's own interpretation. For no prophecy was ever produced by the will of man, but men spoke from God as they were carried along by the Holy Spirit.

- 1 JO 4:6 ~ We are from God. Whoever knows God listens to us; whoever is not from God does not listen to us. By this we know the Spirit of truth and the spirit of error.

Misattribution: I discussed this subject in the Changes section, but I want to elaborate on it in more depth. We infer the intentions and motives of others after observing their actions. We evaluate the distinctiveness and consistency of their behavior and construe meaning via our perception of their traits and their objectives. These are examples of attributions. All too often, these attributions are wrong.

People are generally unscientific when it comes to making attributions or decisions. This is because they do not understand the various factors affecting the situation and contributing to the possible outcomes, not to mention the interrelationships among these variables. One example of this is the illusory correlation. You may think things are related because one follows the other or they occur coincident in time. This does not imply causality.

Take for example the young man who saw a black cat cross the road and then crashed his car into a ditch. He gets a ride in an ambulance and his car is towed to the impound lot. After a while he heals, gets the car fixed, and is back on the road. But when he approaches that same intersection he turns around, or takes another route. It is a way of avoiding the unpleasant memory. Then he starts avoiding black cats simply because the cat was there when the accident happened. It reminds him of the event also. Maybe he develops a full blown phobia of black cats; he associates them with mishaps. The fact of the matter, if he had been watching where he was going and not watching the cat, it never would have happened. The cat had nothing to do with the accident (or maybe black cats are out to get him).

Most of the time we just react without giving it much thought or analysis. It takes a lot of discipline to put your emotions aside and be an unbiased observer. It takes a lot of patience to gather sufficient evidence to increase certainty to a reasonable level. It takes a lot of effort to synthesize the data, perform a cost-effectiveness analysis, and select the alternative with the most merit. Simply put, information gathering requires work.

If you do not invest the time, resources, and effort how can you be sure of yourself? Well, sometimes you get lucky. But uncertainty equates to risk, and the less certain you are the less likely you will obtain the desired result. It gets back to the unrealistic expectations problem. My advice is: when in doubt, don't; gather more information. When you must decide and you are not sure, choose the least risky alternative. Information is power insofar as it reduces uncertainty; and this raises confidence. You make better choices when you are well-informed. And being correct likely will raise your self-esteem.

Misunderstandings frequently occur due to misinterpretation of the information. Someone says something that offends you though they didn't mean to; maybe it just didn't come out right. Or, maybe you didn't hear the entire message, or took part of it out of context, or just heard what you wanted to hear. Because we don't have all the facts we attribute causes that are irrelevant to the problem. "Sister made me do it," the little brother said when he got his hand caught in the cookie jar. Was the sister the primary cause, or the brother's yearning for a cookie? The devil does the same thing: throws the temptation into our path. But it is your choice to follow up on it, so don't say "the devil made me do it."

Talking about causality, what causes major depression? There are a myriad of factors. One of the most overlooked is chemistry. Repeated behaviors, experiences, trauma, drug use, or setbacks create variations in the chemistry of the brain. Many patients are embarrassed or ashamed to take medication because they don't understand that their illness is largely physiological. They'll attribute the cause to divorce, death, trauma, or whatever. While these things do bring us down, and we get depressed, the depression usually goes away after we have had time to heal. But there is rarely a single cause or event that triggers Major Depressive Disorder, which lasts a long time and returns every so often, sometimes without advanced notice or precipitating event. "I'm depressed because my mother died," the patient said. "After twenty years you are still depressed?" the therapist asked. The therapist thought to herself: This cannot be normal; something else must be going on. Yeah, maybe they've been bombarded with unpleasant memories for so long their chemistry is out of whack.

If you explore with your clients the alternatives, discuss the facts, and weigh the benefits against the costs, they will learn to make better decisions. Misattributions lead to blaming; people blame themselves, others, the devil, God, and the list goes on. Like I always say, the cause of suffering is sin, so if you want to blame anything blame that. By blaming others we blame ourselves, for we are just as guilty of sin as they are.

- LUK 6:37 ~ Jesus said, "Judge not, and you will not be judged; condemn not, and you will not be condemned; forgive, and you will be forgiven."

- ROM 2:1 ~ Therefore you have no excuse, O man, every one of you who judges. For in passing judgment on another you condemn yourself, because you, the judge, practice the very same things.

- 1 CO 4:3-5 ~ But with me it is a very small thing that I should be judged by you or by any human court. In fact, I do not even judge myself. For I am not aware of anything against myself, but I am not thereby acquitted. It is the Lord who judges me. Therefore do not pronounce judgment before the time, before the Lord comes, who will bring to light the things now hidden in darkness and will disclose the purposes of the heart. Then each one will receive his commendation from God.

Allow me one final word about superstitious behaviors, belief in old wives tales, consulting mediums, relying on astrological forecasts, following cult leaders, and practicing divination: such things will cloud your vision of truth and are a slight, indeed they are an abomination to God. There is nothing factual or credible about paranormal discovery, insight, or intuition. God, on the other hand, is the perfect and only trustworthy source of indisputable truth. If you seek such a revelation you will find it in God's Word. But you will not find such truth via a single "religious" experience or consulting a witch doctor.

- DEU 18:10-12 ~ There shall not be found among you anyone who burns his child as an offering, anyone who practices divination, tells fortunes or interprets omens, or a sorcerer, charmer, medium or necromancer, or one who inquires of the dead.

- PRO 30:5-6 ~ Every word of God proves true; he is a shield to those who take refuge in him. Do not add to his words, lest he rebuke you and you be found a liar.

- ISA 47:10-14 & JER 10:2-3 (paraphrased) ~ You felt secure in your wickedness. But evil shall come upon you and disaster will befall you. So stand fast in your enchantments, sorceries, and counsels. Let them save you, those who gaze at the stars, divide the heavens, and predict what will happen to you according to the new moon. Fire will consume them and you... Don't learn the ways of unbelievers or be dismayed by signs in the heavens, for the customs of the people are false.

- ACT 17:16,22-28 ~ While Paul was in Athens, his spirit was provoked within him as he saw that the city was full of idols... Standing in the midst of the Areopagus, Paul said, "Men of Athens, I perceive that in every way you are very religious. For as I passed along and observed the objects of your worship, I found also an altar with this inscription, 'To the unknown god.' What therefore you worship as unknown, this I proclaim to you. The God who made the world and everything in it, being Lord of heaven and earth, does not live in temples made by man, nor is he served by human hands, as though he needed anything, since he himself gives to all mankind life and breath and everything. And he made from one man every nation of mankind to live on all the face of the earth, having determined allotted periods and the boundaries of their dwelling place, that they should seek God, and perhaps feel their way toward him and find him. Yet he is actually not far from each one of us, for in him we live and move and have our being, as even some of your own poets have said, 'We are indeed his offspring.'"

- COL 2:8,18-19 ~ See to it that no one takes you captive by philosophy and empty deceit, according to human tradition, according to the elemental spirits of the world, and not according to Christ... Let no one disqualify you, insisting on asceticism and worship of angels, going on in detail about visions, puffed up without reason by his sensuous mind, and not holding fast to the Head, from whom the whole body, nourished and knit together through its joints and ligaments, grows with a growth that is from God.

Decision Making

Decision making is not a simple task. It stands to reason that a complex decision should not be based upon a simple analysis. There are a multitude of factors that affect decisions. The more capable you are at identifying the factors involved, and determining their relative contribution to the desired outcome, the better results you will get. While each situation brings a variety of conditions that affect your choices, there are three factors that are present in almost every decision-making situation: outcomes, risk, and time. Let us analyze each of these briefly and apply them to a hypothetical decision task.

First, we'll consider consequences, or outcomes. They can be good or bad. Every alternative has a possible set of outcomes. If you add up all the positives and subtract all the negatives you will get a relative outcome value for each alternative. It could result in an overall plus or a minus. Clearly, any possible choice resulting in a minus becomes very unattractive, unless the choice is among a bunch of minuses in which case you'll be inclined to select the least negative option. What people typically do is arrange the alternatives in order of relative outcome value and select the top one. They tend to simplify the problem by selecting the best payoff but that is illogical, especially when one considers the relative risks. People seldom consider the risk when they're putting their money on the lottery, for example.

Risk equates to uncertainty; it is the inverse of the probability of getting the desired outcome. In the case of the lottery, the chances of winning are, say about 1/100,000,000. Thus, the risk is extraordinarily high. It is common to deceive oneself into thinking of bettering the chances by buying five lottery tickets. Congratulations, you have increased your chances to 1/20,000,000. You have a better chance of being struck by lightning twice. If you spend a buck for a jumbo candy bar, the outcome isn't nearly as good as winning $100M, but the probability that you'll enjoy it for five minutes is better than 95%.

Some people focus only on outcome, others focus only on risk. They will look at the relative chances of each alternative and just pick the one with the best chance, regardless of outcome value. There are people who simply are not willing to take any risks. You won't see them investing in the stock market, that's for sure. But you'll never get anywhere if you're not willing to take some risks. Just don't be stupid about it, like gambling away your entire paycheck every week hoping to hit the jackpot so you can quit working.

It's easy to see how outcome and risk interact. If there are two alternatives that have the same outcome value, the least risky one will be more attractive. With risks being equal the one with the most valuable outcome becomes the easy choice. But what if outcome values vary among alternatives and so do risk values? You want to maximize your benefit and minimize your risk. One shouldn't focus solely on outcome or risk, but both together. However, that takes a lot more mental resources, and time.

Benefit and certainty also interact with time. People are willing to incur the cost of insurance to protect them from the risk of an automobile accident. While the probability of having a wreck is very low in the near term, it increases over the long term. We pay the premiums month after month so we won't get blitzed by an unexpected loss which may never occur. Sure, you risk losing your investment, but only if you never have to face a significant

174

loss later. It is worth the cost to reduce or remove that risk, unless you drive a jalopy in which case you probably only need the liability insurance.

The risks in the near term are not the same as the long term. Neither are the outcomes. If I want to have fun this weekend and I spend my entire paycheck partying it'll be quite a gala. But what am I going to use to pay the bills at the end of the month? There won't be enough left even for groceries. In that case, the immediate outcome wasn't nearly as big a positive as the overall outcome was a negative. When it comes to my retirement, I am putting away a little money now but it will build up over time; when I get older, it'll be quite a nest egg. It's like insurance: a little cost now with the possibility of a bigger payoff later.

Examine the following table. If we were to pick an alternative based on outcome alone, C would be the obvious choice. If we picked based on confidence (inverse of risk) alone, A would be the clear choice. But if we look at these two variables together (the interaction of outcome and confidence) B would stand out because it has a reasonable outcome value with acceptable certainty.

Alternative	A	B	C
Outcome	.4	.7	.8
Confidence	.8	.7	.4
Combined	.6	.7	.6

Here's a hypothetical decision: who am I going to accompany at the prom. The candidates are as follows: Bachelorette A is captain of the cheerleaders (or captain of the football team depending on your preference); Bachelorette B is a friend that I've known since the sixth grade; Bachelorette C is someone that is rumored to have a crush on me. Let's scrutinize each candidate using the above factors. For the purposes of this exercise we'll assume that all other factors are equal. Therefore, attractiveness, possibility of accepting the date, or any other features that may be pertinent will be controlled for this study.

First we'll look at outcome value alone. Now I'm just an ordinary guy. Being seen at the prom with the cheerleader (candidate A) would definitely be a boost to my ego. But the bigger payoff is that everybody is going to think I'm cool; my popularity will increase because of my increased visibility. Even if we don't hit it off, my social life will get a lift and it may open up more opportunities. The desired outcome is not to find a lover, it's to make an impression. So I'm going to rate that date a 6 on outcome. Candidate B is someone I've gotten to know over the years; some of her friends know my friends, so we're always running into each other at get-togethers. We have hung out some and are friends but I've never asked her out. I figure we'll probably have fun even if we don't make a love connection so I'll give her an 8. Miss C is a mystery. I don't really know her though I've seen her around and had a class or two with her. That she might like me already is a plus for her, but that scares me a little. What if she's psycho or something? Still she intrigues me a little, but since we may not have much in common I'll have to give her a 6. So, Bachelorette B wins round one.

Now let's assess the candidates focusing on confidence (remember, high confidence means low risk). Bachelorette A is relatively low risk. I mean, what have I got to lose? Even if she ditches me at the prom the objective was met: everybody saw us together. The girls are going to wonder what makes me so special as to attract her in the first place. I'll give her a 7. Miss B, however, is higher risk. Since I don't want to lose her as a friend maybe I shouldn't jeopardize our friendship by taking her to the prom. There will be other opportunities to date her in a less public setting. She may assume that it's just a friendly date, so if I fall for her I could get burned. I'll have to give her a 5 because there's a little uncertainty there. Now the mystery girl, she is a little risky also. What if she falls for me and I don't feel the same about her? How am I going to gracefully cut her loose without hurting her? I don't really know her, what if we have absolutely nothing in common? Since I'm still a little apprehensive, I'm going to give Miss C a 6 on confidence. So, A wins round two.

Now we'll throw in time (near versus long term) and look at all three variables together, and how they interact. This will be the final round when I have to make a selection. Thinking about A, I realize that the outcome value fades over time. The visibility helps in the short term but people will forget. Besides, my popularity depends on me, and if I generated interest initially it could fade rapidly. Risk doesn't really change that much over time with Miss A. However, if she goes around and tells everyone what a dull date I was then the long term outcome value really drops. Her overall score is a 4; there simply is not much value in the long run. With Miss B the effect of time is most profound. Since we're friends already, I'd much rather wait until later to ask her out than going to the prom on our first date. That would be like putting all my eggs in one basket. I could invite her for coffee someday when we're hanging out, and we could get to know each other better. There will be other opportunities to see if there is a love connection. I want to reduce the risk of blowing it with her and threatening our friendship. Still, she gets a better grade than Miss A, so I'll give Miss B a 5. Turning to Miss C, there is a huge effect of time. To begin with, the risk fades practically to zero over time. Like, I really have nothing to lose here. Maybe we don't hit it off, or she is stalker, or whatever; it'll get resolved in time. The outcome value goes up significantly over time for the mystery girl. Maybe we don't make a love connection but I gain a friend. Or maybe I gain a lover, or both. If none of this happens I still haven't lost anything. And if we don't hit it off I still can pursue Miss B. I have much to gain and little to lose. Thus, Miss C wins with an overall score of 8. She will be my escort to the prom; she's probably waiting by the phone even as we speak.

The table below shows the result of my thought experiment. Notice how I changed my mind each time I introduced another variable. And then, when I considered all three factors together, I was surprised that Miss C was the clear frontrunner.

Bachelorette	A	B	C
Outcome	.6	.8	.5
Confidence	.8	.5	.6
Time Added	.4	.5	.8
Total Score	18	18	19

To be objective in complex decisions you need to look at the multivariate aspects of the decision. We can look at one variable and decide like many people do; and we probably won't make the right choice, but we'll never know. If we look at two variables we have a basic Analysis of Variance design: main effect of A, main effect of B, interaction effect AB. That design would resemble a square. Looking at all three variables together produces a three dimensional design resembling a cube: A, B, C, AB, AC, BC, ABC.

Employ this decision analysis technique using a spreadsheet to list your alternatives (horizontal axis) and your factors (vertical axis). Ascribe relative weights to factors with respect to how important each is: how much each contributes to strengths or weaknesses of the choices. Some factors may have the same weight; or one may be twice as important as another, and so on. Next rate (say from 1-10) each alternative on each factor in terms of the degree to which that choice possesses that attribute. Then multiply weights times ratings, and sum them across all variables to achieve a composite score for each alternative. The option with the highest total score is a good choice. A computer makes this process quick and easy.

Say you want to buy a car and you're interested in cost, style, color, gas mileage, durability, extras, comfort, etc. Weigh the importance of each criterion and rate the alternatives on them. For me, economy (cost and gas mileage) is very important, comfort next. Extras would probably be lowest as I'm not into frills or gadgets in my car; more expensive cars have more extras. I rate design and color choices about equal. Maybe I find two cars that have the same gas mileage, but one costs less. I'd probably go with the less expensive model as cost rules. I bought a car with good gas mileage, which is comfortable, affordable, has a few extras, and just happened to come in a color I liked. It also had extra steel added for reinforcement in case of a collision, reducing insurance costs and increasing durability. I don't need all that glitzy stuff as it only makes the car a target for thieves, and the insurance goes way up. All I want is to get around safely, comfortably, and economically and I found a car that meets all these criteria.

When you compute the results of your decision analysis, one or two alternatives should stand out in terms of the degree to which they meet your specifications. You can convert your data in such a way as to produce a percentage score; it will give you an estimate of the relative distance between each alternative in terms of total scores. All you have to do is set up your spreadsheet, plug in the numbers, and the computer will calculate the scores. It is very objective, considers all the available data, and reduces the risk of making a bad choice.

Virtually every decision is multidimensional. When you practice analytical approaches to decision making you train your brain to think in more than one dimension. It's a way of tapping into the greater capability afforded by the unconscious: multifaceted thinking, data organization and reduction, and parallel processing. Decision analysis is an excellent way to impartially evaluate alternatives, and make informed, educated decisions. This leads to more confidence, better outcomes, and more contentment. This technique is similar to so-called fuzzy set logic used in computer modeling. Empirical data are plugged in, a computer algorithm crunches the data, and a predicted outcome is produced. While the result isn't totally concrete, it helps decision makers examine the alternatives objectively.

"Thinking is the hardest work there is, which is the probable reason why so few engage in it."
– Henry Ford

Activity

Everyone has engaged in irrational thinking one time or another. What forms of irrational thinking have you engaged in and how? Give examples from your experience. Refer to the table in this section for ideas, or use the ones suggested below.

Overgeneralization _____

_____

Extreme Reasoning _____

_____

Cognitive Conceit _____

_____

Reliability Errors _____

_____

Misattribution _____

_____

Superstition _____

_____

How did these mistakes in thinking or judgment create problems in your life?

1. Problems in Relationships (spouse, children, parents, friends, boss)

_____

_____

_____

_____

_____

_____

How did these mistakes in thinking or judgment create problems in your life (continued)?

2. Identity Problems

_____

_____

_____

3. Self-Esteem Problems

_____

_____

_____

4. Self-Control Problems

_____

_____

_____

5. Spiritual Problems

_____

_____

_____

6. Lost Opportunities

_____

_____

_____

- Overgeneralizing
- Inference Errors
- Insufficient Data
- Selective Sampling
- Jumping to Conclusions
- Preconceived Notions
- Global Labeling
- Stereotyping
- Cognitive Conceit
- Confirmation Bias
- Ignoring Evidence
- Knew It Already Mentality
- 20/20 Hindsight
- Avoidance Behavior
- Extreme Reasoning
- All or Nothing Thinking
- Catastrophizing
- Magnification/Minimization
- Narrow Mindedness
- One-Track Mind
- Emotional Reasoning
- Reliability Errors
- Availability Errors
- Flimsy Sources
- Misattributions
- Illusory Correlation
- Perceptual Bias
- Superstition

IRRATIONAL THINKING

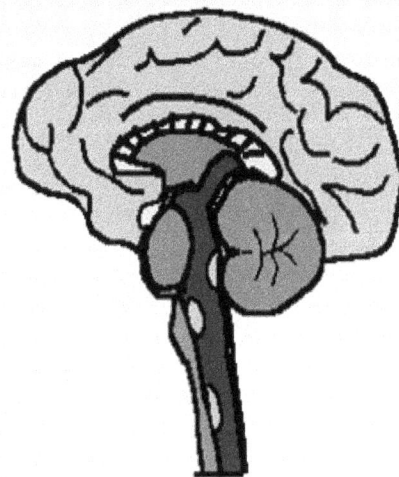

Reality Testing

OBJECTIVE	Introduce the process of being mindful of detrimental or fallacious thoughts by testing their validity in light of what is real and true. Properly discriminate between real and unreal, true and untrue to eliminate confusion prior to acting or reacting. Realize the various ways that negative or irrational thinking contribute to bad decisions and maladaptive behaviors.
INTERVENTION	Examine thoughts, behaviors, and their relationships, especially when they are counterproductive. Determine when and how the thoughts should be modified so that they are consistent with reality prior to deciding or responding.
PLAN	Practice reality testing regularly in order to develop healthy habits such as thoughtfulness, rational thinking, and rejecting irrelevant or irrational patterns of thinking and behavior.

"Reality is that which, when you stop believing in it, doesn't go away." – Philip Dick

"To treat your facts with imagination is one thing, but to imagine your facts is another." – John Burroughs

Reality testing finds its roots in Freud's theory of the personality. Recall that the components of that theory were the id, ego, and superego. The id is governed by the pleasure principle; it seeks immediate gratification of desires and needs. The ego is governed by the reality principle; its purpose is to ensure that societal norms are not violated during the expression of the id. When one's behavior goes against social rules the superego, which is governed by the morality principle, steps in and punishes the ego with guilt. Thus, there is a mental process whereby we choose appropriate behaviors in accordance with the norms and prohibitions of society. In the Motivation section we tied the idea of self-esteem and ego strength to getting our needs met; that is what drives our behavior as Maslow pointed out. When we conduct the reality check we are essentially performing a costs-benefits analysis. We are looking at the pros and cons of a given action in light of possible good or bad outcomes. This brief delay in executing the action is a form of mindfulness.

"Illusions commend themselves to us because they save us pain and allow us to enjoy pleasure instead. We must therefore accept it without complaint when they sometimes collide with a bit of reality against which they are dashed to pieces." – Sigmund Freud

"I can feel guilty about the past, apprehensive about the future, but only in the present can I act. The ability to be in the present moment is a major component of mental wellness." – Abraham Maslow

Cognitive theorists such as Beck, Ellis, and Glasser incorporated these notions into their models and therapeutic approaches; the goal was to enable people to gain insight into the fallacies of their thinking. Beck was a psychiatrist and one of the first to propose cognitive-behavioral interventions such as challenging and analyzing thoughts and behaviors. He identified common cognitive distortions that influenced people to misinterpret reality and make mistakes in judgment. Poor decisions were the result of errors in thinking that could easily be corrected with awareness training and reinforcement. Ellis also broke ground with the development of his rational-emotive technique. He observed that people obtain unsatisfactory results largely because of the irrational beliefs upon which their actions are founded. This is due to misinterpretation of events that affect one's life, which are common to everyone though viewed differently. Ellis would challenge a client's belief system when it was irrational or based on erroneous information, and guide that person towards corrective thinking and behavior modification. Glasser introduced reality therapy as a way to encourage people to stay connected to the here and now. Largely behavioral in concept, the supposition was that everyone wants to get their needs met, but achieving that end is mostly up to them. They need to take control rather than yield it. That is, people have the power to choose, not just behaviors, but thoughts, feelings, attitudes, and yes, reality. Reality testing is an effective therapeutic approach that instructs clients how to redirect emotional energy, positive or negative, in a constructive and appropriate manner. It reinforces the practice of basing behaviors on rationality rather than emotionality.

Reality Tests

Right / Wrong

True / False

Real / Unreal

Reason / Emotion

Belief / Disbelief

Sure / Unsure

Rational / Irrational

Objective / Subjective

Productive / Unproductive

Positive / Negative

Honest / Dishonest

Clearly, there are many variations to this technique, such as differentiating between reality and fantasy, fact and fiction, bad and good, evidence versus bias, conceptualization or imagination. All of the categories listed overlap to some degree, and yet are unique in other ways. Thus, there are any number of ways to use reality testing for thoughtful evaluation of patterns of thinking, alternative behaviors, and likely consequences (positive or negative). It is a trade-off analysis in which relative costs and benefits are examined prior to deciding, speaking, or acting. The practice of reality testing can benefit every client and can be applied to any diagnosis, not to mention its value to the therapist.

The therapist helps the client to identify ineffective or destructive patterns of thinking and behavior. They can perform thought experiments to analyze future scenarios in terms of the probable effects of various approaches, as the client learns how to role play in his or her mind. They discuss conventional reality, social norms, and verifiable truths. Together they examine how internal processes are leading to inaccurate perceptions, poor judgments, unrealistic expectations, maladaptive behaviors, and/or negative results. The two also examine situational context and extenuating circumstances; they evaluate knowledge of results associated with diverse strategies, when particular words are spoken, or after hypothetical or real actions are taken.

The client will soon recognize not only his or her bad habits, but also what the rational mind should think, and what the appropriate response should be, given the available facts. The therapist provides constructive feedback based on sound analysis, factual data, and accepted moral standards. By learning more adaptive patterns of thinking, deciding and behaving, the individual becomes more willing to act, achieves greater success, and is more aware, thoughtful, and resourceful. This will result in raising their self-esteem, confidence, and happiness; and probably raising the bar with respect to personal standards of morality or performance. Three important reasons to perform this self-check are to determine: the degree to which a choice is in accordance with personal standards of behavior or performance; the degree to which the decision benefits the individual, group or corporation; and the degree to which the preferred alternative supports the greater good of the family, society, or humanity.

The feedback aspect, which is a principle aspect of knowledge of results, makes reality testing a particularly effective intervention during group therapy. Participants can discuss social norms and expectations, they can challenge one another's beliefs; they can provide insight and analysis into theirs' and others' thinking, beliefs, and behaviors; they can perform role play functions, and they can act as peer counselors to reinforce appropriate and acceptable responses.

"Nothing ever becomes real until it is experienced." – John Keats

Applications

There are a number of possible applications to reality testing, including treatment of anxiety-related disorders (OCD, phobia, panic disorder, PTSD), psychosis (delusions, hallucinations), anger management, and suicidal depression. Obviously, the degree of pathology will affect the length of treatment, and the amount of practice required to remain in touch with the here and now. In short, the person needs to be reoriented to person, place, time, space, and/or situation repeatedly in order to reconfigure their internal processes and programming, by attributing new responses to well-established triggers, and other preconditions. Some clinical examples are provided below.

While treating a Vietnam veteran with PTSD in an inpatient setting, we developed a plan to test reality whenever he had a flashback. Loud noise was one of his major triggers; he would hit the floor as if being in a firefight in the jungle. This was especially problematic when the maintenance people were testing the building's alarm system. He would immediately form a perimeter with the furniture and would not let anyone penetrate that barrier. I would get on the floor with him in the prone position after helping him build the perimeter, so he would identify me as a "friendly". Then I would walk him through the reality check by appealing to each of his senses. We would feel around on the ground to realize the floor was too hard and smooth to be the jungle. I would appeal to his sight, pointing out tables and chairs. I would draw his attention to the television or other sounds; we would examine the odors which were incongruent with the smell of a battlefield. I would help him examine all sensory input until he could verify that none of them were consistent with combat. Eventually, this routine replaced his usual behavior of establishing a perimeter around him to create a safe zone. I used a similar technique with a soldier of the Iraq war, who had frequent night terrors. It would scare the daylights out of his wife when he would spring up in a deep sleep and engage in defensive behavior. Planning with his wife, they practiced some reality checks so she could walk him through the process at a comfortable pace and reorient him to where he was and who she was. Since he responded to auditory stimuli, she would whisper his name softly a few times to reconnect him to her voice before gently touching his hand. Unfortunately, I never found out whether they were able to repair the damage that his illness was causing their marriage. In dealing with PTSD, specific routines can be established that will tether the individual to the present. In another case, it was as simple as turning the wedding band on the husband's ring finger.

I use reality testing a lot with patients exhibiting phobias or OCD. In either case, the individual engages in avoidance behavior. For the phobic, it is a matter of avoiding the feared object or event that causes the anxiety to escalate. For the obsessive-compulsive, they avoid the anxiety by engaging in the compulsive behavior (rearranging objects, washing hands, or whatever). The action in both cases gives them temporary relief from the anxiety which only serves to reinforce the avoidance behavior. The best treatment for any kind of avoidance behavior, whether due to OCD, PTSD, or phobia is exposure therapy. Clients need to build up more tolerance for the thing they fear, and that means having to face it. Little by little they get stronger and the effect gets weaker, just like when addicts experience greater tolerance for their drugs: more drugs equals less pleasure. Getting the individual to allow themselves greater exposure is where reality testing comes in; they have to admit the irrational nature of the behavior. They retrain their brain to remember that the memory, object, or situation is not to be feared. This is accomplished by exploring the truth through research and evaluation. A fear of the unknown is overcome with additional knowledge; most fears are irrational and the beliefs are usually founded on poor and incomplete information. For instance, a child with school phobia can conquer it via exposure to the classroom using systematic desensitization, whereby he or she becomes less sensitive and more tolerant to that environment.

Applied to anger or stress management, reality testing again takes the form of information gathering. For example, if the husband is always getting mad at the wife because she is pushing his buttons, the two can examine together exactly what each perceives about the situation. I point out how both individuals are acting on the basis of their own state of mind or emotion, and not the other person's. Everybody chooses their own emotional states, so responses such as frustration, anger, aggravation, or irritability are the result of being in a bad mood that we ourselves created. That is to say, she is not responsible for the way he thinks or feels, and vice-versa. Seldom does a person act deliberately to make another angry or upset. If that is the case, then the one causing the friction needs a reality check because his or her behavior is outside the ethical norm. Some problems, misunderstandings, and arguments are the result of poor communication. Clarification, feedback, and information sharing reduces such occurrences significantly just by examining the facts of the matter.

In treating psychosis, it is a matter of discriminating between reality and unreality. Usually, the psychotic client knows that the voices are in his/her head, or the shadowy figures are not real people, or there are no visible bugs to support the feeling they are crawling all over him/her. That is, most of the time they are accustomed to the intrusive thoughts or perceptions and can recognize when they are present. In extreme cases, they may be totally unaware that their behavior is out of touch with reality; such individuals will need a lot more training and convincing for them to realize that they have lost contact with the world. Along with medication, the most important intervention for the psychotic person is reality testing. In combination, medication and reality testing facilitate the learning process. Clients can dismiss the intrusive hallucinations and focus on the correct sensory stimuli; they can rethink the delusions and establish beliefs that are consistent with the truth and the real world. Like every other example, we are talking learning and practice.

Suicidal ideation is a great application for reality testing. The amazing success of suicide hotlines lies in the ability of the operator to engage clients in conversation, and help them identify viable alternatives, examine collateral damage and other repercussions; assist them in rethinking anything and everything, and negotiate a compromise. Like most emotional states, suicidal depression waxes and wanes, so time itself is often sufficient to ease the client towards another direction; all you have to do is to keep them engaged. The very fact they tell someone or call the hotline is because they are reaching out for such an intervention: someone to talk them out of it using reason, truth, and compassion. Certainly, the reality that they are loved unconditionally by Almighty God should help them realize how important they are, and how precious is human life such that our Lord would die for them.

Group therapy is certainly an excellent setting to delve into topics like socially unacceptable actions, unreasonable conclusions or expectations, irrational beliefs, and unverifiable facts; or conversely, topics such as absolute truth, moral behavior, logical explanations, credible evidence, and commonly held beliefs. In groups, whenever someone speaks, behaves, or shares opinions that are illogical or self-destructive, they are typically challenged by enough of their peers to rethink things. Often such interactions are more compelling than just hearing it from the therapist. It is even more fun when role playing is incorporated and persons can see how they come across by witnessing others engaging in the same fallacies in thinking and behavior. The open climate encourages participation, conversation, and sharing. This enables participants to sharpen their cognitive skills. Activities and exercises can be incorporated that promote reality testing, and they always stimulate very interesting, positive, and directional discussions.

"Courage is not simply one of the virtues but the form of every virtue at the testing point, which means at the point of highest reality." – C. S. Lewis

One Final Note

There is another reality check that should be considered, and that is God's reality. Yes, we need to be connected to our reality and stay grounded in the here and now. But we also need to remain connected to God who exists outside of this reality. We need to acknowledge that, though we do not see him, he is always there with us to guide our actions and direct our paths. God is the source of all wisdom and truth; so everything we see and hear must be checked against what he reveals to us by the power of his Spirit, especially through his Word. We need to do the spirit check on anything that seems real but maybe isn't.

- JOB 38:2,4,33,36 & JOB 40:2 (paraphrased) ~ God was speaking to Job when he said, "Who obscures wise counsel using words void of knowledge? Where were you when I laid the foundations of the earth? Tell me if you understand. Do you know the ordnances of heaven? Can you establish dominion upon the earth? Who put wisdom in the inward parts or gave understanding to the mind? Will anyone contend with the Almighty to instruct him? He that criticizes God, let him answer these questions."
- LAM 3:40 ~ Let us test and examine our ways, and return to the LORD!
- 1 CO 2:7-16 ~ But we impart a secret and hidden wisdom of God, which God decreed before the ages for our glory. None of the rulers of this age understood this, for if they had, they would not have crucified the Lord of glory. But, as it is written, "No eye has seen, nor ear heard, nor the heart of man imagined, what God has prepared for those who love him" – these things God has revealed to us through the Spirit. For the Spirit searches everything, even the depths of God. For who knows a person's thoughts except the spirit of that person, which is in him? So also no one comprehends the thoughts of God except the Spirit of God. Now we have received not the spirit of the world, but the Spirit who is from God, that we might understand the things freely given us by God. And we impart this in words not taught by human wisdom but taught by the Spirit, interpreting spiritual truths to those who are spiritual. The natural person does not accept the things of the Spirit of God, for they are folly to him, and he is not able to understand them because they are spiritually discerned. The spiritual person judges all things, but is himself to be judged by no one. For who has understood the mind of the Lord so as to instruct him? But we have the mind of Christ.
- 1 CO 4:16-17 ~ Paul wrote: I urge you, then, be imitators of me. That is why I sent you Timothy, my beloved and faithful child in the Lord, to remind you of my ways in Christ, as I teach them everywhere in every church.
- GAL 1:8 ~ But even if we or an angel from heaven should preach to you a gospel contrary to the one we preached to you, let him be accursed.
- HEB 11:1,3 ~ Now faith is the assurance of things hoped for, the conviction of things not seen. By faith we understand that the universe was created by the word of God, so that what is seen was not made out of things that are visible.
- JAM 1:8 ~ A double-minded man is unstable in all his ways.
- 1 JO 4:1-4 ~ Beloved, do not believe every spirit, but test the spirits to see whether they are from God, for many false prophets have gone out into the world. By this you know the Spirit of God: every spirit that confesses that Jesus Christ has come in the flesh is from God, and every spirit that does not confess Jesus is not from God. This is the spirit of the antichrist, which you heard was coming and now is in the world already. Little children, you are from God and have overcome them, for he who is in you is greater than he who is in the world.

EFFECTIVE COMMUNICATION

OBJECTIVE	Learn effective communication skills and how to be a good listener and observer. Learn how to deliver and receive messages in ways that enhance understanding.
INTERVENTION	Discuss different aspects of communication, to include verbal and nonverbal, and how they contribute to or distract from a message.
PLAN	Practice these skills to improve communications and reduce misunderstandings, and recognize your communication styles via self-monitoring.

"Speech is power: speech is to persuade, to convert, to compel. It is to bring another out of his bad sense into your good sense." – Ralph Waldo Emerson

"Do not say a little in many words but a great deal in a few." – Pythagoras

Everybody can benefit from communication skills training, not just clients but also therapists. In this chapter we will dissect components of communication and explore methods of communicating effectively. Keep in mind that knowing your audience also will determine the manner in which the communication is, or should be, conveyed.

Verbal Communication

- ➤ Active listening
- ➤ Think before you speak
- ➤ Be concise
- ➤ Speak slowly, clearly
- ➤ Control the volume
- ➤ Own the message
- ➤ Feedback
- ➤ Ask questions (wait for an answer)
- ➤ Reflective listening
- ➤ Know your audience

Communication is a two-way street. The lion's share is listening. People have a habit of tuning out a large percentage of a conversation, whether because there are other things on their mind, they are not very interested, they are distracted, they try to anticipate what the other person is going to say, or they are anxious to respond. Learn to be an active listener. Pay attention, convey that you are paying attention, and wait for the speaker to finish before you reply or change the subject. Verify what you heard and give them a chance to rebut.

Transmission of the message leaves a lot to be desired. People are not particularly careful about putting together the message, wording it, and delivering it. Thus, misinterpretations are commonplace. More on this can be found in the Assertiveness chapter, which details the proper way of expressing oneself in a way that produces optimum results.

Usually, the verbal account is far too verbose. Being specific about what you want or what you think is the best course. This requires a bit of forethought. Don't just blurt out what is on your mind because it probably isn't organized or sanitized. You may know what you're thinking but you may not be ready to speak about it. That is, when we talk before we think it seldom comes out right.

Make it short and sweet in a way that explains things precisely or makes an explicit point. Choose words that are easily understood; some words can be ambiguous or have multiple meanings. Don't complicate it with too many words or try to impress others with your sophisticated vocabulary. Speak slowly, clearly, and with sufficient volume. I used to mumble a lot; now people say I'm too loud. Anyway, try to find a reasonable middle ground. If you mumble, you may be ignored; the listener may think you are talking to yourself. If you are boisterous, they may think you are emoting.

Own the message. Speak for yourself. You are communicating your viewpoint not someone else's. It is your opinion, idea, or belief. Nobody else is responsible for the way you think or feel and you are not responsible for the way they think and feel. Although we adopt the ideas or values of others, once we do it becomes ours. It may be theirs too, but that doesn't discount that I chose it for myself.

You have, no doubt, been trained in using "I" messages. If you are angry, say "I am angry because…" Don't say, "You ticked me off." That isn't possible. I can't make you feel anything. We choose our own emotions, attitudes, and outlooks. Train your clients to get into the habit of owning their opinions, feelings, and beliefs. "My personal opinion is…" "I believe that…" "I get upset when…" And don't forget the reason; state the reason you feel or think that way.

Ask for feedback. Get the listener to repeat what you said in his or her own words. You can clarify any errors in transmission. Once both of you have reached an understanding, you have effectively communicated to them. Give feedback. Read back to them what you thought you heard. Allow the communicator to scrutinize your understanding. Once both of you have reached an agreement, he or she has effectively communicated to you.

Misunderstandings occur a lot more often than you think. If not straightened out, long term consequences could arise. You will spend a lot less time elucidating than recuperating. A sure method of determining what is on another person's mind is to ask. Most people are happy to tell you what they think about something. Again, be specific about what part you are trying to refine.

Please don't be one of those people that ask a question and ignore, forget, or do not wait for the answer. I dislike when that happens. Someone asks me something and I answer them, and then they ask me the same question later. Or they don't even let me finish the answer and interrupt me for some other reason. Or I share my answer and they tune it out completely. Okay, I've been guilty of these things myself. But we have to be aware of how we are coming across. This will be explored further in our discussion of body language.

You probably remember the concept of reflective listening. Teach that skill to your clients. This is when you provide feedback, not only about the perceived message in the words, but also about the perceived message in the emotions. "I hear you saying you are ready, but I sense a little uncertainty in your voice." "I can tell you're excited about being selected for the job." "I understand that you're upset about what happened, and I am truly sorry." "I appreciate that you are discouraged; maybe we can explore some other options."

Remember, know your audience. Speak to their level, to their needs, and to their hopes. It is senseless to try to sell someone on something for which they have no use.

Nonverbal Communication

Psychologists argue that possibly 85% of the message is nonverbal (some say even more). This makes sense when you bear in mind the myriad of other stimuli the recipient is seeing and hearing from the communicator.

➤ Tone of voice	➤ Body position
➤ Emotions	➤ Body movement
➤ Eye contact	➤ Posture
➤ Touching	➤ Proximity
➤ Facial gestures	➤ Self-monitoring

Listen to the tone of voice. Modify the amplitude, pitch, tonality, duration, rhythm, rate, and stress and see how many ways the spoken word "no" can be interpreted. There are many words that can be used for different parts of speech, or as a question, exclamation, or statement. Certainly, such modifications can be used to emphasize a point if used selectively and judiciously. When not employed carefully, they also can detract from the point.

I could spend a whole week discussing body language. We will review some of the innumerable ways to express with the body. Note that the body speaks louder than the remark. If the verbal and nonverbal are incongruent, the body language is closer to the truth. Remember when you were a teen and you were being lectured by a parent for twenty minutes? Finally your father asked you, "Is that clear?" You replied, "Sure Dad," as you rolled your eyes. The voice said yes; the body language said I don't care.

There are ways of reinforcing the message through nonverbal language, which includes facial gestures, tone of voice, emotions, body position, arm and hand signals, and so forth. But any one of these characteristics can interfere with or downright contradict the statement. To repeat myself, use love if you want to strengthen the statement; all other emotions should be removed from the communication. Eye contact helps to ensure that you know they are paying attention, and they know you are. Sometimes it is necessary to get at eye level with the listener, especially a child. A little gentle touching also may serve to strengthen the communication. Keep in mind, however, that these methods may not be appropriate for certain populations (depending on the individual). For example, it could be disrespectful to look a Native American or a Japanese person in the eye. But if they avoided eye contact it might be misconstrued as inattention or disrespect. It could be improper to use certain types of touching, like when talking to a member of the opposite sex. Certainly you could use eye contact and touching with your children, loved ones, and close associates. Use these techniques wisely if the situation allows.

Get to know the idiosyncrasies of facial gestures. Notice how many of them work together to collectively suggest a mood or feeling. You can rearrange the muscles in the face into all manner of contortions. Each one implies a different affect. Subtle changes can change the meaning entirely. There are innumerable possible combinations each of which conveys a different emotion or meaning. Get your clients to look in the mirror and watch themselves. It is also fun to have them watch each other and describe what they see in the various expressions. Sometimes there will be a consensus among them; other times there will be as many different interpretations as there are people.

Let's start with the eyes. What do the following gestures suggest?

Eyes Wide	Eyes Half Open
Eyes Narrow	Eyes Looking Up
Eyes Crossed	Eyes Looking Away
Eyes Squinting	Eyes Looking Down
Eyes Shut	Eyebrows Raised
One Eye Closed	Eyebrows Lowered
Eyes Rolling Back	Eyebrows Inward

Does the nose communicate anything? And how about the head and chin?

Nostrils Flared	Nose Pulled Down
Nose Scrunched	Chin Up or Down
Nose to One Side	Head Tilted

Next, check out the mouth. Note that some of these gestures can be used in combination (such as smiling with teeth showing versus without teeth showing). The same is true for most of the lists that follow. Small alterations can mean big differences in meaning. You will see that the mouth is a very dynamic communicator even when it is not speaking.

Smiling	Teeth Showing
Frowning	Biting Lower Lip
Smirking	Biting Upper Lip
Puckering	Crooked Smile
Mashed Lips	Tongue in Cheek
Mouth Shut	Tongue Partway Out
Wide Open	Tongue Completely Out
Half Open	Tongue Pointed
Oval Shaped	Tongue Out to the Side

Now we'll move down to the body. Again, there are countless combinations of body positions and movements, each of which conveys a different mannerism. We'll begin with the shoulders and arms.

Shoulders Back	Shoulders Shrugged

190

Body Slumped	Arms Behind Back
Body Erect	Hands Behind Head
Chest Protruding	Hands on Face
Chest Sunken	One Hand on Face
Arms Crossed	One Hand on Elbow
Arms Hanging Free	Hands Covering Eyes
Arms Outstretched	Hands Covering Nose
Hands on Hips	Hands Covering Ears
One Hand on Hip	Fist Supporting Chin

Let's look at the hands. In particular, the position of the fingers can transform the emphasis or the message dramatically. Much information can be gleaned from a simple handshake, such as dominance, power, and control.

Extended Hand	Scratching Head
Fist Clenched	Palms Up
Wringing Hands	Palms Down
Fingers Parted	Palms Together
Thumb and Finger Touching	Hand Pointing
Fingers in Mouth	Thumb Up
Finger Pointing Out	Thumb Down
Finger Pointing In	Hands Clasped
Biting Fingernails	Hands Folded

Okay, how about sitting or standing positions, especially the position of the legs? The position of the body relative to others is also quite informative, such as whether the tummy or the toes point toward or away from others, which denotes degree of interest.

Legs Crossed	Legs Straight
Legs Extended	Sitting Up
Legs Tucked In	Sitting Back
Legs Apart	Sitting Slumped
Legs Together	Leaning to One Side
Legs Bent	Standing Up

Posture is an arrangement of the positions of several body members. Some postures suggest interest and some disinterest; some suggest tension and others, relaxation. What would an open posture suggest as opposed to closed? Posture, gestures, and movements may intimate patience, annoyance, fatigue, laziness, boredom, frustration, energy, enthusiasm, attentiveness, defensiveness, arrogance, uneasiness, illness, attraction, and more. Looking at limb and body motions separately, contemplate the differences between fast, slow, abrupt, prolonged, smooth, shaky, jerky, and erratic movements.

Obviously, these lists are but a smattering of the various subtleties of body language. Experiment with the lists a little. Try different configurations to see what they might mean. Just pick several of the above characteristics at random, place yourself in that pose, and see what it feels like. What emotions or moods are suggested in the following examples? Put yourself into the exact arrangement. Does it conjure a feeling or state of mind? This is a great activity to use for groups as it generates a lot of participation, discussion, and camaraderie. Have them pick attributes and have another assume the pose, or pick items at random and have them all try the pose. Get the participants to discuss how it looks to the observer and how it feels to the actor. Here are some examples to try.

- Sitting with legs together and tucked under, arms folded, shoulders shrugged, lips puckered, and chin down.
- Sitting with chin down, legs bent, eyes closed, mouth closed, slumped over, with palms together and pointing upward.
- Standing erect, with legs straight and together, arms by the side, chin up, mouth shut, chest protruding, eyes open.
- Standing but leaning a little, with shoulders back, legs apart, one hand on hip, chin up, smiling, thumb pointing inward.
- Standing, leaning forward, eyes wide open, mouth wide open, one hand on face, the other hand pointing.

There are positions that feel different simply by changing one aspect. For example, in the first example above, the feeling may be pondering. But change the shape of the mouth from puckered to frowning and you might feel depressed.

Proximity is another dimension to the body language equation. It's the law of distance: distances vary depending on culture, age, gender, and the nature of the relationship. The more you are brought into the same proximity with someone else the more likely you will develop a relationship with them. I remember in grade school, we were always arranged alphabetically so the teacher could learn our names. Needless to say, I became friends with several who were frequently seated near to me. You usually can gauge what kind of relationship it is by observing the distance between people. Closer distance implies a closer bond. But there are different proximities for different occasions, cultures, and populations.

We fluctuate in our sensitivity to proximity depending on mood, circumstances, and location. People emit vibrations, or proximity cues, when you are getting too close. Clearly, romantic couples have few space restrictions, except perhaps in public. It is socially more acceptable to hold hands in public than to passionately embrace, except maybe at a wedding. A feeling of personal space invasion occurs when the proximity boundary is breached. If the relationship is not intimate, personal space extends to three or four feet (arm length). This would be a normal distance if you were talking to a friend; maybe a little farther if talking to a stranger. You would not want to get as close as two feet if you were talking to a gangster.

Public space is greater, about ten to twelve feet. If you were picking your spot at the beach you would be using the public measurement. People position their site in a way that maximizes the distance from the other visitors. When you are walking through the mall you try to give others as much space as possible (which is impossible if it is the day before Christmas). If people are more dispersed the inclination is to leave as much space between them as possible. When I am driving cross country, I like to center my car between the one in front and the one behind; I will adjust my speed if necessary to accomplish this as long as it is safe. That's what proximity is all about: your personal safety zone.

Which would you prefer? Living in a barracks housing thirty people where there is about eight feet separating each bed. Living in an apartment where there are people living above you, below you, behind you, beside you. Living in a townhouse where you have people on either side, but not much of a yard. Living in a suburb, where the houses are set several feet apart and you have a little extra space in front and back. Living in the country where the next closest cottage is an acre or two away. Living on a ranch where the next hacienda is ten to twenty miles away. Living on the moon.

Conclusions

A great deal of excellent research has been conducted on this topic. Perhaps the most complex communicator is the face. Ekman originally identified seven emotions appearing in facial expressions that are relatively universal across cultures: fear, anger, surprise, sadness, disgust, joy, and contempt. The list has grown since his pioneering work in the 70s and 80s (see Ekman, 2003). The literature suggests there may be literally thousands of recognizable expressions, made possible by selective flexing of the plethora of muscles in the face.

Many emotions are hard to fake for an extended period, noticeable only to the eye of a seasoned observer. The poker player's tell is a common tool used among gamblers to detect when the opponent has a good or bad hand; you will notice that pros always have a completely expressionless look. Take for example lying. Watch for some of these signals when a person's verbalization is suspect: gulping, covering the mouth or eyes, momentary smirk, shifty or beady (evil) eyes, and/or nervousness (leg movements, stuttering, excessive blinking, twitching, scratching).

An astute observer can recognize clusters of nonverbal signals that will have particular meaning within the context of the conversation and the situational conditions; such meaning is fairly consistent across subjects (see Pease, 2004). Examples include so-called "seed gestures" such as shrugging the shoulders, weak in the knees, choked up, cold feet, pain in the neck, looking down one's nose, hot under the collar, getting things off one's chest. Have you noticed the following attraction (i.e., interest) signals in other men or women: eye contact, eye wink, sideways glance, eyebrow jump, smiling, mirroring, small talk, self-grooming, gentle touching, shaking the hips, raising the shoulders, protruding the chest, hair flick, seductive lips, bedroom eyes, head tilt, exposing the neck, opening the legs, pointing the feet?

The more you learn about the subtleties of communication, the sharper you become as an observer. I recommend that you study the subject and develop a keen eye for the details. I also recommend that you observe yourself and teach your clients to do the same. If you are self-aware you will be tuned into the way you come across to others. It is tricky enough to be attentive to the mannerisms of others; it is even more of a challenge to be conscientiously self-monitoring. But both skills will make anyone a better communicator and radically reduce misunderstandings and misinterpretations. Just keep in mind that some mannerisms are unique to the individual and part of his or her style. Body language specialists always try to establish a baseline of the idiosyncrasies of each individual. That way they can tell when the person is deviating from natural.

Don't forget that there are significant cultural differences when it comes to verbal and nonverbal cues. There also are differences due to gender, age, region or geography, personality, situation, location, and so on. While there are similarities among members of a group, population, or culture, communication signals, whether oral or of the body, are not entirely generalizable from one person to another.

As a therapist, we must be careful in the way we come across to those we serve. Helpful nonverbal cues would include a soothing voice, interested expression, smiling, relaxed posture, leaning toward client, eye contact, graceful gestures, and close, comfortable proximity. Immediacy is another useful helping skill that focuses on the here and now experience between the counselor and client. It is a good custom to structure the relationship by setting ground rules, defining roles, establishing boundaries, and explaining the counseling process during key transition points (beginning, end, and during change).

Practice self-monitoring. Notice how you come across to others, and the impact your words and deeds have on those around you. Turn the camera back on yourself and observe your own body language, listen to what you are saying, recognize your intrusive habits, and identify your patterns and distractions.

We can glean a lot of wisdom about effective communication from God's Word. We talk to him through prayer. He talks to us in his Word, and the teachings of Christ. It also is possible to be moved by the Holy Spirit through the words of a devout preacher. Ever had that feeling in church when the sermon seems to be about you, as if the minister knows your life story? The pastor who confirmed me used to say that these avenues of communication represent a heart to heart conversation with God. That is, God communicates with us in a unique way: via his Spirit; and it is comprehended by our spirit. And we communicate with God through our spirits as well (ROM 8:26; EPH 6:18-19; COL 4:2)

- DEU 12:32 ~ God says, "Everything that I command you, you shall be careful to do. You shall not add to it or take from it."

- PRO 8:1,4,21,34-35 (paraphrased) ~ God says, "Doesn't wisdom cry out, and understanding speak? I call to you people; my voice speaks to everyone. I want those that love me to inherit something of substance, for I will fill their treasure troves. Blessed is the person who listens to me, watches daily at my gates, and waits at the door. For whoever finds me finds life, and shall obtain my bountiful favor."

- PRO 30:5-6 ~ Every word of God proves true; he is a shield to those who take refuge in him. Do not add to his words, lest he rebuke you and you be found a liar.

- ISA 55:10-12 ~ As the rain and snow come down from heaven and do not return there but water the earth, making it bring forth and sprout, giving seed to the sower and bread to the eater, so shall my word be that goes out from my mouth; it shall not return to me empty, but shall accomplish that which I purpose, and shall succeed in the thing for which I sent it. For you shall go out in joy and be led forth in peace; the mountains and the hills before you shall break forth into singing, and all the trees of the field shall clap their hands.

- 2 TI 3:16 ~ All Scripture is breathed out by God and profitable for teaching, for reproof, for correction, and for training in righteousness.

- REV 22:18-19 ~ I warn everyone who hears the words of the prophecy of this book: if anyone adds to them, God will add to him the plagues described in this book, and if anyone takes away from the words of the book of this prophecy, God will take away his share in the tree of life and in the holy city, which are described in this book.

The Bible teaches us how to communicate effectively; not just with God, but with others. When you speak to others, be careful what you say and how you say it (1 PE 3:15).

- MAT 5:37 ~ Jesus said, "Let what you say be simply 'Yes' or 'No'; anything more than this comes from evil."

- 1 CO 15:33 ~ Do not be deceived: Bad company ruins good morals.

- EPH 4:29 ~ Let no corrupting talk come out of your mouths, but only such as is good for building up, as fits the occasion, that it may give grace to those who hear.

- COL 4:6 ~ Let your speech always be gracious, seasoned with salt, so that you may know how you ought to answer each person.

- 2 TI 2:24-26 ~ The Lord's servant must not be quarrelsome but kind to everyone, able to teach, patiently enduring evil, correcting his opponents with gentleness. God may perhaps grant them repentance leading to knowledge of the truth, and they may come to their senses and escape from the snare of the devil, after being captured by him to do his will.

"That which we are capable of feeling, we are capable of saying." – Cervantes

"The problem with communication is the illusion that is has occurred." – George Bernard Shaw

References

Ekman, P. (2003). *Emotions revealed*. New York: Times Books.

Pease, A., & Pease, B. (2004). *The definitive book on body language*. London: Orion Publishing.

Activity

Develop an opinion about a particular topic, perhaps a political issue. Write it down. Then edit the statement in a way that communicates the idea with better clarity using fewer words and/or different words.

Original Statement _____

_____

Revised Statement _____

_____

Practice constructing "I" messages about the way you feel. Example emotions include angry, upset, afraid, and excited.

_____

_____

_____

Choose a word or phrase and see how many different meanings you can come up with by changing the way it is spoken, and/or by incorporating different body language styles. Examples could include: "no," "I know," "what," "I'll be seeing you," "okay," "please," "oh my," "do you want to."

Pick some of the words or phrases above and see how many different things they could mean, depending on how they are spoken. For example, "no" could mean: don't do that, I don't want to, oh my God, you don't mean it, why me, yes, etc.

_____

_____

_____

Try different body positions and configurations to see what it feels like to be in that pose.

Determine your proximity boundary with other people. See if you have different distances for different people depending on their gender, age, ethnicity, and/or how well you know them. If they get too close it probably will make you feel uneasy.

COMMUNICATION SKILLS

Verbal
- Active Listening
- Think Before You Speak
- Be Concise
- Speak Slowly, Clearly
- Control the Volume
- Own the Message
- Give & Receive Feedback
- Ask Questions
- Reflective Listening
- Know Your Audience

Non-Verbal
- Tone of Voice
- Emotions
- Eye Contact
- Touching
- Facial Gestures
- Body Position
- Body Movement
- Posture
- Proximity
- Self Monitoring

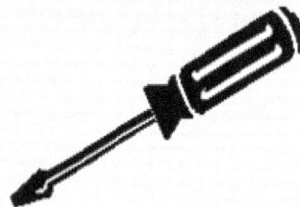

OVERCOMING ADVERSITY

OBJECTIVE	Learn how to rely on the power of God to defeat Satan and the powers of evil.
INTERVENTION	Discuss God's promises, power, and authority, which he freely gives to all who believe and trust in him.
PLAN	Develop a connection to God and maintain that connection to receive his power and overcome temptation, sin, and death.

"No one can make you feel inferior without your consent." – Eleanor Roosevelt

"Success in the affairs of life serves to hide one's abilities, whereas adversity frequently gives one an opportunity to discover them." – Horace

Remember, God is the source of our power. Read the passages below and make a list of the attributes of God and the things that are important to him. These are ways to connect with God who is the highest power, and who bestows certain powers upon us. Hence, they represent our higher powers and lie upon the path of righteousness, to maximize our full potential, growth, and capability.

- ISA 33:22 ~ For the LORD is our judge; the LORD is our lawgiver; the LORD is our king; he will save us.

- MAT 6:22-23 ~ Jesus said, "The eye is the lamp of the body. So, if your eye is healthy, your whole body will be full of light, but if your eye is bad, your whole body will be full of darkness. If then the light in you is darkness, how great is the darkness!"

- LUK 6:32,35 ~ Jesus said, "If you love those who love you, what benefit is that to you? For even sinners love those who love them... But love your enemies, and do good, and lend, expecting nothing in return, and your reward will be great, and you will be sons of the Most High, for he is kind to the ungrateful and the evil."

- LUK 11:33-36 ~ Jesus said, "No one after lighting a lamp puts it in a cellar or under a basket, but on a stand, so that those who enter may see the light. Your eye is the lamp of your body. When your eye is healthy, your whole body is full of light, but when it is bad, your body is full of darkness. Therefore be careful lest the light in you become darkness. If then your whole body is full of light, having no part dark, it will be wholly bright, as when a lamp with its rays gives you light."

- JOH 4:24 ~ God is spirit, and those who worship him must worship in spirit and truth.

- JOH 8:12 ~ Again Jesus spoke to them, saying, "I am the light of the world. Whoever follows me will not walk in darkness, but will have the light of life."

- JOH 14:6,10 ~ Jesus said to him, "I am the way, and the truth, and the life. No one comes to the Father except through me... Do you not believe that I am in the Father and the

Father is in me? The words that I say to you I do not speak on my own authority, but the Father who dwells in me does his works."

- 1 JO 4:7-8 ~ Beloved, let us love one another, for love is from God, and whoever loves has been born of God and knows God. Anyone who does not love does not know God, because God is love.

- 1 JO 5:6-8,20 ~ This is he who came by water and blood – Jesus Christ; not by the water only but by the water and the blood. And the Spirit is the one who testifies, because the Spirit is the truth. For there are three that testify: the Spirit and the water and the blood; and these three agree… And we know that the Son of God has come and has given us understanding, so that we may know him who is true; and we are in him who is true, in his Son Jesus Christ. He is the true God and eternal life.

The powers the Holy Spirit has bestowed upon us equip us to produce good fruit from our spirits. Encourage your clients to tap into these spiritual powers and bear good fruit, overcome setbacks and heartaches, and gain an inheritance that will last forever.

- JOH 15:1-4 ~ Jesus said, "I am the true vine, and my Father is the vinedresser. Every branch in me that does not bear fruit he takes away, and every branch that does bear fruit he prunes, that it may bear more fruit. Already you are clean because of the word that I have spoken to you. Abide in me, and I in you. As the branch cannot bear fruit by itself, unless it abides in the vine, neither can you, unless you abide in me."

- GAL 5:22-23 ~ But the fruit of the Spirit is love, joy, peace, patience, kindness, goodness, faithfulness, gentleness, self-control; against such things there is no law.

- EPH 5:9 ~ The fruit of light is found in all that is good and right and true.

- 2 PE 1:5-8 ~ Make every effort to supplement your faith with virtue, and virtue with knowledge, and knowledge with self-control, and self-control with steadfastness, and steadfastness with godliness, and godliness with brotherly affection, and brotherly affection with love. For if these qualities are yours and are increasing, they keep you from being ineffective or unfruitful in the knowledge of our Lord Jesus Christ.

The prime objective of the profession of Christian Counselor is to set an example. And our example is Christ. We want people to see Christ in us, by radiating his love, serving our patrons, and glorifying God. Someday, when they look into the mirror, they will be able to see Christ in themselves. Next time you look into the mirror don't look at your face but into your heart. If you see Christ there, you are saved. That should raise anybody's self-esteem.

- JOH 13:14-15 ~ Jesus said, "If I then, your Lord and Teacher, have washed your feet, you also ought to wash one another's feet. For I have given you an example, that you also should do just as I have done to you."

- 2 CO 3:18 ~ And we all, with unveiled face, beholding the glory of the Lord, are being transformed into the same image from one degree of glory to another. For this comes from the Lord who is the Spirit.

People that come to you for guidance and encouragement have hit some rough road. They are suffering to the point it has become unbearable in many cases. They don't know how to cope with it, explain it, or even define it. They think they are guilty or they blame others, or both. People want a reason why bad things happen. But what is the true cause of all the suffering, sorrow, and pain in this world? Answer: Sin. Sin is the affliction, and Christ is the remedy.

"I count him braver who overcomes his desires than him who conquers his enemies; for the hardest victory is over self." – Aristotle

Conquering Sin

Sin brings a curse upon every human being and along with it the punishment of death (ROM 6:23). Instead of trying to find blame, we should be giving thanks to God; for his Son overcame the world and its sin, and gave us freedom from its curse.

- GEN 3 (paraphrased) ~ The fall of Adam and Eve brought sorrow, pain, and suffering. That was their reward for sin. And sin became a curse that would affect all human beings.

- JOB 14:1 ~ Man who is born of a woman is few of days and full of trouble.

- 1 JO 5:17 ~ All wrongdoing is sin, but there is sin that does not lead to death.

Isaiah prophesied that Messiah would come to mend broken hearts, to free people from sin, and to bring peace to those who seek the Lord. That was Christ's mission and it is our mission too. We must help others who suffer by lifting them up in the spirit of God's love. That love will change everything, beginning with the heart. And it will empower those it touches to be free of sin by focusing on the payment that was made for it by Jesus Christ.

- ISA 61:1-2 ~ The Spirit of the Lord GOD is upon me, because the LORD has anointed me to bring good news to the poor; he has sent me to bind up the brokenhearted, to proclaim liberty to the captives, and the opening of the prison to those who are bound.

- 2 CO 1:3-4 ~ Blessed be the God and Father of our Lord Jesus Christ, the Father of mercies and God of all comfort, who comforts us in all our affliction, so that we may be able to comfort those who are in any affliction, with the comfort with which we ourselves are comforted by God.

- 2 CO 5:17-21 ~ Therefore, if anyone is in Christ, he is a new creation. The old has passed away; behold, the new has come. All this is from God, who through Christ reconciled us to himself and gave us the ministry of reconciliation; that is, in Christ God was reconciling the world to himself, not counting their trespasses against them, and entrusting to us the message of reconciliation. Therefore, we are ambassadors for Christ, God making his appeal through us. We implore you on behalf of Christ, be reconciled to God.

On earth, everyone will suffer because of sin. But Christ suffered in our place and he paid the ultimate price for sin. Thus, we shouldn't dwell on our afflictions, woes, torments, and sorrows. Instead, we should focus on Christ who makes us strong in the face of persecution, tribulation, and life's stumbling blocks. Remember, he has suffered so that we do not have to suffer. If you think you must suffer you are denying what he has already done. So give your emotional baggage to God; it belongs to him anyway because Christ bought and paid for it. Christ has suffered with us and for us. And though we all have trials and tribulations, they are a result of the fall and not God's judgment, which will come upon those that do not trust in Jesus to be saved. For those that do, their suffering will end, for good.

- JOB 3:20-26 ~ Why is light given to him who is in misery, and life to the bitter in soul, who long for death, but it comes not, and dig for it more than for hidden treasures, who rejoice exceedingly and are glad when they find the grave? Why is light given to a man whose way is hidden, whom God has hedged in? For my sighing comes instead of my bread, and my groanings are poured out like water. For the thing that I fear comes upon me, and what I dread befalls me. I am not at ease, nor am I quiet; I have no rest, but trouble comes.

- JOB 11:13-20 ~ If you prepare your heart, you will stretch out your hands toward him. If iniquity is in your hand, put it far away, and let not injustice dwell in your tents. Surely then you will lift up your face without blemish; you will be secure and will not fear. You will forget your misery; you will remember it as waters that have passed away. And your life will be brighter than the noonday; its darkness will be like the morning. And you will feel secure, because there is hope; you will look around and take your rest in security. You will lie down, and none will make you afraid; many will court your favor. But the eyes of the wicked will fail; all way of escape will be lost to them, and their hope is to breathe their last.

- ROM 8:35,38-39 ~ Who shall separate us from the love of Christ? Shall tribulation, or distress, or persecution, or famine, or nakedness, or danger, or sword? For I am sure that neither death nor life, nor angels nor rulers, nor things present nor things to come, nor powers, nor height nor depth, nor anything else in all creation, will be able to separate us from the love of God in Christ Jesus our Lord.

- 1 PE 1:3-6 ~ Blessed be the God and Father of our Lord Jesus Christ! According to his great mercy, he has caused us to be born again to a living hope through the resurrection of Jesus Christ from the dead, to an inheritance that is imperishable, undefiled, and unfading, kept in heaven for you, who by God's power are being guarded through faith for a salvation ready to be revealed in the last time. In this you rejoice, though now for a little while, if necessary, you have been grieved by various trials.

I frequently remind the reader, a change of heart will lead to a change in belief. Too many people believe that suffering is God's punishment, or that they are being chastised by God for their sins. They think they deserve to be afflicted, grieving, oppressed, or depressed. But God's primary mission on earth is salvation, not judgment. Christ took the punishment upon himself, as well as the grief, and He gives us relief.

- DEU 4:30-31 ~ When you are in tribulation, and all these things come upon you in the latter days, you will return to the LORD your God and obey his voice. For the LORD your God is a merciful God. He will not leave you or destroy you or forget the covenant with your fathers that he swore to them.

257

- LAM 3:31-33 ~ For the Lord will not cast off forever, but, though he cause grief, he will have compassion according to the abundance of his steadfast love; for he does not afflict from his heart or grieve the children of men.

- JOH 16:33 ~ Jesus said, "I have said these things to you, that in me you may have peace. In the world you will have tribulation. But take heart; I have overcome the world."

All people who trust in Christ are found not guilty: this is the definition of justification by faith. Such a faith will change attitudes, behaviors, and entire lifestyles. Hardship is not God's retribution for our disobedience. He knows we are weak and cannot comply no matter how hard we try. That's why he gave us his Son; it was part of the grand design from the start. Yes, there will be punishment for sin when Christ comes in judgment. But remember, you are justified if you depend exclusively on the atonement of Christ. Praise the Lord!

- JOB 4:7-8 ~ Consider this: Who among the innocent ever perished? When were the righteous ever destroyed? I have seen for myself, that those who plow evil and those who sow trouble reap the same.

- ROM 6:1-2,12-16 (paraphrased) ~ Shall we continue to sin, so that God's grace can continue to abound? God forbid! How can we, who were dead in our sins, continue to live a life of decadence? Do not allow sin to reign in your mortal body, influencing you to pursue desires of the flesh. Do not use your body parts as instruments of unrighteousness and sin, but yield to God, and use your body to glorify Him. Sin cannot control you for you are no longer under the Law, but under the grace of God. Does that mean we can sin, because we are under Grace and not the Law? No way! A person obeys whomever they yield to; you can yield to sin unto death, or you can yield to obedience unto righteousness.

- PHP 3:12-13 ~ I (Paul) continue to press on, to grab hold of that for which Christ has grabbed hold of me. I do not claim to have obtained it as yet, but instead I forget those things that are behind, and reach for those things which lie ahead.

It is fruitless to worry about the past as it is no longer a threat. The only thing we need to take from the past is our experience and the wisdom it has taught. It is pointless to worry about the future as there is no way of knowing what is there. The only thing we can be sure to find are the things we left unfinished today. We do have a modicum of control over the present. And we needn't be anxious about now because it is here and God is too. And now is the time to act.

Follow Christ's lead and remain steadfast, leaving your troubles behind, and concentrating on his promises as you look ahead. Let us review some of those promises which we must cling to and trust in.

God promises provision.

- PSA 23:1 (paraphrased) ~ Because the Lord is my Shepherd I have everything I need.

- PSA 145:14-16 ~ The LORD upholds all who are falling and raises up all who are bowed down. The eyes of all look to you, and you give them their food in due season. You open your hand; you satisfy the desire of every living thing.

- MAT 6:31-33 ~ Jesus said, "Therefore do not be anxious, saying, 'What shall we eat?' or 'What shall we drink?' or 'What shall we wear?' For the Gentiles seek after all these things, and your heavenly Father knows that you need them all. But seek first the kingdom of God and his righteousness, and all these things will be added to you."

God promises productivity.

- LUK 1:37 ~ For nothing will be impossible with God.

- JOH 15:3-7 ~ Jesus said, "Already you are clean because of the word that I have spoken to you. Abide in me, and I in you. As the branch cannot bear fruit by itself, unless it abides in the vine, neither can you, unless you abide in me. I am the vine; you are the branches. Whoever abides in me and I in him, he bears much fruit, but apart from me you can do nothing. If anyone does not abide in me he is thrown away like a branch and withers; and the branches are gathered, thrown into the fire, and burned. If you abide in me, and my words abide in you, ask whatever you wish, and it will be done for you."

- PHP 4:13 ~ I can do all things through him who strengthens me.

God promises protection.

- PSA 91:11-12 ~ For he will command his angels concerning you to guard you in all your ways. On their hands they will bear you up, lest you strike your foot against a stone.

- PRO 29:25 ~ The fear of man lays a snare, but whoever trusts in the LORD is safe.

- 2 TH 3:3 ~ The Lord is faithful. He will establish you and guard you against the evil one.

Your patients need to understand that it's normal to have problems. But why swim in your misery? It will pass soon enough. Time is on your side. Don't let life bring you down, let God lift you up. Look where you are going, not where you've been; it's a lot brighter where you are headed even though there is darkness in your past. Seek God in crisis and you will find solutions.

"Life is thickly sown with thorns, and I know no other remedy than to pass quickly through them. The longer we dwell on our misfortunes, the greater is their power to harm us." – Voltaire

"Trust yourself. Create the kind of self that you will be happy to live with all your life. Make the most of yourself by fanning the tiny, inner sparks of possibility into flames of achievement." – Golda Meir

The Armor of God

When it comes to protection, there is a force field which will repel the devil himself. It is the Armor of God. And God gives it to us for free. It is the ultimate safety net, insurance policy, and defense system. Examine the following scriptures to gain an understanding of the potency and durability of this armor. Just remember this: you need all the armor (the whole armor) not just pieces of it, and you need to keep it on at all times.

- ISA 59:17 ~ He put on righteousness as a breastplate, and a helmet of salvation on his head; he put on garments of vengeance for clothing, and wrapped himself in zeal as a cloak.
- EPH 6:10-17 ~ Be strong in the Lord and in the strength of his might. Put on the whole armor of God, that you may be able to stand against the schemes of the devil. For we do not wrestle against flesh and blood, but against the rulers, against the authorities, against the cosmic powers over this present darkness, against the spiritual forces of evil in the heavenly places. Therefore take up the whole armor of God, that you may be able to withstand in the evil day, and having done all, to stand firm. Stand therefore, having fastened on the belt of truth, and having put on the breastplate of righteousness, and, as shoes for your feet, having put on the readiness given by the gospel of peace. In all circumstances take up the shield of faith, with which you can extinguish all the flaming darts of the evil one; and take the helmet of salvation, and the sword of the Spirit, which is the word of God.

First of all, it is important to understand the enemy that we are up against. When I was in the Army, I was trained vigorously to prepare for combat in Southeast Asia. I was confident that I could perform my duty without question, if and when I was summoned to go into battle. Months of education, drills, and practice prepared all of us to the extent that we were ready to execute our mission without hesitation or doubt. Fortunately, I never had to heed that call. My mission was to protect Americans stateside. But all the combat training in the world cannot prepare a person for the battle between right and wrong. We are facing an enemy that cannot be seen. We are talking spiritual warfare here, and the adversary is pure evil. You need training in how to fight this enemy and how to apply the armor.

We are up against principalities, kingdoms, or better said, entire governments; these are entities and territories governed by authority of extreme wickedness, where the prince of darkness is sovereign. Consider some of the nations on earth that despise Christendom and seek to eradicate Christians from the face of the earth; they are merely pawns in this elaborate war. We are up against powers and rulers of gloom and death, some are human some are not. They include innumerable evil spirits: hosts of demons. These are beings with formidable might and cunning. And they follow the command of Lucifer, who was a very high ranking angel before he opposed God and was thrown out of heaven.

- ISA 14:12-15 (KJV) ~ You have fallen from heaven and have been cut down to the ground, Lucifer, who brought down the nations. For you deceived yourself, expecting to be exalted, even above God. Instead, you will be brought down into the depths of hell.

- EZE 28:14-19 (KJV) ~ You were the anointed cherub and lived upon the holy mountain of God. You were perfect from the day you were created until evil was found in you. Your great wealth made you violent inside and you became sinful. Therefore, you were thrown off the holy mountain, and you will be destroyed. You exalted yourself because of your beauty, thereby corrupting yourself. You defiled the sanctuaries with your abominations. You will be destroyed by the fire within you; your terrible deeds will come to an end.

- 1 PE 5:8 ~ Be sober-minded; be watchful. Your adversary the devil prowls around like a roaring lion, seeking someone to devour.

- REV 12:9,12 ~ And the great dragon was thrown down, that ancient serpent, who is called the devil and Satan, the deceiver of the whole world – he was thrown down to the earth, and his angels were thrown down with him… Therefore, rejoice, O heavens and you who dwell in them! But woe to you, O earth and sea, for the devil has come down to you in great wrath, because he knows that his time is short!

- REV 16:14 ~ For they are demonic spirits, performing signs, who go abroad to the kings of the whole world, to assemble them for battle on the great day of God the Almighty.

This is the foe that we will face in battle; and a bloody, gory, horrible clash it will be. But they will be defeated because their weapons cannot penetrate the armor, and because God fights by our side. And when the dust settles and the sun shines, those who wore the whole armor of God will be the only ones who remain standing.

- 1 SA 17:36-37,45-47 ~ David told King Saul, "Your servant has struck down both lions and bears, and this uncircumcised Philistine shall be like one of them, for he has defied the armies of the living God. And The LORD who delivered me from the paw of the lion and from the paw of the bear will deliver me from the hand of this Philistine." And Saul said to David, "Go, and the LORD be with you!" Then David said to Goliath the Philistine, "You come to me with a sword and with a spear and with a javelin, but I come to you in the name of the LORD of hosts, the God of the armies of Israel, whom you have defied. This day the LORD will deliver you into my hand, and I will strike you down and cut off your head. And I will give the dead bodies of the host of the Philistines this day to the birds of the air and to the wild beasts of the earth, that all the earth may know that there is a God in Israel, and that all this assembly may know that the LORD saves not with sword and spear. For the battle is the LORD's, and he will give you into our hand."

- JAM 4:7 ~ Submit yourselves to God. Resist the devil, and he will flee from you.

- 1 JO 4:3-4 ~ Every spirit that does not confess Jesus is not from God. This is the spirit of the antichrist, which you heard was coming and now is in the world already. Little children, you are from God and have overcome them, for he who is in you is greater than he who is in the world.

Let us begin with the helmet of salvation. What does the helmet protect? – Your head, your mind, your thoughts. Salvation is the knowledge that Christ has paid the price for sin and saved you from its curse of death. It is the hope of heaven that keeps us mindful of him, and compels us to do his will. If your thoughts are on Christ, the negative, destructive, and sinful thoughts cannot deceive you, tempt you, or lead you astray. So guard your head from desires of the flesh and from entry by the tempter, by placing God first and seeking his kingdom and his righteousness (MAT 6:33). If your thoughts are on God your mind is safe, and he will give you the knowledge of salvation and the mind of Christ (1 CO 2:16).

The breastplate of righteousness, what does it protect? – Your heart. God's love changes the heart and fills it with his love (2 CO 5:17). We are to radiate that love (MAT 22:39) and continue in virtue, decency, and morality. With Christ living in your heart you will be protected from lusts of this world, and fear which is the devil's power. For the love of God destroys the fear, his Word illuminates the path of righteousness, and his Spirit raises us up and out of danger. Loving God back keeps your heart pure, and your desires set on Christ.

Wrap the belt of truth around you snugly and fasten it securely. The Holy Spirit will encompass you with the light of truth, so that you cannot be tricked, deceived, or fall into a trap. You will always see where you are going, you will always know the right thing to do, and you will always embrace the truth. The Spirit of God will never lie to you, and will tell you what to do or say (LUK 12:12). That Spirit is the source of our conscience, our moral code, and the ability to understand his message and respond in faith. The belt of truth is God's wisdom wrapped around you.

Always follow in God's peace. Do not be one who creates discord, conflict, or ill will (PRO 6:16-19). Be a peacemaker not a warmonger. God provides us with a peace that surpasses all understanding (PHP 4:7), if we remain grafted to the vine which is Jesus. Connected to him we can do anything, but disconnected we can do nothing (JOH 15:5). So put on the shoes of peace and they will prevent your feet from roaming; for if you veer off track you might get lost. That road leads to darkness and destruction, and there is no protection to be found there. Real peace comes by accepting God's forgiveness, which prevents us from worrying today, being anxious about tomorrow, or fretting about yesterday.

Holding firm to the shield of faith, there is nothing the devil can throw at you that you cannot fend off. You possess wonderful powers and gifts because of that faith, which also equips you to bear fruit of the spirit. Faith enables you to perform great feats of strength and endurance, and empowers you to accomplish miracles in Jesus' name. Of course, this implies that you act on your faith, for it is one thing to believe and yet another to put it to work. Satan can never take your shield of faith from you. His temptations, obstacles, and poison darts cannot penetrate the armor or the shield.

- HEB 11:1,3,6 ~ Now faith is the assurance of things hoped for, the conviction of things not seen… By faith we understand that the universe was created by the word of God, so that what is seen was not made out of things that are visible… And without faith it is impossible to please him, for whoever would draw near to God must believe that he exists and that he rewards those who seek him.

- HEB 11:7-38 (paraphrased) ~ With faith, the great prophets were able to endure many hardships and performed great feats, such as subduing kingdoms, escaping certain death, overcoming incredible odds, healing the sick, and even raising the dead.

Clearly, we have the best defense possible. But this is war, and you cannot win a war with only a good defense. So God has given us a weapon: the sword of the Spirit. It is the Word of God, which pierces to the soul. The word of truth will bypass all the mental obstructions to understanding because it places God's undisputable truth right there into the depths of your mind. When you read the Bible, God is speaking directly to you with a wisdom that can only be comprehended by your spirit. When you wield that sword it will cut the enemy all the way through. It will sever their very spirit which is the life force, if they do not accept and believe the Word within their soul. While a literal sword cuts through muscle and bone, this sword cuts more deeply, separating the spirit from the soul. How powerful is that?

- MAT 10:28 ~ Jesus said, "Do not fear those who kill the body but cannot kill the soul. Rather fear him who can destroy both soul and body in hell."

- 1 CO 2:14 ~ The natural person does not accept the things of the Spirit of God, for they are folly to him, and he is not able to understand them because they are spiritually discerned.

- HEB 4:12 ~ For the word of God is living and active, sharper than any two-edged sword, piercing to the division of soul and of spirit, of joints and of marrow, and discerning the thoughts and intentions of the heart.

- HEB 10:39 ~ But we are not of those who shrink back and are destroyed, but of those who have faith and preserve their souls.

Christ overcame the world and so will all believers. We can overcome because he has given us the power to do so through his Holy Spirit that lives in us. You will overcome Satan and his army, because that same Spirit equips you with an authority so mighty, the devil himself will fear you.

- JOH 16:33 ~ Jesus said, "I have said these things to you, that in me you may have peace. In the world you will have tribulation. But take heart; I have overcome the world."

- ROM 8:31 ~ If God is for us, who can be against us?

- ROM 12:21 ~ Do not be overcome by evil, but overcome evil with good.

- 1 JO 5:4-5 ~ For everyone who has been born of God overcomes the world. And this is the victory that has overcome the world – our faith. Who is it that overcomes the world except the one who believes that Jesus is the Son of God?

- REV 21:5-7 ~ And he who was seated on the throne said, "Behold, I am making all things new." Also he said, "Write this down, for these words are trustworthy and true." And he said to me, "It is done! I am the Alpha and the Omega, the beginning and the end. To the thirsty I will give from the spring of the water of life without payment. The one who conquers will have this heritage, and I will be his God and he will be my child."

If you want to understand the power of the Armor of God, look at the story of Shadrach, Meshach, and Abednego (DAN 3). They refused to bow before the Babylonian king's statue and were sentenced to die in the fiery furnace. In his rage, Nebuchadnezzar had the heat raised seven times normal. To his amazement, he observed them biding their time in the midst of the inferno, having a chat with the Angel of God (often considered to be the pre-incarnate Christ). These three men emerged from the flames unscathed; not even a hair on their heads was singed, while the operators of the furnace were burned to a crisp.

- DAN 3:16-28 (paraphrased) ~ The men told the king, "If it be God's will He will deliver us from the burning furnace, and from you. But if it is not his will, understand that we will not worship any other than the Lord God Almighty." Nebuchadnezzar became furious and commanded the three men be bound and tossed into the furnace, after heating it seven times normal. The fire was so hot it killed those who escorted the men to the furnace. The king was astonished to observe the mem walking around in the midst of the blaze, especially when another like the Son of God appeared among them. He called the men to come out of the fiery furnace, and Shadrach, Meshach, and Abednego emerged unscathed. And the princes, governors, captains, and the king's counselors who were gathered there saw these men, whose bodies were unaffected by the fire; not a hair was singed, nor their coats seared, and no smell of fire was upon them. The king announced, "Blessed be the God of Shadrach, Meshach, and Abednego, who has sent his angel and delivered his servants because they trusted in him, and challenged the king's word, sacrificing their bodies so that they might not serve or worship any god except their God."

The Armor of God protects you when you fight the good fight as a Christian soldier called by Christ (1 TI 6:12-13; 2 TI 2:3-5; 2 TI 4:6-8). The Holy Bible is your field manual that explains the mission, tactics, and doctrine; it also instructs you how to employ the armor and the sword. As you become more equipped to serve, your confidence will equally grow, until such time when your supreme commander sends you into battle to defend the weak, defeat the powers of darkness, rescue the captives, and bring home the lost sheep (ISA 61:1-2). And you will not be afraid for God himself directs the battle and fights by your side (DEU 31:6); because the battle belongs to the Lord (1 SA 17:45-51).

- 2 CO 10:3-5 ~ For though we walk in the flesh, we are not waging war according to the flesh. For the weapons of our warfare are not of the flesh but have divine power to destroy strongholds. We destroy arguments and every lofty opinion raised against the knowledge of God, and take every thought captive to obey Christ.

God's Word

The Sword of the Spirit

HOLY BIBLE

Activity

List your blessings here.   List your catastrophes here.

_____

_____

_____

_____

_____

_____

_____

_____

_____

_____

_____

_____

_____

_____

_____

Which list is longer?

If you are truthful to yourself, you won't even be able to count all the blessings.

Describe each component of the Armor of God.

Helmet of Salvation

_____

_____

_____

Breastplate of Righteousness

_____

_____

_____

Belt of Truth

_____

_____

_____

Shoes of Peace

_____

_____

_____

Shield of Faith

_____

_____

_____

Sword of the Spirit

_____

_____

_____

THE ARMOR OF GOD

HELMET — SALVATION

BREASTPLATE — RIGHTOUSNESS

BELT — TRUTH

SHIELD — FAITH

SWORD — WORD of GOD

SHOES — PEACE

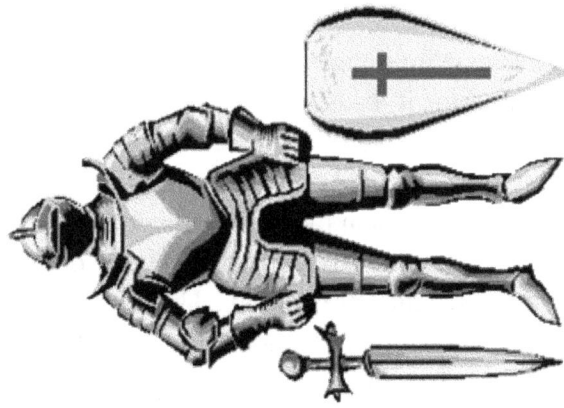

RESISTING TEMPTATION

OBJECTIVE	Learn the schemes of the enemy, recognize the powers of evil, and determine how to defeat them using God's power.
INTERVENTION	Discuss the most common and deadly sins that Satan tempts us with and understand the consequences for giving into them. Identify escape routes from sin.
PLAN	Plan on living a lifestyle pleasing to God and you will have an abundant and fulfilling life. Trust in God to overcome temptation and not give into sin.

"The most formidable attribute of temptation is its increasing power, its accelerating ratio of velocity. Every act of repetition increases power, diminishes resistance." – Horace Mann

"Every conquered temptation represents a new fund of moral energy. Every trial endured and weathered in the right spirit makes a soul nobler and stronger than it was before." – William Butler Yeats

Satan tempts us with things of this world to induce us to stray away from God. Do not succumb to temptation for it leads to sin, which leads to death. You cannot love the world or material things and still love God at the same time (MAT 6:24; LUK 16:13). The big three temptations are lust, greed, and pride. These sins make the greatest men become small, and bring down entire empires. Satan even tried to get Jesus Christ to give into these enticements, as he does with all people. Sin is destructive and just begets more sin; and the sinner becomes more degenerate and the sins more heinous. Unless the individual relies upon Christ to change his or her heart, the end result will be horrific.

- LUK 4:1-13 ~ And Jesus, full of the Holy Spirit, returned from the Jordan and was led by the Spirit in the wilderness for forty days, being tempted by the devil. And he ate nothing during those days. And when they were ended, he was hungry. The devil said to him, "If you are the Son of God, command this stone to become bread." And Jesus answered him, "It is written, 'Man shall not live by bread alone.'" And the devil took him up and showed him all the kingdoms of the world in a moment of time, and said to him, "To you I will give all this authority and their glory, for it has been delivered to me, and I give it to whom I will. If you, then, will worship me, it will all be yours." And Jesus answered him, "It is written, 'You shall worship the Lord your God, and him only shall you serve.'" And he took him to Jerusalem and set him on the pinnacle of the temple and said to him, "If you are the Son of God, throw yourself down from here, for it is written, 'He will command his angels concerning you, to guard you,' and 'On their hands they will bear you up, lest you strike your foot against a stone.'" And Jesus answered him, "It is said, 'You shall not put the Lord your God to the test.'" And when the devil had ended every temptation, he departed from him until an opportune time. And Jesus returned in the power of the Spirit to Galilee, and a report about him went out through all the surrounding country. And he taught in their synagogues, being glorified by all.

- 1 JO 2:15-16 ~ Do not love the world or the things in the world. If anyone loves the world, the love of the Father is not in him. For all that is in the world – the desires of the flesh, the desires of the eyes, and the pride of life – is not from the Father but is from the world.

Through Christ, we possess the power to resist temptation and oppose evil. Without him we are powerless against the wiles of the devil and the cravings of this world.

- PRO 1:10 ~ If sinners entice you, do not consent.

- 1 CO 10:13 ~ No temptation has overtaken you that is not common to man. God is faithful, and he will not let you be tempted beyond your ability, but with the temptation he will also provide the way of escape, that you may be able to endure it.

- JAM 4:7,17 ~ Submit yourselves therefore to God. Resist the devil, and he will flee from you… Whoever knows the right thing to do and fails to do it, for him it is sin.

- 1 JO 4:4 ~ Little children, you are from God and have overcome them, for he who is in you is greater than he who is in the world.

Lust

People are easily enticed by earthly delights. God wants us to pursue yearnings of the spirit, and avoid lusts of the flesh. Evil desires are never satisfied because the pleasure is fleeting; so the person just wants more. But the more one gives in the less enjoyment he or she gets. Therefore, lasciviousness progressively gets worse; and the expression of it more aberrant. It is a slippery slope that leads to promiscuity, sexual deviancy, disease, and death.

A number of mental disorders are launched by lust. The most obvious are examples of paraphilia, which grow from bad to worse: voyeurism, fetishism, exhibitionism, pedophilia. Less obvious is the mental illness that employs sex as a weapon or for power; these people are domineering, hostile, and violent. They commit serious felony crimes with no bother about the consequences. Such is the mind of the rapist, the kidnapper, and the sociopath. Picture the victims of such crimes who have been traumatized beyond belief, and develop long term, often debilitating illnesses such as Bipolar Disorder, Post-Traumatic Stress Disorder, Gender Identity Disorder, or Dissociative Identity Disorder.

Often, sexual deviance begins with an infatuation with pornography; in fact, Internet pornography is becoming an epidemic addiction. This also is a progressive condition which develops into greater lewdness. It may begin with pictures of naked people, and then videos of people fornicating; next comes the viewing of more risqué sexual behavior (I will let you imagine what that might mean); then perhaps an interest in child pornography. The seeing of it, and the constant thinking of it, are scarcely shy of actually doing it; but that is the inevitable end (see PRO 23:7). Addiction to pornography may lead to other impulse control disorders including chemical dependency.

What people don't realize is that lascivious behavior can provoke sexual dysfunction. The reason is this: the person ceases to feel aroused by normal sexual activity, so they require more and more kinkiness to produce the excitement. In time, not even that will get them going; so they turn to the wickedest means of getting their thrills. Sooner or later they lose the desire for anything normal, or possibly anything at all. Although they may still have the desire they cannot get aroused, function, or perform the act. When the equipment stops working a whole repertory of mental illnesses comes into play.

Not only is lust detrimental to your mental health it is toxic to your physical health, and potentially lethal. Countless diseases are transmitted sexually and many are incurable. These include herpes, genital warts, hepatitis C, and HIV. In the case of AIDS, it is always fatal. If you and your lover stay true, the risk is zero that you will get a disease via sex when neither of you are infected. The risk goes up dramatically each time one of you is unfaithful. Remember, when you fool around you are doing so with someone else that fools around. So, multiply your risk times the number of partners they have had, and the ones their partners have had, and so on. You get the point, right?

Monogamous couples find pleasure and fulfillment in their relationship; they stimulate each other in ways that delight their mate. Such people are happier, more satisfied, healthier, and live longer. When you seek alternate ways of generating arousal it is artificial, and it becomes less and less satisfying. Besides, decent and proper intercourse within the confines of marriage has worked fine for centuries without the need for extracurricular activity. If you are truly in love, your honey is your desire and you don't lose your passion for him or her. And the sex is far more powerful. Compare copulation with making love; making love is way more gratifying and lasting. God commands that we remain true to our soul mates. In the seventh commandment we are taught that any sex outside of marriage is unlawful; and injurious, because it destroys the unity and the trust.

- ISA 3:16-26 (paraphrased) ~ The Lord says, "Because the daughters of Zion have exalted themselves with their pride and arrogance, acting carefree and flirtatious, I will expose their nakedness and their sin will come back on their own heads. I will take away their ornaments, jewelry, perfume, hair-dos, and flashy clothes. Their sweet smell will be replaced with stink, their wardrobe with rags, and their beauty with burning. They will be slain by the sword; they will cry and moan over their desolation."

- MAT 5:28 ~ Jesus said, "You have heard that it was said, 'You shall not commit adultery.' But I say to you that everyone who looks at a woman with lustful intent has already committed adultery with her in his heart."

- MAR 4:19 ~ Jesus said, "The cares of the world and the deceitfulness of riches and the desires for other things enter in and choke the word, and it proves unfruitful."

- ROM 1:18-32 ~ The wrath of God is revealed from heaven against all ungodliness and unrighteousness of men, who by their unrighteousness suppress the truth. For what can be known about God is plain to them, because God has shown it to them. For his invisible attributes, namely, his eternal power and divine nature, have been clearly perceived, ever since the creation of the world, in the things that have been made. So they are without excuse. For although they knew God, they did not honor him as God or give thanks to him, but they became futile in their thinking, and their foolish hearts were darkened. Claiming to be wise, they became fools, and exchanged the glory of the immortal God for images resembling mortal man and birds and animals and creeping things. Therefore God gave them up in the lusts of their hearts to impurity, to the dishonoring of their bodies among themselves, because they exchanged the truth about God for a lie and worshiped and served the creature rather than the Creator, who is blessed forever! Amen. For this reason God gave them up to dishonorable passions. For their women exchanged natural relations for those that are contrary to nature; and the men likewise gave up natural relations with women and were consumed with passion for one another, men committing shameless acts with men and receiving in themselves the due penalty for their error. And since they did not see fit to acknowledge God, God gave them up to a debased mind to do what ought not to be done. They were filled with all manner of unrighteousness, evil, covetousness, malice. They are full of envy, murder, strife, deceit, maliciousness. They are gossips, slanderers, haters of God, insolent, haughty, boastful, inventors of evil, disobedient to parents, foolish, faithless, heartless, ruthless. Though they know God's righteous decree that those who practice such things deserve to die, they not only do them but give approval to those who practice them.

- ROM 8:5-7,13 ~ For those who live according to the flesh set their minds on the things of the flesh, but those who live according to the Spirit set their minds on the things of the Spirit. For to set the mind on the flesh is death, but to set the mind on the Spirit is life and peace. For the mind that is set on the flesh is hostile to God, for it does not submit to God's law; indeed, it cannot... For if you live according to the flesh you will die, but if by the Spirit you put to death the deeds of the body, you will live.

- 1 CO 6:18 ~ Flee from sexual immorality. Every other sin a person commits is outside the body, but the sexually immoral person sins against his own body.

- JAM 1:13-15 ~ Let no one say when he is tempted, "I am being tempted by God," for God cannot be tempted with evil, and he himself tempts no one. But each person is tempted when he is lured and enticed by his own desire. Then desire when it has conceived gives birth to sin, and sin when it is fully grown brings forth death.

- 1 PE 2:11 ~ Beloved, I urge you as sojourners and exiles to abstain from the passions of the flesh, which wage war against your soul.

"The expense of spirit in a waste of shame is lust in action." – William Shakespeare

Greed

Striving for material wealth instead of spiritual wealth causes us to neglect or forget God. To chase power, riches, pleasure, or fame is greed. Not that fame and fortune are sins, but the love of them. Like the Lord said, you can't love God and money (MAT 6:24; LUK 16:13), because you will end up despising one or the other. The original sin by Adam and Eve was motivated by greed. They wanted what God had: knowledge, power. But the only knowledge they acquired was the knowledge of sin, and instead of making them powerful like God it made them sinful like Satan. And we too have partaken of that forbidden fruit.

Greed underlies a multitude of other sins such as selfishness, dishonesty, cheating, swindling, hoarding, and stinginess. Greed has no boundaries; everything is fair game. Some people will do whatever it takes to get ahead or get rich, whether by hook or by crook. It matters nothing whether they earned it. I suppose many think they are entitled somehow. And when they amass their riches they maintain "it's all mine." Recall the words of Paul quoting Christ, "It is better to give than to receive" (ACT 20:35). But with the greedy person it's all take and no give.

Like lust, greed is never satisfied. If you are in a hurry to amass wealth and fortune there will never be enough. Greed is covered in the tenth commandment: covetousness. If you desire what someone else has, that is envy. It just makes you dissatisfied with what you have. Even if you had what they have it wouldn't satisfy you; that is the law of greed. The motivation for stealing also is greed, which is covered in the eighth commandment. It is greater in the hierarchy because it is one thing to want what others have and still another to take it. Often, people steal to support other sinful ways, such as lust and sloth.

Disorders such as Factitious and Malingering may be influenced by greed. The factitious person unconsciously seeks secondary gain or attention by playing the poor, sick, pitiful person. The malingerer is much more aware of the motives; he or she deliberately feigns illness to receive monetary compensation or to avoid punishment. The Cluster B Personality Disorders relate to greed as well. These people tend to be control freaks, very manipulative, very selfish. They want to be the center of attention, they want everything their way, they expect immediate gratification, and they are interested in getting their needs or desires met but not so much others'.

- JOB 20:15 ~ He swallows down riches and vomits them up again; God casts them out of his belly.

- PRO 1:18-19 ~ But these men lie in wait for their own blood; they set an ambush for their own lives. Such are the ways of everyone who is greedy for unjust gain; it takes away the life of its possessors.

- PRO 11:4,28 ~ Riches do not profit in the day of wrath, but righteousness delivers from death. Whoever trusts in his riches will fall, but the righteous will flourish like a green leaf.

- PRO 23:5 ~ When your eyes light on it, it is gone, for suddenly it sprouts wings, flying like an eagle toward heaven.

- ECC 5:10-14 ~ He who loves money will not be satisfied with money, nor he who loves wealth with his income; this also is vanity. When goods increase, they increase who eat them, and what advantage has their owner but to see them with his eyes? Sweet is the sleep of a laborer, whether he eats little or much, but the full stomach of the rich will not let him sleep. There is a grievous evil that I have seen under the sun: riches were kept by their owner to his hurt, and those riches were lost in a bad venture. And he is father of a son, but he has nothing in his hand.

- MAT 6:19-21 ~ Jesus said, "Do not lay up for yourselves treasures on earth, where moth and rust destroy and where thieves break in and steal, but lay up for yourselves treasures in heaven, where neither moth nor rust destroys and where thieves do not break in and steal. For where your treasure is, there your heart will be also."

- LUK 12:15-21 ~ And Jesus said to them, "Take care, and be on your guard against all covetousness, for one's life does not consist in the abundance of his possessions." And he told them a parable, saying, "The land of a rich man produced plentifully, and he thought to himself, 'What shall I do, for I have nowhere to store my crops?' And he said, 'I will do this: I will tear down my barns and build larger ones, and there I will store all my grain and my goods. And I will say to my soul, Soul, you have ample goods laid up for many years; relax, eat, drink, be merry.' But God said to him, 'Fool! This night your soul is required of you, and the things you have prepared, whose will they be?' So is the one who lays up treasure for himself and is not rich toward God."

- ACT 8:20 ~ But Peter said to him, "May your silver perish with you, because you thought you could obtain the gift of God with money!"

- 1 TI 6:6-10,17 ~ But godliness with contentment is great gain, for we brought nothing into the world, and we cannot take anything out of the world. But if we have food and clothing, with these we will be content. But those who desire to be rich fall into temptation, into a snare, into many senseless and harmful desires that plunge people into ruin and destruction. For the love of money is the root of all kinds of evils. It is through this craving that some have wandered away from the faith and pierced themselves with many pangs... As for the rich in this present age, charge them not to be haughty, nor to set their hopes on the uncertainty of riches, but on God, who richly provides us with everything to enjoy.

- JAM 5:1-3 ~ Come now, you rich, weep and howl for the miseries that are coming upon you. Your riches have rotted and your garments are moth-eaten. Your gold and silver have corroded, and their corrosion will be evidence against you and will eat your flesh like fire. You have laid up treasure in the last days.

"Poverty wants much, but avarice, everything." – Publilius Syrus

Pride

Pride includes conceit, arrogance, and self-exaltation. God prefers that we be meek and humble. He deserves the glory for your accomplishments, not you. After all, if it wasn't for God you wouldn't even be here. It is God that gives us power, talent, and abilities, so give the glory to him; and brag about the great things he has done for you. If you give him the credit he will prosper you; you will be successful and you will be placed in positions of greater responsibility and authority.

Satan wanted the knowledge, power, and glory of God. His greed and pride got him tossed out of heaven. In a way, Satan was a narcissist; he loved himself. Since he couldn't be God he hates God. If we believe in God, love him, and are modest and unassuming God will give us the kingdom and we will share his glory. Too bad for Satan; he could have experienced the glory if he hadn't wanted it all for himself. It is okay to love yourself as you love your neighbor, but do not place yourself before God or before others (MAT 22:36-40).

The pride of Satan was in violation of the first commandment: Put God first in your life. Satan put himself first. Actually, the first four commandments are about reverencing God. Satan influences people to worship him, idols, or anything but God to steal them away from God, thereby violating the second commandment. Satan cursed God, violating the third. Well, Satan has violated them all. But he is too proud to seek forgiveness from the God he has chosen to oppose. God will forgive you, even if you have violated all ten of the commandments; but you must swallow your pride and trust in him for your salvation. And do try your best to listen to him, and obey him.

- PSA 10:2-4 ~ In arrogance the wicked hotly pursue the poor; let them be caught in the schemes that they have devised. For the wicked boasts of the desires of his soul, and the one greedy for gain curses and renounces the LORD. In the pride of his face the wicked does not seek him; all his thoughts are, "There is no God."

- PSA 12:3 ~ May the LORD cut off all flattering lips, the tongue that makes great boasts.

- PSA 101:5 ~ Whoever slanders his neighbor secretly I will destroy. Whoever has a haughty look and an arrogant heart I will not endure.

- PRO 11:2 ~ When pride comes, then comes disgrace, but with the humble is wisdom.

- PRO 16:18-19 ~ Pride goes before destruction, and a haughty spirit before a fall. It is better to be of a lowly spirit with the poor than to divide the spoil with the proud.

- ISA 10:33 ~ Behold, the Lord GOD of hosts will lop the boughs with terrifying power; the great in height will be hewn down, and the lofty will be brought low.

- LUK 14:7-11 ~ Now Jesus told a parable to those who were invited, when he noticed how they chose the places of honor, saying to them, "When you are invited by someone to a wedding feast, do not sit down in a place of honor, lest someone more distinguished than you be invited by him, and he who invited you both will come and say to you, 'Give your place to this person,' and then you will begin with shame to take the lowest place. But when you are invited, go and sit in the lowest place, so that when your host comes he may say to you, 'Friend, move up higher.' Then you will be honored in the presence of all who sit at table with you. For everyone who exalts himself will be humbled, and he who humbles himself will be exalted."

- LUK 18:9-14 ~ Jesus also told this parable to some who trusted in themselves that they were righteous, and treated others with contempt: "Two men went up into the temple to pray, one a Pharisee and the other a tax collector. The Pharisee, standing by himself, prayed thus: 'God, I thank you that I am not like other men, extortioners, unjust, adulterers, or even like this tax collector. I fast twice a week; I give tithes of all that I get.' But the tax collector, standing far off, would not even lift up his eyes to heaven, but beat his breast, saying, 'God, be merciful to me, a sinner!' I tell you, this man went down to his house justified, rather than the other. For everyone who exalts himself will be humbled, but the one who humbles himself will be exalted."

- EPH 2:8-9 ~ For by grace you have been saved through faith. And this is not your own doing; it is the gift of God, not a result of works, so that no one may boast.

- 1 PE 5:5-6 ~ Likewise, you who are younger, be subject to the elders. Clothe yourselves, all of you, with humility toward one another, for "God opposes the proud but gives grace to the humble." Humble yourselves, therefore, under the mighty hand of God so that at the proper time he may exalt you.

"The greatest of faults is to be conscious of none." – Thomas Carlyle

Deceit

Who in the entire history of mankind has never told a lie (well, except Christ)? Deception is just as bad because it is a deliberate attempt to conceal the truth. Anytime the truth is obscured or tainted it can no longer be truth, for truth is pure. You cannot have several truths about a single fact. If a witness tells one lie the whole testimony is thrown out. That is why the Holy Bible is inerrant; it has to be. If any part of it was untrue, how would you tell the difference between the true and untrue? God is truth, and he wants us to follow him. To lie is to follow Satan, the father of lies. The ninth commandment refers to this sin: bearing false witness. Consider the power of truth over lies. You tell one lie, and then five more to cover that one, and twenty more to cover those, and before you know it there is a mountain of lies that you cannot surmount. Nobody can possibly keep track of all those lies. And a single truth exposes them all and the mountain crumbles. Just like the flicker of candlelight will break the deepest darkness, truth with collapse a tower of tall tales. Lying is an untenable position no matter where you stand.

Always walk in truth for it is the light that illuminates your path (PSA 119:105). The truth exposes everything that is false. Without truth you would get lost in darkness. Remember, Jesus is that light that shows you the way, presents the truth, and gives life (JOH 14:6). This is the ultimate, undisputable fact. God is truth; he is incapable of lying. Jesus Christ never told a lie; he wants us to become like him. And so we will, when we are brought home to live with him forever.

- LEV 19:16 ~ You shall not go around as a slanderer among your people, and you shall not stand up against the life of your neighbor: I am the LORD.

- PSA 12:2 ~ Everyone utters lies to his neighbor; with flattering lips and a double heart they speak.

- PRO 24:28 ~ Be not envious of evil men, nor desire to be with them, for their hearts devise violence, and their lips talk of trouble.

- PRO 19:5 ~ A false witness will not go unpunished, and he who breathes out lies will not escape.

- JOH 8:42-47 ~ Jesus said to them, "If God were your Father, you would love me, for I came from God and I am here. I came not of my own accord, but he sent me. Why do you not understand what I say? It is because you cannot bear to hear my word. You are of your father the devil, and your will is to do your father's desires. He was a murderer from the beginning, and does not stand in the truth, because there is no truth in him. When he lies, he speaks out of his own character, for he is a liar and the father of lies. But because I tell the truth, you do not believe me. Which one of you convicts me of sin? If I tell the truth, why do you not believe me? Whoever is of God hears the words of God. The reason why you do not hear them is that you are not of God."

- JAM 4:11 ~ Do not speak evil against one another, brothers. The one who speaks against a brother or judges his brother, speaks evil against the law and judges the law. But if you judge the law, you are not a doer of the law but a judge.

"Oh, what a tangled web we weave when first we practice to deceive." – Sir Walter Scott

Laziness

This is another sin that breeds a multitude of other sins. When there is nothing to do the mind wanders out of bounds. It begins with vain imaginations which lead to deviant behavior. Be active, productive, responsible, and earn your keep. Stay busy physically, mentally, and spiritually. This is especially true in regards to faith; God wants us to have an active faith.

- ROM 1:21 ~ For although they knew God, they did not honor him as God or give thanks to him, but they became futile in their thinking, and their foolish hearts were darkened.

- 2 CO 10:5 (KJV) ~ Cast out vain imaginations, and every high minded way that inserts itself before God. Bring to captivity every thought in obedience to Christ.

Lazy people do not want to work; they just want to have fun. But they want it for free. They'll resort to deceit, con games, making excuses, whatever it takes to get out of working for it. They want a handout, a free pass, or somebody else to pay. They'll collect welfare even when they are able bodied to hold a job. But they don't get anywhere, or achieve anything, except getting more lazy and fat. They have no ambition. If they spent as much time doing something as they did dodging it, they might become somebody.

- PRO 10:4-5,26 ~ A slack hand causes poverty, but the hand of the diligent makes rich. He who gathers in summer is a prudent son, but he who sleeps in harvest is a son who brings shame… Like vinegar to the teeth and smoke to the eyes, so is the sluggard to those who send him.

- PRO 24:30-34 ~ I passed by the field of a sluggard, by the vineyard of a man lacking sense, and behold, it was all overgrown with thorns; the ground was covered with nettles, and its stone wall was broken down. Then I saw and considered it; I looked and received instruction little sleep, a little slumber, a little folding of the hands to rest, and poverty will come upon you like a robber, and want like an armed man.

- PRO 26:13-16 ~ The sluggard says, "There is a lion in the road! There is a lion in the streets!" As a door turns on its hinges, so does a sluggard on his bed. The sluggard buries his hand in the dish; it wears him out to bring it back to his mouth. The sluggard is wiser in his own eyes than seven men who can answer sensibly.

- ECC 10:18 ~ Through sloth the roof sinks in, and through indolence the house leaks.

"He that is busy is tempted by but one devil; he that is idle, by a legion." – Thomas Fuller

Idolatry

The seven deadliest sins proposed by the Catholic Church (Pope Gregory I) include lust, avarice, pride, wrath, gluttony, sloth, and envy. We'll take a look at each one before we review how they all relate to idolatry.

> Lust: Have you ever desired sex with someone that you were not married to? Example: Imagining being intimate with someone or examining their private parts.
> Avarice: Have you ever acted stingy or greedy? Example – Not sharing your things or your gain with others.
> Pride: Have you ever thought yourself better than someone else? Example – Looking down on someone of perceived low estate.
> Wrath: Have you ever taken your anger out on someone else? Example – Yelling at someone who is not at fault for your bad mood.
> Gluttony: Have you ever overindulged in something? Example – Getting several desserts from the buffet.
> Sloth: Have you ever been lazy or neglected your responsibility? Example – Calling in sick when you simply didn't want to go to work.
> Envy: Have you ever wanted something that was not yours? Example – Wishing that your friend's companion would have chosen you.

These sins are very common, in that everybody has violated them one time or another. However, idolatry is often overlooked as being a commonplace and deadly sin. But it is both. One could argue it is the deadliest sin because it disrespects God. And commonplace: It is likely the most frequently committed sin. And what's more, it is a sin against God directly, whereas the others are often sins against others or our own bodies. Either way, it's putting something before God. The greatest of the Ten Commandments is to love God first, and the second is to refrain from worshipping idols. To violate either is to commit idolatry. God wants to be first in our lives and promises us everything if we do. When we do not put God first we have committed idolatry, and we stand to lose everything.

If you worship, idolize, or adore anyone: a famous person, a person of romantic interest, yourself, even a character in a book, you are guilty of idolatry. Do not yearn to be like or emulate a favorite movie star, athlete, celebrity, or historical figure; strive to be like Christ. Those people we admire the most are frequently people that were reflecting Christ. All glory, praise, and thanks should be directed to the Lord God; to give such adulation to anyone else is to place God second. Anytime you let anyone or anything come between you and God you have committed this grievous sin.

Using God's name in vain is idolatry because it is an insult to God. Blasphemy is idolatry because it is akin to calling God a liar. Neglecting to honor God on the Sabbath is idolatry as it places him lower in priority. Practicing witchcraft, consulting mediums, and all other occultist activity are forms of idolatry and are an abomination to God. Putting faith in astrological forecasts is the same thing. Lust, greed, and pride can be considered forms of idolatry as they favor the flesh over the spirit. The love of riches is idolatry, as is placing any worldly desires and pursuits foremost in your life. Disbelief in God is idolatrous and dangerous; it leads to the second death.

- EXO 20:4-7 ~ God says, "You shall not make for yourself a carved image, or any likeness of anything that is in heaven above, or that is in the earth beneath, or that is in the water under the earth. You shall not bow down to them or serve them, for I the LORD your God am a jealous God, visiting the iniquity of the fathers on the children to the third and the fourth generation of those who hate me, but showing steadfast love to thousands of those who love me and keep my commandments. You shall not take the name of the LORD your God in vain, for the LORD will not hold him guiltless who takes his name in vain."

- LEV 19:12 ~ You shall not swear by my name falsely, and so profane the name of your God: I am the LORD.

- DEU 5:8-9 ~ You shall not make for yourself a carved image, or any likeness of anything that is in heaven above, or that is on the earth beneath, or that is in the water under the earth. You shall not bow down to them or serve them; for I the LORD your God am a jealous God, visiting the iniquity of the fathers on the children to the third and fourth generation of those who hate me.

- DEU 18:10-12 ~ There shall not be found among you anyone who burns his son or his daughter as an offering, anyone who practices divination or tells fortunes or interprets omens, or a sorcerer or a charmer or a medium or a necromancer or one who inquires of the dead, for whoever does these things is an abomination to the LORD. And because of these abominations the LORD your God is driving them out before you.

- JOB 31:26-28 ~ If I have looked at the sun when it shone, or the moon moving in splendor, and my heart has been secretly enticed, and my mouth has kissed my hand, this also would be an iniquity to be punished by the judges, for I would have been false to God above.

- ISA 42:8 ~ God says, "I am the LORD; that is my name; my glory I give to no other, nor my praise to carved idols."

- MAT 4:10 ~ Jesus told Satan, "Be gone, Satan! For it is written, 'You shall worship the Lord your God and him only shall you serve.'"

- EPH 5:1-5 ~ Therefore be imitators of God, as beloved children. And walk in love, as Christ loved us and gave himself up for us, a fragrant offering and sacrifice to God. But sexual immorality and all impurity or covetousness must not even be named among you, as is proper among saints. Let there be no filthiness nor foolish talk nor crude joking, which are out of place, but instead let there be thanksgiving. For you may be sure of this, that everyone who is sexually immoral or impure, or who is covetous (that is, an idolater), has no inheritance in the kingdom of Christ and God.

- COL 3:5 ~ Put to death therefore what is earthly in you: sexual immorality, impurity, passion, evil desire, and covetousness, which is idolatry.

- 1 TI 6:10 ~ For the love of money is a root of all kinds of evils. It is through this craving that some have wandered away from the faith and pierced themselves with many pangs.

- REV 21:8 ~ But as for the cowardly, the faithless, the detestable, as for murderers, the sexually immoral, sorcerers, idolaters, and all liars, their portion will be in the lake that burns with fire and sulfur, which is the second death.

Thus, idolatry covers a lot of ground when it comes to separating oneself from God. The nation of Israel found this out quite often. Whenever they wandered away from God, and after idols or worldly things, they were punished, exiled, enslaved, or destroyed. Whenever they put God first they prospered, grew, conquered enemies, and were greatly rewarded. The same is true in the world today. It seems the farther the USA strays from God the worse is our economy, social problems, hardships, and global standing. Everyone needs to be aware of the destructiveness of this deadly sin and the ease of falling into its clutches.

- PSA 16:4 ~ The sorrows of those who run after another god shall multiply; their drink offerings of blood I will not pour out or take their names on my lips.

- MAT 6:24 ~ Jesus said, "No one can serve two masters, for either he will hate the one and love the other, or he will be devoted to the one and despise the other. You cannot serve God and money."

- 1 JO 5:20-21 ~ We know that the Son of God has come and has given us understanding, so that we may know him who is true; and we are in him who is true, in his Son Jesus Christ. He is the true God and eternal life. Little children, keep yourselves from idols.

Do you remember the story of King David who committed adultery with Bathsheba and murdered Uriah to satisfy his passions? He took a man's life to steal his wife. He thought he got away with it until the prophet Nathan admonished the king. Fortunately for David, he repented and God forgave him. But that did not absolve King David of some devastating consequences; his despicable acts would cost him three sons and inject continuous turmoil into his household from then on (read 2 SA 11 &12). David never forgot God's grace and mercy, however; the king reformed his ways and taught his people the consequences of placing anything or anyone before God. To this day that lesson stands as an example of how everyone, even men of God, can be overcome by lusts of this world, which lead to severe penalties. God will not tolerate idolatry, which is a violation of the first and most important commandment. One final note, the union between David and Bathsheba may already have been part of God's plan as the lineage of Christ would follow through their son Solomon. So it is possible that they would have ended up together without David forcing the situation.

Activity

See how many of the Ten Commandments you can remember. Try to get them in the right order.

1_____ 6_____

2_____ 7_____

3_____ 8_____

4_____ 9_____

5_____ 10_____

When you committed the following sins, how did it affect your life?

Lust _____

Greed _____

Pride _____

Deceit _____

Laziness _____

When others committed the following sins, how did it affect your life?

Lust _____

Greed _____

Pride _____

Deceit _____

Laziness _____

What forms of idolatry have you engaged in? That is, give examples of when you placed something or someone before God in your life.

_____

_____

_____

_____

How did things decline for you when you were not placing God first in your life?

_____

_____

_____

_____

How did things improve for you when you were placing God first in your life?

_____

_____

_____

_____

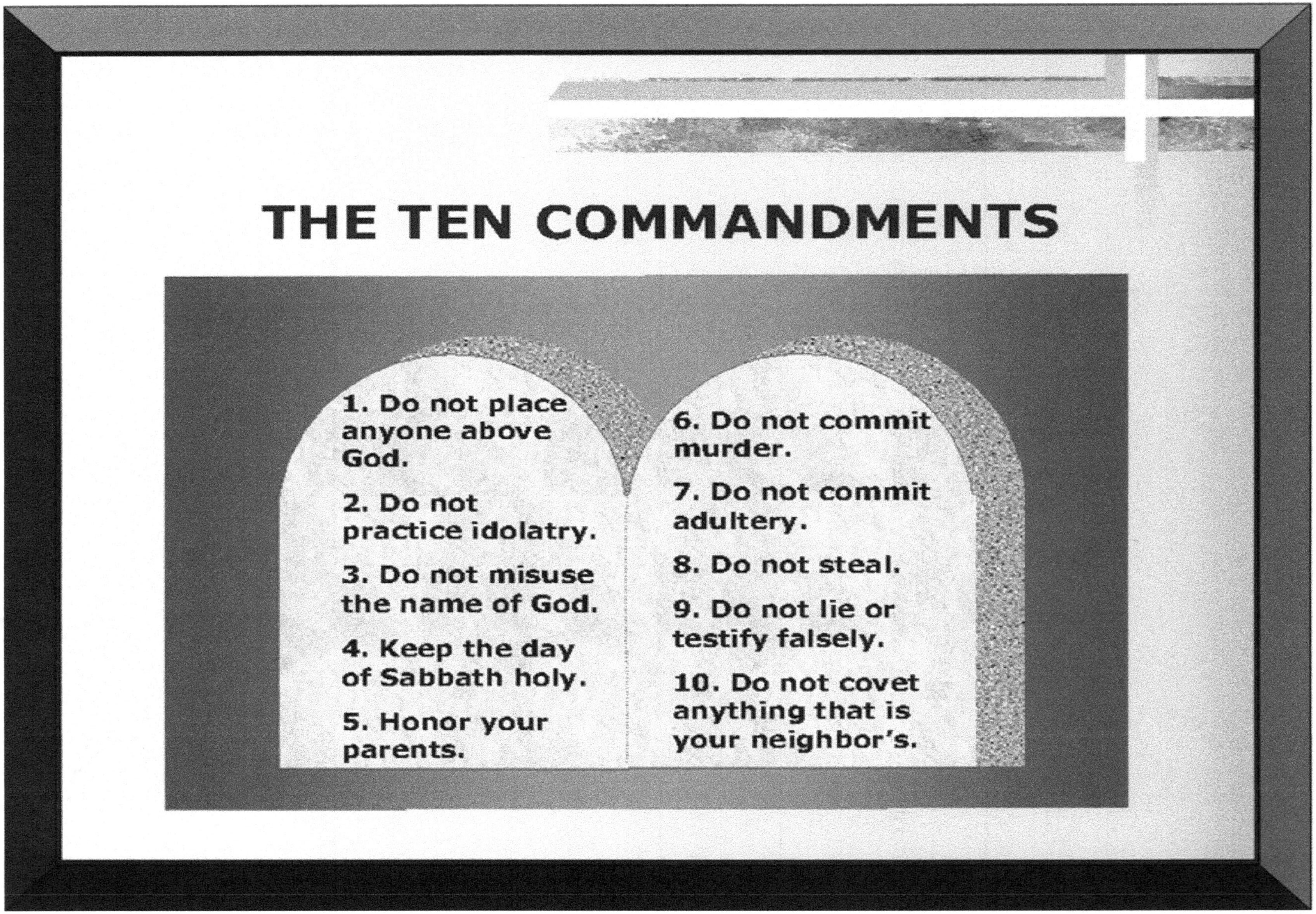
THE TEN COMMANDMENTS
1. Do not place anyone above God.
2. Do not practice idolatry.
3. Do not misuse the name of God.
4. Keep the day of Sabbath holy.
5. Honor your parents.
6. Do not commit murder.
7. Do not commit adultery.
8. Do not steal.
9. Do not lie or testify falsely.
10. Do not covet anything that is your neighbor's.

RESOLVING GUILT

OBJECTIVE	Learn to distinguish healthy guilt from unhealthy guilt. Determine how guilt can be good for you or devastating to you.
INTERVENTION	Discuss guilt, and how it teaches us. Relate this to the sacrifice of Christ. Realize how one should respond to God's loving kindness: contrition, confession, repentance, reform, reparation, forgiveness.
PLAN	Rely on God's forgiveness and freely give it to others. Do not get into the blame game. Make an earnest effort to do the Lord's will and stay focused on the path of righteousness. Let Christ take the guilt away by accepting his sacrifice.

"Guilt is present in the very hesitation, even though the deed be not committed." – Cicero

"Every man is guilty of the good he did not do." – Voltaire

Healthy Guilt

When children develop a sense of morality they become accountable for their own actions. That is, once we have internalized the standards of our parents and our culture, we don't need supervision. We know what not to do, and we know when we have done wrong. Anyone that has a conscience will feel guilty when this happens. Even a child will begin to feel shame when he or she has crossed the line. We all develop a moral code and feel bad when we don't live up to it. Human beings know right from wrong because God has given us the power of discernment. And those who are motivated to please God are displeased with themselves when they don't.

- GEN 2:16 & GEN 3:1-13,22-23 (paraphrased) ~ God gave a command to Adam saying, "You may freely eat of any tree in the garden, but you may not eat from the tree of the knowledge of good and evil; for on the day that you disobey this command you will surely die." The crafty serpent asked Eve, "Did God say you cannot eat from every tree of the garden?" Eve replied, "We can eat the fruit of all the trees, except the tree in the middle of the garden. God told us not to eat from that tree or we will die." The serpent replied, "You will not die. God knows if you eat that fruit it will open your eyes and you will be like gods, knowing good and evil." So Eve gave into temptation, took some fruit and ate it, and gave some to Adam who also was there, and he ate it too. And immediately their eyes were opened and they realized they were naked; and they made aprons of fig leaves. Then God called to them; but they were afraid and hid from him. God again called out to Adam, saying, "Where are you?" And Adam said, "I heard you calling but I was afraid because I was naked; so I hid myself." God replied, "Who told you that you were naked? Have you eaten from the tree I commanded you to leave alone?" Adam blamed it on Eve saying "The woman you brought to me, she gave me some fruit and I ate it." Then God asked Eve, "What have you done?" Eve blamed it on the serpent saying, "The serpent tricked me, and I ate." And God said, "Behold, man has become like us, knowing good and evil. He must not take from the tree of life, and eat, and live forever." So God banished them from the garden.

God laid down the Law so we would know right from wrong. The moment we do wrong we also know sin. His Law gives us the wisdom of obedience. When we disobey God we should feel guilty; this is a natural response to wrongdoing. We also should feel sorry; it would be abnormal to feel no remorse. Even the sociopath knows when they commit evil; they just don't care. Those who don't care about disobeying God will suffer severe punishment. As God pointed out to Adam and Eve, as well as to the rest of us, the punishment for sin is death (GEN 2:16; ROM 6:23; JAM 1:14-15).

- ROM 3:19-21 ~ If you are sure that you are a guide to the blind, a light to those who are in darkness, an instructor of the foolish, a teacher of children, having in the law the embodiment of knowledge and truth – you who teach others, do you not teach yourself?

- ROM 4:15 ~ The law brings wrath, but where there is no law there is no transgression.

- ROM 5:13 ~ Sin indeed was in the world before the law was given, but sin is not counted where there is no law.

- ROM 7:7,14 ~ What then shall we say? That the law is sin? By no means! Yet if it had not been for the law, I would not have known sin… We know that the law is spiritual, but I am of the flesh, sold under sin.

- JAM 2:10 ~ Whoever keeps the whole law but fails in one point has become accountable for all of it.

- 1 JO 3:4 ~ Everyone who makes a practice of sinning also practices lawlessness; sin is lawlessness.

Unfortunately, all people are guilty of sin.

- ECC 7:20 ~ Surely there is not a righteous man on earth who does good and never sins.

- ROM 3:23 ~ All have sinned and fall short of the glory of God.

- 1 JO 1:8 ~ If we say we have no sin, we deceive ourselves, and the truth is not in us.

Since we are all guilty we all deserve to die. That's why we need a Savior. If it wasn't for Christ's sacrifice for sin nobody could be saved. But even though Christ has paid the debt, it doesn't mean you can do whatever you want. Where is the contrition if you keep repeating the misbehavior? That would indicate an unwillingness to amend your ways. God will forgive you if you believe; but with forgiveness comes responsibility. That your guilt has been removed should motivate you to improve; the incentive is that Jesus will reward you handsomely if you stay true to him. And forgive others (note: forgive yourself also).

- LUK 6:37 ~ Jesus said, "Judge not, and you will not be judged; condemn not, and you will not be condemned; forgive, and you will be forgiven."

- ROM 6:1-2,12-16 ~ What shall we say then? Are we to continue in sin that grace may abound? By no means! How can we who died to sin still live in it? Let not sin therefore reign in your mortal body, to make you obey its passions. Do not present your members to sin as instruments for unrighteousness, but present yourselves to God as those who have been brought from death to life, and your members to God as instruments for righteousness. For sin will have no dominion over you, since you are not under law but under grace. What then? Are we to sin because we are not under law but under grace? By no means! Do you not know that if you present yourselves to anyone as obedient slaves, you are slaves of the one whom you obey, either of sin, which leads to death, or of obedience, which leads to righteousness?

- HEB 10:26-29 ~ If we go on sinning deliberately after receiving the knowledge of the truth, there no longer remains a sacrifice for sins, but a fearful expectation of judgment, and a fury of fire that will consume the adversaries. Anyone who has set aside the law of Moses dies without mercy on the evidence of two or three witnesses. How much worse punishment, do you think, will be deserved by the one who has trampled underfoot the Son of God, and has profaned the blood of the covenant by which he was sanctified, and has outraged the Spirit of grace?

- 2 PE 2:20-21 ~ For if, after they have escaped the defilements of the world through the knowledge of our Lord and Savior Jesus Christ, they are again entangled in them and overcome, the last state has become worse for them than the first. For it would have been better for them never to have known the way of righteousness than after knowing it to turn back from the holy commandment delivered to them.

Response to Guilt

A response is required when you are truly sorry for defying God. Remember, parents: children must be taught that disobeying their parents means they are going against God, as stated in the fifth commandment. If you do not try to refine your conduct, trusting in God to do better, the guilt might get worse (if you are listening to your conscience at all). Part of the recovery from guilt is making a commitment to God to develop good habits. It is a small cost, especially when you consider the payoff. You have to feel sincerely sorry, confess your sins to God, ask him for forgiveness, and then make every effort to reform. Repeat this process whenever you have wronged another person, and it will be felt by God (MAT 25:40,45). Refer to the section on Forgiveness for more on this topic.

- PSA 32:5 ~ I acknowledged my sin to you, and I did not cover my iniquity; I said, "I will confess my transgressions to the LORD," and you forgave the iniquity of my sin.

- ISA 57:15 ~ Thus says the One who is high and lifted up, who inhabits eternity, whose name is Holy: "I dwell in the high and holy place, and also with him who is of a contrite and lowly spirit, to revive the spirit of the lowly, and to revive the heart of the contrite."

- EZE 18:30 ~ "I will judge you, O house of Israel, every one according to his ways," declares the Lord GOD. "Repent and turn from all your transgressions, lest iniquity be your ruin."

- HOS 5:15 ~ God says, "I will return again to my place, until they acknowledge their guilt and seek my face, and in their distress earnestly seek me."

- LUK 13:3 ~ Jesus said, "I tell you; but unless you repent, you will all likewise perish."

- ROM 10:10 ~ With the heart one believes and is justified, and with the mouth one confesses and is saved.

- 2 CO 7:9-10 ~ I rejoice, not because you were grieved, but because you were grieved into repenting. For you felt a godly grief, so that you suffered no loss through us. For godly grief produces a repentance that leads to salvation without regret, whereas worldly grief produces death.

- JAM 5:16 ~ Confess your sins to one another and pray for one another, that you may be healed. The prayer of a righteous person has great power as it is working.

- 1 JO 1:9 ~ If we confess our sins, he is faithful and just to forgive us our sins and to cleanse us from all unrighteousness.

God is a loving Father who wants the best for his children. Yes, he will correct us when we are wrong like any loving parent. But he does not impose hardship upon us due to our iniquity; at least not in this life. And he will always give us a way out when we are tempted to do wrong. He gives us every chance in the world to find him, learn his truth, and change our ways. He does not bombard us with burdens we cannot carry or castigate us unmercifully for every sin. But he does give us free will. Those who choose to ignore him, disregard his ways, or despise him – they will suffer the ultimate penalty.

- JOB 5:17 ~ Behold, blessed is the one whom God reproves; therefore despise not the discipline of the Almighty.

- PSA 103:8-12 ~ The LORD is merciful and gracious, slow to anger and abounding in steadfast love. He will not always chide, nor will he keep his anger forever. He does not deal with us according to our sins, nor repay us according to our iniquities. For as high as the heavens are above the earth, so great is his steadfast love toward those who fear him; as far as the east is from the west, so far does he remove our transgressions from us.

- PRO 3:11-12 ~ My son, do not despise the LORD's discipline or be weary of his reproof, for the LORD reproves him whom he loves, as a father the son in whom he delights.

"Whatever guilt is perpetrated by some evil prompting, it is grievous to the author of the crime. This is the first punishment of guilt: that no one who is guilty is acquitted at the judgment seat of his own conscience." – Juvenal

Unhealthy Guilt

"The worst guilt is to accept an unearned guilt." – Ayn Rand

So, feeling guilty is normal, at least if you are indeed guilty of a sin of commission or a sin of omission. But some people blame themselves for things of which they are not guilty or could not control. Either they have a guilty conscience, or they internalize the false accusations of others, or they have endured unreasonable and horrific punishment for the slightest infractions, or they have delusions of persecution, or they were raised by fanatical religious extremists, or they were brainwashed by some ungodly cult, or they want to be a martyr, or they have an overbearing superego, or who knows? None of this is good. Such things are destructive to your self-esteem, your psyche, and your ability to function overall.

Sometimes a client will come to you with a major guilt complex. This can develop in childhood or later on in life. Some kids get blamed for everything, like when the parents fight or hurt one another and take it out on the kids; or the kids blame themselves for a divorce thinking something is wrong with them. Maybe they were chastised endlessly for having feelings, like a teen experiencing hormonal change and having sexual fantasies. Or maybe it was an abusive husband that governed the household with an authoritarian attitude, offensive behavior, and tyrannical rule. Constant yelling and screaming in a home can create a guilt complex, especially if you are the recipient of the verbal abuse. Certainly any kind of abuse will cause disturbances in thinking and mood. These victims need to be reassured that it is not their fault, and that there is consolation in knowing Christ will bear the burden of it.

I had a female patient from Mexico who had been raped by her alcoholic father from ages 10-12 before her mother finally threw him out and they moved to the USA. The patient later married alcoholic men just like her father and was physically abused by them. And she blamed herself for all of this, though she was a devout Catholic. I asked her how she could possibly feel responsible for their irresponsible behavior. She thought she may have coaxed them, or deserved it somehow. She felt like she must have been asking for punishment, that she needed to be reproved for her sins. I told her there is no way a ten year old is emotionally equipped or mature enough to possibly understand incest, and that there is nothing that can justify men who beat up or rape women. I reminded her that Christ had already paid for her sins, as well as for the sins of those who abuse others as she had been abused. But to receive a pardon one must repent, seek God and his forgiveness, and make amends. It would not be an easy ride for this lady as she struggled to give the guilt to Jesus, but she delivered it one parcel at a time. Without her solid faith she would never have gotten relief. She also was fortunate to have found a good man to marry on her third try who had a profound faith. Together they made a formidable team, and defeated the devil's attempt to pierce her soul further with guilt and shame. She was able to forgive herself, and those men.

If you are consumed with guilt it will prevent you from moving forward. And you will dwell on it all the more. Negativity cannot produce anything positive. Swimming in the guilt will produce more guilt; stagnant water just gets more polluted over time. Purification by the blood of Jesus cleanses the soul of impurities such as guilt, shame, and worthlessness. Give it to Christ. He earned it. It belongs to him. He will give you peace, righteousness, and life in return. Only a fool would pass up such a bargain. But God's wisdom is not discerned with our feeble minds; it is discerned by the spirit (1 CO 2:7-16). So don't take God for granted (JAM 1:25), don't deny him (MAT 10:32-33), and remember that you cannot do anything without him (JOH 15:4).

- EPH 1:4 ~ He chose us in him before the foundation of the world, that we should be holy and blameless before him.

- PHP 2:13-15 ~ It is God who works in you, both to will and to work for his good pleasure. Do all things without grumbling or disputing, that you may be blameless and innocent, children of God without blemish in the midst of a crooked and twisted generation, among whom you shine as lights in the world.

- JDE 1:24-25 ~ To him who is able to keep you from stumbling and present you blameless before the presence of his glory with great joy, to the only God, our Savior, through Jesus Christ our Lord, be glory, majesty, dominion, and authority, before all time, now and forever. Amen.

In conclusion, there are two types of guilt: healthy and unhealthy. Healthy guilt is our conscience reminding us when an offense falls below our standards of morality. It is normal to feel remorse for hurting another person, or to be disappointed when we have disobeyed God, because it teaches us. To resolve the situation acknowledge the wrong, repent with genuine sorrow, make amends, and change the behavior. Don't forget to forgive; and don't forget that you forgave. The guilt will subside; but the lesson will survive.

Unhealthy guilt is unresolved. An earned guilt might be unresolved because the person continued to repeat the sin, never paid the debt, or didn't face the consequences. In the case of unearned guilt it is impossible to make amends or discontinue the wrongdoing. How can you resolve that for which you are not responsible? In such cases, the best way to release the guilt is to focus on the truth. Remind clients to listen to their spirit as it will always know the right thing to do and it will never lie to them. Have them perform a reality check by examining their experience, the circumstances, and lingering beliefs.

A common example of unhealthy, unearned guilt is survivor's guilt; a phenomenon experienced by many a soldier who has witnessed the horror of war. It is often a delayed reaction for a great number of veterans who suffer from PTSD or related adjustment disorder. The full brunt of the anxiety, guilt, and fear usually hits them after their deployment and it continues to bury them in negativity. For some, the darkness drives away the light and they feel locked in a dungeon from which there is no escape. But the entire syndrome is based upon a lie, that somehow those who fell were better men and women than they. What these victims need most are frequent helpings of God's grace and truth.

If you have done the right thing you should not feel guilty; if you do, something is terribly amiss. You know in your heart when you've done wrong; if you've messed it up then fix it. If you haven't, but you believe you have, you are lying to yourself. Guilt that is carried too long will cause serious mental health problems because it gets heavier. Resolve it and let it go. Whether real or not, we must thank and praise God through Jesus Christ, who has taken the guilt of sin upon himself and covered it with his righteousness. But though he has forgiven us we are obligated to repair the damage, adjust our conduct, and listen to the truth. A final point: if you can't make amends or pay it back, you actually can, by paying it forward.

"To show resentment at a reproach is to acknowledge one may have deserved it." – Tacitus

"He declares himself guilty who justifies himself before accusation." – Thomas Fuller

"The greatest incitement to guilt is the hope of sinning with impunity." – Cicero

Activity

How can guilt be good for you?

_____

_____

_____

Do you still carry any guilt for past offenses against others? If so, what offenses?

_____

_____

_____

What things can a person do to be relieved of guilt?

_____

_____

_____

Describe how guilt can be unhealthy.

_____

_____

_____

Christ accepted the guilt for all the sin in the world. When he took your sins upon himself, what did he give you in return?

_____

_____

What should you do in response to the loving sacrifice that Christ made for you?

_____

_____

RESENTMENT AND FORGIVENESS

OBJECTIVE	Learn how resentment creates negativity that prevents forward progress, inhibits positive thinking and growth, and damages relationships. Recognize the power of forgiveness to change the belief system and to let go of resentment.
INTERVENTION	Discuss the process of resentment and how it leads to destructive thinking and behavior. Then discuss the process of forgiveness and illustrate how it allows one to get unstuck and move on.
PLAN	Acknowledge how resentment begins and grows, and be prepared to stop it in its tracks. Practice forgiveness to overcome resentment, initiate acts of kindness, and mend relationships.

"He who requires much from himself and little from others, will keep himself from being the object of resentment." – Confucius

The Process of Resentment

Resentment is a destructive condition that festers like an open wound which will not heal. It builds up over time until it becomes a wall that blocks everything out, and in. That is, it so dominates our thoughts that nothing else can enter the mind, especially anything positive. A person can literally become stuck, thereby inhibiting forward progress or growth.

Resentment leads to equally destructive feelings and behavior because hurtful thoughts often result in harmful actions. The things we think about will be the things we act upon, positive or negative. As long as resentment lurks in the heart one can never achieve peace of mind. Nothing good can come from a tormented soul, and it can get progressively worse the more you dwell on it.

The process of resentment begins with a precipitating event. However, it is not the event that causes resentment but one's belief about the event. All too often, we assume that the reason we are upset is because someone else was deliberately mean to us. Whatever happened we have taken personal; so we blame them for our emotional pain.

For example, I was driving down the middle lane on the freeway a few years back. In my rearview mirror I spotted some fool weaving in and out of traffic, tail-gaiting people, cutting them off, driving recklessly and in a big hurry (which was futile considering the traffic congestion). He came up behind me about to climb up my bumper, swerved around me and back into my lane, causing me to brake.

In my earlier years I might have become angry and done something stupid. I might have let the incident get to me, and I would have arrived at work in a bad mood. A sour attitude can be contagious; if my patients sensed it they might become cranky as well. I've seen examples of road rage in the news. The self-appointed victim pulls the same act with the other driver. A cat and mouse game ensues which turns into a war. And the rage escalates until someone is running another off the road, or grabbing a gun and shooting the other driver. But I stopped to think, and I realized it wasn't personal. It wasn't as if he spotted a blue car up the road and decided to single me out. He was discourteous to everybody, regardless of the make, model, or color of the car, or whether the driver was male, female, old or young.

I left it alone, figuring he won't get away with that kind of behavior for long, when the police impound his vehicle. I didn't need to be the judge, jury and executioner. I preferred to let it go. That decision came after examining the belief that I could choose to take it personal and take my anger out on him, or not. I opted for the alternative: I choose to drop it because he didn't even know my name. Besides, there were other logical explanations for his behavior: maybe he was late to work and had already been chewed by the boss for that very problem. He might have been in an emergency situation, trying to get to a hospital, maybe a sick child in the backseat. It's possible he was high on drugs, fantasizing that he was in a stock car race. Maybe he was having a bad day, angry and driving like a madman. Or maybe he is a jerk all of the time to everybody. Clearly, the reason for his behavior had nothing to do with me. Besides, I could see myself doing the same thing; it's not like I've never been guilty of speeding or cutting someone off, whether it be due to an emergency or for no good reason.

It is very easy to interpret events the wrong way, especially when they spark an emotional response because emotion interferes with reason. It is also easy to jump to conclusions and believe that others are responsible for the hurting inside me. When we hurt, we become judgmental and want justice, and we act blameful. But this is irrational. Take a moment to rethink it and you'll discover that the person you are holding responsible is seldom interested in hurting you. They may be having a bad day, they are in an emergency situation, they are in a panic, or just plain aren't thinking straight. Certainly, we don't intend to hurt those we love. Would they really do something hateful to you on purpose just to see if you get upset?

- MAT 7:1-2 ~ Jesus taught, "Judge not, that you be not judged. For with the judgment you pronounce you will be judged, and with the measure you use it will be measured to you."

- ROM 2:1 ~ You have no excuse, every one of you who judges. For in passing judgment on another you condemn yourself, because you, the judge, practice the very same things.

When the hurting phase kicks in, the pain is compounded by dwelling on it. Remember when you were a kid playing outside and having a great time, until you noticed you were bleeding, then you ran home crying to your mommy? It didn't hurt before that because you weren't paying attention to it; but once you saw blood it hurt like crazy. Emotional pain is no different. If you dwell on it, it hurts all the more, to the extent that you cannot feel anything else. I've commented before that pain (emotional and physical) is said to be 75% psychological. Thus, you can reduce the pain significantly by not dwelling on it.

That's when the anger starts to swelter. Now, anger itself is not necessarily a negative thing, but what you do with it might be. Apparently, even God dispenses wrath; he will exact vengeance upon the wicked. It's not my job. Some believe that anger is one of the seven deadliest sins; I would submit that hate is far more dangerous. Hate can be a byproduct of anger and it leads to even deadlier sins such as murder. Nevertheless, if the anger erupts it can be very devastating. Anger can be quelled, vented, or released in a constructive manner; or it can be used in a destructive manner which only makes the situation worse. This will engender more negativity, leading to frustration, irritability, mistrust, poor self-esteem, abominable acts, even physical ailments.

- PRO 14:17 ~ A man of quick temper acts foolishly, and a man of evil devices is hated.

- PRO 15:1,18 ~ A soft answer turns away wrath, but a harsh word stirs up anger... A hot-tempered man stirs up strife, but he who is slow to anger quiets contention.

- PRO 26:24-28 ~ Whoever hates disguises himself with his lips and harbors deceit in his heart; when he speaks graciously, believe him not, for there are seven abominations in his heart; though his hatred be covered with deception, his wickedness will be exposed in the assembly.

- ECC 7:9 ~ Be not quick in your spirit to become angry, for anger lodges in the heart of fools.

- MAT 5:22 ~ Jesus said, "I say to you that everyone who is angry with his brother will be liable to judgment; whoever insults his brother will be liable to the council; and whoever says, 'You fool!' will be liable to the hell of fire."

- EPH 4:26-27 ~ If angry do not sin; do not let the sun go down on your anger, and give no opportunity to the devil.

If I get chastised by my boss, and go home angry, I might yell at my wife, and she might punish the kid, and he might kick the dog, and the dog might pee on the floor, and then I might get mad at the dog for messing the floor, and before you know it, the whole household is getting angrier and angrier. That's why the Bible teaches us to deal with the anger and reconcile with one another, so it doesn't evolve into a fiasco.

As the prophet James asserts: lust when conceived brings forth sin, and sin when finished brings forth death. The temptation is presented before you, and if you give it a second thought (i.e. give birth or conception to the idea), then you have sinned in thought. The next step is to act on it. The Lord said you are guilty of adultery if you lust after another in your heart, and John wrote you are guilty of murder if you hate another person. The constant thinking of the evil act will eventually lead to the doing of it; but either way you are still guilty of sin. The message is this: Don't think about it and you won't be inclined to do it, or anything else that could be wrong or bring trouble upon you.

- MAT 5:28 ~ Jesus said, "Everyone who looks at a woman with lustful intent has already committed adultery with her in his heart."

- JAM 1:14-15 (paraphrased) ~ Everyone is tempted when they are enticed by their sinful desires, which when conceived, brings forth sin; and sin when finished brings forth death.

- 1 JO 3:15; 1 JO 4:20 ~ Everyone who hates his brother is a murderer, and you know that no murderer has eternal life abiding in him... If anyone says, "I love God," and hates his brother, he is a liar; for he who does not love his brother whom he has seen cannot love God whom he has not seen?

Surely the evil deed is more dreadful than the thought; but in God's Law all sin deserves the death penalty. The reason for this is the slippery slope that evil thinking creates. Take hate, for instance, which leads to prejudice, racism, bigotry, assault and battery, perhaps murder. Or consider lust, which leads to promiscuity, voyeurism, fetishism, sexual deviancy, and pedophilia. The persistent negative thought eventually leads to the inevitable evil deed.

As resentment progresses, growing disdain seriously alters thinking. A grudge settles in and all the person can think of is to even the score. So they start contemplating ways of getting revenge, in order to make the perceived perpetrator suffer as they have. Unfortunately, revenge is never about getting even, because the response is always designed to inflict a little more pain than initially experienced.

- LEV 19:18 ~ You shall not take vengeance or bear a grudge against the sons of your own people, but you shall love your neighbor as yourself: I am the LORD..

- JAM 5:9 ~ Do not grumble against one another, brothers, so that you may not be judged; behold, the Judge is standing at the door.

When I was a young man I had friends that I would party with, and we would kid around, and playfully smack one another. And this was followed by another playful slap, followed by a hit, then a punch, and then a brawl. Each blow would tip the scales in the other direction and a balance was never achieved. The same principle is at work in an argument where each nasty comment is followed by a nastier one, and the scales get tipped in one direction and then the other, and nobody gets even. The scales just get farther out of tilt. Each participant feels the need to get in the last word. You might shake hands, or kiss and make up, but someone usually has to get in one more comment or condition.

Clearly, revenge never enables you to forget about it, even the score, or move on. The negativity seethes, the wall grows higher, and the scales become farther out of balance. Payback is that slippery slope. Equity cannot be restored with punishment, but it can with forgiveness. Forgiveness enables you to even the score, dismantle the barriers, grow in your relationships, and continue becoming all you can be.

The Bible provides examples of the destructiveness of resentment. Remember the case of Cain (see GEN 4:2-16)? Cain was a farmer and his brother Abel a shepherd. They both presented offerings to the Lord, for it was the custom to give the first fruits of one's increase to show appreciation to God and obtain his forgiveness. Abel's sacrifice from his flock was excellent, but Cain's offering from his crops was unacceptable. Cain tried to shortchange God by offering a substandard and/or insincere sacrifice and this displeased God. So God did not accept his offering. Cain became angry at God, feeling rejected. Fuming with resentment, Cain took it out on his brother; he murdered his brother and tried to hide the act from God. Now God was really displeased and he put a curse on Cain, and Cain became an exile and an outcast. The error of Cain demonstrates precisely the process of resentment and the harm that it engenders. It just makes a person get more and more incensed, and clouds their thinking. And it leads to heinous acts.

- HEB 11:4 ~ By faith Abel offered to God a more acceptable sacrifice than Cain, through which he was commended as righteous, God commending him by accepting his gifts. And through his faith, though he died, he still speaks.

- 1 JO 3:12 ~ We should not be like Cain, who was of the evil one and murdered his brother. And why did he murder him? Because his own deeds were evil and his brother's righteous.

When you share the love of God you become more like him: holy. Consider the process of sanctification. Little by little you are being conformed into the image of Christ. Eventually, you become the perfection of Christ, receiving a glorified body that will never die because it is free of sin. You are without sin because God has forgiven you if you believe.

- PHP 3:20-21 ~ But our citizenship is in heaven, and from it we await a Savior, the Lord Jesus Christ, who will transform our lowly body to be like his glorious body, by the power that enables him even to subject all things to himself.

- 1 JO 3:1-2 ~ See what kind of love the Father has given to us, that we should be called children of God; and so we are. The reason why the world does not know us is that it did not know him. Beloved, we are God's children now, and what we will be has not yet appeared; but we know that when he appears we shall be like him, because we shall see him as he is.

- 1 TH 5:23 ~ Now may the God of peace himself sanctify you completely, and may your whole spirit and soul and body be kept blameless at the coming of our Lord Jesus Christ.

- HEB 2:10-11 ~ For it was fitting that he, for whom and by whom all things exist, in bringing many sons to glory, should make the founder of their salvation perfect through suffering. For he who sanctifies and those who are sanctified all have one source. That is why he is not ashamed to call them brothers.

"Mankind must evolve for all human conflict a method which rejects revenge, aggression, and retaliation. The foundation of such a method is love." – Martin Luther King Jr.

Forgiveness is an act of love. It is one of the numerous means by which God extends his grace to us, by pardoning our sins. It is a gift of the Holy Spirit, which once bestowed empowers you to forgive others. So if you want to get even with someone, let go of the resentment. Let go of the past and you can begin to enjoy the present. Radiate the love and you can dispose of the anger and the hate, and forgive. Forgiveness conquers resentment; and your life becomes more fulfilling and purposeful.

PROCESS OF RESENTMENT

- Event
- Belief
- Hurting
- Anger
- Dwelling
- Grudge
- Hate
- Revenge
- Heinous Act

Getting Stuck Not Even

The Process of Forgiveness

Forgiveness is a process of healing. It relieves us of the pain we would otherwise feel if we believed the lie: that others are to blame for our suffering. Sure, people deliberately hurt others, even themselves. We all do, save Jesus Christ. Strive to be like him, think like him, and act like him. God is love. We possess that love. Forgiveness is an act of love and kindness.

Remember, the cause of suffering in this world is sin. If you want to blame something for your pain, blame sin, for without it, nobody would suffer. And since we all are to blame for sin, why blame anybody? Everyone is guilty and you definitely don't have the time to blame everybody, so don't waste your time playing the blame game. Let it go. It will just develop into more emotional baggage that weighs you down. You will find that forward progress is facilitated when you lighten the load.

Thus, forgiveness helps me more than the one I am forgiving. He or she might not even care that I forgave them. But it enables me to heal and to let go. It doesn't condone their actions. It doesn't absolve them of consequences; it absolves me of being the one to administer judgment. If they are guilty, it will catch up with them someday. But leave it to law enforcement to investigate and the courts to decide. Ultimately, the Lord will judge everyone. Trust in Christ if you want to be found not guilty. Jesus said not to judge others or you will be judged yourself, and by the same standards you levy upon them (LUK 6:37).

Like resentment, the process of forgiveness begins with an event. The second step is to rethink your belief. An assessment is in order, from which you will gain a better understanding. I assessed the other driver's behavior and considered possibilities that made more sense to me than my gut reaction. I also assessed my own behavior and realized I'm just as guilty as that other driver, given that I've done the same thing. If I would have responded with a kneejerk reaction, I would have been every bit as much a jerk as he was.

It's about listening to your heart. It will tell you the truth and it will tell you the right thing to do. You have a choice. When you logically examine the information, the situation, the conditions, etc., you will realize that your initial thought was probably based upon a lie. It was a response to an emotion that was unrepresentative of the circumstances. It is pointless to let such a thing get under your skin. Sometimes it is so trivial it makes you wonder why you used to let that kind of thing bother you.

Of course, how big or small the problem is relative to the beholder. What is trivial to you may not be to me. If they see it as a big deal you should not trivialize it. If they see it as a small affair, it probably could be. If it is perceived by either party as a major issue it could build a wall between you. And your defenses will grow more and more formidable and permanent. It's not easy to give in, to change your opinion, or to modify your belief; or so it seems. It surely cannot be easier to seek revenge and return one injury for another. But if that is your course, you will not be able to heal emotionally or grow spiritually. Reverse course and you will gain insight.

The next step in the process will be acceptance. Stuff happens; it's not a big deal. It certainly isn't a show-stopper; at most, an inconvenience. Like the apostle Paul wrote to the Romans, these setbacks (big or small) teach us patience. And patience is way more virtuous than anger. So there may be a positive aspect to it. Look on the bright side. All things work to our good, Paul also taught the Romans. Every experience has value, even the negative, because it teaches us.

- ROM 5:1-5 ~ Since we have been justified by faith, we have peace with God through our Lord Jesus Christ. Through him we have also obtained access by faith into this grace in which we stand, and we rejoice in hope of the glory of God. Not only that, but we rejoice in our sufferings, knowing that suffering produces endurance, and endurance produces character, and character produces hope, and hope does not put us to shame, because God's love has been poured into our hearts through the Holy Spirit who has been given to us.

- ROM 8:28 ~ And we know that for those who love God all things work together for good, for those who are called according to his purpose.

Correct thoughts are based on the truth, such as that written in God's Word. Dwell on the truth and you will be in a positive state of mind. Let the Lord take control and the resulting actions will be positive. Not only will your basic belief structure change, so will your attitude. And that will change your behavior. Don't forget, if you want to change your behavior you must first change your mind.

It's a simple task really; all you have to do is stop and think. If you don't, you will just react on whatever emotion you are experiencing. That feeling is based on a belief that is generally wrong. Maybe it was conditioned into you, or maybe it is just a common human trait; perhaps a notion that you didn't deserve to be in that situation. Life isn't fair we suppose, so why should I be? And you want to take it out on someone else for no apparent reason; because you feel uncomfortable you want someone else to feel that way. Like they say, misery loves company. Such thinking is simply unacceptable.

Be constantly mindful, every second of the day, and you will make the right choices. Here is the definition of righteousness: doing the right thing. You know in your heart what is true and right because you have the gift of discernment, same as everybody else. It takes effort to pause the program, invoke cognitive control over the process, and reroute it. This will result in a revision, a correction in the action: a righteous act. Remember, forgiveness is an act of love; it develops over time (just like revenge is an act of hate that develops over time). Once again, if you challenge your beliefs you will see some changes, beginning with changing your mind. In due course, your attitude will change followed by your behavior, and also your character and disposition. Your motivation should be to seek a purpose that has real value, not one with an exorbitant cost.

- 1 CO 13:2-8,13 ~ And if I have prophetic powers, and understand all mysteries and all knowledge, and if I have all faith, so as to remove mountains, but have not love, I am nothing. If I give away all I have, and if I deliver up my body to be burned, but have not love, I gain nothing. Love is patient and kind; love does not envy or boast; it is not arrogant [5]or rude. It does not insist on its own way; it is not irritable or resentful; it does not rejoice at wrongdoing, but rejoices with the truth. Love bears all things, believes all things, hopes all things, endures all things. Love never ends. As for prophecies, they will pass away; as for tongues, they will cease; as for knowledge, it will pass away... So now faith, hope, and love abide, these three; but the greatest of these is love.

Therefore, forgiveness is a healing process that makes me whole. Such healing will result in a corresponding action, usually designed to make amends. For instance, you might be compelled to apologize, even if it isn't your fault. Or make a sacrifice to save the relationship by recommitting yourself, and not hold the wrongdoing against the other person. We are obligated to God to confess our sins, and repent with true contrition; to seek his forgiveness and obtain absolution. By forgiving others we are forgiven by God, and by not forgiving others we remain unforgiven. So consider giving and seeking forgiveness.

- MAT 6:9-15 ~ Jesus taught them to pray then like this: "Our Father in heaven, hallowed be your name. Your kingdom come, your will be done, on earth as it is in heaven. Give us this day our daily bread, and forgive us our debts, as we also have forgiven our debtors. And lead us not into temptation, but deliver us from evil. For if you forgive others their trespasses, your heavenly Father will also forgive you, but if you do not forgive others their trespasses, neither will your Father forgive your trespasses."

- MAT 18:21-22 ~ Then Peter came up and said to him, "Lord, how often will my brother sin against me, and I forgive him? As many as seven times?" Jesus said to him, "I do not say to you seven times, but seventy-seven times."

Like Christ we sacrifice ourselves for others as he did for us. If you are compelled to think via the spirit, you will perform acts of love and altruism. Such a change in attitude advances the opportunity to make amends, possibly even achieve reconciliation. But don't expect reconciliation from someone that doesn't care about or want your forgiveness, or that is unwilling to forgive you even if you are sorry. God offers us forgiveness in Christ, but you have to want it to receive it. If you confess and repent he will forgive you and reconcile you unto God our Heavenly Father. Those that reject this gift will not be forgiven, or saved.

Some bridges cannot be rebuilt, some connections cannot be reestablished, and some wounds cannot be mended. People move on, move out, or die. Others give up or just don't care. But we still can make amends by changing the way we treat others, the way we communicate with people, and the way we conduct our affairs in the future. Forgiveness allows me to let go and to move on, but not always to make up.

When you place conditions on love there will be restrictions on the possibilities. But don't have expectations about how people will react, or whether the bridge can be rebuilt, or when your paths may cross again. Just expect that God will notice, and may reward your good deeds with greater responsibility or purpose. The proper actions are the fruit of a revised belief system, founded on Jesus Christ, who himself was forgiving the very people who had just nailed him to the cross. Can you think of a better, more profound example of forgiveness? The episode was moving enough even for the centurion to reexamine the entire event and declare, "Surely he was the Son of God" (MAT 27:54). Everyone who has accepted Christ as the Son of God will receive his forgiveness and the inheritance that is his. That choice is available to you.

Forgiveness is something you must give to yourself as well. If you have asked God to forgive you and you believe he has forgiven you, but you haven't forgiven yourself, you are basically denying what God has done. All too often the resentment we carry is against ourselves. It is every bit as destructive as the resentment we hold against others. If we can forgive them we have the power to forgive ourselves. If we do not forgive others, or ourselves, should God forgive us? God's forgiveness is a free gift that you receive if you believe. It also should be given just as freely. To withhold forgiveness from anyone, including you, is to be selfish with a gift God has given to you for free. Besides, if you give forgiveness you receive it; and as you freely give, so shall you receive (MAT 10:8; LUK 6:38).

One final word about letting go: unlike God we do not forget so easily. While he will forgive us and wipe our slate clean, we cannot simply erase a misdeed or mistake from our memory. But by unloading the emotional baggage, the memory will be allowed to fade as many do after they cease to be of value. That is, as soon as the correct meaning is found, the learning will have taken place and that has value. And that is the part worth keeping and carrying forward.

You will discover how the experience worked to your good when you arrive at the greater purpose that lies ahead, for which you were being trained and prepared all the while. Then it all will make sense, both the evil and the good, but possibly not before then. And instead of forgetting what happened, you will understand why it had to happen that way; and that is wisdom. Therefore, it is not necessary to forget, recognizing that God will use the incident for your betterment and learning. Besides, you mustn't forget that you forgave.

- PSA 130:3-4 ~ If you, O LORD, should mark iniquities, O Lord, who could stand? But with you there is forgiveness, that you may be feared.

- JER 31:34 ~ "No longer shall each one teach his neighbor and his brother, saying, 'Know the LORD,' for they shall all know me, from the least of them to the greatest," declares the LORD. "For I will forgive their iniquity, and I will remember their sin no more."

"We shall not cease from exploration, and the end of all our exploring will be to arrive where we started and know the place for the first time." – T. S. Eliot

Conclusions

Practice forgiveness. Don't put it off. Let go of the past. Stay in the present and build steps towards a brighter future. Learn the process; get a visual map of it. See the positive changes it produces. Pray for others. Radiate the love; it will draw people towards you. Push them away and they may not come back. Base your actions on love and you will feel it in your heart and so will others. And God will reward you in ways you cannot envisage.

"Nobody ever forgets where he buried the hatchet." – Kin Hubbard

Resentment will destroy relationships; forgiveness can rebuild them. Forgiveness is, therefore, the higher power. It is a product of God's love which he freely gives to all who desire it. That love empowers you to overcome evil, and the hurt and agony it produces. Forgiveness enables you to learn the lessons of life and let go of the obstacles to insight and understanding. You need not forgive and forget. Forgive and remember. That is, once a transgression has been forgiven, resentment should not resurface, and you must remember this to prevent that from happening. It is easier to forget that you let it go than to remember that you did.

With respect to resentment: you can stop the process at any stage and reverse course. But if you have committed the heinous act it is too late; the damage has been done and it will be very difficult to repair. Awareness of the resentment process makes it easier to recognize what's going on, stop it in its tracks, and change your mind. Of course, it becomes more difficult after each stage to undo it, so practice halting resentment at the belief stage. Perform the reassessment of your beliefs and reactions, and this should immediately trigger the forgiveness process.

- MAT 6:14-15 ~ Jesus said, "For if you forgive others their trespasses, your heavenly Father will also forgive you, but if you do not forgive others their trespasses, neither will your Father forgive your trespasses."

"Forgiveness is the sweetest revenge." – Isaac Friedmann

"To err is human, to forgive, divine." – Alexander Pope

Have you studied the story of Hosea the prophet? Hosea is a lesser known book in the Old Testament which has a profound message. The name Hosea is translated as "salvation," and his character appropriately reflects that of God. This prophet's marriage also represents God's relationship with Israel. The Bible frequently illustrates the love of God for his people in terms of a groom and a bride, respectively. It just so happens that the wife of Hosea was unfaithful to him, and they lived in a time when Israel was unfaithful to God. Despite her infidelities, Hosea continued to love his wife, forgive her, and take her back. Similarly, God forgave the Israelites after they committed spiritual infidelity with their idol worship, and the defilement of God's holy places with prostitutes. Hosea warned the Israelites that their idolatry and contempt for sacred things were an abomination to God and implored the people to return to faithfulness and righteousness. Unfortunately, they would not and ended up being conquered by the Assyrians. God had forgiven them countless times and withheld his wrath. Eventually the unfaithful of God suffer the consequences of their sin and disobedience. Remember, forgiveness does not mean there will be no consequences. Though we have been forgiven of our sins, Christ still had to suffer and die because of them. The story of Hosea and his adulterous wife points to the unfailing love of God for humanity, and the ultimate example of that love in the sacrifice and salvation afforded by Christ's offering for sin.

Activity

List a few past events that caused you to be resentful.

What someone did: _____

What someone failed to do: _____

Analyze the resentment that developed within you.

Your belief about the event: _____

What you felt: _____

What you did: _____

Do you still hold a grudge? _____

Did you plan or take revenge? _____

What is the current status of that relationship? _____

What could they do (or what could they have done) to make amends?

_____

What action could you take to repair the relationship?

_____

How long have you been stuck (or how long were you stuck before moving on)?

_____

What will you do in the future to let go of resentment?

_____

_____

PROCESS OF FORGIVENESS

- Event
- Assessment
- Understanding
- Acceptance
- Modified Belief
- Positive Attitude
- Patience
- Letting Go
- Loving Act

Getting Even and Unstuck

BUILDING RELATIONSHIPS

OBJECTIVE	Learn the dynamics of different relationships, and how to improve bonds and nurture those relationships you wish to preserve.
INTERVENTION	Discuss types of relationships and building relationships, with emphasis on integrating spirituality to strengthen them. Identify connections and disconnections with respect to the different layers of existence and associated relationships.
PLAN	Develop relationships that are healthy, lasting, and which radiate God's love. Discontinue relationships that are unhealthy.

"Let us be grateful to people who make us happy, they are the charming gardeners who make our souls blossom." – Marcel Proust

Friendship

Friendship develops largely because the relationship is based upon sharing things in common, such as living in the same neighborhood, going to the same school or church, being in the same class or occupation, playing on the same team, or just being at the same place at the same time. Thus, the relationship begins as the result of proximity. You are brought together due to circumstances and events and this provides common ground. But for it to develop there must be a common bond.

The relationship grows the more things you find in common; and it grows when both of you happen to be in the same place or situation again and again. Sometimes relationships cease when you don't find commonality on particular issues, or when proximity decreases. Beliefs about a relationship that are incompatible among the partners will create discord. This is particularly true with respect to marriage, but it also applies to friendship. That doesn't mean everyone in the relationship must believe exactly the same. Sometimes the differences help to strengthen the bond or the interest. As long as there is mutual respect the friendship will last. But long term friendships are built primarily upon trust.

Peer pressure is an obstacle to healthy relationships. Oftentimes, we feel pressured into doing things that are against our better judgment. Sometimes we give in just to fit in. The greatest conflict comes when we must sin to please someone else whose company we value. God warns us to be careful about associating with people that can influence us in a detrimental way.

- 2 CO 6:14 ~ Do not be unequally yoked with unbelievers. For what partnership has righteousness with lawlessness? Or what fellowship has light with darkness?

Identity confusion is a significant issue with adolescents who are still trying to determine who they are. This is especially the case when it comes to sexual orientation and

303

spiritual orientation. It may cause confusion in terms of one's perspective about morality and how this tracks with others' outlooks; this is a major source of conflict for many teenagers. Identity issues are worth exploring during counseling especially if the teen has a guilty conscience about a current or anticipated sexual relationship (heterosexual or homosexual). Involvement in drugs and alcohol is another moral issue that teenagers face which leads to conflict, with peer pressure being a significant influence.

Determining where the client stands on such issues as premarital sex, abortion, birth control, marriage, and divorce is important. Discuss with the client his/her definition of love, dating, "hooking up," and what constitutes sexual intercourse. What are the client's expectations regarding intimacy? One of the goals of adolescent counseling could be, and probably should be, helping the client determine his/her spiritual identity. This will help him/her establish a sexual identity as well. Naturally, people of any age can benefit from such an analysis.

Compatibility issues loom large, especially in a society where variations in beliefs and where differing definitions of morality exist. Whether the relationship is one of friendship, "going steady," or marriage, there are many dimensions of compatibility that could make or break the potential for longevity. Some of these dimensions are listed at the end of this lesson in the activity. The degree to which these issues are important to the members of a group, or the partners in a relationship, will vary from person to person and as a function of time and maturity.

Marriage

"Marriage means expectations and expectations mean conflict." – Paxton Blair

Marriage is a religious rite ordained by God in his Law. Marriage is not a command but a privilege. Marriage allows us to satisfy our emotional, physical, and worldly needs while still obeying God. Marriage represents a commitment to one's spouse, similar to the commitment made to God through participation in the Holy Sacraments, and the commitment made by Christ to his church. Thus, marriage is a covenant between husband and wife and is not to be broken any more than God's covenant with mankind. But to maintain it for life requires constant, sincere effort. The marriage is in danger of collapse if any of these destructive forces get in the way of true sharing: infidelity, abuse, jealousy, possessiveness, mistrust, inequality.

- GEN 2:18,21-22,24 ~ Then the LORD God said, "It is not good that the man should be alone; I will make him a helper fit for him." So God caused a deep sleep to fall upon the man, and while he slept took one of his ribs and closed up its place with flesh. And the rib that God had taken from the man he made into a woman and brought her to the man. Therefore a man shall leave his father and his mother and hold fast to his wife, and they shall become one flesh.

- PRO 5:18 ~ Let your fountain be blessed, and rejoice in the wife of your youth.

- PRO 18:22 ~ He who finds a wife finds a good thing and obtains favor from the LORD.

- PRO 19:13-14 ~ A foolish son is ruin to his father, and a wife's quarreling is a continual dripping of rain. House and wealth are inherited from fathers, but a prudent wife is from the LORD.

- PRO 31:10-12,25-30 ~ An excellent wife who can find? She is far more precious than jewels. The heart of her husband trusts in her, and he will have no lack of gain. She does him good, and not harm, all the days of her life... Strength and dignity are her clothing, and she laughs at the time to come. She opens her mouth with wisdom, and the teaching of kindness is on her tongue. She looks well to the ways of her household and does not eat the bread of idleness. Her children rise up and call her blessed; her husband also, and he praises her: "Many women have done excellently, but you surpass them all." Charm is deceitful, and beauty is vain, but a woman who fears the LORD is to be praised.

- 1 CO 7:1-5,8-9,28,39 ~ Now concerning the matters about which you wrote: "It is good for a man not to have sexual relations with a woman." But because of the temptation to sexual immorality, each man should have his own wife and each woman her own husband. The husband should give to his wife her conjugal rights, and likewise the wife to her husband. For the wife does not have authority over her own body, but the husband does. Likewise the husband does not have authority over his own body, but the wife does. Do not deprive one another, except perhaps by agreement for a limited time, that you may devote yourselves to prayer; but then come together again, so that Satan may not tempt you because of your lack of self-control. To the unmarried and the widows I say that it is good for them to remain single as I am. But if they cannot exercise self-control, they should marry. For it is better to marry than to burn with passion. But if you do marry, you have not sinned, and if a betrothed woman marries, she has not sinned. Yet those who marry will have worldly troubles, and I would spare you that. A wife is bound to her husband as long as he lives. But if her husband dies, she is free to be married to whom she wishes, only in the Lord.

- EPH 5:22-25,28,33 ~ Wives, submit to your own husbands, as to the Lord. For the husband is the head of the wife even as Christ is the head of the church, his body, and is himself its Savior. Now as the church submits to Christ, so also wives should submit in everything to their husbands. Husbands, love your wives, as Christ loved the church and gave himself up for her. In the same way husbands should love their wives as their own bodies. He who loves his wife loves himself. Let each one of you love his wife as himself, and let the wife see that she respects her husband. (see also COL 3:18-19)

- TIT 2:4-6 ~ Train the young women to love their husbands and children, to be self-controlled, pure, working at home, kind, and submissive to their own husbands, that the word of God may not be reviled. Likewise, urge the younger men to be self-controlled.

- 1 PE 3:1,7 ~ Wives, be subject to your own husbands, so that even if some do not obey the word, they may be won without a word by the conduct of their wives... Husbands, live with your wives in an understanding way, showing honor to the woman as the weaker vessel, since they are heirs with you of the grace of life, so that your prayers may not be hindered.

Certainly, being joined in marriage requires major adjustments to lifestyle, duties, and decisions. It is a partnership not unlike a business arrangement, where equal partners share the labor, the hardships, the good times, and the rewards. Emotional security is essential, because if someone doesn't feel safe in the relationship, or there is not a full commitment, the marriage will be a rough ride downhill. You are commending your heart to the other and you need to feel certain it is safe with him or her. Security opens the doors for intimacy, freedom, and creativity. And trust will follow.

Some advice for men: talk to your wife and touch her often, but without any sexual connotations. Women tend to be verbal and kinesthetic by nature. Her insecurity is more related to your lack of emotional and physical attendance than to the size of your bank account. She wants to feel close to you all the time, whether you are at home together, in bed, or apart. She will not think about sex as often as you do and will not be ready whenever you say so (so don't insist); but she will enjoy it just as much as you if you use gentle foreplay and take your time (hint: try talking and touching). Give her your devotion even when she is in a bad mood. Give her compliments, recognize her accomplishments, tell her she is pretty, and say, "I love you."

Some advice for women: don't assume your man knows what you want or what he did wrong. He is more ignorant about your needs and desires than you think. Just tell him and be specific (don't beat around the bush). I recommend that you do not make fun of him in public as he will feel embarrassed but won't admit it. Act sexy when you are alone together, as men tend to be visual by nature. Go ahead and initiate the sex once in a while; your desire for him gives him confidence in his commitment. Note that the man will feel rejected when you are unresponsive to him and this will be destructive to his ego. Give him your respect, even when he hasn't earned it. Tell him what a good provider he is, and how he makes you feel complete. When he is troubled, he desperately needs your emotional support and reassurance, because you are better equipped emotionally just as he is physically.

Sex is an extraordinary way to experience the passion of a deep and sincere love. It is a lovemaking ritual, and not merely a means for procreation. Take your time building up the mood, talk about what excites your spouse, and be imaginative by using your brain (which is by far the most important sex organ). Keep in mind that sexual intercourse doesn't always require copulation. Intercourse is an intimate communication and includes regularly hugging, kissing, romancing, and caressing one another. Focus on pleasing your partner and you are guaranteed a good time: that is, enjoy each other. If the husband is crazy about his wife it will kindle her passion; she will invite him sexually, which reaffirms his desire and love for her. This reciprocal validation keeps the unity intact and makes the sex amazing.

Planning sexual encounters helps to raise the anticipation. Although the act is often spontaneous, you can still create the prospect via a romantic date, getaway, or regularly scheduled time for just the two of you. The desire grows through expectation as you progress in greater intimacy and sharing, thereby enhancing the quality of the experience. Plan everything together, including being together for everything and always, making time for lovemaking and for others whose relationships are important to the two of you. Make all of that time of the highest quality by integrating God's love into yours.

Marriage was instituted by God to allow a person to engage in sex without being guilty of fornication. Adultery is infidelity in marriage, or sex outside of marriage. God commands us never to break apart a couple joined together in marriage, because marriage results in a man and wife becoming one flesh (GEN 2:24).

- MAL 2:15-16 ~ Did God not make them (husband and wife) one, with a portion of the Spirit in their union? And what was God seeking? Godly offspring. So guard yourselves in your spirit, and let none of you be faithless to the wife of your youth.

- MAT 19:3-9 ~ And Pharisees came up to him and tested him by asking, "Is it lawful to divorce one's wife for any cause?" He answered, "Have you not read that he who created them from the beginning made them male and female, and said, 'Therefore a man shall leave his father and his mother and hold fast to his wife, and the two shall become one flesh'? So they are no longer two but one flesh. What therefore God has joined together, let not man separate." They said to him, "Why then did Moses command one to give a certificate of divorce and to send her away?" He said to them, "Because of your hardness of heart Moses allowed you to divorce your wives, but from the beginning it was not so. And I say to you: whoever divorces his wife, except for sexual immorality, and marries another, commits adultery."

Adultery may not appear to defy the laws of nature but there are negative consequences. These days, promiscuous behavior is very high risk; for example, sexually transmitted disease is a real hazard. This in itself is a sufficient reason to stay monogamous. Adultery also breaks down the trust, love, and respect in a marriage thereby destroying the unity. The result is that the couple is no longer one flesh and one mind. Perhaps this is why adultery and abandonment are permissible reasons for getting divorced (according to the Bible) because the unity often cannot be restored.

- MAT 19:9 ~ Jesus said, "I say to you: whoever divorces his wife, except for sexual immorality, and marries another, commits adultery."

- 1 CO 7:14-16 ~ The unbelieving husband is made holy because of his wife, and the unbelieving wife is made holy because of her husband. Otherwise your children would be unclean, but as it is, they are holy. But if the unbelieving partner separates, let it be so. In such cases the brother or sister is not enslaved. God has called you to peace. For how do you know, wife, whether you will save your husband? Or how do you know, husband, whether you will save your wife?

- 2 CO 6:14 ~ Do not be unequally yoked with unbelievers. For what partnership has righteousness with lawlessness? Or what fellowship has light with darkness?

The practice of polygamy is akin to adultery. Nowhere in the Bible is the taking of multiple wives (or husbands) condoned. In fact, the opposite is true. Considerable evil came upon individuals because they had multiple wives (see GEN 21:9-14; DEU 21:15-17; 1 KI 11:4-9). Scripture encourages people to have their own spouse; this implies that a married person is not to share that spouse with another. References to marriage in the Bible regard one wife and one husband; the Bible never says to take wives or husbands (in the plural).

Jesus said that a person is guilty of adultery if that person looks with lust in their heart upon someone other than their spouse. So how could anyone possibly consider it to be acceptable taking on additional spouses? If two people that marry become one flesh, how can a married couple become one flesh with multiple partners? Further, a male cannot be of one flesh with another male, and a female cannot be of one flesh with another female. It makes me wonder why anybody would want to define marriage in that way as it is not the same.

Scripture indicates that kings, priests, and deacons are to live by example and that example includes having only one spouse. We also have the example of Christ. A husband should not seek multiple wives any more than Christ would seek multiple churches. It would be like Christ being the head of the Christian church, the Moslems, Buddhists, Hindus, etc. God accused his people of infidelity whenever they worshipped other gods. The Bible makes it clear that there is only one bride and one groom.

- DEU 17:15-17 ~ You may indeed set a king over you whom the LORD your God will choose. One from among your brothers you shall set as king over you. You may not put a foreigner over you, who is not your brother. Only he must not acquire many horses for himself or cause the people to return to Egypt in order to acquire many horses, since the LORD has said to you, 'You shall never return that way again.' And he shall not acquire many wives for himself, lest his heart turn away, nor shall he acquire for himself excessive silver and gold.

- 1 CO 7:10-11 ~ To the married I give this charge (not I, but the Lord): the wife should not separate from her husband (but if she does, she should remain unmarried or else be reconciled to her husband), and the husband should not divorce his wife.

- 1 TI 3:2,12 (paraphrased) ~ The directions Paul gave to Timothy about pastors, deacons, and elders included that they must be the husband of only one wife (see also TIT 1:6).

A note on Abortion: God forbids the sacrificing of children to pagan gods. This was a common practice among the Ammonites, who sacrificed their children to Molech (god of fertility). According to the Mosaic Law, the shedding of innocent blood deserved the death penalty, and innocent blood included a pregnant woman's fetus (see EXO 21:22-23).

- GEN 9:6 ~ Whoever sheds the blood of man, by man shall his blood be shed, for God made man in his own image.

- EZE 16:20-21 ~ You took your sons and your daughters, whom you had borne to me, and these you sacrificed to them to be devoured. Were your whorings so small a matter that you slaughtered my children and delivered them up as an offering by fire to them?

- AMO 1:13 ~ Thus says the LORD: "For three transgressions of the Ammonites, and for four, I will not revoke the punishment, because they have ripped open pregnant women in Gilead, that they might enlarge their border."

Some people believe that abortion is not the same as murder; they argue that the fetus is not a living human being. Let's review what the Bible says.

- PSA 139:13-16 ~ You formed my inward parts; you knitted me together in my mother's womb. I praise you, for I am fearfully and wonderfully made. Wonderful are your works; my soul knows it very well. My frame was not hidden from you, when I was being made in secret, intricately woven in the depths of the earth. Your eyes saw my unformed substance; in your book were written, every one of them, the days that were formed for me, when as yet there was none of them.

- ISA 46:3-4 ~ God says, "Listen to me, O house of Jacob, all the remnant of the house of Israel, who have been borne by me from before your birth, carried from the womb; even to your old age I am he, and to gray hairs I will carry you. I have made, and I will bear; I will carry and will save."

- JER 1:4-5 ~ Now the word of the LORD came to me, saying, "Before I formed you in the womb I knew you, and before you were born I consecrated you; I appointed you a prophet to the nations."

- LUK 1:13-15,44 (paraphrased) ~ God told Zachariah that his wife Elisabeth would bear a son, and to name him John. That son would be filled with the Holy Spirit, even from his mother's womb... Elisabeth said to Mary, "The moment you said hello, the baby in my womb leaped with joy."

Clearly, the Bible teaches that a fetus is a living being, loved by God, and capable of emotion. Abortion must be devastating to God. Nature's law of survival does not include the killing of innocent babies. Further, the act of abortion can be harmful to the woman's reproductive system, sometimes resulting in sterility. There may be special circumstances or reasons when abortion might be a viable alternative; however, the following are not acceptable excuses: birth control, medical research, fetal tissue transplants, and pagan rituals. This is further proof of the importance of being faithful and monogamous. God designed the family so that children would have a mother and father to guide and teach them.

Parenthood

"There are no illegitimate children, only illegitimate parents." – Leon Yankwich

Parents must set an example for their children to follow. God the Father is our model of unconditional parental love, and Christ sets the perfect example of a child's obedience. Children imitate their parents so parents must provide an appropriate model of behavior for their children. The best way to accomplish this is by loving one another sincerely as an example to your kids. Parents should practice honor and respect in the home. Spouses must show respect to one another and parents must show respect to their children. Without mutual respect, children will not learn to respect their parents, much less others or even themselves.

- TIT 2:1-8,11-12 ~ But as for you, teach what accords with sound doctrine. Older men are to be sober-minded, dignified, self-controlled, sound in faith, in love, and in steadfastness. Older women likewise are to be reverent in behavior, not slanderers or slaves to much wine. They are to teach what is good, and so train the young women to love their husbands and children, to be self-controlled, pure, working at home, kind, and submissive to their own husbands, that the word of God may not be reviled. Likewise, urge the younger men to be self-controlled. Show yourself in all respects to be a model of good works, and in your teaching show integrity, dignity, and sound speech that cannot be condemned, so that an opponent may be put to shame, having nothing evil to say about us… For the grace of God has appeared, bringing salvation for all people, training us to renounce ungodliness and worldly passions, and to live self-controlled, upright, and godly lives in the present age.

Setting an example involves considerable self-control. Parents must demonstrate discipline and must execute discipline in the home. Disciplining a child may include reinforcement, and at times punishment. When children are disobedient parents should discipline them, just as God disciplines his children when we disobey him. But discipline should never be administered in anger and it should come with an explanation. Further, discipline should never harm or maim but only make a point without causing injury.

- DEU 8:5 ~ Know then in your heart that, as a man disciplines his son, the LORD your God disciplines you.

- JOB 5:17 ~ Behold, blessed is the one whom God reproves; therefore despise not the discipline of the Almighty

- PRO 3:11-14 ~ My son, do not despise the LORD's discipline or be weary of his reproof, for the LORD reproves him whom he loves, as a father the son in whom he delights. Blessed is the one who finds wisdom, and the one who gets understanding, for the gain from her is better than gain from silver and her profit better than gold..

- PRO 13:24 ~ Whoever spares the rod hates his son, but he who loves him is diligent to discipline him.

- PRO 29:15-17 ~ The rod and reproof give wisdom, but a child left to himself brings shame to his mother. When the wicked increase, transgression increases, but the righteous will look upon their downfall. Discipline your son, and he will give you rest; he will give delight to your heart.

- HEB 12:7-11 ~ It is for discipline that you have to endure. God is treating you as sons. For what son is there whom his father does not discipline? If you are left without discipline, in which all have participated, then you are illegitimate children and not sons. Besides this, we have had earthly fathers who disciplined us and we respected them. Shall we not much more be subject to the Father of spirits and live? For they disciplined us for a short time as it seemed best to them, but he disciplines us for our good, that we may share his holiness. For the moment all discipline seems painful rather than pleasant, but later it yields the peaceful fruit of righteousness to those who have been trained by it.

By setting an example of godliness and obedience to God children also learn obedience, both to their parents and to God. Christ was the example of God, and we as counselors and parents are the example of Christ, and our kids will follow our example and their kids too.

- PRO 28:7 ~ The one who keeps the law is a son with understanding, but a companion of gluttons shames his father.

- EPH 6:1-4 ~ Children, obey your parents in the Lord, for this is right. "Honor your father and mother" (this is the first commandment with a promise), "that it may go well with you and that you may live long in the land." Fathers, do not provoke your children to anger, but bring them up in the discipline and instruction of the Lord.

- COL 3:20-21 ~ Children, obey your parents in everything, for this pleases the Lord. Fathers, do not provoke your children, lest they become discouraged.

In addition to setting an example and teaching children right from wrong, parents must teach their children the ways of the Lord. When parents punish their children, it is because they love them and want no harm to come to them. It is a teaching tool. Parents also must teach children the Word, especially the Gospel of Jesus Christ.

- DEU 4:9 ~ Take care, and keep your soul diligently, lest you forget the things that your eyes have seen, and lest they depart from your heart all the days of your life. Make them known to your children and your children's children.

- PRO 1:7-10 ~ The fear of the LORD is the beginning of knowledge; fools despise wisdom and instruction. Hear, my son, your father's instruction, and forsake not your mother's teaching, for they are a graceful garland for your head and pendants for your neck. My son, if sinners entice you, do not consent.

- PRO 22:6 ~ Train up a child in the way he should go; even when he is old he will not depart from it.

Parents should remind their children that they have a Heavenly Father who loves them as much or more than their own parents do. Children should be taught to love their Heavenly Father and Jesus; and to love their parents as well as all people. They should be taught that God is love and that love is their higher power (JOH 3:16; 1 CO 13:4-13; 1 JO 4:7-21).

- 1 PE 1:22-23 ~ Having purified your souls by your obedience to the truth for a sincere brotherly love, love one another earnestly from a pure heart, since you have been born again, not of perishable seed but of imperishable, through the living and abiding word of God.

- 1 JO 2:15 ~ Do not love the world or the things in the world. If anyone loves the world, the love of the Father is not in him.

Parents need to be well versed in God's Word. Children need to begin learning about the Bible, God, and Jesus Christ at an early age. In fact, young children are especially able to understand the love of God and can possess a strong faith in Jesus Christ. The best guide to parenting is the Holy Bible. The best example of a loving parent is God our Father. The best illustration of an obedient child is Jesus Christ. Study the Bible together as a family regularly;

daily devotions is a great way to spend quality time together in the presence of the Lord (MAT 18:20).

- MAT 18:3-6 – Jesus said, "Truly, I say to you, unless you turn and become like children, you will never enter the kingdom of heaven. Whoever humbles himself like this child is the greatest in the kingdom of heaven. Whoever receives one such child in my name receives me, but whoever causes one of these little ones who believe in me to sin, it would be better for him to have a great millstone fastened around his neck and to be drowned in the depth of the sea."

- LUK 18:15-17 ~ Now they were bringing even infants to him that he might touch them. And when the disciples saw it, they rebuked them. But Jesus called them to him, saying, "Let the children come to me, and do not hinder them, for to such belongs the kingdom of God. Truly, I say to you, whoever does not receive the kingdom of God like a child shall not enter it."

Parents must make themselves available and accessible to their children from birth to death. This is critical. It begins with the initial attachment without which the child will be unable to develop stable connections with others. Children need love, affection, discipline, and direction. Who will they get this from if not their parents? I wouldn't trust others to fill that need as there's no telling what they might learn or become. Talk to your kids often; ask them what's going on, what interests them, what they want, and what they need. Give them praise, help them with problems, and work on things together. Make time for each child, give them equal attention and unconditional love, and teach them to share with others. If you do these things they will be more likely to talk to you if they are in trouble, share their secrets with you, and keep you posted on developments in their lives. Above all, listen to them; never tune them out. If you are busy, tell them when you can make time for them and always follow through.

Parenting is the most important role you will ever play in your lifetime. It helps to get some training; read some books and/or take some classes before having children. Most parents learn how to be a mom or a dad by trial and error; they don't get it right the first time, if ever. You wouldn't hire a nanny without experience, education, or references would you?

Either way, have a game plan and include your kids in the planning. Together you can win the game. If they try to make it by themselves, they will often lose out. This is because your family is more powerful and capable collectively, than anyone of you are individually. Set the boundaries, make the rules, establish the privileges, assign the chores, and determine the consequences. Have a routine that includes family entertainment, distributes quality time, and ensures that everyone is responsible for something.

Be consistent but flexible. Be reasonable but firm. Show respect, love, and support; offer encouragement and praise. Let them explore within practical boundaries so they can discover their identity; don't provide it for them. Don't do everything for them; let them try on their own and allow them to make mistakes. Hold them accountable when they violate the rules, breach the borders, or behave in an irresponsible or immoral fashion. Provide reinforcement, reproof, and punishment if necessary. Make the penalty fit the crime; allow the children an opportunity to be part of such decision making.

Help them when they ask and back off when they ask; intervene if there is danger to their health or safety and tell them why you are getting involved. Don't be overprotective or overly permissive; research has shown that the democratic style of parenting is the most effective. Keep a close eye on them without being snoopy, inquisitive, or invading their privacy. Responsible behavior should be rewarded with more freedom; irresponsibility should result in a loss of certain freedoms or narrowing of the borders. Be an example of responsible behavior; that is, practice what you preach.

Relationship with God

Everyone has freedom of choice, including choosing God to be their Father. God chooses us to be his children. God has chosen those who seek and obey him to be his own. It is a great privilege to be chosen by God who also chose rulers (DEU 17:15; 1 SA 10:24; 1 KI 3:8), judges (JDG 2:16-18; JDG 13:5), ministers (NUM 1:50; DEU 21:5), and prophets (NEH 9:7; ISA 6:8; JER 1:5). Jesus Christ continued this tradition by choosing his apostles (JOH 6:70; ACT 1:2; ACT 9:15). Christ also chooses us to be his witnesses and to serve one another (MAT 20:1-16).

Those people who set an example of God's love, understanding, fairness, and wisdom are placed in positions of authority over his sheep, so that others may follow his example. In the same way, God ordained his Son to be an example before all the world of his unconditional and steadfast love. Jesus Christ was ordained from the beginning of time to show all people who he was and how we could be like him (JOH 1:1-14). If we follow him we shine his light, showing the way for others who are lost and cannot find their way (PSA 119:105; JOH 8:12).

- PSA 89:3-4,27,29,34 (paraphrased) ~ God says, "I have made a covenant with my chosen people, and I have sworn to my servant David that the throne of my blessed servant (Messiah) will be established forever before all generations. He will be my firstborn, higher than all of the kings of the earth, and his seed will live forever. And I will never break that covenant."

- ISA 42:1 ~ God says, "Behold my servant, whom I uphold, my chosen, in whom my soul delights; I have put my Spirit upon him; he will bring forth justice to the nations."

- ISA 43:10-12,15 ~ "You are my witnesses," declares the LORD, "and my servant whom I have chosen, that you may know and believe me and understand that I am he. Before me no god was formed, nor shall there be any after me. I am the LORD, and besides me there is no savior. I declared and saved and proclaimed, when there was no strange god among you; and you are my witnesses," declares the LORD, "and I am God. Also henceforth I am he; there is none who can deliver from my hand; I work, and who can turn it back? I am the LORD, your Holy One, the Creator of Israel, your King."

- MAT 12:15-18 (paraphrased) ~ Jesus Christ is the fulfillment of the prophecy of Isaiah who wrote: Behold my servant, whom I have chosen; he is my beloved, who pleases my soul. I will put my Spirit upon him, and he will show judgment to the Gentile nations.

God chose Christ who in turn chooses you. Everyone is called to be a child of God, but God chooses only those who call upon him to be their Lord. If you choose to seek the Lord you will find him through his only Son Jesus Christ. If you follow Christ he will lead you to the Promised Land, where all his chosen people will live in God's house forevermore. Once called however, it is important to remain faithful, and to set an example for others to see. This is not an easy thing to do because to be faithful to God is to be at odds with the world.

- DEU 14:2 ~ For you are a people holy to the LORD your God, and the LORD has chosen you to be a people for his treasured possession, out of all the peoples who are on the face of the earth. (also PSA 135:4)

- JOH 15:16,19 ~ Jesus said, "You did not choose me, but I chose you and appointed you that you should go and bear fruit and that your fruit should abide, so that whatever you ask the Father in my name, he may give it to you... If you were of the world, the world would love you as its own; but because you are not of the world, but I chose you out of the world, therefore the world hates you."

- 1 PE 2:9 ~ But you are a chosen race, a royal priesthood, a holy nation, a people for his own possession, that you may proclaim the excellencies of him who called you out of darkness into his marvelous light.

To be chosen by God is a wonderful thing indeed. What great rewards God has promised to those who love him and who try to keep his commandments. His joy and peace are bestowed upon his people on earth and again in heaven. There is no end to his loving kindness, which can be enjoyed the moment one dedicates his or her life to the Lord and which endures for eternity. Therefore, to choose God and to choose to follow his Son is to choose life, and that life lasts forever. To choose not to seek God or to follow him is to choose death, and that death is permanent (DEU 30:19-20).

- PSA 33:12 ~ Blessed is the nation whose God is the LORD, the people whom he has chosen as his heritage!

- ISA 66:4 ~ I also will choose harsh treatment for them and bring their fears upon them, because when I called, no one answered, when I spoke, they did not listen; but they did what was evil in my eyes and chose that in which I did not delight.

- EPH 1:4-5 ~ God chose us in him before the foundation of the world, that we should be holy and blameless before him. In love he predestined us for adoption as sons through Jesus Christ, according to the purpose of his will.

- 2 TH 2:13 ~ We ought always to give thanks to God for you, brothers beloved by the Lord, because God chose you as the firstfruits to be saved, through sanctification by the Spirit and belief in the truth.

- REV 17:13-14 ~ These are of one mind, and they hand over their power and authority to the beast. They will make war on the Lamb, and the Lamb will conquer them, for he is Lord of lords and King of kings, and those with him are called and chosen and faithful.

- REV 20:14; REV 21:8 ~ Then Death and Hades were thrown into the lake of fire. This is the second death, the lake of fire... But as for the cowardly, the faithless, the detestable, as for murderers, the sexually immoral, sorcerers, idolaters, and all liars, their portion will be in the lake that burns with fire and sulfur, which is the second death.

The Household of Saints

The family of God includes all believers who are adopted into his family and become heirs to the kingdom of heaven. God's people include anyone who desires a relationship with him and who strives to be joined with his Holy Spirit. That relationship is based on God's love for us and our faith in him. You are members of God's household simply by believing in his promises. God's children are equal heirs with Jesus Christ, God's only Son, regardless of nationality.

- ISA 14:1 ~ For the LORD will have compassion on Jacob and will again choose Israel, and will set them in their own land, and sojourners will join them and will attach themselves to the house of Jacob.

- ROM 4:13,16; ROM 9:6-7 ~ For the promise to Abraham and his offspring that he would be heir of the world did not come through the law but through the righteousness of faith... That is why it depends on faith, in order that the promise may rest on grace and be guaranteed to all his offspring – not only to the adherent of the law but also to the one who shares the faith of Abraham, who is the father of us all... But it is not as though the word of God has failed. For not all who are descended from Israel belong to Israel, and not all are children of Abraham because they are his offspring, but "Through Isaac shall your offspring be named."

- GAL 3:6-29 (paraphrased) ~ Paul wrote: Just as Abraham believed God, and it was accounted to him for righteousness, so also are those that are of faith children of Abraham. The scriptures foretold that God would justify the heathen through faith, as preached before the Gospel of Christ to Abraham himself through the words, "In you all nations shall be blessed" (see JOH 8:56-58). Therefore, those who have faith are blessed along with Abraham. Nobody is justified by the Law, but by faith. Christ redeemed us from the curse of the Law through his crucifixion on the cross. This he did to enable the blessing given Abraham to be given to the Gentiles as well, so that they too could receive the promise of the Holy Spirit through faith (ISA 49:6). I am talking about a contract that cannot be annulled any more than a contract between men can be annulled. Now to Abraham and his seed these promises were made. God didn't say, "to seeds," as of many, but "seed" as in one. And that seed is Jesus Christ. If the inheritance was to be the Law, it wouldn't be in the form of a promise; but God gave it to Abraham by promise. So what good is the Law? It was given to us to show us our sins until the promised Messiah would come who is the mediator of God's covenant. Is the Law contrary to the promise? Absolutely not! If there had been a law that could bring life, then righteousness could have been earned by obedience to the Law. But the scriptures told us that, because of sin, faith in the promise of Jesus Christ would be provided to all who would believe. Before faith came we were kept according to the Law until the time that faith would be revealed. Thus, the Law was our teacher of the promise of faith that would bring us to the knowledge of Christ. So we are all children of God by faith in Jesus Christ, for anyone who has been baptized by the Spirit bears the name of Christ. Therefore, there is no such thing as Jew or Greek, slave or free, male or female, for we all are equal in Jesus Christ. And if you belong to Christ then you are Abraham's seed, and heirs according to God's promise (see also LUK 16:19-31).

Heaven is our Home. When you leave home for extended periods do you ever get homesick? Most people miss their loved ones. Why is it that we don't miss God? Why is it that we never get homesick for heaven? After all, our citizenship is in heaven not here on earth. Christians need to have a greater passion for that day when we can finally go home to be with our Heavenly Father, and Christ our brother. Let that joy live in your heart and shine.

- ISA 56:5-8 ~ God says, "I will give in my house and within my walls a monument and a name better than sons and daughters; I will give them an everlasting name that shall not be cut off. And the foreigners who join themselves to the LORD, to minister to him, to love the name of the LORD, and to be his servants, everyone who keeps the Sabbath and does not profane it, and holds fast my covenant – these I will bring to my holy mountain, and make them joyful in my house of prayer; their burnt offerings and their sacrifices will be accepted on my altar; for my house shall be called a house of prayer for all peoples." The Lord GOD, who gathers the outcasts of Israel, declares, "I will gather yet others to him besides those already gathered."

- JOH 1:11-13 ~ He came to his own, and his own people did not receive him. But to all who did receive him, who believed in his name, he gave the right to become children of God, who were born, not of blood nor the will of the flesh nor the will of man, but of God.

- EPH 2:19 ~ So then you are no longer strangers and aliens, but you are fellow citizens with the saints and members of the household of God.

- 1 JO 3:1-2 ~ See what kind of love the Father has given to us, that we should be called children of God; and so we are. The reason why the world does not know us is that it did not know him. Beloved, we are God's children now, and what we will be has not yet appeared; but we know that when he appears we shall be like him, because we shall see him as he is.

The world is full of evil and corruption. We have to be careful not to fall into its trap and be led astray from our home.

- 2 CO 4:4 ~ The god of this world has blinded the minds of the unbelievers, to keep them from seeing the light of the gospel of the glory of Christ, who is the image of God.

- EPH 2:1-2 ~ And you were dead in the trespasses and sins in which you once walked, following the course of this world, following the prince of the power of the air, the spirit that is now at work in the sons of disobedience.

If we do get sidetracked and wander down the road of condemnation, we can always return home to God our Father where we will be welcomed with open arms. How comforting it is to know that he is always there for us. He loves us unconditionally even when we stray or disobey, just as we love our children in the same manner.

- PSA 46:1 ~ God is our refuge and strength, a very present help in trouble

- MAT 11:28 ~ Jesus said, "Come to me, all who labor and are heavy laden, and I will give you rest."

- LUK 15:11-32 (paraphrased) ~ Jesus told the parable of the prodigal son, who asked his father for his share of the inheritance. The father gave the son the inheritance, and the son left for a foreign land where he squandered all his money on wine and women. Meanwhile, a great famine arose in that country. The son had to feed pigs to make a living. Even his father's servants were better off than this, so he returned home to confess everything to his father, and apologize. His father saw him coming, ran out to meet the son, and embraced him. The son told his father that he was not worthy of being called a son and should be treated as a servant. But the father had his servants prepare a great feast to celebrate. The elder son became angry and refused to enter the house. The father consoled him saying, "You are always with me and all that is mine is yours. But it is fitting to celebrate, because your brother was lost but now he is found; he was dead but now he is alive again."

- 1 JO 4:3-4 ~ Every spirit that does not confess Jesus is not from God. This is the spirit of the antichrist, which you heard was coming and now is in the world already. Little children, you are from God and have overcome them, for he who is in you is greater than he who is in the world.

Among the many choices we have in this life, the one that impacts our future the most is whether we choose to be part of this world or part of God's kingdom. We tend to get distracted by this world and often neglect God. Yet there is nothing in this world that can compare to the treasures awaiting us in heaven. So there is no reason to make worldly things or material wealth our primary focus; instead we should keep focused on the Lord. There are no guarantees in this world but there are in heaven.

- MAT 6:19 ~ Jesus said, "Do not lay up for yourselves treasures on earth, where moth and rust destroy and where thieves break in and steal, but lay up for yourselves treasures in heaven, where neither moth nor rust destroys and where thieves do not break in and steal."

- JOH 14:2 ~ Jesus said, "In my Father's house are many rooms. If it were not so, would I have told you that I go to prepare a place for you?"

- 2 PE 1:3-4 ~ His divine power has granted to us all things that pertain to life and godliness, through the knowledge of him who called us to his own glory and excellence, by which he has granted to us his precious and very great promises, so that through them you may become partakers of the divine nature, having escaped from the corruption that is in the world because of sinful desire.

When we leave home we often can't wait to get back to our homes where we feel safe, comfortable, and happy. But such feelings are only fleeting due to constant interference from the world and the many problems, trials, and sorrows we face on earth. Our home in heaven will be much more enjoyable and comfortable because the joy, comfort, and peace will never end.

- ISA 32:17-18 ~ The effect of righteousness will be peace, and the result of righteousness, quietness and trust forever. My people will abide in a peaceful habitation, in secure dwellings, and in quiet resting places.

- ISA 65:17-19 ~ God says, "Behold, I create new heavens and a new earth, and the former things shall not be remembered or come into mind. But be glad and rejoice forever in that which I create; for behold, I create Jerusalem to be a joy, and her people to be a gladness. I will rejoice in Jerusalem and be glad in my people; no more shall be heard in it the sound of weeping and the cry of distress."

- ZEC 8:3,5-8 ~ Thus says the LORD: "I have returned to Zion and will dwell in the midst of Jerusalem, and Jerusalem shall be called the faithful city, and the mountain of the LORD of hosts, the holy mountain… And the streets of the city shall be full of boys and girls playing in its streets. If it is marvelous in the sight of the remnant of this people in those days, should it also be marvelous in my sight, declares the LORD of hosts? Behold, I will save my people from the east country and from the west country, and I will bring them to dwell in the midst of Jerusalem. And they shall be my people, and I will be their God, in faithfulness and in righteousness."

- REV 21:1,4 ~ Then I saw a new heaven and a new earth, for the first heaven and the first earth had passed away, and the sea was no more… God will wipe away every tear from their eyes, and death shall be no more, neither shall there be mourning, nor crying, nor pain anymore, for the former things have passed away.

"How far you go in life depends on your being tender with the young, compassionate with the aged, sympathetic with the striving, and tolerant of the weak and strong. Because someday in your life you will have been all of these." – George Washington Carver

Activity

The following areas of compatibility affect how a relationship starts and develops. Weigh how important each dimension is to you regarding relationships, using a scale of 1 to 10 (prioritize them). Note: the same weight can be ascribed to more than one attribute.

Weight/Rating

__/__ Spiritual (religious beliefs, dedication to God, church affiliation)

__/__ Ethical (moral standards, definition of right and wrong, views on contentious topics)

__/__ Physical (attractiveness, fitness, health)

__/__ Sexual (preferences, boundaries)

__/__ Behavioral (mannerisms, demeanor, attitude)

__/__ Emotional (temperament, openness, compassion)

__/__ Cultural (ethnicity, community, heritage)

__/__ Social (friends, activities, entertainment)

__/__ Developmental (maturity, identity, responsibility)

__/__ Political (liberal versus conservative, political affiliation, activism)

__/__ Intellectual (education, conversation, interests)

__/__ Educational (classes, background, knowledge)

__/__ Occupational (careers, place of work, skills and abilities)

__/__ Organizational (housekeeping, roles, responsibilities)

Next rate your significant other (or the person that interests you) on each attribute (from 1 to 10). That is, to what degree does he or she meet or fulfill that compatibility dimension for you? To obtain a composite score, multiply the dimension weight times the rating, and compute the total sum across all dimensions. There may be perfect compatibility in one or more dimensions but not all, so there are no "perfect tens". Rate other relationships using this method. Compute the overall scores for those relationships.

Have your partner weigh the dimensions and rate you on them. Compare your results on each dimension and overall. This will help you both to understand desires, and one another.

The Impact of Relationships

Without relationships we could not survive. However, relationships have either a positive or a negative impact upon our lives depending on whether they are healthy or unhealthy. The best way to guarantee that a relationship is beneficial is to ensure it is in accordance with God's will: upright, proper, honorable, virtuous. Carefully examine your relationships by truthfully answering the following questions.

> Do others impact you positive or negative?

> Is your impact on others positive or negative?

> Do you feel connected or disconnected?

> Are communications or connections a one way or a two way street?

> How strong is the connection between each component or each member?

> Are responsibilities, benefits, investments, participation, and credit shared equitably?

> Is the relationship built upon genuine, mutual love?

I find there are three types of people that impact our lives.

> Supportive – These are people who truly love you, support you, and relish in your success. They want to be part of your team, and to help you develop and execute your game plan. They are your real family; they want to take the journey with you. And the same is true regarding the way you feel and care about them.

> Problematic – These are people who get in the way; they'll bring you down, or even sabotage your success. They don't want you to be free, to excel, or to grow because it makes them feel small, or they are not interested in change period. Such relationships are destructive and may need to be discontinued.

> Indifferent – Some people fall in-between. They are not willing, desiring, or able to be part of your team, to go to bat for you or fight for you. But they care about you and you care about them. It is not necessary to abandon such relationships, but you cannot depend on their support, though they will want to be kept informed.

Keep in mind that we relate, not just to people but also to our environment. Each sphere of influence in our lives can impact us in a positive or negative manner. We also can impact each layer of our existence positively or negatively. Assess the Systems Model illustrated below; it depicts the various realms of influence in our environment. Notice how every concentric circle represents a much larger domain which encompasses all those within it; the corresponding impacts on one's life can be equally enormous. Each outlying layer produces effects that flow all the way down to you. And what you do, whether right or wrong, big or small, can have a ripple effect that flows all the way through to the outer layers.

You produce effects upon your life, the lives of your loved ones, and others around you, your community, society, the planet, and even God. And it works the other way around as well. So if you do the right thing the impact will be positive overall. That is, goodness results in positive outcomes and evil in negative outcomes. If you seek happiness, success, or fulfillment; if you want a desirable outcome for you and for all; you will need to evaluate your alternatives and make your choices based on what is right for you, for your loved ones, and for the greater good. Consequently, doing the righteous thing is quite a complicated matter; it requires one to be thoughtful and mindful, every waking minute and for every decision. Okay, granted; nobody is perfect (well, except Christ). The most important choice of all is to invite Christ to live in you, and he will come; and everything in your life will change for the better. Respond to him by raising the bar on yourself: recalibrate your moral compass; improve your standards of behavior, and give your best performance.

The Systems Model

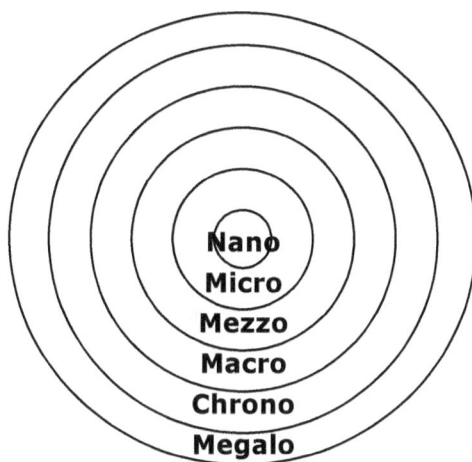

- ➤ Nano – You (Personal)
- ➤ Micro – Inner Circle (Parents, Kids, Spouse, Family, Friends)
- ➤ Mezzo – Institutional, Organizational, Community (Church, Work, School)
- ➤ Macro – Society, Government, Culture (Religion)
- ➤ Chrono – Time, Space, Nature (Universe)
- ➤ Megalo – Heaven, Eternity (God)

Observe how God encompasses it all; how he operates outside of the universe as well as within it. In fact, he exists and resides in all people, places, and things, especially you. That makes you pretty special, doesn't it? He has created everything and it all belongs to him; and he has created us in his image. Yet he has placed us in the middle of it because it was all done so that we could love him, live for him, and live with him. God is a living, spiritual, nonmaterial, invisible, and supernatural being. Who but God could create the living, the material, the visible, and the natural? God has given us similar qualities, as well as associated gifts: natural, supernatural, cognitive, and spiritual: like life, love, morality, ability, consciousness, and free will.

- ISA 45:12 ~ God says, "I made the earth and created man on it; it was my hands that stretched out the heavens and I commanded all their host."

- JOH 1:16 ~ From his fullness we have all received, grace upon grace.

- COL 1:15-17 ~ Jesus is the image of the invisible God, the firstborn of all creation. For by him all things were created, in heaven and on earth, visible and invisible, whether thrones or dominions or rulers or authorities – all things were created through him and for him.

Activity

Evaluate your relationships using the model presented above. Identify where you have connections or disconnects. Determine how you impact each environment and whether it is impacting you positive or negative.

Evaluate your relationship with yourself. Do you like yourself? How is your self-esteem? Do you send negative messages to yourself? Are you a happy person? What is not right about how you feel about yourself?

_____

_____

_____

Evaluate your relationship with your inner circle. How do you get along with your spouse, your children, your parents, your family? Do you have many friends? How often or how much time do you spend with loved ones and friends?

_____

_____

_____

Evaluate your relationship with your immediate environment. Do you like your job, your school, your church, your neighborhood? Do you get along with your fellow employees, students, or parishioners? Do you feel connected in these environments? If not, why?

_____

_____

_____

Evaluate your relationship with your community, your society, your culture. Are you proud of your heritage, your country, your town? Do you like where you live? What do you like or dislike about the people around you? Would you like to meet and talk with some of them? How would you rate your government, the laws of the land, and the norms of society?

_____

_____

_____

Evaluate your relationship with the universe. Are you connected to nature, and to God's creation? Can you have a positive impact on it? If so, how? How does it impact you? Are you able to contribute to humanity, help the planet, or change the space-time continuum with what you do? If so, how?

———————————————————————————————————————

———————————————————————————————————————

———————————————————————————————————————

Evaluate your relationship with God. Do you feel connected to him? Is he a part of you (inside of you and/or part of your inner circle)? Do you pray to the Lord, study the scriptures, and worship God? How often or how much time do you spend doing these things? If you don't do these things, why not?

———————————————————————————————————————

———————————————————————————————————————

———————————————————————————————————————

What could you do to improve upon or repair some of the following relationships? How could you make the world a better place for yourself and others?

Personal _____

Interpersonal _____

Community _____

Society _____

World _____

God _____

BUILDING RELATIONSHIPS

- Friendship
- Marriage
- Parenthood
- Relationship with God
- Household of Saints

CONFLICT RESOLUTION

OBJECTIVE	Learn how to avoid conflict and resolve conflict more effectively.
INTERVENTION	Discuss methods to avoid confrontation, quell arguments, and reduce discord. Recognize what to do before, during, and after a disagreement, as well as throughout the relationship.
PLAN	Identify interpersonal conflicts and apply resolution techniques and principles in order to prevent arguments and strengthen bonds.

"Pick battles big enough to matter, small enough to win." – Jonathan Kozol

Internal Conflict

Everyone has problems in this world due to sin. Because of our sinful flesh, we experience conflict in our lives, not just with others, but within ourselves. In fact, the Bible teaches that our flesh is in constant conflict with our spirit. According to the holistic health perspective we possess a spiritual, mental, and physical component. If the physical and the spiritual are at war with each other, what are they fighting over? Answer: the mental. The battle is over control of the mind, the thoughts, beliefs, and ultimately the actions. Do not let the flesh win this battle or you will risk damnation. But if you allow the spirit to prevail, you will find life.

- PRO 23:7 (KJV) ~ As he thinks in his heart, so is he …

- JOH 6:63 ~ Jesus said, "It is the Spirit who gives life; the flesh is no help at all. The words that I have spoken to you are spirit and life."

- ROM 7:18 - ROM 8:7 ~ I know that nothing good dwells in me, that is, in my flesh. I have the desire to do what is right, but not the ability to carry it out. For I do not do the good I want, but the evil I do not want is what I keep on doing. Now if I do what I do not want, it is no longer I who do it, but sin that dwells within me. So I find it to be a law that when I want to do right, evil lies close at hand. I delight in the law of God in my inner being, but I see in my members another law waging war against the law of my mind and making me captive to the law of sin that dwells in my members. Wretched man that I am! Who will deliver me from this body of death? Thanks be to God through Jesus Christ our Lord! So then, I serve the law of God with my mind, but with my flesh I serve the law of sin. There is therefore now no condemnation for those who are in Christ Jesus. For the law of the Spirit of life has set you free in Christ Jesus from the law of sin and death. For God has done what the law, weakened by the flesh, could not do. By sending his own Son in the likeness of sinful flesh and for sin, he condemned sin in the flesh, in order that the righteous requirement of the law might be fulfilled in us, who walk not according to the flesh but according to the Spirit. For those who live according to the flesh set their minds on the things of the flesh, but those who live according to the Spirit set their minds on the things of the Spirit. For to set the mind on the flesh is death, but to set the mind on the Spirit is life and peace. For the mind that is set on the flesh is hostile to God, for it does not submit to God's law; indeed, it cannot. Those who are in the flesh cannot please God.

- GAL 5:17-18 ~ For the desires of the flesh are against the Spirit, and the desires of the Spirit are against the flesh, for these are opposed to each other, to keep you from doing the things you want to do. But if you are led by the Spirit, you are not under the law.

- 1 PE 2:11 ~ Beloved, I urge you as sojourners and exiles to abstain from the passions of the flesh, which wage war against your soul.

What about those who allow the flesh to control their thoughts? They are constantly seeking to fulfill their desires via this world. But like the addict, they are never satisfied. That's because the flesh is never fulfilled. You will get hungry, thirsty, tired, and/or craving passions of the flesh again and again. You can never get enough relief and fulfillment satisfying worldly desires.

- ECC 1:8-9 ~ All things are full of weariness; a man cannot utter it; the eye is not satisfied with seeing, nor the ear filled with hearing. What has been is what will be, and what has been done is what will be done, and there is nothing new under the sun.

- PHP 3:17-19 ~ Brothers, join in imitating me, and keep your eyes on those who walk according to the example you have in us. For many, of whom I have often told you and now tell you even with tears, walk as enemies of the cross of Christ. Their end is destruction, their god is their belly, and they glory in their shame, with minds set on earthly things.

We went to the all-you-can-eat buffet one day. Like always, I piled the food up to the ceiling and then had seconds. I went back to the dessert counter a second time also, knowing that I would probably regret it. My hunger was gratified but still I wanted more; the dessert was so good and I wanted to get my money worth, and so forth. These rationalizations were designed to convince my mind to go ahead and have more, though my conscience was warning me not to. But I did anyway, and I got a bellyache. I learned the lesson, though.

Let your conscience be your guide, the saying goes; and it's true. I should have followed my conscience. It wasn't lying to me; unfortunately, my thoughts were being guided by my stomach. Those who let the lusts of the flesh distract them from the needs of the spirit are losing the war. You need to let the spirit win the battle over your brain, and you will be happy, fulfilled, and right. When you overindulge in things of this world you are trying to fill a void that will never be filled because it is a spiritual emptiness. More on this subject can be found in the lesson on Bad Habits.

It is difficult to resolve this internal conflict on your own. But with Christ, you will ultimately overcome the world. We must remember that we are spiritual beings, not merely physical, and that our home is in heaven not on earth.

- JOH 16:33 ~ Jesus said, "I have said these things to you, that in me you may have peace. In the world you will have tribulation. But take heart; I have overcome the world."

A good Biblical episode illustrating the internal conflict between the physical and the spiritual is the judge Samson. He was groomed to be a Nazarite while still in the womb. A Nazarite was one who had been dedicated to God and separated from others to become a person of discipline, example, and virtue (see NUM 6:2-21). Such a person would not cut his hair, would not drink alcohol, and would be a model of righteousness and morality. But Samson fell for the temptress Delilah, and she seduced him into giving up his vows and exchanging them for pleasures of the flesh. After exploiting the weaknesses of his flesh, she would betray him to the Philistines to be ridiculed, tormented, and blinded. In time, he would renew his vows to God. Then, in one fell swoop he took down the Temple of Dagon and the thousands that had mocked him and God (see JDG 16:1-31). Beware: desires of the flesh are very compelling; Satan will use them to draw you away from your convictions and follow him into the pit, because he desires company in the fall. Note how powers of the spirit are greater and can defeat those of the flesh.

Conflict with Others

First I would like to suggest that, as a Christian, you will find conflict with the world. Secularists will attempt to persuade you that you do not need God or that you can be your own god. The worldly view is that the Bible is a joke and believers are either idiots or crazy; but it is those who deny God that are deluded. You can witness to them if the situation allows, but it is unlikely that they will listen; if that be the case, this is a conflict that can be avoided.

- 2 TH 3:10-12 ~ The coming of the lawless one is by the activity of Satan with all power and false signs and wonders, and with all wicked deception for those who are perishing, because they refused to love the truth and so be saved. Therefore God sends them a strong delusion, so that they may believe what is false, in order that all may be condemned who did not believe the truth but had pleasure in unrighteousness.

But when it comes to your loved ones, conflict needs to be faced; you cannot just pass it off or ignore it because the problem can intensify. There are a number of strategies for resolving conflict and preventing an argument from escalating into a full blown confrontation. We will review some of them in this lesson but it is in no way an exhaustive list.

These strategies are particularly necessary for the security of relationships that we value. I have often said: Those who are not part of your support could be part of your problem. People who belong to your true family are not always your blood. In other words, those who are there for you when you need them, and who are people you can trust, are the relationships worth keeping, protecting, and repairing.

Therefore, some obstacles in our path we must face while some we can avoid. Internal conflict must always be faced, such as fear and doubt, and the war between the flesh and spirit. Sometimes we can bypass the external barriers to forward progress; such barriers might include people, places, and things that are unnecessary for our success or happiness. But if the conflict is with a person whose companionship I value, I will have to face them sooner or later.

BEFORE: Preventing a Confrontation

➢ Plan Ahead

➢ Teamwork

➢ Practice, Rehearse

➢ Seek Help, Support

➢ Give Help, Support

Let's begin with what we can do beforehand to prevent future conflict. First of all, we should plan ahead. If you are in a significant intimate relationship you should discuss your plans together. This is a good way of spending quality time with one another; it is fun planning your life together. Plan everything, including whose responsibility is whose, and how you will divide up the chores, and what to do for entertainment: all the what, when, how, who, and where stuff. If you are a parent, conduct regular family meetings; discuss the rules, consequences, privileges, and boundaries. Include all the members of the family and allow children to voice their opinions. Take turns choosing what to do during family fun time. Naturally, for the key decisions it should be understood that the parents' vote pulls more weight than the children.

When I first got married both my wife and I had a career. Therefore, it wasn't fair for one to do more household chores than the other. So we divided it up. Since I had been a bachelor for years I knew how to cook. She didn't like to cook but didn't mind cleaning, whereas I hated cleaning because that was my duty when I was growing up. It was an easy division; she did the laundry, dishes, and housework, and I did the grocery shopping and the cooking. That didn't mean I would never clean or she would never cook. We simply planned how to divide the chores in a way that was agreeable to both of us. Try fairness and you will see it always works. You and your partner should take turns choosing, like what movie to watch. Men will discover that sometimes they actually like the chick flick and women will sometimes like the science fiction one; either way you will enjoy the quality time together.

And you parents, plan together how you will discipline your children. Your kids won't be able to play one parent against the other when they realize both are playing from the same sheet of music. Involve your kids in the decision making and the punishment. If everyone in the relationship is part of the decision, all will take ownership of the results and/or the consequences. If the responsibilities, consequences, rules, etc. are mapped out there won't be any misunderstandings about the course of action. And the penalties will always relate directly to the misdeeds.

- PRO 22:6 ~ Train up a child in the way he should go; even when he is old he will not depart from it.

- EPH 6:1-4 ~ Children, obey your parents in the Lord, for this is right. "Honor your father and mother" (this is the first commandment with a promise), "that it may go well with you and that you may live long in the land." Fathers, do not provoke your children to anger, but bring them up in the discipline and instruction of the Lord.

- COL 3:20-21 ~ Children, obey your parents in everything, for this pleases the Lord. Fathers, do not provoke your children, lest they become discouraged.

When my son was little he used to love video games; he knew if he misbehaved the games would be the first thing to go. One day I asked him what would be a fair consequence for playing video games while neglecting to do his homework, and then lying about it. He said I should take his machine away for two weeks, one for each infraction. I agreed, and he counted the days keeping score each day to remind me, "Just 10 more days," then 9, 8, 7. After one week I gave back his machine as a reward for enforcing the rule himself (I was planning on one week anyway). He learned the lesson and enforced the rule because he was part of the decision. There was no possibility for misunderstanding.

Planning involves teamwork. Paul writes: Do not be unevenly yoked with unbelievers. A yoke is that wooden frame which holds two oxen together as they pull the plow or the cart. If unevenly yoked, one is pulling in one direction and the other in another direction. Or you have the two pushing against each other; or one doing all the work and dragging the other behind. If you are equally yoked both have a common direction, a common goal, a common vision. Both equally share the load, the responsibility, the purpose, and the rewards.

- 2 CO 6:14 ~ Do not be unequally yoked with unbelievers. For what partnership has righteousness with lawlessness? Or what fellowship has light with darkness?

In marriage you are a team. Certainly, you should maximize upon the natural abilities of each spouse; for instance, moms are generally better at nurturing and dads at discipline. But both need to know how to do the other's job especially if one spouse is working, sick, or otherwise indisposed. The Bible teaches the manner in which a wife and a husband should behave, giving sound doctrine in ensuring a successful marriage (see the Relationships section). The bottom line is to want to be together and to do everything together (within reason of course, as you don't need to go to the bathroom together). Certainly, there should be time allocated to all your loved ones in different combinations, including personal time for yourself, and of course, God. But most important to your partnership is to block out some time to be alone with your partner. If you have a routine or a schedule, everyone will know what to expect or to do. So plan it out to the extent that you can, allowing opportunities for spontaneity, discovery, and personal growth.

Another strategy is to rehearse, practice. It's like preparing for an exam, job interview, stage performance, or speech. As a teen, did you ever gather your words and rehearse them in front of a mirror before calling someone on the phone? You wanted the words to come out just right. In this day of email I find myself editing a message several times before sending it. Have you ever sent a message on your phone and then wanted to retrieve it, but you were too late? Then you sent two more messages to rebut or clarify the previous message. If that has happened to you before you will be more careful before pressing the send button, so that the message is received as it was intended, and there is no inflammatory verbiage or confusing language.

Simply stated, think before you speak. Remove the emotion from the message. The only emotion that I am sure will reinforce a message is love. Remember when you were getting lectured by an irate parent, who was yelling at you and spitting all over you? You didn't hear a word they said; the only message transmitted was the anger. The same is true when someone is overjoyed; he or she tries to tell you something and they are so excited that you have to insist they calm down because you have no idea what they are talking about. We need to extract the emotion from the message and insert reason. Most people, even children, are reasonable. They might not agree with your reasoning but will respect that you have a reason.

- PRO 13:3 ~ Whoever guards his mouth preserves his life; he who opens wide his lips comes to ruin.

- PRO 15:28 ~ The heart of the righteous ponders how to answer, but the mouth of the wicked pours out evil things.

- PRO 17:27-28 ~ Whoever restrains his words has knowledge, and he who has a cool spirit is a man of understanding. Even a fool who keeps silent is considered wise; when he closes his lips, he is deemed intelligent.

- MAT 12:37 ~ Jesus said, "By your words you will be justified, and by your words you will be condemned."

- JAM 3:13-17 ~ Come now, you who say, "Today or tomorrow we will go into such and such a town and spend a year there and trade and make a profit" – yet you do not know what tomorrow will bring. What is your life? You are a mist that appears for a little time and then vanishes. Instead you ought to say, "If the Lord wills, we will live and do this or that." As it is, you boast in your arrogance. All such boasting is evil. So whoever knows the right thing to do and fails to do it, for him it is sin.

How about this scenario? "Quit that!" "Why?" "Because!" "Because why?" "Because I said so, that's why!" "That's not a reason." "I don't need a reason because I'm the parent you have to do as I say." The following would work better. "Son, the reason I get angry when you jump on the furniture is I'm afraid you could hurt yourself or maybe break something." With calmness and firmness the message is conveyed in love, with a little touching and eye contact perhaps, and with reason not emotion. Notice also to keep it short, simple, and to the point (25 words or less is a good practice).

To wrap up the discussion of prevention, consider getting and giving help. Patients who are hospitalized or clients that come to your office are making a sound decision to seek help. They know they can't figure out how to proceed so they look towards a professional or expert in the field. I encourage clients to seek marital counseling, or family counseling, or psychiatric evaluation. Certainly, seeking God's counsel is a smart course of action. If you are struggling to carry a heavy load, Jesus beckons you to give it to him and he will carry it for you (MAT 11:28).

People that think they know all the answers or can do everything without anyone else's help eventually become very lonely. But when seeking help consider the source. For example, would you rather seek medication consultation from a psychiatrist, a drug dealer, an addict, or a friend who is taking medications for a similar reason? Would you prefer advice about your marriage from a bachelor friend, a divorced friend, a married friend, or a marriage counselor?

In matters of individual differences in a relationship, one can invite their partner to help them understand, diagnose a problem, or explore the alternatives. One can likewise assist by freely communicating opinions, ideas, thoughts, or feelings. Help others understand you and seek to understand them. But if you constantly seek help from someone who consistently lets you down you are undoubtedly wasting your time. It may surprise you who is there for you and who is not when you experience a crisis or a conflict. The ones that will support you in your vision, decision, or plight – they are your true family and belong in your inner circle.

DURING: Averting a Fight

- ➤ Leave
- ➤ Time Out
- ➤ Let Go, Give In
- ➤ Positive Thinking, Imagery
- ➤ Make Peace

Now let us turn to the next phase, when a conflict is developing. Again, we want to prevent it from becoming a war. There are certain escape routes available. Not that we are going to run away from the conflict, but we are trying to avoid allowing it to get out of hand. Of course, if the relationship is not of value then the better part of valor might be to leave. For example, if there is someone at your workplace that is a gossip, or tattle tale, or creates discord, or shaves hours off the work day, or doesn't pull his or her weight – it may be better to stay away from such a person. They might try to get you into trouble, or compete with you for some position, or talk behind your back. If you don't need to work with them, or be their friend, then avoid that person. Revisiting the example I gave above, if they are part of your problem you don't have to continue the relationship. In order to avoid the decadent lifestyle of the seventies, I eventually chose to stay away from certain places and people as I didn't need the temptation. Some "friends" became expendable; because it turned out they really weren't true friends, just bad influences.

- PSA 1:1-2 ~ Blessed is the man who walks not in the counsel of the wicked, nor stands in the way of sinners, nor sits in the seat of scoffers; but his delight is in the law of the LORD, and on his law he meditates day and night.

- PRO 6:16-19 ~ There are six things that the LORD hates, seven that are an abomination to him: haughty eyes, a lying tongue, and hands that shed innocent blood, a heart that devises wicked plans, feet that make haste to run to evil, a false witness who breathes out lies, and one who sows discord among brothers.

- ROM 16:17 ~ I appeal to you, brothers, to watch out for those who cause divisions and create obstacles contrary to the doctrine that you have been taught; avoid them.

- JDE 1:19 ~ It is these who cause divisions, worldly people, devoid of the Spirit.

If you value the relationship, you can escape temporarily by calling a timeout. The purpose of the timeout is to gather your thoughts, remove the emotion, and come back to the table with a clear mind and a cool head. It is a good rule of thumb for partners and families to use the timeout method. Anybody in the relationship should have the right to call a timeout, for 5, 10, or 15 minutes (you set the rule), with the intention of reasonably discussing the issue at the end of the timeout. Just like in a sports event; they take a timeout, figure out a strategy, and then the game is on again.

It is pointless to try to work it out when both or either partner is emotionally distraught. Often, it takes only a few moments to calm down, other times it will take longer. But do not put it off indefinitely or the issue may escalate. Agree on a time to talk it over and wait until that time, and be ready for it. Sometimes when my wife and I have a little spat, and we take time to cool off, the problem just goes away (if it is trivial to us both). We make up and forget about it, if it isn't already forgotten by then. Of course, trivial is a relative term. If either partner thinks it important then it should be considered important to the other partner, and it warrants being addressed. Question: So what should you do when the matter is trivial to you but a big deal to your partner? Answer: Give in. Remember, it's a small matter to you, and thus requires minimal sacrifice. What if the matter is a big deal to you but a small matter to him or her? Answer: Let go. It might not be that big a deal after all.

Other ways of letting go include the following: vent the emotions in a constructive manner, use positive thinking or imagery (place yourself in an upbeat state of mind or go to a favorite place in you mind), pray about it, and practice forgiveness. As I have repeated throughout this text, the positive will drive away the negative because it is more powerful. Thinking "I can" is more powerful than "I cannot" not to mention the fact that it is the truth. And if I can and you can, then we can too.

The more you practice being positive, thoughtful, level-headed, and relaxed the more you become the peacemaker. Who doesn't look up to such a person? My most admired character was my maternal grandfather. I never saw him lose his temper. Sure he may have gotten angry, who doesn't? But he always kept his cool and resolved the issue with love and understanding. An attitude of compassion combined with a demeanor of temperance can quell the fire of another's anger quicker than anything I know.

- PRO 15:13 ~ A glad heart makes a cheerful face, but by sorrow of heart the spirit is crushed.

- ECC 7:9 ~ Be not quick in your spirit to become angry, for anger lodges in the heart of fools.

- ROM 12:16-21 ~ Live in harmony with one another. Do not be haughty, but associate with the lowly. Never be wise in your own sight. Repay no one evil for evil, but give thought to do what is honorable in the sight of all. If possible, so far as it depends on you, live peaceably with all. Beloved, never avenge yourselves, but leave it to the wrath of God, for it is written, "Vengeance is mine, I will repay, says the Lord." To the contrary, "if your enemy is hungry, feed him; if he is thirsty, give him something to drink; for by so doing you will heap burning coals on his head." Do not be overcome by evil, but overcome evil with good.

- GAL 6:10 ~ So then, as we have opportunity, let us do good to everyone, and especially to those who are of the household of faith.

- PHP 2:14 ~ Do all things without grumbling or disputing.

AFTER: Communicating

➢ Compromise

➢ Restore Equity

➢ Collaboration

➢ Ask Questions, Don't Assume

➢ Get and Receive Feedback

Next, what should we do after a conflict has started, or ended? The prime objective: communication. The Communication and Assertiveness lessons previously presented also relate to this discussion. Naturally, communication should occur throughout the relationship. But there are things that we can do to figure out what is wrong and correct the wrong. Compromise is a very good custom: coming together and working out a deal. Our nation was founded on the art of compromise. The left-wingers on one side and the right-wingers on the other sit across the table and hammer out an agreement, and it becomes legislation – this is the democratic process. Relationships can be handled in the same manner.

What you're looking for is a 50/50 deal where both parties give up something to get something, or meet half way. A technique I frequently use in marital counseling is the like/don't like list. Each partner lists half a dozen things they like and they dislike about the other. They prioritize the lists and then exchange them. It usually comes as a surprise to each the way the other partner feels about them. And this makes it very easy to meet in the middle. You may start at the bottom of the list; agree to give up one on your list if they'll do the same. For example, the man agrees not to leave dirty socks on the floor if the woman will quit hanging wet stockings in the shower. They both give up something that takes little or no effort. Often, both may perceive that they got the better end of the deal. In the case I cited above, since I preferred cooking and my wife preferred cleaning, the benefit exceeded the cost for both of us. It was more like a 75/75 deal.

Keep working your way up the list and you may be able to compromise on every point. A 50/50 setup is usually enough to sustain any relationship. But you eventually want to work up the ladder until you achieve 100/100. That's a win-win situation for both of you. After all, love is supposed to be unconditional, no strings attached, total commitment. If you achieve that kind of love you will be happy, and you won't need to expect it in order to give it; you'll know it's always there. But less than 50/50 seldom works. It will gradually work down to 40, 30, 20, 10. My first marriage failed largely because it dwindled to 10/10. We were so busy we both put in the bare minimum and got the same out of it; eventually neither of us was getting enough of our needs met so we split up.

An important theory in Social Psychology concerns equity. It is based on the presumption that relationships involve a social exchange, not unlike an economic one. I give the clerk a buck and get a bag of chips. That's an even exchange. Healthy relationships require equity too or they will eventually end. If someone feels they are giving more than they are getting they will be unhappy. We think in terms of equal costs and benefits, though we all like when our benefits outweigh the costs. That will work in a monetary investment but not an emotional one. When the scales are tipped equity must be restored, for if they stay out of balance too long it will cause damage to the relationship. And psychological equity will not be sufficient in the long run because most people will want to see something tangible, especially when promises are not followed through. Communication helps us to get feedback from our significant other as to how he or she perceives the give and take, and how we can make them feel better through fairness and understanding.

If you practice compromise and equity you will build up to the level of collaboration. As with teamwork, you become partners in every aspect: emotional, sexual, social, financial, business, spiritual, and so forth. You can bring your kids in on the discussion, or other family members, when appropriate. Get into the habit of collaborating on all important decisions, thereby improving communication, strengthening relationships, removing misunderstandings, and avoiding conflicts. Collaboration results in a decision that is acceptable to all involved parties. And every participant owns the decision, so each partner gets credit for the results.

Another important part of communicating is asking questions. Don't assume, jump to conclusions, or have unrealistic expectations. Your spouse may know you better than anybody; but not 100% (I don't even know myself that well). It's a sensible request that he or she ask before assuming what you are thinking or feeling. Maybe we are right most of the time guessing what others think or feel, but when we are not right a misunderstanding is inevitable. It takes little effort to ask first; a lot less than explaining later. The other side to that is to give feedback. Volunteer the information and they won't have to ask. Give feedback and ask for feedback and you can circumvent conflict in many cases.

THROUGHOUT: Education

- Examine the Other Side(s)
- Rethink Things
- Research and Evaluation
- Humility and Sacrifice
- Self-Awareness, Self-Monitoring

There are approaches we can follow before, during, and after quarrels to mitigate the emotional impact. In fact, all of these are worthwhile strategies at any time during the relationship. It's all about education: becoming knowledgeable about what makes others tick, or get upset, or feel good. We learn quickly how to push others' buttons, it seems, which turns them off; but we need to know how to turn them on as well, and how to soothe their pain, and how to get them to open up about their feelings. So take the time to learn about your significant other and educate them about you and your peculiarities.

Be willing to examine the other side or sides to a matter. If there are eight in the relationship get all eight points of view. You may discover there is an octagon behind the theme and not three sides staring you in the face. The more information you have the better equipped you are to understand the entire puzzle, and this may result in a modification to your own position or viewpoint. Seldom do others think, feel, or behave as you do. Flexibility seems a better option than to be unwavering in how we perceive the situation and how we perceive their view of it. Besides, as pointed out earlier, if you can articulate the opposing viewpoints you will be more equipped to defend yours.

The objective of positive change is to change your mind. This will result in a corresponding adjustment to your beliefs. When a change is in order it's typically because the thinking is not based on the facts. If you want the truth, the Word of God is a perfect start. If what you are hearing or what you are telling yourself is contrary to what God says, I would go with God on that one. Be thoughtful at all times and be prepared to rethink it. You may need to rethink it often, until you have done enough research, gained enough information, obtained extensive experience, and have the insight to be sure. If your action is in concert with God's Word you can be absolutely certain.

As we make ourselves aware of the thoughts, needs, and desires of others we improve in our decision making regarding those relationships. We should likewise become aware of our own thoughts, desires, and needs and communicate these to others. Such awareness involves self-monitoring. If you tune into yourself you will know when your emotions are getting the better of you, when your body language is inconsistent with your spoken message, when others are turned off by your behavior, and when a timeout is in order.

One final word about commitment: a little bit of humility will go a long way. Many clashes can be averted by a simple "I love you." Or say you're sorry; even if you're not to blame say it anyway. It's not an admission of guilt. Such statements of genuine caring represent a small sacrifice; in fact, most sacrifices are. And the benefit is well worth the effort. Letting go and giving in are also ways of being humble and making small sacrifices. You don't always need to get your way to be happy; usually if they are happy that will make you happy. Remember, small sacrifices often yield large payoffs. Christ made the ultimate sacrifice for us, so it is important to make sacrifices for others and to be a reliable part of their support system. And each time you do you reflect God's love.

- ROM 12:1 ~ I appeal to you therefore, brothers, by the mercies of God, to present your bodies as a living sacrifice, holy and acceptable to God, which is your spiritual worship.

335

Activity

Identify some things that you and a loved one have disagreed about.

_____

_____

Identify some things that you and a loved one have argued about.

_____

_____

Identify some things that you and a loved one have fought about.

_____

_____

How could you have employed some conflict resolution strategies during these circumstances?

_____

_____

_____

_____

List some strategies that you have used successfully in the past.

_____

_____

List some strategies that you intend to try in the future. Refer to the table for ideas.

_____

_____

STRATEGIES FOR
AVOIDING CONFLICT

BEFORE

- Plan Ahead
- Teamwork
- Practice, Rehearse
- Seek Help, Support
- Give Help

DURING

- Leave
- Time Out
- Let Go, Give In
- Positive Thinking
- Imagination

AFTER

- Compromise
- Restore Equity
- Collaboration
- Ask Questions
- Give/Get Feedback

THROUGHOUT

- Examine All Sides
- Rethink Things
- Humility
- Sacrifice
- Self-Monitoring

SUPPORT TEAMS

OBJECTIVE	Review the various support systems available, identify desired attributes of team members, recruit people that are invested in your success, and apply planning and implementation processes.
INTERVENTION	Identify areas where help is needed to accomplish goals, and establish support teams to assist. Discuss the dynamics and responsibilities of support teams.
PLAN	Put together an action plan that incorporates support teams and create a strategy of building and utilizing several support systems.

"If everyone is moving forward together, then success takes care of itself." – Henry Ford

The TEAM is an organized assembly of unique individuals with a common interest, purpose, and/or bond. The TEAM congregates periodically to confer, collaborate, and plan in order to achieve an objective that benefits the whole. Individuals with varying talents, skills, and experience come together to accomplish goals or arrive at solutions that are for the collective good as well as the good of each member of the group. The performance of the TEAM exceeds that reachable by the individuals independently; thus the TEAM is greater than the sum of its parts.

Case in point: At a major football championship awhile back an inferior team beat a superior team skillfully. The superior team had a lot of superstars and beat all of their opponents handily; the general consensus was that they would go undefeated for the season. The inferior team didn't have many superstars, and lost several games; but they won enough to make it to the finals. Then they proceeded to the championship by knocking off a few conference victors, but they were always the underdogs. When the big game came, the inferior team had a solid game plan to thwart any big plays by the opposition's superstars. When the favored team started struggling and falling behind, their superstars tried to step up and win the game all by themselves. But that played right into the underdogs' game plan; what's more, they were able to make a few big plays themselves. And that is why the favorites lost the championship. You see, the inferior team was a more formidable opponent collectively than the superior team was as bunch of individual stars. Had the favored team held together as a cohesive entity, they might have wiped the floor with the underdogs.

The moral of the story is this: If you want to win the game you need a good team backing you and a solid game plan. The bottom line: you can't do it all yourself; you need help. Even things you can accomplish solo still require God, because without God nothing is possible (MAT 19:26). Your patients and clients can use all the support they can get in order to realize their goals, hopes, and dreams. Each separate goal or task could require a completely different support team. For instance, for physical health goals you might have a different team than for spiritual health goals, or mental health goals. Some of the different support systems that could be part of one's repertory of teams are listed below. I encourage every client to develop an action plan that includes many support systems, and identifies how they can be utilized.

> Treatment Facility: The treatment team is a great example of a diverse collection of professional talent equipped to help the client accomplish his or her goals. Typically there is a physician/psychiatrist, nurse, therapist, case manager, and client. Places I have worked have variations on this basic scheme, to include identifying a different team member to facilitate team meetings.

> Inner Circle: Team members might include the parents, kids, siblings, extended family, and close friends. Remember, your true family doesn't have to be only blood relatives. Anyone who wants you to succeed and is willing to take the journey with you comprises your true support (those that do not want to take part may be indifferent, if not part of the problem).

> Church: Certainly, there is a lot of support available in a good church. There may be men's and women's groups, singles groups, Bible study group, prayer groups, social events, even focus groups like divorcees, depressed people, grieving people, etc. This resource provides the added advantage of spirituality; and spiritual support is frequently the greatest need. The pastor or priest is another person you can turn to.

> Anonymous Group: Alcoholics, Narcotics, or Gamblers Anonymous, Weightwatchers, etc. can be a great support system and a good place to make friends with others in the same boat as you. They will understand you better because they know exactly what you are going through. These groups usually have a spiritual component such as twelve step programs.

> Veterans Administration: This is a great resource for military veterans. They have all kinds of support groups such as Trauma/PTSD, drug/alcohol rehabilitation, marital counseling, individual counseling, psychiatric care, and medical care. The VA is one of many government, social, and private entities that can be resources for improving your health and meeting your goals. There are similar agencies for the underprivileged, elderly, and handicapped that are supported by the government and covered under Medicare/Medicaid.

> Communities: There are social groups and services available that cater to specific types of demographics (race, age, gender), diagnoses (depression, OCD, PTSD), and purposes or goals (success, growth, health, motivation, spirituality). These communities have a particular focus such as dieting, second language, citizenship, yoga, body building, or whatever. Take a look at the resources available in your community. Group therapy represents an excellent community support system.

> Other Support Groups: You can find a support group for just about anything, all over the country: in communities, government agencies, through private practitioners, even on the Internet. Support groups have the advantage of being cohesive, insofar as they are often comprised of people experiencing the same problem; although that may not

be a requirement for one to benefit from the group setting. Sometimes just engaging in social activities can be therapeutic.

> Employer: Many reputable businesses and corporations have employee assistance programs. Therefore, your place of work may be a resource to you, as the company is invested in you and wants you to succeed. And this will benefit the company as much as you, because you become a better, more productive employee; and hence, you are an asset not a liability.

- PRO 27:17 ~ Iron sharpens iron as one man sharpens another.

Requirements of Members

"Synergy: the bonus that is achieved when things work together harmoniously." – Mark Twain

A good team has an assortment of individuals, each with a specific area of expertise they can bring to bear when implementing the plan. Like a football team, the group cannot function effectively unless each position is filled, preferably by a well-qualified player. The quarterback can't do everything. Who is he going to pass the ball to if he has no receivers? How is he going to execute the play if he has no blockers? Every participant plays a unique role for the entire system to succeed, and no part is more important than any other. Each member is equally invested in the plan, has an equally important role to play, and equally shares the credit for the results, whether good or bad, win or lose. Consider the following treatise by St. Paul to the Corinthians.

- 1 CO 12:4-31 (paraphrased) ~ There are a variety of spiritual gifts, but only one Spirit. There are different ways of administering but only one Lord. There are different operations, but the same God works through them. The Spirit is manifested in some way in everyone to use productively. Some people have received wisdom, some knowledge, some faith, all from the same Spirit. Some people have the ability to heal, others to work miracles, others to prophesy, others to discern spirits, others to speak foreign tongues; but all of them are working with the same Spirit, who divides power among everyone as he chooses. Just as the body is one though it has several members, likewise we are all members of the body of Christ, regardless of race or status. There should be no inner conflict in this body; but all members should equally care for one another. If one member suffers, all suffer; if one member is honored all members rejoice. For the body is not one member, but many. Can the foot say, "I am not a hand and so I am not part of the body?" Can the ear say, "Since I am not the eye then I am not part of the body?" If the entire body was an eye, how would we be able to hear? If the body was built only for hearing, how would we be able to smell? But God placed each member in the body for a particular purpose. If they were all one member, where would be the body? But there are many members, yet only one body. And the eye cannot say to the hand, "I don't need you." Nor can the head say to the feet, "I don't need you." Every member of the body, no matter how minor, is needed. God has assembled the body together so that there would be no division within it, and so that all members of the body would receive equal recognition and

340

importance. Just like our physical body, each member of the body of Christ has a particular function. We can't all be apostles, prophets or teachers; we can't all be healers and helpers. But we all hold dear our best gifts, especially the gift of God's excellent Holy Spirit.

The list below provides a number of attributes that team members should possess. It is kind of a wish list; because seldom, if ever, will your team meet all of these criteria. You may notice some overlap among these traits as they are not mutually exclusive.

> ➢ Commitment: If any member is uncommitted then their function in the group will not be adequately performed. Those people you select for your support team need to be loyal to the cause. If parents are not committed to their kids, the kids will go astray or run amok; parents have to make themselves accessible to their kids.

> ➢ Accountability: People need to be held accountable for non-performance. In healthy support systems the members will take the initiative and be accountable for their actions and to the group. If members are invested in the outcome they will pull their weight. It's not a matter of getting a reward commensurate with the contribution; if there is insufficient contribution you will miss the goal. Nonperformers may be invited to leave the team; in most for-profit enterprises that means getting fired.

> ➢ Cohesiveness: A cohesive group has unity. They all fit together like a jigsaw puzzle. In some teams, such as marriage, loss of unity often leads to disbanding the team. There should be a common bond, a shared goal, and equitable distribution of credit and responsibility. A mob of rioters is not what I would call a cohesive group, though they share a common result.

> ➢ Initiative: Members need to be self-motivating. They should have no question as to their individual role, and no qualms about performing it. They were selected precisely because they have what it takes, and have been entrusted to lay it on the line when it is their turn. Such a philosophy means they do not need to be supervised, reminded, or prompted. This individual skill will open doors and get you ahead more quickly. If you don't take the bull by the horns you're likely to get trampled.

> ➢ Diversity: Everybody brings their distinct talents so their duties should match up with their gifts. Diversity also brings a variety of viewpoints to get a better look at the big picture. The more perspectives you have the more likely you'll see all sides, angles, and curves. A combat infantry fire team might consist of a leader, riflemen, machine gunner, and grenadier, so that they can engage the enemy in a way that best meets the demands from the terrain, weather, camouflage, range, and threat.

> ➢ Cooperation: It goes without saying that a lack of cooperation or conformity will eventually lead to conflict and discord. There should be mutual participation, interest, and dedication. There should be compromise and collaboration, so that agreement can be reached on every issue or decision. If the parts in a machine do not work together it will either self-destruct or it won't run at all.

> Stability: Instability in any component or member can cause the system to fail. There should be a stable organization, platform, and footing in order to proceed in an orderly, controlled, and purposive manner. If a building has a weak foundation it will not hold up in an earthquake. There's nothing more useless than a dysfunctional team.

> Direction: Probably more important than the target goal is the direction. If you are heading in the right direction you'll reach your destination. That route may lead to a purpose other than the one you embarked upon, but it will still yield a positive outcome. If the goal was to get a degree in sociology but you end up with a degree in criminal justice it will not be a disappointment. It was just a minor change in direction; but the end game of getting a college education was still met.

> Structure: The team needs organization, design, possibly a chain of command. Sports teams usually have strata: unit captains, assistant coaches, head coach, maybe general manager, in addition to specific players. On the other hand, your team may be set up to be self-governing. This can be accomplished easily if there is high accountability.

> Equality: Remember, everyone is valuable and nobody is indispensable. You need the ammo bearer just as much as the machine gunner. You need the center just as much as the quarterback. You need a mom just as much as you need a dad. If everyone is treated as equals, nobody will try to jockey for a more powerful position, for greater prestige, or for personal gain. This concept is not unlike God's unconditional love for all humanity; he loves us regardless of age, race, sex, or social standing.

> Supportiveness: I am always impressed by the way members in a therapy group edify one another. When one is down the others band together to lift them up. After all, that's what a support group is all about isn't it? If one leg in the chair is not supporting your weight, you might keel over and bang your head.

> Privacy: Depending on the group, you may want to keep what goes on in the meetings confidential. This is an implied rule in most therapy groups, though I often remind the members anyway. Keeping things private requires all to adhere to this principle; this is very difficult to enforce in a mixed therapy group. But the members of the group need to agree on how important this issue is. When I was a defense analyst, leaking information could've landed someone in jail. The same is true for therapists.

> Selflessness: Each member makes certain sacrifices to be a member, because the main focus is on the team not on its individual members. It impresses me when I see a gifted athlete being interviewed and he or she acknowledges that the victory was a team effort; they refuse to take credit for the win even when some reporter is offering it. But if they lose they will acknowledge their contribution to that loss, by identifying personal errors which led to defeat. Humility, personal sacrifice, ascribing credit where credit is due, mutual respect, elevating others over self – these are qualities of high character.

"Gettin' good players is easy. Gettin' 'em to play together is the hard part." – Casey Stengel

Obstacles to Success

Now that we have considered some positive attributes that promote strong teams, let's take a look at some of the negatives that can be destructive to the team. Of course, you could correctly point out that the opposite characteristics of those listed above would be potentially lethal to the success or longevity of the team. But there are a few concepts worth examining in more detail. Below are some of the common enemies of team decision making. Note that the best prevention against these pitfalls is education; teach these principles to the group members so they can be aware of the symptoms.

You have, no doubt, studied phenomena from the field of Social Psychology with respect to group influence. A principal tenet is the notion of Social Facilitation. The presence of others affects the way people behave and perform, especially if they believe they are being observed, compared, and/or evaluated. So then, if others are present I might be preoccupied about making mistakes, resulting in hesitation, nervousness, hypervigilance, or panic; and this may actually increase errors. For example, I find it extremely difficult typing on a computer keyboard when someone is watching; I will make significantly fewer errors if they wait for me to finish instead of reading over my shoulder. Social Facilitation can aid performance or detract from it depending on the personality and emotional state of each individual, their relationship with one another, and the situation. Decisions made under certain circumstances will not be optimal and possibly will be counterproductive.

> Groupthink: This is when the group strives to reach total consensus or absolute conformity. Members tend to agree just to avoid disagreement to the detriment of considering plausible alternatives. If the climate is such that dissent is frowned upon, then some members will not speak up when they have an opposing opinion. Thus, there exists the pretense of unanimity, when in fact people are just feeling the pressure to concur or get along. They don't want to be perceived as rocking the boat, and they don't want to be put down or ridiculed. Evidence or viewpoints that run contrary to the mainstream may be dismissed out of hand. I've seen groupthink occur in many leadership meetings where the tendency was to agree with whatever the CEO or certain revered members said. I have felt the brunt of raising issues that are not being properly addressed, and have gotten flak for it even when there was a clear violation of policy or a legitimate safety concern for the hospital. To prevent the groupthink syndrome leaders must remain impartial and objective. They must guard against people voting to please rather than voting their conscience. Obtain a secret ballot to find out where individuals stand independently, before having a group debate or vote. The suggestion box is a great idea. Appoint members to research the various options for relative merit, or bring in subject matter experts to explain the pros and cons.

> Social Loafing: Oftentimes, individuals will be there just for show; they really do not wish to participate they just want to appear supportive. In reality they expect a free ride, enjoying the benefits without having to make contributions. They feign cooperativeness but are not committed, accountable, or selfless. Loafing and complacency can be avoided when members are obliged to be accountable, responsible, and self-motivating. I saw social loafing a lot as a professor when assigning group projects to students. A few students ended up doing the lion's share of

the work, which became readily apparent when the group gave their oral presentations. If those freeloaders had read the syllabus they would have noticed that the group grade included an overall group performance score and an individual performance score. Many were surprised when they discovered that some members of their group got better grades for the same project.

> Polarization: Group discussions may strengthen a member's position or weaken it; or at least alter the perception. The team may end up dividing according to sides of the issue; like-minded people tend to flock together. When people agree with you there is a tendency to hold them in higher esteem; many will agree with those they want attention from. Social influences like attractiveness, aggressiveness, persuasion, and coercion influence what people are willing to do to look good or be favorably judged. Some individuals change their personal opinion to conform to members having more prestige or power, especially if their outlook is unpopular or they are in the minority. The schism can become even greater as debates carry on and positions move to even more extremes. Moderates in the group turn into extremists, as is often the case in politics. Resulting decisions are too far from center and therefore unrepresentative of the members' original positions, much less the mainstream view.

> Risky Shift is related to polarization. Research has shown that a group decision is often riskier than it would be if individuals made the decision independently or by secret ballot. This is largely due to the decline of individuality in a group. A bad consequence will be felt less by individuals because the responsibility of the outcome is shared or distributed among the members. In essence, they feel less guilty for a poor decision because they have convinced themselves they are not that responsible. I recall a tragedy a few decades ago when three middle school boys murdered a teacher mercilessly. They didn't particularly like the teacher and they each had their own reasons. But none of these boys were rotten kids, and never had they contemplated privately that they would actually harm the teacher. But when they got together they opted to punish the teacher. Extreme positions prevailed and their decision shifted to the most egregious mistake of their lives.

> Leveraging: You see this quite a lot in organizations where people are jockeying for a position of greater influence or power. This may result in downright conspiracy, underhandedness, and backstabbing. Certain things break down the unity of the team such as competition, conflict, internal power struggles, and enmity. There can be no cohesiveness, supportiveness, or equality in such a hostile environment. It will only lead to greater division and disdain. The whole point of the team is to work together for a common end, not to use the group for your personal advantage. This is largely the duty of political lobbyists who try to get a foothold in government policy making. They have no interest in the common good of the country, but for pushing their personal agenda into legislation.

> Sovereignty: By this I mean doing your own thing regardless of what the group has decided, or which responsibilities were ascribed to you. You may have experienced

344

this in the workplace when the supervisor assigns duties, and some people just do the stuff they like, or the stuff that is easy, or the stuff they think is important to or benefits them. They leave the rest of the work for others because they cannot see the point, or they have decided it is unnecessary or not their problem; or they don't want to make the effort or invest their time. It's similar to social loafing, when somebody really doesn't do much of anything to contribute, and it's also similar to leveraging. The autonomous member doesn't want to achieve a group goal; they just want to do it their way, or on their terms, or make it personal. The example given in the introduction, how certain team members tried to win the championship game by themselves, is a perfect example. Some people think they know better than the group, or feel superior to the others for whatever reason, or are just selfish. Extreme deviations from the plan, tasks not being completed, or schedules not being met may result. Missing important milestones or deadlines lead to either complete failure of the mission or to negative results.

Definitions

Moving on, I will now present aspects of the group/team requiring definition. First, you need to define the membership: who do you want to take part, what skills are necessary, how large of a group is about right. When I conduct a process or encounter group, eight participants seems perfect; more than twelve or less than five really doesn't lend to good interactions. Second, identify whether you need structure, a chain of command, a leader, a secretary, a sergeant at arms, or whatever. Elect officers or ask for volunteers; rotate these responsibilities every so often if you like. In a therapy group, there is no chain of command. Even though I may be facilitating I still regard myself as an equal member and no more important than the others. The participants seem to like that approach, and are more comfortable expressing themselves as they know they will not be judged for what they say, and that all opinions will be valued and respected.

Lay down the ground rules, time limits, expectations, and boundaries to ensure meetings run smoothly and digression, arguing, missing the point, wasting time, and other exercises in futility are minimized. Preparing an agenda in advance will help to organize the topics, maintain a smooth flow of events, and maximize the use of time. Establish a format for group meetings: old business, new business, future issues worth considering, small group discussions, results of ongoing projects, individual reports; well, you get the idea. Allocate adequate time for discussion, collaboration, negotiations, and compromise. Develop a schedule: how often to meet, when, and where. Keep accurate and complete records such as minutes, progress reports, research results, performance obstacles, milestones achieved, etc.

Have a purpose or end game in mind. Identify the goals, objectives and steps using the SMART technique. Work together to breakdown the goals, develop a flow chart, establish milestones, and determine the timeline. Prepare a taxonomy of tasks and ascribe them to members in accordance with their abilities. Capitalize upon individual differences, personal trust, fairness, and diversity of ideas. Members should already know how their talents can be applied to meet goals, and should step forward when they are confident of tackling a task. You may allocate some of these functions to smaller groups or subcommittees. Identify resources that are available to assist the team such as experts, subcontractors, financing, equipment, supplies, tools, and time. Identify also constraints, potential obstacles, or whatever could impede progress or cause interference. Prepare the plan of action, with contingency plans in the event that roadblocks or unforeseen events occur.

Process

The following generic process is recommended during the execution of the action plan. Like all of the presentations in this lesson, this is a guideline. Utilize aspects that apply or are practical. Note that some stages may be repeated, occur in a different order, be simultaneous, or not be required. Whatever fits into your scheme is what you're looking for.

- ➤ Outcome: This is your end game or purpose. Once fulfilled, establish the next destination.

- ➤ Goal Development: Determine goals that need to be met to achieve the desired end result.

- ➤ Resource Review: Identify options, assets, liabilities, money, supplies, equipment.

- ➤ Breakdown: Use the proposed SMART technique to break down goals into components. Create a flow or tree diagram of how the process should proceed.

- ➤ Measurement: Develop measurement tools, quantitative and qualitative, to track and report progress.

- ➤ Schedule: Determine the timeline, establish milestones, and plug in anticipated dates for tasks/steps to begin and end. Use the GANTT chart method to schedule and follow progress.

- ➤ Plan: Publish the first draft of the proposed plan. Have the team review it. Make recommended changes and distribute the revision. Then have the plan approved by the group. Repeat as often as necessary.

- ➤ Budget: Create a budget that delineates how you will spend your time and money, and how and when you will allocate your resources. Track expenditures regularly to see how you stand in terms of the remaining assets available and/or required.

- ➤ Implementation: Execute the plan as designed.

- ➤ Monitoring: Measure progress and report on progress at regular meetings.

- ➤ Managing: Administer, direct, coordinate, and supervise the execution of the plan. Intervene as needed, or call an emergency meeting if progress is slow or stagnated.

- ➤ Evaluation: Conduct performance and progress evaluations periodically to see what is working or not working, and to develop additional contingency plans as needed. Evaluate when a milestone is met or a goal is reached in terms of time and accuracy.

➤ Revision: The plan is a living document; it should be revised if the evaluation results indicate that things are not going according to plan. Thus, you may need to go back and repeat a few stages.

➤ Completion: Once all the goals are accomplished the end game should be met. Thus, the process ends at the same stage in which it began.

Jesus Christ sure put together an awesome team. Comprised of ordinary men, they would take the Gospel to all the earth (ACT 13:47), and would sacrifice everything in doing so. You need to make Christ the captain of your team. Otherwise, you might miss the mark, or maybe you won't get anything done. But with him in the lead you can do anything (PHP 4:13) and, more likely, will exceed your goals.

• JOH 15:4-5 ~ Jesus said, "Abide in me, and I will abide in you. As the branch cannot bear fruit by itself, unless it abides in the vine, neither can you, unless you abide in me. I am the vine; you are the branches. Whoever abides in me and I in him, he it is that bears much fruit, for apart from me you can do nothing."

Read the story of Gideon and his defeat of the Midianites (JDG 6 – 8). The Israelites were downtrodden due to the oppression, poverty, and violence imposed upon them. God sent an angel to Gideon to inform that he would engage and destroy their enemy. At first Gideon was skeptical; he complained that his people were disadvantaged, and denied that he had the ability to carry out this mission. After God assured him, Gideon was still afraid and uncertain; he wanted proof from God. But he was not satisfied with just one sign; it took several signs to convince Gideon to place his confidence in the Lord. God instructed Gideon to select men that drank from the river using their hands and exclude those that lapped the water like a dog. Three hundred such men were chosen for battle. They surrounded the Midianite encampment, equipped with a trumpet and a clay pitcher in which a lamp was hidden. When Gideon signaled, the men at once blew their trumpets; then they broke the pitchers exposing the lanterns. They continued to make noise, blow trumpets, and swing their lanterns to the extent that they appeared to the Midianites as thousands of men, not hundreds. In a panic the men of Midian began fighting amongst themselves in the dark; others fled the scene. All were chased down and massacred, along with their princes and kings. The Israelites were freed and Gideon became their judge for forty years. Gideon's success can be attributed to two principles: trust in God to lead your team, and recruit dedicated, courageous, and honorable people to help you execute God's plan in your life. With God you can accomplish a lot more than you think; and he will give you everything you need to do it.

"We must all hang together or most assuredly we shall all hang separately." – Benjamin Franklin

"Remember, upon the conduct of each depends the fate of all." – Alexander the Great

Activity

Make a list of possible support systems that could help you accomplish your goals.

_____

_____

_____

_____

_____

Who from your inner circle would you like to have on your team?

_____   _____

_____   _____

_____   _____

_____   _____

Give a few examples of how solid teamwork accomplished a significant goal. It can be a personal experience, something you have observed, a story you read, or a show you watched.

_____

_____

_____

_____

Give a few examples when a lack of teamwork fell short of a significant goal. It can be a personal experience, something you have observed, a story you read, or a show you watched.

_____

_____

_____

_____

BEREAVEMENT

OBJECTIVE	Learn about bereavement and how to cope effectively with death and loss. Understand the stages of grieving, death and dying in order to recognize where you or a loved one is in the process.
INTERVENTION	Discuss each phase of the grieving process and give examples of healthy and unhealthy ways of dealing with loss. Identify normal and abnormal responses to death and loss.
PLAN	Allow yourself and your loved ones to grieve sufficiently and to gain acceptance of the loss. Facilitate the process when appropriate to aide loved ones in healing and moving on.

"The bitterest tears shed over graves are for words left unsaid and deeds left undone." – Harriet Beecher Stowe

"The pain passes, but the beauty remains." – Pierre Renoir

Everyone experiences loss of a loved one either by death, divorce, or abandonment. It is normal to feel grief and it is normal to mourn. Bereavement is a healthy response that results in emotional healing. In the Old Testament the traditional period of grieving and mourning a death was 40 days. That seems a reasonable period of time, though for some it takes longer. Like they say, time heals wounds; when it doesn't something is wrong. It depends on the individual; but neither insufficient nor excessive grieving is good for you.

- GEN 50:1-3 ~ Joseph fell on his father's face and wept over him and kissed him. And Joseph commanded his servants the physicians to embalm his father. So the physicians embalmed Israel. Forty days were required for it, for that is how many are required for embalming. And the Egyptians wept for him seventy days.

Loss

If the person experiencing the loss has not allowed himself or herself to grieve, or the grieving continues beyond what is normal, it is unresolved. Unresolved grief can lead to guilt, depression, poor self-esteem, physical illness, and suicidal ideations. Grieving should begin relatively quickly, continue several weeks, and gradually taper off. Waiting years to grieve or grieving for years interferes with mental healing. If normal symptoms do not eventually fade away the individual may develop long-term mental illness such as chronic depression, anxiety disorders, addiction, even psychosis.

Normal emotions during the grieving process include sadness, anger, fear, loneliness, despair, regret, and helplessness. Normal thought processes include disbelief and denial, guilt, confusion, disorientation, poor insight, poor coping, dwelling on the past, dreams that include the deceased person, and worry about unfinished business. Normal behaviors include crying, nervousness, poor appetite, insomnia, isolation and withdrawal, anhedonia, calling out to them, hearing your name called, and digging through memorabilia. Normal physical responses include fatigue, dizziness, headache, stomachache, muscle tension, and super-sensitivity in the auditory, visual, and tactile domains. Normal spiritual responses include increases or decreases in spiritual awareness, prayer, worship, giving, and/or mourning rituals.

Remember, if these symptoms are prolonged for a lengthy period of time it can affect brain chemistry and mood, thereby resulting in additional mental and physical problems. The important thing is that the individual allows himself or herself to grieve and mourn, and receives encouragement to do so. Sometimes others interfere by telling them, "Don't cry," "It's going to be all right," "Be strong," "Don't let it drag you down," "Stay in control." What the grieving person needs to be hearing is that it's okay to cry all you want, to feel sad and blue, and to give yourself time to heal. The griever should not be in a hurry to get over it, go back to work, forget, or get used to living without their lost loved one. You don't really get back to normal with respect to the way it used to be, you move on to the way it is going to be. It is unnecessary to completely let go as if the loss will someday cease to be.

If you want to console someone who has suffered loss the last thing they need is to be inundated with attention. These people need healing not distractions. Certainly it is good for them to be occupied but not to be overwhelmed; they already are overwhelmed. Imagine how uncomfortable to have everybody and their cousins calling to extend their condolences, and have to explain over and over what happened to your loved one, how you are doing, and how they can help. If you want to help the grieving family pray for them, love them, and mourn with them. It might be more appropriate to send a card or some flowers with a written sentiment. The person who is bereaved needs mostly only their inner circle of support. They don't need a line of people that extends around the block, each one bringing a casserole dish for dinner. To coin a cliché: it's the thought that counts. Keep them in your thoughts, hopes, and prayers. You can be available without being present; if they need your presence or assistance they will tell you.

- JOB 16:6 ~ If I speak, my pain is not assuaged, and if I forbear, how much of it leaves me?

- JER 45:3 ~ You said, "Woe is me! For the LORD has added sorrow to my pain. I am weary with my groaning, and I find no rest."

- LAM 3:31-33 ~ The Lord will not cast off forever, but, though he cause grief, he will have compassion according to the abundance of his steadfast love; for he does not afflict from his heart or grieve the children of men.

Stages of Grieving

Kubler-Ross was a Swiss physician who studied death, dying, and bereavement. She laid the foundation for understanding the grieving process in her famous book, *Death and Dying*. While different people process grief differently, her model provided a reasonable starting point from which others have followed. Some of the common stages include shock, denial, isolation, anger, bargaining, depression, and acceptance. The degree to which a person gets bogged down or even experiences a given stage will vary. Also, people may cycle back and forth between stages or experience them in a different order. Understanding the process allows the therapist to help the client cope, to deal with each stage and associated crises, and to transition in a controlled and deliberate manner.

Social scientists differ in how they identify and define the stages largely because there is no specific process that all people undergo. We will examine some of the familiar phases of bereavement. Keep in mind that phases may overlap, may not occur, and/or may be repeated. The entire process should take about six weeks, give or take a week or two. If it takes longer, say three to six months, it might be time to seek professional help.

Shock/Denial: The initial response can be disbelief. "This is not happening," or "This can't happen to me." Oftentimes the person just feels numb. They shut down and shut out the world around them. This should pass in a few days after which reality will set in. And that reality brings emotional pain.

Depression: Again, this emotion will wax and wane throughout the process. Keeping busy mind, body, and spirit is the best way to deal with depression. It's perfectly natural to feel down; but sometimes down can go really deep into a rut. There is nothing wrong with seeing a doctor and getting a prescription for antidepressant or antianxiety medication to help moderate the mood. The depression should subside within a few months; but the doctor likely will want to continue the medication for some period beyond that. Allow yourself to be weaned off of the medication gradually; don't just quit as it could result in mood variations.

Isolation/Withdrawal: Usually the griever is not in the mood for lots of company, or to go out, or to have to deal with all the logistics of a funeral. While loved ones will be concerned and want to extend their condolences, it can become inundating to the griever. It's probably better to have minimum but solid support around as the family gears up for the upcoming events. That is, help them with the chores and talk to them, but don't try to fill the emptiness. Occasionally, they will need to use public institutions and agencies and this is when some companionship would be welcome to help them run errands and such.

Anger/Blame: Individuals may get angry at or blame the deceased, God, others, or themselves. This may come and go as the grieving continues. In fact, depression and anger are closely related and they may occur interchangeably. The mourner may ask, "Why did you have to die now?" or "Why did you take him God?" They may believe, "He had so much more to give," "I could have done more," "I should have noticed she was ill," "If only I had been there." Such a response is a plea to understand, to find a reason or cause. Unfortunately, there is no clear reason and nobody caused it. Everything happens in accordance with God's plan; he may have a reason but it won't make sense during the grieving. Remember, everything works towards your good if you trust in the Lord.

Unfinished Business: The griever often will become preoccupied with unsettled issues pertaining to the deceased. They dwell on things they should have said or done, or things that the deceased should have said or done. They think about how they could have spent more time together, gone on a trip, phoned, wrote letters, or just talked. It is all right to jot down some of these things that you wish you had said or wish you could hear. In fact, journaling is a great way to express thoughts and feelings during bereavement. Write the dialogue in your journal that you need (wanted) to have and you will gain insight. Imagining that you are tying up loose ends really does help to move on. Any creative outlet will enable the processing of emotions, thoughts, and cognitive dissonance, and might result in building something positive from the memories, confusion, and strain.

Bargaining: There are many different opinions about what this entails, or if it even occurs. Basically, it is a desire to make a deal with God as if there was a way to reverse or halt time. It's a little like having unfinished business with God; it can provide some assurance that God is in control and knows what he's doing. It is another way of trying to understand what purpose is made possible by the loss of a loved one. This stage especially relates to an impending death, not only a loss.

Acceptance: There will be a point when the person begins to adjust to the new reality; accepting the loss will follow. This is a gradual process in which the griever gains a little more strength every day, modifying his or her perspective concerning the loss, taking on more responsibility, and fulfilling important roles. It is a good practice to start becoming active in business and society after the initial phases have passed, but not to take on too much too soon. That is, activity is helpful, but making important life decisions should be put off for a while, at least until the final stages of grieving. For example, it is not recommended that a person rush into a new relationship to replace the old one as it could result in more emotional pain; or to move away before the estate is settled as many important decisions may fall through the cracks; or to liquidate the assets only to invite a lawsuit from disgruntled relatives. A sure way of prolonging the agony of bereavement is to allow further chaos to infiltrate your peace of mind. Important resolutions are better made when clarity of thought has returned and the pests, strangers, and scroungers are out of the picture.

- JOB 19:25-26 ~ I know that my Redeemer lives, and at the last day he will stand upon the earth. And after my skin has been thus destroyed, yet in my flesh I shall see God.

- ECC 3:1-2 ~ For everything there is a season, and a time for every matter under heaven: a time to be born, and a time to die…

- ECC 7:1 ~ A good name is better than precious ointment, and the day of death than the day of birth.

Therapeutic interventions for the grieving include individual therapy, support groups, venting (journaling, art, music), activity and exercise, mourning rituals, short vacations or getaways, and of course, spirituality and faith. Church attendance, Bible study, and Christian fellowship will be especially uplifting. Christians are generally better at grieving because they have a greater sense of hope, particularly if they can picture their loved one in heaven with God. Visual imagery therapy, especially of a religious nature, is an excellent technique to aid the client in acquiring a positive frame of mind. Anything that facilitates a forward looking, positive outlook is beneficial. A good place to start is to remember the grief that Christ bore; he didn't just suffer in our stead but rewards us because of it.

- ISA 53:4-6 ~ Surely he has borne our griefs and carried our sorrows; yet we esteemed him stricken, smitten by God, and afflicted. But he was pierced for our transgressions; he was crushed for our iniquities; upon him was the chastisement that brought us peace, and with his wounds we are healed. All we like sheep have gone astray; we have turned – every one – to his own way; and the LORD has laid on him the iniquity of us all.

- JOH 14:2-3 ~ Jesus said, "In my Father's house are many rooms. If it were not so, would I have told you that I go to prepare a place for you? And if I go and prepare a place for you, I will come again and will take you to myself, that where I am you may be also."

- JOH 16:20,22,33 ~ Jesus said, "Truly, truly, I say to you, you will weep and lament, but the world will rejoice. You will be sorrowful, but your sorrow will turn into joy... You have sorrow now, but I will see you again, and your hearts will rejoice, and no one will take your joy from you… I have said these things to you, that in me you may have peace. In the world you will have tribulation. But take heart; I have overcome the world."

The account in the Book of Job illustrates how one can overcome extreme grief and loss. The devil brought more suffering and hardship on Job than most people can bear, trying to prove that Job would turn against God if he lost all that God had blessed him with. Job's children died, he lost his fortune, his wife abandoned him, and he became terribly ill. But Job never gave up on God despite the scorn and blame levied upon him by his friends. He admitted to God that he couldn't possibly understand God's ways and reasons; he apologized for trying to second-guess God. God acknowledged Job's unrelenting faith and patience and rewarded him with a new wife and family, and double the wealth he had before. And the devil lost his bet.

- JOB 42:10,12 ~ And the LORD restored the fortunes of Job, when he had prayed for his friends. And the LORD gave Job twice as much as he had before. And the LORD blessed the latter days of Job more than his beginning…

- JAM 5:9-11 ~ Do not grumble against one another, brothers, so that you may not be judged; behold, the Judge is standing at the door. As an example of suffering and patience, brothers, take the prophets who spoke in the name of the Lord. Behold, we consider those blessed who remained steadfast. You have heard of the steadfastness of Job, and you have seen the purpose of the Lord, how the Lord is compassionate and merciful.

"Only people who are capable of loving strongly can also suffer great sorrow, but this same necessity of loving serves to counteract their grief and heals them." – Leo Tolstoy

Activity

Recall a recent or significant loss. Indicate how you experienced the stages and how you dealt with these stages of bereavement.

Shock/Denial

_____

_____

Depression

_____

_____

Isolation/Withdrawal

_____

_____

Anger/Blame

_____

_____

Unfinished Business

_____

_____

Bargaining

_____

_____

Acceptance

_____

_____

DUMPING THE EMOTIONAL BAGGAGE

OBJECTIVE	Learn ways to channel affective material in a positive manner. Exercise the imagination and cultivate the creativity in order to use the emotional baggage to build rather than to destroy.
INTERVENTION	Discuss physical, mental, and spiritual avenues for venting negative emotional energy in constructive ways. Recognize that processing negative memories or feelings results in the disclosure of new meaning.
PLAN	Explore different outlets in each domain to discover what works for you to process the experiences and unload the emotional baggage. Examine the contents of the baggage to uncover greater understanding. Bring that wisdom forward, leaving the baggage behind.

Each event, every experience, whether positive or negative, prepares us for a greater goal. In other words, all experience has value. God can turn any tragedy, trauma, loss, defeat or setback into a victory, just as Christ did on the cross. Great examples can be found in Jesus' own lineage, for although Christ's parents descended from sinful men and women, their treachery and depravity did not circumvent or delay God's elaborate plan. (It is recommended that the reader study the Old Testament stories of Judah and Tamar, the prostitute Rahab, and David and Bathsheba). Remember, everything works together for your good if you love God and heed his call (ROM 8:28).

- MAR 9:17-27 (paraphrased) ~ A man asked Jesus to cast the demon out of his child. Jesus told the man, "All things are possible to those who believe." The man replied, "I believe, Lord; help me overcome my unbelief." Then Jesus ordered the demon to leave the child.

- JOH 9:1-41 (paraphrased) ~ As Jesus passed by he saw a man who was blind from birth. And his disciples asked him, "Master who sinned, this man or his parents, causing him to be born blind?" Jesus answered, "Neither did this man sin nor his parents, but so that the works of God would be shown through him." Jesus proceeded to make clay from his spittle, placed it on the man's eyes, and told him to wash in the pool of Siloam. The man did this and immediately he could see. Everyone that knew him marveled and they brought him before the Pharisees who didn't believe him, so they summoned his parents who affirmed that the man was born blind. And still they didn't believe, and called the man a sinner as well as Jesus who had healed the man. After explaining to them enough times how he came to see, the man told the Pharisees, "Isn't it a marvelous thing? Have you ever heard of anything like this happening before? We know that God listens to those who believe and come to him in faith; if the man who healed me was not from God he couldn't have done this." The Pharisees threw him out saying that he was not in a position to teach them anything. The man discovered that Jesus was the Son of God and worshipped him, whereas the Pharisees did not believe and therefore, were not forgiven.

I had a female patient who was very bitter about her mother's tragic death. She blamed God for not being merciful, while her mom endured an arduous battle with terminal cancer and excruciating pain. Her mom died in the hospital after a lengthy, futile struggle. I asked the lady what kind of person was her mother; she replied that her mom was kind, loving, good-humored, compassionate, and understanding. I asked the lady what her mother was like during her suffering; she said her mom was the same person. Everyone was amazed at her strength and courage, for her mom inspired many people. I explained how the lady had found an answer to her dilemma. I quoted the above scripture from St. John and she realized that God had a greater purpose. Though her mother had a rough time, she was the one person who could rise above it and be an example to others. I told her she was lucky to have such a wonderful mother. Once she appreciated the newfound meaning to her mother's death (and life), she understood. No longer would she dwell on the tragedy, but on the encouragement and hope her mother's life offered to those who had the pleasure and honor to witness it. This gave her the will to move forward, and tell others what a gift from God is longsuffering.

Another example was a soldier who returned with posttraumatic stress after two deployments in Iraq. He was filled with fear, prone to violent outbursts and uncontrollable rage; he had frequent flashbacks, high anxiety, with night terrors and nightmares. And yet, he wanted to go back solely for the extra money allotted with hazardous duty. Plus, he couldn't adjust to his new life as it didn't seem to be as important a mission. I assured him he was not ready to go back just yet, because he hadn't dealt with the fear and anger sufficiently to keep a cool head in a combat situation. You see, the enemy is on a mission to torment, terrorize, and bombard you with fear, I explained. If a soldier doesn't fall in battle, but returns tormented in his mind, the enemy has produced another casualty. Their tactics are evil because they are depending on the devil's power: fear. But the love of God is more powerful and can cast out the fear (1 JOH 4:18); greater is Christ that lives in you than Satan that is in the world (1 JOH 4:4). Former president Franklin Roosevelt once declared, "We have nothing to fear but fear itself." I told him: Once you face your fears, understand them, and overcome, you might be a candidate to return and maybe lead others; for you will not panic or hesitate, take foolish risks that would jeopardize your comrades or your mission, or let emotions get the better of you. The bottom line, he hadn't grasped the true meaning to his experiences and trauma, which manifested fear, anger, guilt, and torment. Constant bombardment from horror and evil had desensitized him to what is right, and darkened his spirit. He was killing the enemy out of hate rather than duty. This became an obstacle to understanding and growth. It was his goal from that point to overcome; to get back into his spiritual life and the love, which had almost been driven away until then. Whether he is redeployed or terminated from service is irrelevant. If he learns to conquer fear with love he will be trusting in the greater power; and that will point to a greater purpose and a worthwhile mission.

As is often the case with PTSD, the individual wants to reclaim who he or she was prior to the trauma. They are convinced they will never find that person again. But they don't need to. Instead, what they need to claim is who they are destined to become. While war and terror change a person, so does everything else. But nothing produces such a drastic change as love. In fact, love enables us to start over; once the change begins it continues without end (2

CO 5:17). Help motivate clients to discover the person God wants them to be, and they may appreciate it more than the self they lost. Additionally, one never loses the ability to love; if they loved before they can love and be loved again. Sometimes it takes a bit of reconditioning, particularly when fear and anger have been the routine.

These case studies exemplify how one can take a bad situation or setback and turn it into a steppingstone, bringing them ever closer to fulfilling God's plan. That's what St. Paul and St. James meant when they said they welcomed the trials and tribulations of life (ROM 5:1-5; JAM 1:2-3). Such challenges teach us patience, prepare us for additional tests of courage, and give us the character and experience to carry out a loftier mission, and then another, and another. That is the perfect work God has assigned for you to do.

- ROM 5:1-5 ~ Since we have been justified by faith, we have peace with God through our Lord Jesus Christ. Through him we have also obtained access by faith into this grace in which we stand, and we rejoice in hope of the glory of God. Not only that, but we rejoice in our sufferings, knowing that suffering produces endurance, and endurance produces character, and character produces hope, and hope does not put us to shame, because God's love has been poured into our hearts through the Holy Spirit who has been given to us.

- 2 CO 12:9-10 ~ God said to me (Paul), "My grace is sufficient for you, for my power is made perfect in weakness." Therefore I will boast all the more gladly of my weaknesses, so that the power of Christ may rest upon me. For the sake of Christ, then, I am content with weaknesses, insults, hardships, persecutions, and calamities. Because when I am weak, then I am strong.

- JAM 1:2-4 ~ Count it all joy, my brothers, when you meet trials of various kinds, for you know that the testing of your faith produces steadfastness. And let steadfastness have its full effect, that you may be perfect and complete, lacking in nothing.

If you are stuck in the past, carrying emotional baggage, or repressing unpleasant memories you haven't realized its value or meaning. You must process the information, and not hide it or hide from it. It finds its way into consciousness anyway no matter how many ego defense mechanisms you employ to prevent that from happening. If you are going to think about it you might as well do so in a way that helps you to better understand why. The alternative is to spend a lifetime expending substantial time, energy, and resources to avoid dealing with it, which will only make you progressively more mentally ill in the long run.

That we are physical, mental, and spiritual beings implies all three need to be healthy and nurtured. Everybody should have a routine that ensures they are engaging themselves in each area. It follows that all three can be used to channel the negative energy. After all, it's just energy; it's what you do with the energy that can be either constructive or destructive. Taking the baggage out on loved ones is certainly not good; neither is beating yourself over the head with it. However, venting it in a positive direction not only is an effective way to unload it, it also is good for you because it builds something in addition to lightening the load. Explore the possibilities in all three domains and discover skills, interests, and solutions of which you were unaware because you hadn't tried them. Everybody needs physical, mental, and spiritual outlets. And there are literally thousands available for us to utilize.

The payoff from processing the baggage is the meaning that is derived. Every time the person goes back and processes more, it generates incremental wisdom that ultimately leads to revelation. Once insight is gained the person can apply it, and the memory will not disturb them. It is best to dump the baggage early and not wait until the full brunt of the message is acquired. Either way, processing it will lighten the load. It's like unpacking the baggage and discarding the irrelevant contents piece by piece. Then you can fill it with positive things that lift you up and over the hurdle.

For example, I experienced significant trauma in my twenties. Sparing the details, I can assure you that it was terrible and I wouldn't wish it upon anyone. I want that it never happened. Yet, if it hadn't, I wouldn't have been sufficiently prepared to work with trauma patients, who thought that nobody understood them or what they had been through. I assured them that I understood emotional pain and trauma, but invariably they would ask, "What can you possibly know about my ordeal?" I would tell them a little about mine and they would begin to trust me. It mattered not that I had education, credentials and experience; only that I could relate to them, having walked in their shoes in a way. Such understanding cannot be acquired through a class or a book; it has to be experienced firsthand. Now, one could argue that everyone experiences trauma of some kind and that statement would be largely true. But I am not talking about tragedy, loss or death, or everyday setbacks.

My unfortunate trauma turned out to be part of my preparation for a greater purpose that God had planned all along. That is, God used a bad experience for my good. Sometimes we have to learn things the hard way to get the full impact of the lesson. Once I saw the value I realized that the experience was part of my training. Though I was able to forgive, and let go of the anger and fear, the memory continued to disturb me until I could apply the knowledge it produced. After that, the memory failed to conjure any negative emotion.

One thing this has taught me is to have a greater appreciation of the utter torture and torment that our Lord endured during Holy Week. He would be betrayed by a friend; dragged before a kangaroo court; falsely accused, convicted, and sentenced to die; and tortured to death via crucifixion. Before his horrific execution, he would be beaten, whipped, scourged, mocked, and humiliated. And for that to culminate with the burden of the entire sin of mankind being dumped on his back is unimaginable. What's more, he knew this was going to happen and accepted it with dignity and obedience. The agony of Christ sure makes our suffering seem trivial by comparison. And it makes me want to love him all the more.

Consider also the apostle Paul (formerly Saul): before he converted to Christianity he was persecuting and murdering Christians. Case in point: he was supervising the stoning of St. Stephen (ACT 7:58). He was on his way to Damascus to continue his villainous undertaking when called by Christ to cease and desist (read ACT 9). Paul had a great zeal for God but was misguided. Once Christ turned him in the right direction Paul became the greatest evangelist that ever lived. Talk about total reversal: Saul the persecutor becomes Paul the proselytizer. He would endure more suffering, distress, and anguish than what he executed upon his victims. But he would relish in it, knowing that he was experiencing trials for Jesus' sake; he was proud to die a martyr's death like the one who called him into the ministry. He faced adversity with courage, boldness, confidence, and peace. That vigor can only come from God, and enables mere mortals to face the most horrendous of challenges. Paul wrote that those trials revealed his weaknesses, which were replaced by the strength of his Lord upon whom all trust was placed, enabling him to overcome serious tribulation.

"We should be careful to get out of the experience all the wisdom that is in it – not like the cat that sits on a hot stove lid. She will never sit down on a hot lid again – and that is well; but also she will never sit down on a cold one anymore." – Mark Twain

One day I was surfing through TV channels, finding nothing of interest to watch. I stumbled upon a show about treasure hunters: *American Diggers*. The team dug for treasure in the most unlikely places; this time their target was outhouses from the early 1900's ("The Bowels of Brooklyn" aired on Spike TV on 04/25/12). The leader had an old map revealing where a number of well-to-do immigrants once abided; each manor had a "privy" in back. Comparing the map to the current layout of Brooklyn enabled him to locate a parking lot. He convinced the proprietor to allow him to dig, with the promises of putting everything back the way he found it and sharing 20% of his profit. Reluctantly, the man agreed. The team set out with ground penetrating radar looking for the right signal and found one. They ripped up the pavement, dug, hit a dead end, repaired the damage, and began searching again. Lo and behold, they found what they were looking for: a tunnel of dirt going down a score of feet indicating it was once the site of an outhouse. They excavated a few feet, sifting through every inch of dirt, and found a bunch of old, stained and discolored bottles: valuable, but not enough to fund the excursion. I imagined some sot tossing his empty pint into the commode while doing his business. Digging deeper, they found a tie pin; in those days they didn't use tie clasps but pins. And this one was made of gold. Further down, they unearthed a corroded .38 special from around the 1920's. It was worth a pretty penny. Again, I imagined some gangster popping someone and ditching the gun. Still, the team was far from recovering their expenses. Digging all day, they finally hit bottom. The last pail of sifted dirt netted them a wedding ring from the turn of the century. Three diamonds surrounding a ruby, set in solid gold, and worth ten grand. An unfortunate woman must have lost it while wiping, I thought.

You are probably wondering what this has to do with our lesson. It's about digging through your dirt and finding that hidden gem of wisdom. Most of the time, when the memory returns with all its baggage, we reach in and find something unpleasant: like the guilt, horror, anger, or fear. We promptly put it back and shove the memory into its hiding place. However, that emotional response is often incorrect. Take the soldier who blamed himself for his buddy's death, because he called in sick after puking his guts out. His buddy took his place in a vehicle that was struck by a roadside bomb. Clearly, it was not the soldier's fault he got sick or that his friend died. But certain triggers caused the memory to return with guilt. As we sifted through his emotional baggage he finally came to realize that the guilt was irrelevant and untrue. What was true was that he and his buddy knew the risks and were well prepared for them. What was true was that his buddy laid down his life just as he would have. After examining the contents of the baggage, and tossing out the clutter and debris, the veteran found some truth and wisdom, and disposed of the garbage: unwarranted guilt. It was as if his comrade wanted him to live free, for that was what he died to preserve.

HOLISTIC EXPRESSION
Body, Mind, and Spirit

ACTIVITIES

Spiritual

Daily Prayer
Bible Study
Weekly Worship

Mental

Truthful Thoughts
Positive Imagery
Forward Looking

Physical

Exercise and Sports
Chores and Errands
Personal Hygiene

"Getting over a painful experience is much like crossing monkey bars. You have to let go at some point in order to move forward." – C. S. Lewis

"Lay a firm foundation with the bricks that others throw at you." – David Brinkley

Physical Outlets

You must exercise your body, eat healthy, and get enough sleep. If you are physically fit you can endure a lot more mental strain; if you are not, you will become fatigued a lot more easily and a lot more often. Everyone needs a system; the tough part is sticking to it. Use the physical domain to burn off negative energy. Remember, it's only energy; and energy is valuable. Take a gallon of gas. You can put it in your motorbike and drive to work for a week, or you can pour it on the weeds in your yard and kill all the grass with them. Likewise, emotional energy can be used to build or to destroy.

When he was young, my son used to get frustrated learning the tricks of a new video game. Eventually, he would get angry and throw his controller. I warned him to stop, because if he broke it he'd really get mad for he wouldn't be able to play the game after that. Since he liked football I suggested he put down the controller, go outside, and throw the football. After thirty minutes he would have forgotten about being mad, he would have practiced a useful skill, and he would have gotten some exercise in the process. Well, it didn't work because he didn't follow through, and finally broke the controller. And I wasn't about to go out and buy him another one; he had to wait three months until his birthday. So he learned that one the hard way. Afterwards, he began practicing football a lot more often; and he became accomplished at the quarterback position.

I also got my son a punching bag. He used it a lot. I've read that some psychologists think it violent to release anger in this fashion, but I have to disagree. You don't have to imagine you're busting your boss in the chops; you merely need to let it out. I must confess, I found myself using the punching bag as much as he did. After releasing the negative energy I didn't feel angry anymore; I felt pumped. Oftentimes, I couldn't even remember what I was angry or frustrated about. It took us two years to demolish that punching bag. What a great investment that was.

If you feel like running away, put on your jogging shoes and run around the block five times. Or go to the park or the track; just run until you are tired. You won't be angry anymore; no, you will actually feel good. Maybe your kid is the type that kicks holes in walls to vent. Buy a soccer ball and let them kick the you know what out of it. Imagine if they did that every time they felt angry, afraid, or whatever. Pretty soon they'd be awfully good at soccer, which is an ability they might value. They probably would find a lot more gratification from it, and they wouldn't have to spend a month's allowance paying to repair the wall or the door they damaged.

It's about finding out what works for you. Certainly, continue to practice things that have worked in the past. But also explore methods you haven't tried. I play golf. You might say, "Are you kidding; that looks boring?" Well it is a lot more fun to play than to watch.

After walking eighteen holes, I feel great. And I love the feeling I get when I really connect, and whack the little white ball 275 yards down the fairway. It's all good; and it doesn't hurt anybody. Try golf, tennis, jogging. Join a gym. Go walking with your spouse, or kids, or dog. Burn off the negative energy and return to your life refreshed – and healthier physically and emotionally.

For this to work, you have to be purposeful about it. You need to get the exercise anyway; you are simply directing some of that emotional energy into it, with the purpose of burning it along with the calories. Everyone needs several outlets that work; perhaps some outlets may work better for some emotions and some may work better for others. And it will not get boring because you will consistently improve in whatever pastime you have chosen. Any activity that expends energy can be used to produce something whether it is exercise, housework, gardening, construction, athletic agility, isometrics, weight lifting, you name it.

My favorite outlet is music. I play a variety of instruments, but when it comes to burning negative energy like anger or frustration the drums do the trick. I may come home from a long, intense, and draining day. And though I am emotionally spent, I'll escape to my music room and beat the daylights out of the drums for thirty minutes. I get my arms and legs going, and my heart beating; it's very aerobic. After that I pump iron for about five minutes. And I feel great; it hurts so good. Plus, I play the drums better now than when I played in a rock band back in the seventies. The more I practice, the better I get. This is good for me and it doesn't hurt anybody. Maybe that would work for you too.

Mental Outlets

Why do you suppose they employ recreation therapy at many hospitals and institutions? Because: it works to channel the negative energy. That's why we also employ occupational therapy, art therapy, and journal therapy. While physical exertion enables you to burn the energy, mental exertion helps you to express it. I've had patients tell me they have no talent for art, drawing, etc. My reply: you don't need to be good at it for it to work. Besides, if you don't like to draw try painting or sculpture, or any of the hundreds of other media. Who knows, eventually you might learn to like it.

I encourage every client to begin a journal. Again, they'll come up with excuses not to, like "I don't know how to write" or "I've tried it and it doesn't work." My answer to them is "bunk." It most certainly does work. And if you can't write that good now, you eventually will, because you are practicing a useful skill (something you can use for any career or job). Usually, after they start the journal they get excited and tell me all the things they are writing about, sometimes asking me to read it and comment. Creating and recording their action plan is always an assignment that keeps them busy and occupied, so they won't be preoccupied. Once they see it in writing it makes more sense and they will remember it better. One group participant said that journaling helped him hear what he was thinking. It was like pulling teeth to get him to start journaling and then he really cut loose with it, because he could find meaning to the thoughts racing around in his head. He was able to organize his thoughts and view them more objectively. He became an advocate for journaling and got others to try it.

I first discovered the power of creative expression while I was working on my masters in counseling. It was the late seventies. I was a caseworker at the local runaway center, where kids from all over the country passed through my town trying to escape the awfulness of their upbringing. We didn't have a lot of time to work with them (average length of stay was eight days) before we had the kid before a judge to get him or her back home or to a safe environment in their home state. One young lady, about fifteen, had been molested and raped by a trusted loved one. She was a basket case – just one chaotic bag of emotions ready to implode. I was running out of ideas and time to help her. One afternoon I suggested she write a letter to the perpetrator. She liked the idea. I told her to work on it and I would see what she came up with when I returned the next morning. She produced a seven page letter on legal paper ripping this guy from here to eternity. As I read the letter aloud to her in the privacy of my office I was amazed. The anger, hate, shame, guilt, fear, despair – it was all in there, everything she could possibly tell him and more: how he was going to burn in hell, and what a scumbag he was. I asked her if she would like me to mail it to the guy. She thought about it, then promptly tore the letter to shreds, dropped it in the waste paper basket, and stated boldly, "I don't need it anymore." I was floored. How in the world did she process all of that overnight and then just let go of it?

Needless to say, I was suggesting clients put their thoughts and feelings into writing long before journaling became a popular form of therapy. Art therapy was in its infancy, but I was using that regularly as well. It was unbelievable to me how these kids could communicate their troubles so easily in this manner, but could not express them orally at all. In fact, I was using these techniques for my own mental health. It came natural to me having majored in Art and minored in English as an undergraduate.

As you might imagine, working at the runaway center was very wearisome. I began to swell in my own anger towards adults that abuse children in unspeakable ways, and depression was increasingly creeping in on me as well. These symptoms would have led me to the proverbial burnout if it hadn't been for my art, poetry, and music. I actually wrote a song about my experience and would play it for the runaways. If you were to hear my song you would not see the connection (had I not just explained why I wrote it). It's about a kid who grew up and became a man during the Civil War era, whose life was a living hell; and his only recourse was to hit the road and start over after each setback. To this day, I can go into my music room, shut the world out, crank up the amplifier, and hammer out that song to vent any negative emotions. It has prevented me from burning out more than once.

About ten years ago, during one of the many phases when I was in private practice, some parents brought their six year old son to my office. They left him there for about an hour as if to say "fix my kid." (You know what I'm talking about.) "What's wrong with him I asked?" They explained that he gets up every night at dark-thirty and crawls into bed with them, disrupting their sleep. So I invited the boy to speak privately with me, and he explained that he would get scared late at night. Scared of what? "Monsters," he replied. As it turned out, the kid loved horror movies; he couldn't get enough of them. His parents even let him watch stuff that wasn't fit for youngsters. I asked him if he literally saw monsters in the bedroom. He admitted that they had to be in his head, as it was illogical to believe they were there physically. I informed him that if they were in his head they were his monsters. He could make them dance if he wanted them to. Well it just so happens that this kid was quite a talented artist, so I got him to draw a picture of one of his monsters. "Wow, this is a cool monster," I responded. "Where did you get the idea for that one?" He said it was in his head, from his imagination; he invented it. I had him draw another one. It was just as cool as the first. I suggested the boy continue to draw pictures of his monsters and write little cameos about them, including name, powers, where they live or came from, etc. And I told him to affix them to his bedroom wall and display them for all to see. When he would awaken scared, he was to direct the monsters to get back on the wall and he would see them in the morning. I saw him about six times and then he stopped coming. After a few more weeks had passed the parents stopped by to thank me, and they gave me an Easter card the boy had created just for me in appreciation. The parents said that they didn't know what I'd done, but their son was sleeping in his own bed, all night through, with the light off, bedroom door shut. I explained that it wasn't what I did but what he did. He had turned his fear into inspiration. Instead of being afraid of monsters he was inspired, inventing them, and producing his own storyboard. Before, they were controlling him; now he was controlling them. And he was practicing useful skills: drawing and writing. It wouldn't surprise me if he makes a million bucks from his own monster movie or comic book someday. At only six years old he was already pretty talented in drawing and writing. Imagine how good he will be at twenty-one.

The main point to understand here is that once you have fully processed the emotion, memory, trauma, or whatever, it will take on new meaning. Often that meaning is directly opposite to what it was beforehand. You can take the wisdom forward with you and leave the baggage behind. The memory will possibly fade since it was the baggage that kept it afloat in the first place. It's as if the unconscious is trying to bring you a message from the depths of the baggage that you have yet to realize. Regardless, the event will not be upsetting anymore because the value of it will have been realized, and that is the only part that you need to keep.

Expressing the stuff is far more therapeutic than keeping it inside. That's why talk therapy is so effective. But you don't always have someone to talk to so find alternate ways to express it. Any creative avenue that stimulates the imagination is fair game: arts and crafts, music, drama, song, dance, prose and poetry. Keep on writing your memoirs, your story; maybe you can sell it. Before you know it you're working on act four, scene five. It will evolve and take on a greater importance as you recognize the patterns and trends.

As an expressive arts enthusiast I have encountered and dabbled in all kinds of media. I have yet to find one I didn't like. See what you like; you'll discover a lot of things that work which you'd never tried before. People have been known to create beautiful sculpture out of garbage, even dung. That's what I'm talking about: taking your emotional garbage and turning it into something beautiful. Dig through the dirt and find the hidden jewel of wisdom.

Spiritual Outlets

Spiritually, we can release the baggage. As a Christian, the most obvious solution is to give it to God. Jesus said he will provide rest from all your laboring; he will carry the heavy load for you (MAT 11:28). Just imagine carting the baggage up the mountain, dropping it off at the foot of the cross, leaving it behind, and giving thanks. And receive peace and rest in return! What a bargain! A great weight will be lifted off your shoulders. For more on letting go, the reader is directed to the lesson on Forgiveness.

We connect with God the same way we connect with one another: speak and listen. Prayer is the best way to get things off your chest, enumerate your desires, and thank God. And if it is answers, solutions, or wisdom you seek, you will find them in God's Word. Worship is another great way of connecting with God; you can connect with other believers as well, who also could be part of your support system. The Holy Spirit is the Great Comforter (JOH 14:26); he provides a peace that surpasses all understanding. Talk to him; he is also a wonderful listener and Counselor (ISA 9:6). And pay attention when he replies.

- PSA 50:15 ~ The Lord says, "Call upon me in the day of trouble; I will deliver you, and you shall glorify me."

- ISA 55:10-11 ~ God says, "As the rain and the snow come down from heaven and do not return there but water the earth, making it bring forth and sprout, giving seed to the sower and bread to the eater, so shall my word be that goes out from my mouth; it shall not return to me empty, but it shall accomplish that which I purpose, and shall succeed in the thing for which I sent it."

- ISA 65:24 ~ God says, "Before they call I will answer; while they are yet speaking I will hear."

- JER 33:3 ~ The Lord says, "Call to me and I will answer you, and will tell you great and hidden things that you have not known."

- PHP 4:6-7 ~ Do not be anxious about anything, but in everything by prayer and supplication with thanksgiving let your requests be made known to God. And the peace of God, which surpasses all understanding, will guard your hearts and your minds in Christ Jesus.

- HEB 10:25 ~ And let us consider how to stir up one another to love and good works, not neglecting to meet together, as is the habit of some, but encouraging one another, and all the more as you see the Day drawing near.

People of different religions and faiths can benefit from spiritual release just as much as Christians. For example, meditation, yoga, and martial arts might help one to access his or her spiritual side. These techniques also exercise the mind and body. Whenever the spiritual dimension is introduced, the thought, word, and act become more powerful and positive. So tap into that power and witness its extraordinary effect. It is written: whatever you choose to do or not do, let God be the reason. As pointed out in the literature review, spirituality is an essential component of a successful treatment regimen.

- ROM 14:5-8 ~ One person esteems one day as better than another, while another esteems all days alike. Each one should be fully convinced in his own mind. The one who observes the day, observes it in honor of the Lord. The one who eats, eats in honor of the Lord, since he gives thanks to God, while the one who abstains, abstains in honor of the Lord and gives thanks to God. For none of us lives to himself, and none of us dies to himself.

- COL 3:16-17 ~ Let the word of Christ dwell in you richly, teaching and admonishing one another in all wisdom, singing psalms and hymns and spiritual songs, with thankfulness in your hearts to God. And whatever you do, in word or deed, do everything in the name of the Lord Jesus, giving thanks to God the Father through him.

A man came to my office several years ago, distraught and desperate. He had lost his teenage son tragically from an accidental overdose. He was a man of strict Catholic convictions, and did not question that his son was with the Lord, because his son loved Christ as his father had taught him. But after eighteen months, the man still could not enter into his son's room. He was stuck, he was lost. He was filled with anger, guilt, fear, hopelessness, depression. Well it just so happened that this man was quite handy with his hands. So I suggested that he build something in honor of his son's memory. He liked the idea. To make a long story short, he transformed his son's room into a chapel. He kept enough of his son's belongings there to remind him of who he was and what he liked, but there were a few additions: an altar, a place to sit and to kneel, with crucifix, icons, rosary, candles, and other items one might find in a small chapel. The man came to realize: if he wanted to find his son, he would not find him by looking back; he had to look forward, and up. And not only would he find his son waiting ahead in heaven, but he would see the Lord there also, patient until the day he too would be summoned home. The man was able to exercise all three components: physically he built the furniture and varnished it, and rearranged the room; mentally he designed the chapel and pictured how it would eventually turn out. Spiritually, it was his greatest achievement. He had a place to worship and rejoice. He would frequently retreat to connect with God's Son, and his son. Thus, instead of being afraid of going into his son's room he was driven there. Instead of feeling despair he was renewed each visit with redeeming hope. Instead of feeling lost, he had again found his son, and himself, not to mention reconnecting with his Savior. And this brought him joy. It was an enormously uplifting journey for the man. His son's room will continue to be a place of refuge and sanctuary for many years to come I would imagine.

Conclusions

Everyone needs outlets to vent; I recommend at least three outlets within each domain. That way you won't get bored with one and you will have choices. Some avenues work better, depending on the emotions or memories being reprocessed. The processing is what causes an evolution in the significance of the experience. You may not realize the importance of the message until later in life; but rest assured God has a reason. Not that he wants anyone to suffer, but he can use even that to make you wiser and prepare you for his service. Remember, everything works together for good as long as you trust that the Lord has a plan. And no matter how many monkey wrenches the world tries to throw into the works, God's purpose prevails.

- ROM 8:28 ~ We know that for those who love God all things work together for good, for those who are called according to his purpose.

- PRO 19:21 ~ Many are the plans in the mind of a man, but it is the purpose of the LORD that will stand.

You can carry the baggage for a lifetime but it will only slow your progress in reaching your destination; and many potential destinations you will have to forgo as a result. You wouldn't pack ten pieces of luggage for a weekend in the Bahamas would you? You'll be spending all your time packing and unpacking. You'll be lugging the bags so much you'll be too tired and too busy to have any fun. Try jumping over the hurdles with that load. You cannot. My advice is to travel light.

Do you remember what Jesus told his disciples before sending them off to witness and gain converts? He commanded them to travel light; don't drag a whole bunch of stuff with you, he told them. Endear yourselves to others and give them the option and opportunity to welcome you and your message. If they reject you, dust off your feet when leaving town and move onto the next destination. Ignore the harassment, the defiance, and the rudeness; do not carry it forward. Shake the very dust off your feet when you depart as you don't need any excess weight dragging you down (read LUK 9:1-6).

God will give you what you need to make it; and you will find a lot of it along the way. What you need to bring is the knowledge and experience you gain when processing the events and associated emotional material. Discard the rest as it is of no value and only gets in the way of the truth. You will apply your newfound understanding when you approach the challenge that requires such knowledge. More on disposing of emotional baggage can be found in the lesson on Trauma.

"Sometimes good things fall apart so better things can fall together." – Marilyn Monroe

Lighten
The
Load

367

Activity

Physical Activity: On the left side, list activities you have enjoyed in the past to stay physically fit or active. On the right side list things you are willing to try that you have not explored before.

_____   _____

_____   _____

_____   _____

_____   _____

_____   _____

Mental Activity: On the left side, list things you have enjoyed in the past to express yourself creatively, and to exercise your imagination. On the right side list things you are willing to try that you have not explored before.

_____   _____

_____   _____

_____   _____

_____   _____

_____   _____

Spiritual Activity: On the left side, list spiritual ways in which you have connected to God in the past. On the right side list things you are willing to try that you have not explored before.

_____   _____

_____   _____

_____   _____

_____   _____

DUMPING
EMOTIONAL
BAGGAGE

....

SPIRITUAL **Release it**

....

MENTAL **Express it**

....

PHYSICAL **Burn it**

TRAUMA TREATMENT

OBJECTIVE	Learn the degrees of trauma, ways of managing the emotional material, and techniques for processing traumatic experiences.
INTERVENTION	Discuss the deleterious effects of trauma on long term mental health, and determine which strategies work to reduce the destructive emotional reactions and behavioral responses.
PLAN	Process traumatic events, develop coping strategies, and find ways of moving beyond the stigma of trauma. Deconstruct the memory or event, reprocess it, and reconstruct it to derive new meaning and understanding.

- JER 45:3 ~ Job said, "Woe is me! For the LORD has added sorrow to my pain. I am weary with my groaning, and I find no rest."

It is beyond the scope of this text to get into the many ramifications and treatment of trauma; but we're talking long and intense therapy in most cases. This is because severe trauma is life changing. Effective trauma treatment programs use proven techniques such as Cognitive Processing Therapy, which requires many sessions and very focused reprocessing of memories. Therefore, this lesson will center on effective techniques that the therapist can employ to help mixed groups and individuals deal with trauma in general.

It is fruitless to try to console a trauma patient as if you had any idea how they are feeling. It is better to show empathy and genuine regard. Sure, everybody has experienced trauma to some degree. But the more serious the devastation to the self-esteem, and the greater the frequency and duration of the bombardment, the more permanent is the damage and the more injurious it is to the psyche.

Different kinds of trauma do not produce the same types or degrees of malfunctions. For example battlefield trauma is internalized differently than trauma from rape. Experiencing a natural disaster, violent act, or horrific accident will affect someone differently than living constantly in terror. Factors such as age, gender, and culture also influence the impact of trauma; so does whether the trauma was experienced personally or vicariously. Further, the longer one carries it without expression the longer will be the treatment, especially if dragged from childhood through adulthood. Given the immense time and resources required for a lengthy recovery, many victims never get sufficient help. Although trauma is treatable the effects are often incurable.

One of the reasons that trauma disorders are so resilient to treatment is because memories of trauma are difficult to reprocess and the responses to it difficult to restructure. Traumatic experiences are stored in a primitive part of the brain where the fight, flight, and freeze programming is triggered (i.e., the amygdala). As such, they are time irrelevant, so they tend to linger for years as emotional baggage. The victim reacts automatically when the incident is triggered, without forethought, because the executive functioning area of the brain (prefrontal cortex) becomes disabled (since the limbic system which governs emotion has taken control). To reprogram the maladaptive response one must necessarily dig into the baggage and revisit, reprocess, and reconstruct the memory or experience. This can be a grueling journey for the client, and for the therapist who will need to be as patient as the client is determined. In the words of famed psychiatrist Victor Frankl, who endured the Nazi concentration camps, "What is to give light must endure burning."

I'd like to start the discussion with a verse from a thirteenth century Persian poet and philosopher. You may have heard this saying before; I have seen it quoted in a variety of essays and applied to a number of diagnoses. But, processing of emotional baggage in general and trauma treatment in particular seem the most appropriate applications. Rumi writes, "That which haunts us will always find a way out. The wound will not heal unless given witness. The shadow that follows us is the way in." My interpretation of this message follows the context of trauma treatment. Each statement will be addressed in sequence.

Firstly, memories of trauma can continue to haunt a person for years; and no matter how hard they try to hide them, these memories will not remain repressed. Situational conditions, certain sensations or perceptions, or even unrelated events can trigger the memory and it returns to awareness, baggage and all. Since there are no defense mechanisms in the world that can fully hide it, the person may attempt to build a locker for it via dissociation. That can lead to hidden ego states, or distinct personalities, as found in Dissociative Identity Disorder (DID). Avoiding problems make a person progressively more neurotic. In every case of DID I have encountered, extreme trauma, in the form of sexual and/or physical abuse, has been the common denominator. So, if the disturbing memory is going to find its way up, it is best that the victim find a way to get it out. This is effectively done via cognitive processing.

Secondly, the story must be told. Grueling as it is to relive past horror, it is a necessary path if the person is ever to get it all out. With DID, each closet has to be opened and its skeleton allowed expression to integrate the host personality with the others; otherwise they will take turns expressing themselves and the individual will be oblivious to it. Talk therapy and psychodrama; art, music, and journal therapy; play therapy; these are among the variety of creative ways of disclosing the contents of emotional baggage. In particular, projecting the episode(s) in a way that the individual can dissociate from it can be very therapeutic since the victim's ability to dissociate is already well established. They examine the memory and its circumstances in an objective fashion and still maintain a safe distance from it.

Thirdly, the treatment should have both a conscious and an unconscious processing component. The memory that lurks in the subconscious is given full analysis and expression at the conscious level, as the individual deliberately attends to the material in a non-threatening manner. But the reprocessing and cognitive restructuring of the memory should also occur at the source: the unconscious. This can be done using the imagination to view scenes differently, to role play, or to project oneself backwards or forwards in time. Accessing the programming and performing reframing and restructuring also can be facilitated with positive imagery, hypnosis, EMDR, introspection, meditation, or any technique that accesses the internal database. The maladaptive response is habitual and automatic; the person doesn't think about his or her reaction, it just happens. The program itself is an avenue into the very guts of the haunting memory or image. It can be accessed in a safe and controlled manner by creating the ideal environment for exploration. The client may suggest how to setup the ambience in a way that makes him or her feel calm, secure, comfortable, and confident, while the contents are examined.

I remember a patient responding to an analogy I gave regarding the third statement in the Rumi quote. I suggested that we search for the elusive wisdom of her haunting experience which all the while had been following her. She surmised that she probably needs to turn around and face it. It was a profound insight. The worst thing one can do is to avoid it. This is how some mental disorders develop. The avoidance behavior is reinforced by the temporary relief from anxiety, fear, or hurt. But when the pain never goes away, the avoided emotion gets stronger while the victim gets weaker. The treatment must allow the person to gain strength thereby weakening the fear. Otherwise it will control him or her. Gradually gaining tolerance and control will result in greater confidence and purpose.

The main reason people are afraid or unwilling to go into the baggage is simple. Whenever they reach their hand into the memory they grab hold of the guilt, fear, anger or whatever destructive force lurks there. When they pull it out they feel the hurt and immediately shove it back into the bag, and lock the baggage in its hiding place. But it comes back to trip them up anytime the event is remembered. So they cram it back into its hole until the next occasion the memory is triggered. The individual needs to get past the emotionally charged storm and find the truth that is hidden amongst the rubble. As unpleasant as this will be it is not as grueling as getting bashed over the head with it over and over indefinitely. The negative reaction rarely reflects the truth, relevance, or reality of the experience, but once this is learned, it lightens the load significantly.

Some of the effective techniques for dealing with trauma are listed below. This is by no means an exhaustive list but it does represent a useful procedure. Clearly, these phases overlap to a large extent, and may be repeated each session or in sequential sessions.

Exposure: The individual will have to revisit the trauma to some degree. The conditions for such an invasion into the victim's vault must be well structured to ensure the process is safe, sound, and maintains a comfortable pace. The therapist must avoid fishing, probing for details, suggesting specific items to process, or controlling the direction the client should take; instead let the client disclose to the extent he or she is willing, and follow it where the client's unconscious mind needs to go. Repeated, small doses of the fear will make it more tolerable over time. But if they never face the fear it will consume them. Avoidance behavior is very compelling as it temporarily reduces the anxiety; so periodic redirection may help the client to change focus. Anxiety, worry, and fear often relate to the unknown. The victim doesn't really know why they feel this way or act that way. The best way of overcoming an unknown is knowledge. Thus, such mysteries need to be investigated, researched, queried, and dissected. I remember as an undergraduate I learned about stress inoculation therapy. It's like injecting someone with a small dose of a benign strain of the flu to help them circumvent a full blown viral infection during flu season. Little by little, the person builds up tolerance to stress, fear, or guilt. It's like treating a child who has school phobia. You might begin with having his mom escort him to the class, introduce him to the teacher, maybe sit in the desk next to him for a while. After a few days, she can drop him off at the classroom door and the teacher can escort him to his desk. Before long, she's dropping him off at the entrance to the school, and then at the curb. Who knows, maybe in time he'll be taking the bus. It's called systematic desensitization. You have to build tolerance; like when you wade slowly into a swimming hole that is colder than you like, edging your way carefully into deeper water. It is inadvisable to dive in, as the water is possibly over your head, and there may be hidden obstructions.

Expression: Often, non-verbal techniques (such as art therapy) allow expression more profoundly than actually talking through it. It is the same principal behind the utility of projective tests to uncover hidden traits and states. By gradually telling the story in writing or art the plot may evolve, and the ending may take on a different slant or meaning. Encourage the client to document feelings and thoughts in a journal each time the memory haunts them. Patterns of expression will emerge, as if the unconscious is trying to let something escape from the darkness. Usually, the awareness of the event is unpleasant; that's why the client is hiding it. But the wisdom will surface in subtle ways as it finds its way into the conscious domain, by moving away from the fictional aspects of the memory which will lose strength and eventually can be discarded. Using imagination can facilitate non-threatening exposure, allow the creation of positive replacement images, and enable adaptive role playing. Discussion of key components that emerge will enhance the deconstruction process. Putting the pieces back together usually results in a different picture or new insight. This is a lot more enjoyable than trying to shoo the thoughts away, fearing they will attack you later like a wasp does when you aren't looking.

Analysis: There should be periods of questioning beliefs, reality testing, and scrutinizing interpretations or outcomes. Different meaning, understanding, acceptance, even forgiveness can be entertained reasonably; remember, it's about rationality not emotionality. Examine feelings analytically such as anger, fear, sadness, grief, guilt, shame, despair, helplessness, or worthlessness. This opens the doors for entertaining alternate explanations, exploring coping strategies, and further dissecting events or emotions into pieces for further inspection. By disassembling the baggage in this way, one can reduce the significance of the contents; and possibly find some hidden truth to keep, allowing disposal of the trash. It reminds me of my son who used to turn his playroom into a disaster area. When he had to gather all his toys he'd toss them into boxes without sorting the stuff; so if he wanted to rebuild one of his puzzles he had to exclude pieces that didn't belong in the picture. The client has to perform such an analysis. By removing components that are irrelevant, untrue, or unnecessary, and arranging and joining those that are, the final product reveals an entirely different picture or ending.

Processing: Since the entire process involves cognitive processing, this phase could more appropriately be labeled "reprocessing" or "restructuring" as it is about rethinking things. Of course, that requires one to stop the old program in its tracks, which has become an automatic stimulus-response pattern that will not be broken easily. Considerable discipline will be required in order to recognize when the triggers are present, refocus on different aspects of the experience, conjure a positive thought or image, download an adaptive response to replace the maladaptive one, and practice the new program sufficiently for the old one to fade away. It's like rewriting your internal software through uploading, debugging, and reprogramming. Such restructuring will ultimately reside in the lower levels of consciousness. Thus, both bottom-up and top-down methods will help to build and reinforce adaptive cognitive structures. It may take several iterations before the information is sufficiently reorganized. Thus, the process is staged, with different goals at each stage that moves the client to the next challenge. The partnership between therapist and client turn it into a team effort whereby both agree when it is time to proceed to the next phase of treatment. People who seek counseling must be careful in their selection of a therapist to guide this process, as many who claim to be qualified for such therapy may have underestimated their limitations. I recommend anyone who intends to serve this population get extensive training and knowledge, especially if they have not experienced severe trauma firsthand.

Maintenance: The primary component of maintenance is stress management. Teach the client as many different techniques as possible so they can hone in on the ones that reduce stress and anxiety the best. Clearly, relaxation, breathing, and imagery techniques should be at the top of the list. Most people can benefit from at least one of these methods. When it comes to imagery, help the person determine which of these modalities seem natural to them: visual, auditory, kinesthetic. It will take considerable practice for some clients to master self-relaxation techniques. Once they learn how to get into their zone it will come more naturally and rapidly. They also should continue to utilize creative and constructive outlets to vent such as journaling, art, music, exercise, spirituality, etc. Support systems are essential, to include family, support groups, church/prayer, and trauma counseling (individual, group, family). And don't forget psychiatric follow-ups; psychotropic medication can be very helpful, especially antidepressants (like an SSRI), beta blockers (to subdue the arousal response), anxiolytics (to moderate anxiety and hypervigilance), and sleep aids (as needed). Rehearsing the modified behaviors and programs is required to continue reinforcement of the adaptive processes and extinction of the maladaptive ones. So encourage practice and homework, and rehearse the strategies regularly during follow-ups.

Comorbidity: Given that a number of issues develop as a result of the trauma, therapy may take a few turns. Often the victim is experiencing some combination of the following: substance abuse/dependency problems, marital discord or family conflict, financial problems or unemployment, eating and/or sleeping disorders, nightmares, flashbacks, emotional lability or blunting, forgetfulness or memory lapses, poor motivation, social withdrawal, cognitive malfunctions, and physical ailments. Continued therapy helps the individual to deal with multiple stressors, to reinforce adaptive behavior patterns, to further progress in growth and development, and to realize his or her full potential. Treatment should be well integrated to include mental, educational, social, physical, medical, and spiritual components. Victims need to get out of their comfort zones, to some degree, in order to break isolation, withdrawal, and avoidance behaviors. They need to look forward and move in that direction.

Impress upon the victim that people who terrorize, traumatize, or torment others will suffer a far more terrible fate. This may be small consolation after being victimized; but you can assure victims that they will be found innocent and their perpetrators guilty in the great courtroom in the sky. Victims need to know that they are not guilty, they are not being punished or persecuted by God, they did not deserve what happened to them, and that Christ will bear the burden of the shame and the sin. He will carry them to an eternity free of sorrow, pain, and suffering (REV 21:4). Evil, abusive people do not get away with it for there will be consequences. And their reward will include an eternity of torment if they reject Christ. But the innocent will be lifted up by God.

- PSA 7:16 ~ His mischief returns upon his own head, and on his own skull his violence descends.

- JER 20:11 ~ But the LORD is with me as a dread warrior; therefore my persecutors will stumble; they will not overcome me.

- EZE 11:21 ~ But as for those whose heart goes after their detestable things and their abominations, I will bring their deeds upon their own heads, declares the Lord GOD.

- MAT 13:41-42 ~ The Son of Man will send his angels, and they will gather out of his kingdom all causes of sin and all law-breakers and throw them into the fiery furnace. In that place there will be weeping and gnashing of teeth.

You who attend to the exploited, abused, and oppressed are doing God's work (read the story of the Good Samaritan: LUK 10:29-37). There is a great reward for those who minister to the downtrodden and shine the light of Christ. While we cannot feel what the victims feel we understand hurting better than most, and we hurt along with them. Your clients can sense that. Caring and empathy opens your heart, and promotes a feeling of safety, trust, and confidence enabling your clients to open up. This nurturing environment of love and sharing is conducive to disclosure and growth without the agony and trepidation.

- ROM 8:16-17 ~ The Spirit himself bears witness with our spirit that we are children of God, and if children, then heirs – heirs of God and fellow heirs with Christ, provided we suffer with him in order that we may also be glorified with him.

- 1 CO 12:18-20,26 ~ God arranged the members in the body, each one of them, as he chose. If all were a single member, where would the body be? As it is, there are many parts, yet one body… If one member suffers, all suffer together; if one member is honored, all rejoice together.

- HEB 13:2-3 ~ Do not neglect to show hospitality to strangers, for thereby some have entertained angels unawares. Remember those who are in prison, as though in prison with them, and those who are mistreated, since you also are in the body.

- JAM 5:10 ~ As an example of suffering and patience, brothers, take the prophets who spoke in the name of the Lord.

"Painful as it may be, a significant emotional event can be the catalyst for choosing a direction that serves us, and those around us, more effectively. Look for the learning." – Louisa May Alcott

Conclusions

Exposure therapy is designed to enable the client to tolerate and eventually conquer fear. The associated anxiety becomes debilitating precisely because the person has been avoiding it; they are afraid of it. It causes psychological pain, panic, phobia, conversion disorder, and physical ailments. Flight might be a useful tactic to deal with real fear, but such fear is a result of known danger which can only occur in the present. But when the unbearable memory, situation, or emotion is activated, they try to run from it rather than face it even when there is no actual threat. However, another viable reaction to fear is fight; this response is especially appropriate when the fear is imagined. Fear is maladaptive when danger is not present. So why should we fear the unknown? The truth cannot hurt us; but it can instruct. Unfortunately, people will come up with every excuse in the book to keep it at bay. I redirect every client that begins to recite their list of what ifs, because they are unattached to truth and reality. They make up things to worry about or to justify not trying, as if that would be easier. In the long run, disposing of emotional baggage will serve the person better than carrying it, which only allows it to get heavier and more of a burden.

Remember, more exposure equates to more tolerance. During psychotherapy, I help powerless individuals gain strength via systematic desensitization. Gradually, they build up sufficient vigor to absorb themselves into the very thing they resist. It is a mild form of flooding. I like that term; it congers the perfect analogy. One patient that responded well to the idea was exploring the cold, murky depths of a standing, traumatic memory. He waded into it further and further until he was neck deep in it. Finally, he allowed himself to completely submerge. It was over his head but he forced himself to remain enveloped and fight it. I assured him that he was not alone; I would stand by him in battle and so would God. And his anxiety got a lot worse before it started subsiding. Of course, this method requires an experienced therapist, a safe environment, and an acceptable pace for the client; also, a solid trust in God is extremely helpful if not essential. Otherwise, the submerging itself can be traumatic.

These victims need to accept the anxiety and fear, not refuse it, in order for it to become extinct. That is, when they face it, gain strength, and overcome it they can control the fear, manage the anxiety, and quarantine the memory. The above mentioned client came to the point that he owned the experience, like a landlord. So we explored options: he could sell the land, give it away, or develop it into something else. Since a portion of his childhood had been destroyed, he chose to turn the swampy, muddy, lake of fear into a playground. Using visual imagery, he progressively filled it in with dirt, planted grass and trees, and emplaced equipment. The memory would conger a kid in a park playing with other children on a swing set, seesaw, or monkey bars. He was not escaping the experience, he was replacing it.

- JOS 1:9 ~ God said, "Have I not commanded you? Be strong and courageous. Do not be frightened, and do not be dismayed, for the LORD your God is with you wherever you go."

- PSA 23:4 ~ Even though I walk through the valley of the shadow of death, I will fear no evil, for you are with me; your rod and your staff, they comfort me.

- PRO 12:25 ~ Anxiety in a man's heart weighs him down, but a good word makes him glad.

- MAT 6:34 ~ Jesus said, "Do not be anxious about tomorrow, for tomorrow will be anxious for itself. Sufficient for the day is its own trouble."

- PHP 4:6 ~ Do not be anxious about anything, but in everything by prayer and supplication with thanksgiving let your requests be made known to God.

- 2 TI 1:7 ~ God gave us a spirit not of fear but of power and love and self-control.

"Each one has to find his peace from within. And peace to be real must be unaffected by outside circumstances." – Mahatma Gandhi

"The struggle of life is one of our greatest blessings. It makes us patient, sensitive, and godlike. It teaches us that, although the world is full of suffering, it is also full of the overcoming of it." – Helen Keller

- JOH 16:20,33 ~ Jesus said, "Truly, truly, I say to you, you will weep and lament, but the world will rejoice. You will be sorrowful, but your sorrow will turn into joy… I have said these things to you, that in me you may have peace. In the world you will have tribulation. But take heart; I have overcome the world."

BAD HABITS

OBJECTIVE	Learn to be moderate in all things and avoid temptations of the world that would draw you away from God. Recognize bad habits and how they proceed without conscious awareness.
INTERVENTION	Discuss overindulgence, addiction, and the destruction that comes upon those who place worldly desires above spiritual. Identify areas of your life where you may be losing control and the associated consequences.
PLAN	Let your spirit control your thoughts and not your sinful flesh. Plan on a life of sobriety and temperance. Reprogram unwanted behavior by being mindful of the triggers, executing alternative responses, and practicing the new behavior diligently.

"It is easier to prevent bad habits than to break them." – Benjamin Franklin

"The chains of habit are generally too small to be felt until they are too strong to be broken." – Samuel Johnson

Overindulgence

Bad habits often lead to addictions. Addictions reflect overindulgence: abuse of a substance or an activity. Given this definition, the following could be considered forms of addiction: overeating, smoking, alcoholism, drug dependency, sexual promiscuity, pornography, gambling, and even habitual Internet or electronic media usage. These examples can be linked to lust for they relate to the desire for immediate gratification of the flesh. Therefore, such addictions could be considered idolatry, because the individual has placed their worldly desires before God.

- JOB 31:26-28 ~ If I have looked at the sun when it shone, or the moon moving in splendor, and my heart has been secretly enticed, and my mouth has kissed my hand, this also would be an iniquity to be punished by the judges, for I would have been false to God above.

- PRO 23:21 ~ The drunkard and the glutton will come to poverty, and slumber will clothe them with rags.

- MAT 6:24 ~ No one can serve two masters, for either he will hate the one and love the other, or he will be devoted to the one and despise the other. You cannot serve God and money.

- COL 3:5 ~ Put to death therefore what is earthly in you: sexual immorality, impurity, passion, evil desire, and covetousness, which is idolatry.

- 1 JO 2:15 ~ Do not love the world or the things in the world. If anyone loves the world, the love of the Father is not in him.

God wants to be the center of our lives. He demands in his Ten Commandments that we do not have any other gods before him, neither are we to worship, praise, or adore anything other than God. Unfortunately, for most addicts, that is precisely what they are doing.

- MAT 23:25 ~ Jesus said, "Woe to you, scribes and Pharisees, hypocrites! For they clean the outside of the cup and the plate, but inside they are full of greed and self-indulgence."

- PHP 3:17-19 ~ Brothers, join in imitating me, and keep your eyes on those who walk according to the example you have in us. For many, of whom I have often told you and now tell you even with tears, walk as enemies of the cross of Christ. Their end is destruction, their god is their belly, and they glory in their shame, with minds set on earthly things.

Everything in this world is a gift from God; he has given us all things. God intends for us to use and enjoy his creations. But God did not create the world for us to abuse, and he did not create our lives for us to destroy. Therefore, bad habits and addictions are sins against God as well as against one's own body.

- GEN 1:29-30 ~ God said, "Behold, I have given you every plant yielding seed that is on the face of all the earth, and every tree with seed in its fruit. You shall have them for food. And to every beast of the earth and to every bird of the heavens and to everything that creeps on the earth, everything that has the breath of life, I have given every green plant for food."

- 1 CO 3:16-17; 1 CO 6:19-20 ~ Do you not know that you are God's temple and that God's Spirit dwells in you? If anyone destroys God's temple, God will destroy him. For God's temple is holy, and you are that temple… Your body is a temple of the Holy Spirit within you, whom you have from God. You are not your own, for you were bought with a price. So glorify God in your body.

- EPH 5:18,29 ~ Do not get drunk with wine, for that is debauchery, but be filled with the Spirit… For no one ever hated his own flesh, but nourishes and cherishes it, just as Christ does the church.

There is nothing wrong with eating, drinking, using medications, and having sex, as long as they are enjoyed within the limits set forth in God's Word. When these limits are exceeded, God's gifts cannot be enjoyed to their fullest extent. That is, when excessiveness is required to maintain the pleasure level the activity is not fully satisfying. If it was you could quit when you were satisfied. When you still demand more, it doesn't give more pleasure but more misery. The Bible teaches moderation in all things so that we don't overdo it.

- ECC 7:18 (NIV) ~ It is good to grasp the one and not let go of the other. The man who fears God will avoid all extremes.

"Habit is stronger than reason." – George Santayana

- 1 CO 6:12; 1 CO 10:23 ~ All things are lawful for me, but not all things are helpful. All things are lawful for me but I will not be dominated by anything. All things are lawful, but not all things build up.

- PHP 4:5 ~ Let your reasonableness be known to everyone.

Slippery Slope

A hardcore addict will sacrifice anything to feed the habit. The first things to go will include honesty, integrity, self-esteem, and morality. After surpassing the stages of lying, stealing, and worse, the addict begins to sacrifice his or her job, belongings, home, friends, marriage, and children. Eventually, an addiction could cost the addict his or her freedom, life, and very soul. It is amazing the lengths to which addicts will go to fulfill their cravings. This is a trap set by the devil to lure people away from God

- PSA 49:7-8 ~ Truly no man can ransom another, or give to God the price of his life, for the ransom of their life is costly and can never suffice.

- MAT 16:26 ~ Jesus said, "What will it profit a man if he gains the whole world and forfeits his soul? Or what shall a man give in return for his soul?"

- LUK 12:19-20 ~ I will say to my soul, "Soul, you have ample goods laid up for many years; relax, eat, drink, be merry." But God said to him, "Fool! This night your soul is required of you, and the things you have prepared, whose will they be?"

- LUK 21:34-35 ~ Jesus said, "Watch yourselves lest your hearts be weighed down with dissipation and drunkenness and cares of this life, and that day come upon you suddenly like a trap. For it will come upon all who dwell on the face of the whole earth."

- 1 PE 2:11 ~ Beloved, I urge you as sojourners and exiles to abstain from the passions of the flesh, which wage war against your soul.

The Bible makes it clear that wickedness will lead to death and hell. People that continue in their sinful ways will lose everything, not only earthly treasures but also spiritual ones. Individuals that hang around with addicts or constantly engage in lustful pursuits are playing in the devil's den. Those who belong to Satan's lair include idolaters, fornicators, sexual deviants, murderers, gluttons, blasphemers, occultists, and dishonest and deceitful people. People that dabble in such evil will find themselves quickly sinking deeper into the abyss. They must be warned that if they continue, Satan will succeed in dragging them down to hell. There is a way out for them, however: confession, repentance, and the forgiveness that only Christ can give. What should follow is abstinence.

- EZE 3:18-19 ~ God says, "If I say to the wicked, 'You shall surely die,' and you give him no warning, nor speak to warn the wicked from his wicked way, in order to save his life, that wicked person shall die for his iniquity, but his blood I will require at your hand. But if you warn the wicked, and he does not turn from his wickedness, or from his wicked way, he shall die for his iniquity, but you will have delivered your soul."

- LUK 5:32 ~ Jesus said, "I have not come to call the righteous but sinners to repentance."

- 2 CO 12:21 ~ Paul wrote: I fear that when I come again my God may humble me before you, and I may have to mourn over many of those who sinned earlier and have not repented of the impurity, sexual immorality, and sensuality that they have practiced.

- 1 PE 4:1-3 (paraphrased) ~ Even though Christ has done away with sin, you must not continue to sin as you have in the past when you practiced lewdness, lust, drunkenness, overindulgence, orgies, and idolatry.

In many cases, the person who has developed a deep dependency for a substance or an activity is trying to fill a void in their lives – a spiritual void. When this void is filled with worldly things it becomes an addiction, because the victim can never be satisfied by physical pleasures. Thus, addiction is like demon possession since a spiritual void cannot be replaced with evil and sin. In fact, you may have noticed how addiction makes a person mean, hateful, and wicked. That person develops a dual personality with a good side and an evil side. Unfortunately, the evil side prevails when they are intoxicated, they experience withdrawals, or they lose control. These people need to know that Christ alone can fill the void. He can chase away the demons of addiction and allow his Holy Spirit to replace the emptiness in a person's life. Christ can satisfy every craving of the heart.

- EZE 16:28-30,36-38 (paraphrased) ~ You played like a whore with the Assyrians, with your insatiable lust which could never be satisfied. You further multiplied your sinful lust in the lands of Canaan and Chaldea, and still were not satisfied. You obviously have a weak heart because you behave like an arrogant whore. Since you were so terribly filthy, with your fornication, your idol worship, and the sacrificing of your children, God will gather those you have had sex with, along with those you hate, so that they can see you naked and ashamed. And God will judge you the way he judges murderers and adulterers.

- MAT 26:41 ~ The spirit indeed is willing, but the flesh is weak.

- ROM 13:13-14 ~ Let us walk properly as in the daytime, not in orgies and drunkenness, not in sexual immorality and sensuality, not in quarreling and jealousy. But put on the Lord Jesus Christ, and make no provision for the flesh, to gratify its desires.

- GAL 6:8 ~ For the one who sows to his own flesh will from the flesh reap corruption, but the one who sows to the Spirit will from the Spirit reap eternal life.

Obviously, to be addicted to the world is to ignore God. He has promised to provide our needs if we seek him first (MAT 6:31-34). We are to value spiritual riches above earthly riches (MAT 6:19-21). While it is possible to overdose from worldly things, we can never overdose on God's love. God's love will gratify our deepest desires eternally.

- GAL 5:22-23 ~ The fruit of the Spirit is love, joy, peace, patience, kindness, goodness, faithfulness, gentleness, self-control; against such things there is no law.

- EPH 5:9 (KJV) ~ The fruits of the Spirit originate in goodness, righteousness, and truth.

- 2 PE 1:5-8 ~ Make every effort to supplement your faith with virtue, and virtue with knowledge, and knowledge with self-control, and self-control with steadfastness, and steadfastness with godliness, and godliness with brotherly affection, and brotherly affection with love. For if these qualities are yours and are increasing, they keep you from being ineffective or unfruitful in the knowledge of our Lord Jesus Christ.

God should be the desire of everyone. Let us become addicted to God's love; let us strive for spiritual gratification. If we crave him alone we will not be obsessed with worldly cravings. And we will receive all that we need to satisfy our worldly yearnings.

- PSA 37:4 ~ Delight yourself in the Lord and He will give you the desires of your heart.

- PRO 11:23 ~ The desire of the righteous ends only in good; the expectation of the wicked in wrath.

- ISA 26:7-8 ~ The path of the righteous is level; you make level the way of the righteous. In the path of your judgments, O LORD, we wait for you; your name and remembrance are the desire of our soul.

- GAL 5:17-18 ~ The desires of the flesh are against the Spirit, and the desires of the Spirit are against the flesh, for these are opposed to each other, to keep you from doing the things you want to do. But if you are led by the Spirit, you are not under the law.

- ROM 8:26-27 ~ The Spirit helps us in our weakness. For we do not know what to pray for as we ought, but the Spirit himself intercedes for us with groanings too deep for words. And he who searches hearts knows what is the mind of the Spirit, because the Spirit intercedes for the saints according to the will of God.

- 1 JO 5:14-15 ~ This is the confidence that we have toward him, that if we ask anything according to his will he hears us. And if we know that he hears us in whatever we ask, we know that we have the requests that we have asked of him.

Bad habits result from the weakness of our sinful flesh and the desire to feed on earthly delights. They become bad habits because the behavior is repeated as we strive to fill an emptiness that can never be filled by the world. Such addictive behavior is destined to continue, as the victim becomes a slave to the sin, erroneously believing that the insatiable desire can be gratified. But there never is satisfaction which becomes more elusive as the addiction grows. All it is doing is dragging the person farther away from God and down the road to destruction, until they can see no way out.

Only the Holy Spirit can fill the void in our lives with a sense of fullness and completeness that lasts forever. God fulfills the desire of every living thing through a steadfast love that is wholly satisfying. If we seek his love we will never want or need anything; for all these things will be provided. Any good parent will provide for his or her children; in the same manner it is instinctive for God to provide for his children.

- PSA 145:15-16 ~ The eyes of all look to you, and you give them their food in due season. You open your hand; you satisfy the desire of every living thing.

- EZE 7:19 ~ They cast their silver into the streets, and their gold is like an unclean thing. Their silver and gold are not able to deliver them in the day of the wrath of the LORD.

They cannot satisfy their hunger or fill their stomachs with it. For it was the stumbling block of their iniquity.

Help your clients perform a cost-benefits analysis. Enable them to see that the perceived benefits of their bad habits are nothing compared to the costs. It is not a fair exchange at all. Help them analyze the process from beginning to end: circumstances prior to onset of the program, triggers that prime the unwanted habit, how the thought process proceeds to the unwanted behavior, and the negative consequences that result.

Choices

Be careful of your thoughts, for your thoughts become your words.
Be careful of your words, for your words become your actions.
Be careful of your actions, for your actions become your habits.
Be careful of your habits, for your habits become your character.
Be careful of your character, for your character becomes your destiny.
– Author unknown

People make choices, and these choices can have near term and long term repercussions that can last for years. Some of these choices affect our lives, the lives of others, even our eternal life. God has given us free will, desiring that we choose him and do his will. However, the way we conduct ourselves, the direction we take in life, and the way we spend our time is mostly up to us. We can seize control over ourselves and our destiny, despite the fact that there are many things that are beyond our control.

The exercise I use concerning this subject generates a lot of debate and discussion. First, I read the above quote and get the participants' reaction to that. Most if not all of them agree completely with the saying. I write each item from the quote on the whiteboard as things we have control over. Then I write on the board other things we can choose, according to the opinions of the group members. Participants tend to reach a general consensus on most of the items on the list.

In the words of Aristotle: We are what we repeatedly do. But, notice how everything begins with the thinking doesn't it? You keep thinking something long enough you'll end up doing it; and if you do it enough times it will become a habit, which will eventually define who you are if you don't change the behavior. You can find a platform for this underlying premise in the Bible, which basically states: What you think, you are (PRO 23:7). So if you want to change anything in the list that follows, begin by changing your thinking.

Things We Can Choose or Control

Thoughts	Character	Lifestyle
Words	Destiny	Direction
Deeds	Friends	Activities, Behavior
Habits	Partner, Spouse	Emotions, Feelings

Consequences	Style	Productivity, Success
Communications	Expectations	Battles
Interests, Hobbies	Residence	Effort
Education	Fitness, Health	Decisions
Money	Attitude	Courage
Priorities	Appearance	Boundaries
Beliefs	Identity	Possibilities
Standards, Morality	Satisfaction	Roles, Responsibility
Imagination	Entertainment	Willpower
Views, Politics	Possessions	Treatment
Desires, Goals	Healthcare	Here and Now

Next, I generate a list of things we cannot choose or control; a sampling is listed below. Clearly, it is easier to identify more things you can control than those that you cannot control. This gives the participants a sense of power, that they can manage their lives and choose happiness, and elect not to let things get to them. Further, the things we cannot choose or control usually do not need to be changed or controlled, and/or they are things that nobody has or needs control over. For example, you don't need to change your age, ethnicity, gender, or other people in order to succeed or to be happy.

Things We Cannot Choose or Control

Birth	Death
Parents, Blood, DNA	Other People
In-Laws	Race, Ethnicity
Age	Gender
Physical Attributes	Ailments, Pain
Events	Space-Time
Climate	Weather
Past, History	Truth, Facts

"Twenty years from now you will be more disappointed by the things that you didn't do than by the ones you did do." – Mark Twain"

Finally, we talk about things that can be listed in either category. That is, there are things that we can control sometimes and that we cannot control other times. As we generate the above two lists, and the discussion divides the group, I circle those items or list them under the heading below. You can get a lot of opinions about these dilemmas as they present a paradox to many. It makes for an interesting interchange.

Things That We Choose Sometimes and That We Do Not Choose Sometimes

Free Will	Rights
Events	Suffering, Illness
Dreams	Experience
Personality	Responsibility
Roles	Talent

The point is this: regardless of your bloodline, where you were born, whether you had a good or bad upbringing, or your demographics (age, race, sex) everyone has the potential to succeed, be happy, and live their lives the way they choose. It depends on what they believe to be possible, how much dedication they possess, how much effort they expend, and determination. While freedom of choice is accessible in the USA it is not everywhere. Consider other countries where choices are made for people, or denied to them. It helps one to appreciate the gift of freedom and the rights that God has bestowed upon all mankind.

In conclusion, change is possible but you have to believe in it. Happiness is achievable but you have to pursue it. Success is inevitable but you have to wait for it. Eternal life is available but you have to choose God. And if you choose God you will receive all of these things.

The Serenity Prayer

God grant me the serenity to accept the things I cannot change; courage to change the things I can; and wisdom to know the difference. Living one day at a time; enjoying one moment at a time; accepting hardships as the pathway to peace. Taking, as He did, this sinful world as it is, not as I would have it; trusting that He will make all things right if I surrender to His will; that I may be reasonably happy in this life and supremely happy with Him forever in the next. Amen. – Reinhold Niebuhr

Activity

List some of your bad habits.

_____   _____

_____   _____

_____   _____

_____   _____

How have these bad habits affected your family (spouse, children, parents)?

_____

How have these bad habits endangered you or your loved ones? Examples could include reckless driving, fighting or violence, hitting or hurting, yelling or arguing.

_____

How have these bad habits affected your friends, neighbors, coworkers, or social life?

_____

How have these bad habits affected your job or schooling?

_____

How have these bad habits created legal problems or financial problems?

_____

How have these bad habits affected your health (physical and mental)?

_____

_____

How have these bad habits affected your spiritual life?

_____

_____

_____

List some things that you tend to overdo or overindulge in.

_____   _____

_____   _____

_____   _____

_____   _____

List some of the things that trigger that behavior or activity. These might include thoughts, feelings, memories, events, sensations or perceptions, situational conditions or circumstances.

_____   _____

_____   _____

_____   _____

Describe the process from beginning to end. What happens prior to the triggers or under what circumstances are the triggers present. What are you thinking when the trigger occurs, and how do those thoughts lead to the unwanted behavior? What are the consequences or results of that behavior?

_____

_____

_____

_____

_____

How do the triggers and the intrusive thoughts distract you from what you should be doing?

_____

_____

What should you do to remove these distractions from your walk with God?

_____

_____

ADDICTION

OBJECTIVE	Learn about addiction and ways to prevent it. Recognize how addiction interferes with functioning and prevents success.
INTERVENTION	Discuss the characteristics of addiction and the thought processes involved. Introduce best practices regarding treatment.
PLAN	Understand the destructiveness of bad habits and the losses realized because of addiction. Give up any behavior or substance that could drive a wedge between you and God.

"Habit, if not resisted, soon becomes necessity." – St. Augustine

Addiction is primarily a learned behavior which perpetuates largely due to negative reinforcement. Escaping from an unpleasant reality, numbing the pain, or forgetting about the past can be very compelling motivators. Who wouldn't want to feel good, especially if they were feeling bad at the time? The addiction gives them immediate gratification, or so they think. But all it does is postpone a more severe state of discomfort and unpleasantness.

Addicted people are out of control because the substance, activity, or obsession is controlling them. Once control is lost, they never will be able to control that substance or behavior again. In other words, one drop of vodka, one more view of pornography, or one more visit to the casino will set the addiction in motion again. There is no such thing as completing recovery, returning to the behavior, and maintaining moderation. The importance of the twelve steps to recovery is to relinquish control to God (higher power).

Addiction has many features of idolatry, because it becomes the focus of one's life and the reason they get up in the morning. But the individual never seems to be fully satisfied by it. They continue the behavior chasing a level of pleasure that is never reached, which only leads to greater use and less gratification. It is an attempt to fill a void that is never filled because it is a spiritual void. God alone can fill that emptiness and move that mountain.

Characteristics of Addicts

Let us assume that Aristotle was right: we are what we repeatedly do. Then if you drink every day you are an alcoholic; if you consistently abstain from further drinking you are an alcoholic in recovery. Recall that any behavior, activity, experience, or ingestion of a substance that is repeated enough times will alter the chemistry in the brain. Therefore addiction, like depression and psychosis, becomes a physiological or chemical phenomenon, in addition to a mental and emotional one. If left unchecked, addiction becomes a wall that the victim cannot see beyond.

Loss of Control – If the individual's behavior has been controlled by the addiction for a year or more, he or she is likely out of control; for some people and for some substances, the timeframe is shorter. Participation in the addictive behavior continues to increase at the detriment of other, more responsible behaviors. The person engages in high risk behavior, and becomes a higher risk for relapse. Impulse control issues become apparent in other aspects of the person's life (illicit drug use, irregular eating habits, gambling, sexual promiscuity, Internet pornography, etc.). Thus, control ultimately is lost in other areas of their life.

Time Deficits – The person expends considerable time locating, preparing, abusing, and recovering from the addictive substance or activity. This leads to reduced role fulfillment, often resulting in loss of job, dropping out of school, divorce, eviction, or incarceration. The individual also neglects behaviors that once brought enjoyment, interest, or pleasure such as hobbies, exercise, personal hygiene, socializing, and learning or reading. Eventually they give up eating and sleeping as well. They just don't have the time for these things.

Tolerance – Since the body (especially the brain) adapts to any substance or behavior, the addict increases the exposure, duration, and frequency in an attempt to maintain the experience, excitement, or level of intoxication. Thus, not only does the addict expend enormous amounts of time, but also money on the addiction. Despite the investment of all these resources, the addict is never fully gratified because satisfaction is momentary and fleeting. That is, more results in less.

Withdrawals – The state of withdrawal usually produces the opposite feeling of the addiction; so if the person feels euphoric when intoxicated he or she will feel despairing during withdrawals. This causes extreme anxiety, which is relieved by engaging in the addictive behavior thereby reinforcing the maladaptive behavior. The substance or activity becomes the motivator to the addict, who seeks to reduce the anxiety, pain, or sadness, or to reverse the symptoms of withdrawal. Unfortunately, not only are these problems still there when the person withdraws, but they are worse because these symptoms are also the consequences of withdrawal.

Distortions in Thinking – The addict will experience lapses in concentration, will have problems gathering thoughts before acting or speaking, and will have difficulty remembering. This affects other cognitive functions that require communication, planning, recalling, focusing, or imagination. Naturally, when they are engaged in the addictive behavior the impairment in reasoning, judgment, and rational decision making becomes even worse.

Denial – Though the negative consequences are apparent, addicts persist in engaging in the addiction knowing full well that it is destroying everything they hold dear. They ignore or repress the fact that every problem they are having in their lives can be linked to the habit. They also tend to deny that they have an addiction, that they are out of control, or that they cannot stop. They may alternate between periods of addictive behavior and abstinence, which is perceived as control. For example, a weekend binger may deceive himself into thinking he has it under control, but the abuse will continue to progress. The addict is in denial if he or she thinks the habit can be controlled. The phrase "functional addict" is an oxymoron.

Obsessive-Compulsive Behavior – Obviously, the addiction becomes the central focus of the person's life. They will turn to the addictive behavior as a response to anything. For example, they will do it to escape, to self-medicate, or to celebrate. They tend to obsess about other things as well, such as dwelling on the trivial things that people say or do, being over-controlling and demanding, or engaging in acts of desperation. Impulse control issues mentioned above eventually become obsessions.

Mood Swings – Addicts experience abrupt changes in mood. Depression and anxiety are prevalent conditions as the addict sometimes feels lonely, abandoned, guilty, ashamed, hopeless, fearful, and/or worthless. At other times he or she may appear insensitive, unsympathetic, unremorseful, or hateful. These changes in mood can lead to anger, angst, aggression, and violence, especially if the person is experiencing withdrawals. Addictive behavior usually is a response to mood. They may be trying to suppress feelings of sadness, loneliness, heartache, or anxiety by elevating the mood, forgetting their worries, self-medicating, or destressing. But it only exacerbates their problems and that increases the frequency and intensity of mood swings.

Family History – Children of addictive parents are more likely to become an addict from learning the behavior than from inheriting it. They may have an addictive propensity or personality, as indicated by past polysubstance exploration, other obsessive activities, or a pattern of out-of-control behavior. There may be evidence of neglect or abuse during childhood or adulthood. The addict may be a product of a broken home, may have gone through a nasty divorce, or may have experienced an unexpected death. The person may have destroyed any close ties as revealed by social isolation, lack of attachments, and estrangement from family and friends. While there may be a genetic component suggesting a proclivity to addictive behavior, the environmental aspects are far more influential.

Treating Addicts

The National Institute on Alcohol Abuse and Alcoholism (go to *www.niaaa.nih.gov*) informs that alcoholics are 90% likely to relapse within four years of treatment (Polich, et. al, 1981). The Drug Abuse Treatment Outcome Studies website (go to *www.datos.org*) reports that only 25% of those with serious chemical dependency issues ever seek treatment, and of those that do only 18% remain clean after one year. Thus, national statistics suggest that the odds of staying in recovery are very poor, especially within the first year. If the person never seeks treatment in the first place the chance of successful recovery is practically zero.

It is obvious from the literature that some treatment is better than no treatment in reducing the risk of relapse. Generally, longer treatment yields better treatment outcomes. Further, intensity of treatment equates to better outcomes and the likelihood of completing the program (Yih-Ing, et al., 2003). If more treatment and intense treatment translate into relapse prevention, a long-term program in an intensive inpatient setting will give individuals the best chance to kick their habit.

According to Marlatt and Gordon (1985), the probability of relapse is influenced by many factors, both internal and external. A high-risk environment, replete with triggers, bad influences, social pressures, and interpersonal temptation, is a major contributor. Internal

334

factors are equally important such as coping skills, perceived control, frustration and anger levels, and the anticipation of feeling good or intoxicated.

Appropriate goals convert into positive treatment outcomes, to include modifying the lifestyle, identifying and responding to internal and external triggers, and self-control strategies (ibid). Simpson (2003) asserts that treatment effectiveness is a function of patient motivation, severity of problems, therapeutic engagement (intensity of services), and linkage to community based support programs. Clearly, if a person wants to change they not only have to change their belief system and learn some basic skills, but a corresponding change in the environment is required. Obviously, involvement in Alcoholics Anonymous (AA) or Narcotics Anonymous (NA) would be a key social network connection (NIAAA).

An effective inpatient program must address and reinforce lifestyle and corresponding environmental changes, establish solid support systems, develop appropriate life skills (coping, anger management, self-control), and identify, face and/or avoid triggers. This should be combined with frequent therapeutic interventions; a milieu that promotes camaraderie, edification, and structure; considerable personal homework and assignments that promote self-assessment, growth, and goal setting; developing alternate sources of gratification and support; finding new directions; confidence building and motivation enhancement; and activities that exercise the mind, body, and spirit.

Such a program will keep patients occupied and engaged throughout the day, every day they are in treatment. A secure, safe, and structured environment of care that provides comprehensive assessment, diagnosis, treatment, and medication management is advised. Continuity of care that progresses through detoxification, rehabilitation, outpatient services, and follow-up helps keep the momentum going.

Successful programs combine therapy, education, group work, individual work, AA/NA groups, community meetings, and exercises that promote individual skills, goals, and growth. Programming is scheduled every day throughout the day, so the participants keep busy being occupied with recovery and not preoccupied with how they ended up in the hospital or treatment facility. Even during their personal time they will be reflecting upon their recovery, what they have learned, and future aspirations via journaling and homework.

These principles were adapted into a 28-day program that I helped build and direct at a local psychiatric hospital. I was recruited by a corporate representative that wanted to establish the most powerful program in our area. It was designed to incorporate an evidence-based curriculum, the twelve steps, AA/NA meetings, a full schedule seven days per week, factors gleaned from empirical research, and the collective experience that he and I possessed.

The program included a mix of therapeutic interventions: individual, family, group, art, ropes, journal, recreation, and peer therapy. We had a staff of highly qualified, experienced, and credentialed professionals: therapists, psychiatrists, nurses, and technicians providing comprehensive assessment, diagnosis, treatment, tracking, and medication management. It was a secure, safe, and structured environment of care, with a continuity of care philosophy that progressed through detoxification, rehabilitation, outpatient services, and follow-up. Follow-ups were conducted on everyone that participated, whether they completed the program or not; we also had reunions for graduates of the program up to twice a year. This mix of programming and interventions proved very effective.

The success of the program was evidenced by the high percentage of graduates that were still in recovery at follow-up. Of the 90 follow-ups attempted in the first six months, contact was successful with 37 previous participants (41%). Of those that were hospitalized just for detoxification, 55% were still in recovery; of those that participated in the rehabilitation program, 75% were still in recovery. The average length of sobriety was 4.5 months. Given the percentage of previous participants that could not be located, these statistics may be subject to scrutiny; but even if those not contacted were computed with those that had relapsed, the success rate would still have been 35%. Nevertheless, we met the objective of being the best and most successful rehabilitation program in the area, and it continues to be. Understand this: It was the formula we used, the teamwork, and the professionalism of the staff which led to our success, so I do not take credit. Remember, credit for your success as a helper belongs to God, so thank him.

Since its inception, AA has proven to be the most important aftercare resource for recovering addicts. The primary ingredient is a solid connection to the higher power. Bill Wilson, founder of AA, derived much of his philosophy from the work of famed Swiss Psychiatrist Carl Jung. Through correspondence shared between these two men the following foundation was gleaned (see Wigmore, 2009).

Jung argued that craving for alcohol was similar to our desire for spiritual oneness with God. Unfortunately, worldly things can never fill a spiritual emptiness. Jung considered it somewhat ironic how the former desire is for the spirits of alcohol and the latter for the Holy Spirit. They are at opposite ends of the spectrum he surmised. But as any hardcore addict will tell you, alcohol or drugs is like an evil spirit: hence the phrase, the demon of addiction. Jung held that God alone could overcome this evil power. The impetus of the twelve steps is that the addict cannot beat the habit alone; he or she needs help, especially from their higher power.

- 2 SA 22:22-24 ~ For I have kept the ways of the LORD and have not wickedly departed from my God. For all his rules were before me, and from his statutes I did not turn aside. I was blameless before him, and I kept myself from guilt.

- PSA 42:1 ~ As a deer pants for flowing streams, so pants my soul for you, O God. My soul thirsts for God, for the living God. When shall I come and appear before God?.

- PRO 3:5-7 ~ Trust in the LORD with all your heart, and do not lean on your own understanding. In all your ways acknowledge him, and he will make straight your paths. Be not wise in your own eyes; fear the LORD, and turn away from evil.

Jung proposed three paths towards successful recovery: an act of grace, education, and edification. Successful recovery usually involves all three. Most addicts first experience the act of God, which appears as a wakeup call. And when they get such a call who do you suppose is trying to get their attention? They begin to realize that only by the grace of God are they still alive, and have been given another chance. As Jung proposed, the addiction is like a predator out to capture one's very soul. God shows up when they hit rock bottom; it is then they acknowledge that God alone can save them out of it. For many, it can be a religious experience indeed. The event provides the incentive to remain connected with God, not just when feeling down but always.

Education in addiction is extremely important for modifying beliefs and behaviors. Instruction describes the course in which the addiction proceeds and the consequences that result; the relevant personality traits, attributes, attitudes, feelings, and thought processes; the conditions, triggers, and changes that affect your life and those around you. The addict must recognize and dispatch the monster within; practice more adaptive and appropriate coping strategies; learn to avoid certain situations, people, places, and things; seek alternative sources of gratification; identify and establish supports and networks; prepare a solid relapse prevention plan; and ultimately change their direction and lifestyle. These are essential components of an effective treatment program as stated previously.

Critical to the success of AA/NA are healthy relationships that provide encouragement and edification. The recovering addict should fellowship with loved ones and recovering addicts; he or she also should develop a partnership with a strong sponsor. It is about interacting with people who are sharing, caring, and nonjudgmental: people that will accept them for who they are, who will be there to support them in their recovery and accompany them in the journey. Without a solid support system, relapse is inevitable. Recovery is a team effort that involves a well-informed pupil, God, and other positive influences.

"The unfortunate thing about this world is that good habits are so much easier to give up than bad ones." – Somerset Maugham

References

Marlatt, G. A., & Gordon, J. R. (1985). *Relapse prevention: Maintenance strategies in the treatment of addictive behaviors*. New York: Guilford Press.

National Association on Alcohol Abuse and Alcoholism (NIAAA). www.niaa.nih.gov.

Polich, J., Armor, D., & Braiker, H. (1981). *Stability and change in drinking patterns*. In The course of alcoholism: Four years after treatment. New York: John Wiley & Sons, 159-200.

Simpson, D. (2003). Special section: 5-year follow-up treatment outcome studies from DATOS. *Journal of Substance Abuse Treatment, 25*(3), 123-186.

Wigmore, B. (2009). Caught between the devil and deliverance. *Recovery Today* (www.recoverytoday.net).

Yih-Ing, H., et al. (2003). *California Treatment Outcome Project (CATOP)* Final Report. UCLA Integrated Substance Abuse Programs (ISAP).

Activity

Are you or someone you know struggling with any of the following activities? Place a check mark by those that apply.

___ Drinking alcohol

___ Using drugs

___ Viewing pornography

___ Gambling

___ Sexual promiscuity

List and describe your behaviors or activities that consume too much time. (Note: outside of work, school, or sleep there shouldn't be any one activity that expends 6-8 hours of the day.)

_____

_____

_____

Do you or does a loved one possess any of the following characteristics? Check those that apply. If you checked tolerance, withdrawal, and any other three, it is definitely an addiction. If you checked six or more it is either an addiction or an addict in the making.

___ Loss of Control

___ Time Deficits

___ Tolerance

___ Distortions in Thinking

___ Denial

___ Obsessive-Compulsive Behavior

___ Mood Swings

___ Withdrawal

___ Family History of Addiction

Circle all of the items below that were lost or that you stand to lose due to addiction.

Health, Self-Esteem, Relationship, Job, Faith, Time, Belongings, Morality, Freedom, Identity, Respect, Trust, Senses, Money, Sanity, Happiness, Awareness, Dignity, Life.

SIGNS OF ADDICTION

- **Losing Control**
- **Time Deficits**
- **High Tolerance**
- **Withdrawals**
- **Cravings**
- **Distortions in Thinking**
- **Denial, Rationalization**
- **Obsessive-Compulsive**
- **Mood Swings**

SUICIDE PREVENTION

OBJECTIVE	Learn about suicide, the warning signs, and means of prevention. Be able to recognize when people are at risk and get them some help.
INTERVENTION	Discuss suicide openly to include the risk factors, treatment options, and consequences for those affected by it.
PLAN	Identify the warning signs to be ready to intervene before a person becomes a victim of suicide. Develop safety plans with your loved ones and open the doors of communication.

About 1.2% of annual deaths in the USA are confirmed suicides; that makes it the eleventh largest cause of death. The numbers may actually be higher if we bear in mind that many "accidental" overdoses and other unexplained deaths may be deliberate. The most common denominator for suicide victims is Major Depression (includes Bipolar Depression). As depression worsens suicidal ideations increase. Studies vary, but about 80% of successful suicides are by depressed persons. Major Depressive Disorder is usually associated with recent or recurrent setbacks and stressors; it resurfaces periodically and lasts a long time. Thus, the depression tends to be persistent and pervasive.

Suicide is typically an act of desperation by those who have no hope. Total despair can be experienced by people who feel lonely, helpless, worthless, angry, guilty, or shamed. They probably are suffering physical and/or emotional pain, and possibly have been traumatized. Additional deteriorating mental states include dementia, delusional/psychotic disorder, and delirium. Addiction and intoxication contribute to a declining mental state as well. Loss of physical functioning also may be present. These people obviously hate themselves, their lives, and/or who they have become. Their black hole may be real, exaggerated, or imagined. Either way, they see no way out.

Usually the state of despair subsides in time at least enough for the individual to change his or her mind. Most have not made up their mind until moments prior to the act; others plan it for weeks. They don't really want to die; they just want some relief and peace. That is one of the reasons suicide hotlines are so effective: suicidal individuals usually can be talked out of it. Another reason is that hotline operators are skilled at establishing rapport and striking up a conversation. The best way to prevent suicide is communication. Just beware of a response that is too quick or seems contrived. A victim might try to trick you into thinking all is well to prevent you from changing his or her mind. You must keep them engaged until they are thinking somewhat rationally; at least 20-30 minutes.

It is a good rule of thumb to perform a suicide assessment with every depressed patient, if not all patients. Discuss the topic openly and honestly with the patient. Persistent ideations and prior attempts are significant risk factors. The greatest risk factor is when the individual has a current plan or intent. More lethal prior attempts and current plans drastically increase risk. Prior family history of suicide, parental mental illness, and previous psychiatric treatment are other risk factors. If they have death wishes, find out if they have thought of how, when, where, and why they would do it; risk grows higher for each of these to which they have an answer. Probe more deeply when any of the above risk factors are confirmed. I have developed my own suicide risk assessment provided at the conclusion of this lesson. I recommend you use this tool or another objective measurement tool from the many good ones out there. Comprehensive assessments (such as the tool provided) offer a better picture than subjective self-report measures. I have found that patients often report low risk when they are, in fact, high risk because they want to be discharged from the hospital. The converse is also true: those saying they are high risk are often not; they just want to stay in the hospital. Unreliable self-report measures will not suffice in the event of a lawsuit, because clients may say that they are not suicidal when they are, and vice-versa.

However, studies suggest that 80% of suicide victims do give warning signs. They give verbal warnings: "I wish I was dead," "You'd be better off if I wasn't around," "I hate my life," "You'll miss me when I'm gone." They give behavioral warnings: prior attempts, giving away prized possession(s), destroying things, quitting enjoyable activities, abrupt changes in personality or demeanor, isolation and withdrawal, making final arrangements (guardianship, last will and testament, advanced directives), writing or drawing pictures about death, disinterest in faith and religion, not eating, not sleeping, poor hygiene.

Therapists need to be familiar with the warning signs and contributing factors. A simple risk assessment can be conducted by establishing the number of red flags that a client exhibits and the severity of these conditions. The factors listed below are suggested based upon sound research and associated empirical data. For more information on this topic the reader is referred to the National Institute for Mental Health (NIMH), Center for Disease Control (CDC), and the National Alliance on Mental Illness (NAMI) websites.

Contributing Factors

➤ Mental illness: Clinical depression is the biggest concern as discussed earlier. To a lesser degree, psychosis is a factor particularly if they are experiencing command hallucinations and/or delusions of persecution. The third major illness that relates to suicide is alcoholism and other drug problems, which obviously contribute to both depression and psychosis, not to mention irrational behavior.

➤ Physical illness: Loss of functioning (mental, sexual, physical) is a common denominator, especially for the elderly and those who have become disabled or disfigured. A chronic medical condition may be present for which there is no cure such as cancer, dementia, or AIDS. Another debilitating condition is relentless and excruciating pain. Medical illness is associated with over half the suicides in the 50-85 age bracket.

➤ Age: Statistically, a higher risk is present for those under age 19 and over 65. Suicide is most prevalent among those in the 65-85 range. It may arise in those who have lost a mate or lost functionality. Suicide is still the third largest cause of death among youth 15-24 (after accidents and homicides), largely due to the pressure and stress experienced due to being bullied, rejected, not making the grade, or anything that seriously drives down the self-image.

➢ Race: White males are generally higher risk, black male teens are even higher risk, and Native Americans are higher risk than other demographics.

➢ Gender: Males are three times more likely to kill themselves than females; females are three times more likely to attempt it than males. The fact is, males choose more lethal means. Females prefer pills or other non-violent means; males turn to guns or violent means. Violent means are more permanent because they are immediate, as opposed to nonviolent means which take longer, thereby increasing the chances of being revived. Women around 40-55 have increased risk due to the change of life, perception of decreased attractiveness, and loneliness (divorce, empty nest).

➢ Marital status (numbers are rounded): Single (20%) people are twice as likely to commit suicide than married (10%). Singles that end their lives are more often divorced or separated (40%), or widowed (20%).

➢ Psychosocial factors include death/loss of a loved one, divorce/separation, losing a job, financial straits, family history, and peer pressure or bullying as noted above.

➢ Personality factors include low self-esteem, obsessive, impulsive, agitated, panicky, hateful, immoral/evil, failure oriented, risk seeking, antisocial, and unattached.

➢ Religious orientation: Belief in Christ, Biblical knowledge, church affiliation, devoutness of faith, and an active prayer life reduce the prevalence. However, cult membership does not.

➢ Trauma: Sexual, physical, and/or emotional abuse (especially during childhood) can contribute to long term mental illness such as Major Depression and PTSD. The major culprits include molestation, rape, assault, and kidnapping. Significant trauma also occurs from vicariously experiencing abuse/assault, murder, dismemberment, natural catastrophe, and war. Clearly, experience in combat and witnessing the gore and horror of it is another common cause of PTSD and suicide.

➢ Stressors: Suicidal ideations can be brought on by excessive worry, conflict, morbid fear, frustration, neglect, doubt, and needs not being met. Another major factor is a recent, devastating loss; whether by death, abandonment, or divorce.

Therapeutic Interventions

➢ Education: Everyone can benefit from awareness of the risk factors, interventions, and treatment options to include clinicians, teachers, parents, and individuals.

➢ Crisis Intervention: Hotlines help to reduce the impulse by establishing rapport, clarifying the problem, assessing the seriousness of the threat, identifying available resources and support groups, considering the collateral damage to loved ones, and helping the individual develop a plan that provides a way out (alternatives).

➤ Risk Assessment: Several good measurement tools are available that assess suicide risk, which consider the factors presented in the above discussion. Certainly, a skilled therapist should know the warning signs and contributing factors and should be comfortable discussing this with clients in a non-threatening way.

➤ Medication: Often, serotonin levels are very low in the suicidal patient, which make the SSRI effective at moderating severe depression. Some antidepressants tweak more than one neurotransmitter or are more potent than others. Anxiolytics are also used to help the person destress and sleep. Antipsychotics help to subdue destructive and intrusive thoughts or ideas. A number of effective medications are also available to reduce cravings in the addict or alcoholic. Medication is an effective intervention and should not be viewed as weakness.

➤ Counseling: Treatment goals include ego strengthening, goal setting, cognitive restructuring, and disputing illogical beliefs. Reassess risk periodically. Develop a safety contract with at-risk individuals and provide essential emergency contact information.

➤ Environmental Modifications: The individual may need to alter certain people, places, and things in their environment (see lesson on Changes). A change of location may also help, as well as a change of scenery.

➤ Spiritual Edification: Suicidal individuals should establish a connection and stay connected to God through prayer, worship, and Bible study. Fellowship with other Christians is also beneficial. Help them refocus on the hope that lies ahead and the promises of God that he has a purpose, and that purpose does not include taking one's own life.

The Dilemma

Suicide is a sin. It violates the sixth commandment: do not murder. Some people of faith presume that suicide is an unpardonable sin; that those who kill themselves will not be allowed in heaven. But this is not necessarily true in many cases.

Certainly, there are some who commit suicide as a means of evading the law; they refuse to accept punishment for their heinous crimes. They know full well they are guilty and are not about to be captured. If they think they can avoid judgment they are mistaken. Their sentence will be far more terrible than that imposed by civilized society. That is because they already have rejected the gift of salvation that would have saved their soul.

- EXO 20:13 ~ God's sixth commandment: You shall not murder.
- NUM 35:16-31 (paraphrased) ~ Murder was defined in no uncertain terms in the Law of Moses, and a murderer was to be put to death.

Take the pedophile or the serial murderer who refuses to repent and change their evil ways; when finally caught they end their lives instead of face the music. Their only motive is to escape the penalty for their crimes. It is a rational decision. But they cannot escape God. They will certainly suffer the fires of hell, because they never sought the forgiveness and deliverance promised by a merciful and loving God. They spent their lives doing the very things God despises while despising God at the same time.

- 1 SA 31:1-6 & 1 CH 10:13 (paraphrased) ~ King Saul was wounded in battle and ordered his armor bearer to run him through, but he could not. So Saul fell on his own sword to avoid the shame of being killed by a Philistine; and the armor bearer did likewise. So Saul died for sins committed against the Lord, for not keeping God's Word, and for seeking counsel from a witch possessed with an evil spirit.

- MAT 26:20-25 (paraphrased) ~ Jesus told the disciples that one of them would betray him and they were very worried. He said it would have been better for that man if he had never been born. When Judas asked if it was him, Jesus said yes.

- MAT 27:1-10 (paraphrased) ~ Judas Iscariot realized he had betrayed an innocent man and returned the blood money to the elders. Instead of repenting or seeking Jesus, he went away and hanged himself. If he had truly known Jesus, he would have known that Jesus would have forgiven him, but he chose to take his own life than suffer the shame.

On the other hand, there are those who are not in their right mind whether due to insanity, an organic malady (like a tumor in the brain), dementia, mental illness, or some other affliction that prevents them from thinking rationally. Do you think God will hold that sin against them if they had an unrelenting and sincere faith prior to losing their minds? I think not. Most people who kill themselves are not in their right mind, but not all as explained before.

- JOB 4:6-9 ~ Is not your fear of God your confidence, and the integrity of your ways your hope? Remember: who that was innocent ever perished? Or where were the upright cut off? As I have seen, those who plow iniquity and sow trouble reap the same. By the breath of God they perish, and by the blast of his anger they are consumed.

The Bible teaches that there is only one unpardonable sin: blasphemy against the Holy Spirit. The Holy Spirit is the truth so those that blaspheme the Holy Spirit are essentially calling God a liar. They reject Christ and choose to go to their graves in disbelief rather than accept the free gift of salvation. Since they never rely on our Savior to absolve them of their sins they will have to make payment; and the payment is death.

- PRO 8:34-36 ~ Blessed is the one who listens to me (wisdom), watching daily at my gates, waiting beside my doors. For whoever finds me finds life and obtains favor from the LORD, but he who fails to find me injures himself; all who hate me love death.

- MAT 12:31 ~ Jesus said, "Therefore I tell you, every sin and blasphemy will be forgiven people, but the blasphemy against the Spirit will not be forgiven."

- ROM 1:20-22 ~ For his invisible attributes, namely, his eternal power and divine nature, have been clearly perceived, ever since the creation of the world, in the things that have been made. So they are without excuse. For although they knew God, they did not honor him as God or give thanks to him, but they became futile in their thinking, and their foolish hearts were darkened. Claiming to be wise, they became fools.

- ROM 6:23 ~ The wages of sin is death, but the free gift of God is eternal life in Christ Jesus our Lord.

Although Christ died for the sins of the world only those who believe receive atonement. Christ said he will forgive the sins of those who call on him, trust in him, and try to do better. People who continue to sin without repentance deny that he has the power to save them. Most of the time, they don't even care. They choose sin over faith and death over salvation, and therefore cannot be forgiven. Why? Because they don't want to be forgiven; they flatly refuse to believe, and therefore do not ask for forgiveness. Ask and you will receive (MAT 7:7); don't ask and you won't.

- ECC 7:20 ~ Surely there is not a righteous man on earth who does good and never sins.

- EZE 18:24-27; EZE 33:12-13 ~ God says, "When a righteous person turns away from his righteousness and does injustice and does the same abominations that the wicked person does, shall he live? None of the righteous deeds that he has done shall be remembered; for the treachery of which he is guilty and the sin he has committed, for them he shall die. Yet you say, 'The way of the Lord is not just.' Hear now, O house of Israel: Is my way not just? Is it not your ways that are not just? When a righteous person turns away from his righteousness and does injustice, he shall die for it; for the injustice that he has done he shall die. Again, when a wicked person turns away from the wickedness he has committed and does what is just and right, he shall save his life... And you, son of man, say to your people, The righteousness of the righteous shall not deliver him when he transgresses, and as for the wickedness of the wicked, he shall not fall by it when he turns from his wickedness, and the righteous shall not be able to live by his righteousness when he sins. Though I say to the righteous that he shall surely live, yet if he trusts in his righteousness and does injustice, none of his righteous deeds shall be remembered, but in his injustice that he has done he shall die."

- ROM 5:19 ~ For as by the one man's disobedience the many were made sinners, so by the one man's obedience the many will be made righteous.

Suicide seems the easy way out for the victim but leaves a heavy load for the survivors. In fact, it becomes a risk factor for those left behind. I have worked with countless patients who were suicidal, as well as loved ones of suicide victims. The former are much easier to treat than the latter. It is simpler to explain hope to someone who wishes to die because there is still time; but not so easy for those who have lost someone by suicide because time has already run out. How do you convince them that there is hope and a reason to keep going? Sometimes the following argument will help people with a death wish to reconsider taking their life: Remind them, if they don't care about their own life at that moment, they probably care about somebody who won't take their death so casually.

"The mass of men live lives of quiet desperation." – Henry David Thoreau

Scripture can be a comfort to those who are grieving such a loss. The passages below may serve to bring the bereaved new hope: though their beloved one took his or her life, they did not lose their soul if they believed. Looking backward, the grieving person will not see clearly; but looking upward, they will. They need to trust God who will bring all believers home when it's our time. So we must wait for him and cling to the hope of his promises (PSA 130:5). And luckily, as long as there is breath it's never too late to find him and be saved. For all we know, the loved one they just lost did precisely that; like the thief crucified at the Lord's side who repented with his last wish.

- PSA 130:5 ~ I wait for the LORD, my soul waits, and in his word I hope.

- LUK 23:42-43 ~ And the thief said, "Jesus, remember me when you come into your kingdom." And he replied, "Truly, I say to you, today you will be with me in Paradise."

- 1 CO 13:12 ~ For now we see in a mirror dimly, but then face to face. Now I know in part; then I shall know fully, even as I have been fully known.

- EPH 1:5,11-14 ~ God predestined us for adoption as sons through Jesus Christ, according to the purpose of his will… In him we have obtained an inheritance, having been predestined according to the purpose of him who works all things according to the counsel of his will, so that we who were the first to hope in Christ might be to the praise of his glory. In him you also, when you heard the word of truth, the gospel of your salvation, and believed in him, were sealed with the promised Holy Spirit, who is the guarantee of our inheritance until we acquire possession of it, to the praise of his glory.

- 1 PE 1:2-5 ~ According to the foreknowledge of God the Father, in the sanctification of the Spirit, for obedience to Jesus Christ and for sprinkling with his blood: May grace and peace be multiplied to you. Blessed be the God and Father of our Lord Jesus Christ! According to his great mercy, he has caused us to be born again to a living hope through the resurrection of Jesus Christ from the dead, to an inheritance that is imperishable, undefiled, and unfading, kept in heaven for you, who by God's power are being guarded through faith for a salvation ready to be revealed in the last time.

Probably the most famous suicide in the Bible was that of Judas Iscariot. After betraying the Lord his guilt overwhelmed him, so he returned the blood money and hanged himself (MAT 27:5). This is an interesting case study as it depicts someone who sees no way out, has condemned himself, and rejected the very one who could save him. If he knew he had betrayed innocent blood why didn't he seek forgiveness? It is a paradox, insofar as Judas knew Christ was pure and faultless but was afraid to ask forgiveness of his former friend. We are told that the devil was firmly established in the heart of Judas (JOH 6:71-72; JOH 12:4), and like the devil himself, he knew Jesus was the Christ and yet denied it. Did he go to his grave committing the unpardonable sin? Jesus said his betrayer would be better off had he never been born (MAR 14:21).

"The defects of the mind are like wounds of the body. Whatever care we take to heal them the scars ever remain, and there is always danger of their reopening." – Francois de la Rochefoucald

SUICIDE RISK ASSESSMENT

Factors Indicating a Proclivity for Suicidal Ideation (Part 1)

Add up the points to determine inclination: 0-11 = Low; 12-22 = Medium; 23-31 = High.

- Previous Psychiatric Hospitalizations: Once = 1; Twice = 2; Three or more = 3.
- Behavioral Warnings (Add one point for each behavior that is present)
    - Give away or destroy prized possessions;
    - Total withdrawal from social, recreational, spiritual activity;
    - Writing/Drawing/Role Playing of death scenarios;
    - Making final arrangements (last will and testament, do not resuscitate order);
    - Self-mutilation (self-inflicted cuts, wounds, bruises).
- Emotional Warnings (Add one point for each one presented)
    - Major Depression;
    - Loneliness and Worthlessness;
    - Hopelessness/Despair;
    - Intense Terror/Fear;
    - Anhedonia/Very low interest in life.
- Verbal Warnings ("I wish I was dead, the world would be better off without me, I hate my life"): Once = 1; Few =2; Several = 3.
- Comorbid Diagnoses (Add one point for each one presented)
    - Addiction (drugs, alcohol, gambling, pornography);
    - Chronic Pain;
    - PTSD;
    - Dementia, Psychosis (i.e., command voices; persecution, guilt, or failure complex);
    - Antisocial personality (i.e., immoral, evil, sociopathic/psychopathic).
- Severe Setbacks and Traumatic Events (Add one point for each one presented)
    - Rape/Molestation;
    - Physical Abuse/Gross Neglect
    - Recent Death/Loss;
    - Divorce;
    - Fired from job/Bankruptcy;
    - Disabling disease, surgery, or injury
- Demographic Factors (Add one point for each one)
    - Male;
    - Single/Divorced;
    - Unemployed;
    - 15-24 years old or 65+ years old.

Escalating Risk Factors (Part 2)

These factors increase the risk of suicide dramatically. Add up the scores to compute relative risk: 0-6 = Mild Risk; 7-12 = Moderate Risk; 13-18 = Major Risk; 19-24 = Profound Risk.

If the individual demonstrated Medium inclination as indicated in Part 1, bump up to next highest risk level; if the individual demonstrated High inclination as indicated in Part 1, bump up two risk levels.

- Death Wishes: Brief = 1; Occasional = 2; Persistent = 3.
- Suicidal Ideations with a Current Plan: No Plan = 1; One or more = 2.
- Lethality (if there is a plan)
  - Overdose = 1;
  - Crash Car/Run into Traffic = 2;
  - Stab Self or Slash Wrists = 3;
  - Hang/Asphyxiate/Shoot Self = 4.
- Elements of Plan (Add one point for each one elaborated): How; When; Where; Why.
- Prior Suicide Attempts: Once =1; Twice = 2; Three or more = 3.
- Lethality of Prior Attempts: Low = 1; Medium = 2; High = 3.
- Family History of Suicide
  - Distant Relative/Friend = 1;
  - Close Relative/Friend = 2;
  - Parent, Child or Sibling (Immediate Family/Inner Circle) = 3.
- Religious or Spiritual Foundation
  - Atheist = add 2 points
  - Agnostic = add 1 point
  - Believes in God = subtract 1 point
  - Has an active spiritual, religious, or church life = subtract 2 points

Activity

Suicide is akin to murder. What is your opinion concerning suicide and the law?

_____

_____

_____

What is your position on physician assisted suicide?

_____

_____

How do you think God judges the suicide victim?

_____

_____

_____

Have you ever contemplated suicide? If so, what changed your mind?

_____

_____

_____

What could you do or say to prevent someone from killing themselves?

_____

_____

_____

SUICIDE RISK FACTORS

- Depression, Psychosis
- Sexual, Physical Trauma
- Severe, Multiple Stressors
- Hopelessness, Worthlessness
- Extreme Guilt, Shame
- Addiction, Intoxication
- Physical Illness, Pain
- Loss of Functioning
- History of Suicide, Loss
- Persistent Death Wishes
- Verbal Warnings
- Suicide Plan
- Prior Attempts
- Lethality of Means
- Preparations for Death

CURBING VIOLENCE

OBJECTIVE	Learn about violence, the warning signs, treatment and prevention.
INTERVENTION	Discuss violence openly to include risk factors, consequences, and therapy and treatment options for offenders and victims.
PLAN	Identify the indications that you or someone else is prone to violence so that preventive measures and interventions can be implemented before something goes horribly wrong.

Violence is defined as an act or intention to harm or injure oneself, another person, or group of people. It is an unprovoked and unwarranted expression of internal turmoil converted into a destructive and forceful physical response meant to hurt, ruin, or spoil the target victim(s). With terrorism running rampant in the world, a great many people have become victims of violence. Using religion as a legal position does not justify violence. Refer to the section on Trauma for more about treatment for victims of violence.

- PSA 11:5 ~ The LORD tests the righteous, but his soul hates the wicked and the one who loves violence.
- MAT 26:52 ~ Then Jesus said to Peter, "Put your sword back into its place. For all who take up the sword will perish by the sword."

Violence has been a human problem since Cain murdered his brother Abel. Imagine that, the first two sons of Adam and Eve, and one is murdered and the other banished (GEN 4:1-15). There are innumerable contributing factors to violent rage; in the case of Cain it was a combination of jealousy, anger, and greed. Cain was dishonest with God when he offered a substandard sacrifice from the increase of his crops. But Abel's offering was from the best of his flock. Because God accepted Abel's offering and not his, Cain became jealous of his brother. This fueled anger towards his brother and towards God, which ultimately led him to hate and then to murder. Thus, violence begins with other sins, ignited by destructive thoughts which are not only negative but also irrelevant or false. If Cain had been repentant, and offered God a more excellent sacrifice, probably God would have accepted that offering and forgiven Cain. It wasn't Abel's fault because he was obedient to God; and it wasn't God's fault because he desired a proper offering. It was Cain's fault for being disobedient and blaming it on someone else. Rather than holding himself accountable and taking responsibility, he lost control and took his wrath out on his innocent brother. Maybe he inherited that trait from his parents, since Adam blamed Eve and she blamed the serpent for their original sin. They attempted to hide from God rather than taking responsibility and confessing (GEN 3:1-13).

- MAT 5:21-22 ~ Jesus said, "You have heard that it was said to those of old, 'You shall not murder; and whoever murders will be liable to judgment.' But I say that everyone who is angry with his brother will be liable to judgment; whoever insults his brother will be liable to the council; and whoever says, 'You fool!' will be liable to the hell of fire."

- 1 JO 3:15 ~ Everyone who hates his brother is a murderer, and you know that no murderer has eternal life abiding in him.

Violence is the road to total destruction which begins when we do not listen to our conscience but follow the lusts of our flesh instead. It is the result of distortions in cognition whereby a person ignores what is right, gives into temptation, deliberately does what is wrong and tries to justify it, cover it up, or otherwise deny it. The more a person engages in such counterproductive thinking the greater the chance it will lead to harmful and damaging behavior, not to mention death. So anything that promotes a lapse in judgment, cognitive impairment, disinhibition, or immoral behavior can steer one towards violence. Plainly put, it is another effect of "stinking thinking." Such thinking is usually a product of instrumental conditioning which fosters bad habits.

- PRO 29:7 ~ A righteous man knows the rights of the poor; a wicked man does not understand such knowledge.

"There are only two forces in the world, the sword and the spirit. In the long run the sword will always be conquered by the spirit." – Napoleon Bonaparte

"Nonviolence means avoiding not only external physical violence but also internal violence of spirit. You not only refuse to shoot a man, but you refuse to hate him." – Martin Luther King Jr.

Clearly, cognitive dysfunction is the principal underlying factor. There are numerous intertwining causes for distorted, irrational, and obscured thinking. Repetition of destructive relationships; a history of neglect and abuse; vengeful and hateful thinking; and/or illness or injury that predisposes a person to develop a negative mindset; a pessimistic view of life and humanity; a tendency towards iniquitous behavior; religious fanaticism; and/or dislike and disregard for others. Common reasons for such counterproductive thinking are as follows.

➤ Mind altering substances: drugs, alcohol, toxins, poison
➤ Mental illness: mood disorder, affective disorder, psychosis, impulse control disorder, personality disorder (especially antisocial and other Cluster B traits); childhood disorders such as conduct disorder, oppositional defiant disorder, and intermittent explosive disorder
➤ Organic problems affecting the brain: dementia, lesions, traumatic injury, illnesses that cause damage, certain degenerative diseases (like Alzheimer's, general paresis)
➤ Environmental conditions: violent background, bad neighborhood (places), gang activity, bullying, bad influences (repeated exposure to violent people)
➤ History of violence, neglect, abuse, trauma, abandonment, brainwashing

Probably the greatest contributor to a violent disposition is past history, beginning with prenatal care and postpartum nurturing. Many children are unwanted, uncared for, unappreciated, and/or unloved. The critical period is when the child should be developing a healthy attachment to the parents; of course, this is up to the parents. Poor attachments early in life often result in poor attachments later in life. Abuse and neglect experienced during childhood may be recreated when that person becomes an adult. Those who were victimized, terrorized, or abandoned will find it very hard to trust anyone, and unable to develop solid relationships. And because they were hurt terribly by the very ones they loved the most, they become likely to hurt others, especially the ones to whom they feel connected. The amount, severity, and frequency of the hurt and fear experienced are correlated with the amount of violence, fear, and hurt that person might exact upon others. Therefore, the greater the extent to which the psyche has been wounded the greater the possibility that the conscience will be degraded and the greater the likelihood of major self-control issues. It will take a lot of education and therapy for such a person to recalibrate his or her moral compass, and to keep their emotions and behaviors in check. Often, the negative conditioning leads a person into violence and crime; considerable reconditioning is required to reverse that programming.

Crimes that are considered the most violent in the criminal justice arena are murder, rape, aggravated robbery, and aggravated assault. Assaults occur twice as often as robberies, which occur four times more often than rape, which occurs five times more often than murder. Men comprise almost 3/4 of violent offenders. Ninety percent of attempted or completed rapes are committed by males; roughly 1/6 of women in the USA have been a victim of attempted or completed rape. The most prevalent form of assault has to do with domestic violence. It is the leading cause of injury to a woman, with approximately 1/4 of all women in the USA having been a victim of domestic violence; over six million children each year are victimized. Domestic violence is one of the most common calls that law enforcement responds to, as well as being the most dangerous. Another growing epidemic in America is youth violence. Youth murders in the USA outnumber by a factor of 10 other advanced countries in the world.

The following signs are an indication that a person may become violent without provocation. That is, violent offenders will display some combination of these factors.

- Bad childhood, sordid upbringing, deprivation, poverty, abandonment, abuse
- Poor care, living in squalor, bad environment, no supervision
- Product of a broken home (raised by single parent or neither parent)
- Victim of bullying in school, work, neighborhood
- Poor performance in school, work
- Cruelty to animals, vandalism, problems with the law, fighting
- Gang affiliation, carrying weapons, jail time
- Few friends, unhealthy relationships, low support, peer pressure
- Past experiences (victim, witness, perpetrator)
- History of mental illness; abrupt changes in mood
- Isolative and withdrawn; loner; stalker
- Easily angered, frustrated; short fuse
- Extreme thinking, overreacting, fanaticism
- Cold, controlling, and/or callous demeanor
- Easily distracted, disrespected or insulted; often feeling threatened, paranoid
- Lack of discipline and self-control; inappropriate in social situations
- Lack of empathy and respect for others; egoistic
- Substance abuse, chemical dependency; drug trafficking
- High risk behavior (drive fast, push the limits, sensation seeking, excessive spending)

> Fascination with articles, movies, music, Internet sites, and programs about horror, tragedy, violence, war, cruelty
> Argumentative; bossy, pushy; overly critical; loud and boisterous; verbally abusive
> Physical acting out (breaking things, throwing things; kicking, pounding; aggression)
> Dishonesty, lying/deception, betrayal

"The roots of violence: wealth without work, pleasure without conscience, knowledge without character, commerce without morality, science without humanity, worship without sacrifice, politics without principles." – Mahatma Gandhi

Treatment

It takes an experienced and confident therapist with a lot of patience on the one hand and courage on the other to treat violent offenders and victims of violence. Naturally, the usual client-centered skills and attributes are essential: empathy, genuineness, respect, honesty, positive regard, and acceptance. A non-directive approach is most effective, coupled with delicate direction, assigned homework, and inherent structure. The client must be given a sense of control, and the therapist must be flexible yet firm. The client also will need to be willing to listen and learn, because a great deal of the treatment will be instruction on coping with anxiety, guilt, shame, and/or anger; channeling the negative energy in a positive direction; and self-control/self-regulation techniques. A lot of the interaction will be examining behaviors, consequences, vulnerabilities, triggers, and emotions; unpacking the baggage and repressed memories; as well as developing alternative explanations and substitute behaviors.

- JAM 1:19-22 ~ Know this, my beloved brothers: let every person be quick to hear, slow to speak, slow to anger; for the anger of man does not produce the righteousness of God. Therefore put away all filthiness and rampant wickedness and receive with meekness the implanted word, which is able to save your souls. But be doers of the word, and not hearers only, deceiving yourselves.

Treatment is very much a team effort which is why it is critical that the client feels comfortable and safe, and develops rapport, mutual respect, and trust with the therapist. Offenders and victims have difficulty with relationships, so building the therapeutic relationship will be very edifying. It will be necessary to delve into sensitive material like issues of attachment and abandonment; trauma and abuse; arousal and reactivity. Sometimes spontaneous crisis intervention or redirection will be required. The pace should be mostly set by the client, and so should the agenda; certainly, the counselor can guide the client in the direction he or she needs to go if it is done with subtlety and supportiveness. Many of the humanistic attributes will be foreign to the client, but he or she will become receptive to a counselor who is gentle, caring, and sincere.

Additional important and effective treatment interventions will be group therapy and establishing support systems. Violent offenders *or* victims will do well in groups of people that have similar experiences and behaviors: people that they can identify with. Just make sure that they are not mixed groups of offenders *and* victims. There will be similarities in approaches and interventions between these two groups, as well as profound differences. For example they both need renewed hope, trust, and rational thinking; improved judgment, better decision making, and a capacity for intimacy. They both need to feel less guilty, isolative, withdrawn, and negative. But offenders need to learn to crank it down and be less pushy and aggressive; whereas victims need ramp it up, to be more assertive and less passive. Offenders need to exercise humility, compassion, and patience; victims need to become braver, courageous, and assertive. Victims need to become less fearful and offenders need to become more accepting. Victims need to feel less helpless and offenders need to feel less vulnerable.

"I object to violence because when it appears to do good, the good is only temporary; the evil it does is permanent." – Mahatma Gandhi

There will be severe judgment for those who are violent and hateful towards others. We are commanded to love one another as much as we love ourselves. We are not to place ourselves above others or regard others as below ourselves. There are many instances in the Bible where God's vengeance fell upon mankind, because they were vigorously opposed to God and all that he stands for. Those who live a life of violence usually suffer a violent end.

- GEN 6:11-13 ~ The earth was corrupt in God's sight, and was filled with violence. And God saw the earth, and behold, it was corrupt, for all flesh had corrupted their way on the earth. And God said to Noah, "I have determined to make an end of all flesh, for the earth is filled with violence through them. Behold, I will destroy them with the earth."

- PSA 7:16 ~ His mischief returns upon his own head, and on his own skull his violence descends.

- REV 18:21,24 ~ Then a mighty angel took up a stone like a great millstone and threw it into the sea, saying, "So will Babylon the great city be thrown down with violence, and will be found no more… And in her was found the blood of prophets and of saints, and of all who have been slain on earth."

A final note about dealing with violent offenders: many cannot be helped, treated, or rehabilitated. They are resistant to therapy and intervention. Some sociopathic personalities, pedophiles, and psychopathic deviants resist treatment because they don't care, they don't want to change, they cannot be saved, and they seldom are taken alive. Death is their solace or relief, or that is their delusion; regardless they do not fear death and have no remorse.

References

www.apa.org/topics/violence (American Psychological Association)
www.bjs.statistics (Bureau of Justice)
www.cdc.gov/violenceprevention (Center for Disease Control)
www.fbi.gov/stats-services/crimestats (Federal Bureau of Investigation)

ABUSE AND NEGLECT

OBJECTIVE	Learn the warning signs exhibited by those who have been victims of abuse/neglect or who are otherwise vulnerable to it.
INTERVENTION	Discuss neglect, physical abuse, and sexual abuse and recognize the warning signs, contributing factors, and preventative measures.
PLAN	Identify the symptoms of neglect and abuse and be prepared to intervene or report criminal activity. Develop measures to prevent you and your loved ones from becoming a victim.

Definitions

Any form of aggression against or exploitation of another individual can be viewed as abuse, be it sexual, physical, financial, emotional, or verbal. Obviously, the degree of intrusion and the extent of physical, psychological, and economic harm are correlated, and will vary according to how despicable the perpetrator and the act. The destruction from abuse of any kind can have long term deleterious effects for victims (and at times, perpetrators).

Sexual abuse is a grievous behavior that can cause permanent mental distress and often physical injury for the victim. It represents a forcible act by a deranged person to gratify lewd and sadistic desires. The abusive act could involve indecent exposure, presenting pornography, taking pictures or creating pornography, inappropriate touching, sexual contact (with the victim's genitalia and/or by perpetrator's genitalia), and penetration using any body part (into oral, anal or genital areas). Such a tragedy traumatizes the sufferer for life, regardless of age.

Physical abuse against children, the elderly, the handicapped, or a spouse is a very frequent and serious crime. To repeat, domestic violence is the most prevalent call that police receive, and it is considered one of the most dangerous. Physical abuse is a deliberate action that causes injury, pain, hurt or harm, or otherwise creates a dangerous or hazardous environment. It doesn't always include physical attack, assault, or battery. It can involve confinement, administering drugs, terrorism, and violent acting out behavior (breaking or throwing things, punching holes in walls, waving guns or knives, etc.). Transmitting toxins to a fetus is considered physical abuse of a child in many states in the USA.

Verbal abuse is less likely to invite law enforcement unless it disturbs the peace or is otherwise persistent and threatening. Especially in today's society, terrorist, suicidal, and homicidal threats are taken seriously. Emotional abuse is even harder to define and to prove but can be equally destructive over time. Insulting, ridiculing, blaming, criticizing, ignoring, isolating, denigrating, intimidating, humiliating, condemning, oppressing, and constant yelling are but a sampling of verbal and emotional abuse. Certainly, all forms of abuse can cause emotional damage. Over time, victims of such abuse can experience serious depression, poor self-image, and a broken spirit.

Neglect occurs anytime an adult who is responsible for another human being does not provide adequate care. Obviously, that duty includes providing food, clothes, shelter, nurturing, medical attention, financial support, and education.

There is a disastrous end awaiting those who abuse or molest another human being, especially a child.

- PSA 7:16 ~ His mischief returns upon his own head, and on his own skull his violence descends.

- PRO 11:17-18 ~ O LORD, you hear the desire of the afflicted; you will strengthen their heart; you will incline your ear to do justice to the fatherless and the oppressed so that man who is of the earth may strike terror no more.

- MAT 18:6 ~ Jesus said, "But whoever causes one of these little ones who believe in me to sin, it would be better for him to have a great millstone fastened around his neck and to be drowned in the depth of the sea."

- 1 CO 6:9-11 ~ Do you not know that the unrighteous will not inherit the kingdom of God? Do not be deceived: neither the sexually immoral, nor idolaters, nor adulterers, nor men who practice homosexuality, nor thieves, nor the greedy, nor drunkards, nor revilers, nor swindlers will inherit the kingdom of God. And such were some of you. But you were washed, you were sanctified, you were justified in the name of the Lord Jesus Christ and by the Spirit of our God.

Warning Signs

Parents, children, teachers, caregivers, pastors, health professionals, counselors, and therapists need to be well-informed about the warning signs for neglect and abuse. These signs apply to most all populations, but especially kids. Look for indicators in potential victims and possible perpetrators. The presence of particular signs, or a certain combination of signs, is a good enough reason to notify authorities. Remember, all reports of neglect and abuse should be taken seriously and need to be investigated.

Note that the signals of neglect are often present in physical abuse, and the signs of physical abuse are often present in sexual abuse. Therefore, the person may exhibit signs from all three lists. We will review each area respectively.

Neglect

➢ Poor hygiene (unkempt; bad breath, body odor; filthy body, hands, or hair)

➢ Frequent physical illness, infections, or infestations

➢ Needing dental work, glasses, immunizations

➢ Soiled or shabby clothes; inadequate protection during inclement weather

➢ Frequent absences or tardiness

- Begging, shoplifting, kleptomania
- Vulnerability behavior (risky decisions; hanging around unsafe environments)
- Unsupervised; left alone a lot; loners
- Indifference or constant excuses by caregiver/parent

Physical Abuse

- Presence of visible injuries
- Visible signs of prior injuries
- History of illness, broken bones, bruising, scars
- Inability to explain, or insufficient explanation for injuries
- Abject fear of specific people or places
- Discomfort around particular types of people (gender, age, etc.)
- Aversion to being touched or getting too close
- Easily startled; shrinks or flinches often
- Extremely anxious/apprehensive in some situations
- Cries when going home or to certain places
- Isolative and withdrawn
- Detached (especially from caregiver/parent)
- Running away from home (especially overnight, out of town)
- Inappropriate or regressive behavior
- Extreme behaviors/acting out (demanding, passive-aggressive, submissive)
- Lack of desire to do routine tasks
- Learned helplessness
- Sleep disturbance and frequent nightmares
- Not interested in eating; eating makes them sick
- Constant verbal abuse (excessive criticism, insults, yelling)
- Severe punishment or disciplinary methods
- History of abuse or domestic violence
- Caregiver's refusal to allow interviews, examinations
- Frequent relocating
- Police and/or protective services interventions

Sexual Abuse

- ➢ Difficulty walking, sitting, and/or exercising
- ➢ Physical pain or discomfort in the genitals
- ➢ Constant adjustment, or scratching in the genitals
- ➢ Sexual acting out or bizarre behavior
- ➢ Unusual knowledge of sexual phenomena
- ➢ Venereal disease, or other rare diseases/infections
- ➢ Dread of disrobing
- ➢ Frequent bathing, washing
- ➢ Bedwetting
- ➢ Lack of friends, no social life
- ➢ Age progression or regression; delayed development
- ➢ Suicidal ideations or attempts
- ➢ Overprotective, controlling, or secretive caregiver/parent

Contributing Factors and Consequences

Violence is a major factor; refer to problems contributing to violence previously reviewed. A history of family violence or sexual/physical abuse may be present, either in the immediate family or over generations. It doesn't matter whether one is the victim or an observer of the abuse, or both. Remember, trauma can be experienced personally as well as vicariously; both can have caustic effects on the psyche. Street violence is another variable, especially for kids that grow up in rowdy neighborhoods, are the target of bullies, or are involved in gang activity. Traumatic experience could include witnessing or experiencing a horrible accident, catastrophic event (manmade or natural), indiscriminant violence (like a drive by shooting), or combat. In short, repeated exposure to violence can condition one into a negative mindset leading to becoming a victim, a perpetrator, or an observer.

Another significant factor is substance dependency. Past and current substance abuse predisposes some persons to commit acts of violence and abuse. There may be a family history of alcohol/drug abuse by the parents or immediate family, exposing one to the lifestyle or the environment. The victim might develop his or her own chemical dependency problem. Intoxication breaks down inhibitions, promotes confused or irrational thinking, and leads to deviant behavior. Prolonged use can result in irreversible mental illness.

Mental illness itself is a common factor. I mean, you almost have to be crazy to commit monstrous acts against others, particularly a loved one or a child. It is not uncommon to find perpetrators with depression, dissociative disorder, or mood disorder. Psychosis also is a prevalent condition; look for paranoid or erotic delusions and command hallucinations. Certainly, a great number of perpetrators have antisocial personalities as suggested earlier.

There may be other ailments of an organic nature that cause a person to be deranged such as brain malformations, infectious diseases, or traumatic brain injury.

There is probably a proliferation of stressors in the perpetrator's environment (past and present) to include divorce, broken home, or lack of supervision; relationship conflict; social or economic problems; legal issues, incarceration, arrests/warrants; and/or medical or psychological problems. The person may have been raised or is currently living in unsatisfactory conditions, or is being deprived of essential needs. Perhaps the perpetrator was abused or traumatized, or witnessed the depraved behavior of others close to them.

Being constantly exposed to violence or stress makes some people think and act in strange ways, but that still does not justify immoral behavior. Maybe there is such a thing as temporary insanity but that is an inadequate defense for abusive, criminal, or deviant behavior which is seldom random. Perpetrators are either insane or not. However, abuse and neglect are premeditated, since they occur repeatedly over time.

Sometimes the abuse is a result of untrained or unskilled caregivers, or people that are simply unable to give the necessary care. Obviously, the young, handicapped, and elderly have special needs and this requires special abilities; it is not easy dealing with the demands, workload, or intensity of working with special needs populations. Some people are just not cut out for it; unfortunately they refuse to admit it or get help. Others just don't care because the field is lucrative and it's easy to do the bare minimum without getting caught. So the victim suffers due to their incompetence, disinterest, or laziness.

The long term effects of abuse and trauma on victims include a multitude of debilitating problems. These include, but are not limited to, the following.

➤ Anger and fear
➤ Guilt and shame
➤ Self-disdain or blame
➤ Poor self-esteem
➤ Attachment problems
➤ Adjustment problems
➤ Suicidal thoughts or attempts
➤ Disturbance in sleep
➤ Nightmares and/or night terrors
➤ Flashbacks
➤ Disturbance in eating or an eating disorder
➤ Sexual dysfunction
➤ Chronic pain
➤ Alcohol and/or drug addiction

- Major Depressive Disorder
- Anxiety Disorder, Panic Disorder, and Phobias
- Post-Traumatic Stress Disorder
- Dissociative Identity Disorder
- Conversion Disorder
- Personality Disorder (dependent or borderline)

Prevention

With respect to crimes against children, most penal codes include the infractions of the law listed below. Certainly, these laws would apply to any other age group, but likely under a different title. As a professional, you are obligated to inform law enforcement or Child Protective Services if you are aware of any criminal activity against, abuse of, or sexual behavior with a minor. All of the states have statutory regulations regarding sexual intercourse with someone below a certain age. To protect the elderly and handicapped you are obliged to report evidence of harmful activity to the authorities, such as Adult Protective Services or law enforcement.

- Solicitation of a Minor/Child
- Kidnapping and/or Aggravated Kidnapping (to include a family member)
- Indecency with a Child
- Improper Relationship with a Child (teacher or trusted adult)
- Photographing/Videotaping a Child (especially in various stages of undress)
- Injury to a Child
- Child Abandonment
- Child Endangerment or Neglect
- Physical Abuse of a Child
- Sexual Assault of a Child
- Sexual Contact with a Child
- Sexual Penetration of a Child
- Sexual Performance by a Child
- Enticement of a Child
- Distribution or Display of Material to a Child (i.e., pornography)
- Possession of Child Pornography
- Promotion of Child Pornography
- Statutory Rape

Certain precautions should be taught to potential victims of crimes, maltreatment, or exploitation, especially children. Every child should memorize their address and phone number. They should know and keep a list of names and phone numbers of trusted family, friends, and/or neighbors. They need to know who they can trust and who they can call. Even though someone may have visited the house, are a relative, or are familiar to the family in another way, that doesn't make them a trusted person. The fact that someone knows the names of family members is not evidence they know the family. Most of the time the trust list is a short and practical one, with contacts who are available, close, and who you would entrust with your life.

Kids need to know how and when to dial emergency 9-1-1; the rule of thumb is, when in doubt make the call. Kids should know never to go anywhere alone or without supervision, especially at night. They should be taught not to wander off at the mall, the playground, or the park. They should be accompanied to the bathroom in public places. It is okay to instruct them about the consequences of getting nabbed, running away, or disregarding rules. There should be a set of rules with respect to strangers such as keeping your distance, staying away from parked vehicles (especially vans), and not going near remote, dark, or hidden areas. The parents should cover typical scenarios like someone looking for a lost puppy, saying that their parent is in the hospital, or trying the candy temptation.

For latchkey kids, they should have rules about not answering the door or the phone. If it is the parent, the answering machine will identify the parent and the kid can then pick up the phone. There should be a list of names and numbers that the kid can call including how to contact the parents at any given time. Emergency instructions should be spelled out and rehearsed regarding fire, injury, or possible intruder. Hopefully there is someone they can trust in the neighborhood. Sometimes parents and children create a secret code system, which is fun and effective.

Let us now address crimes of abuse against adults (elderly, handicapped). Loved ones of these people should be taking an active role in the monitoring of services being rendered, especially by people they don't know. Do not count on the government or law enforcement to detect fraud or criminal activity. You need to do the legwork and call them or Adult Protective Services if you have some evidence. All too often, the family cannot be bothered and just dump the person in a foster home or nursing home. After that, the contact is limited if at all, and the poor soul just fades into obscurity. Of course, when the person dies, the relatives will be right there to ransack their belongings. This situation is ripe for exploitation. A great number of victims have been abandoned by the people they need and love the most.

Inadequate Care – This is the most frequent example of adult abuse, whether intentional or unintentional. Oftentimes, the caregiver doesn't care, doesn't have the time, or doesn't possess the necessary skills or knowledge to adequately address the individual's needs. Group and foster homes are often overcrowded, understaffed, or poorly equipped. They feed the patrons cheap food that is not very nutritious, the conditions are sometimes bordering on squalor, and there is often nothing for the guests to do.

Controlling and Overbearing Caregivers – These people take over the charge's very life in a dictatorial fashion. They force the defenseless victim into submission who has no recourse or anyone to rescue them or intervene. To keep the ward under control they might sedate the person or restrain them while they attend to their own agendas. They prevent loved ones or other professionals from visiting or talking to the patient, giving every lame excuse in the book. The victim becomes more dependent and less functional, and that is by design.

Financial Exploitation – This involves extorting money or goods by the caretaker to include forging checks, abusing credit cards, withdrawing cash, and forcing the individual to turn or sign over assets. They will steal expensive belongings, take money and claim it is for something it is not, and neglect paying the individual's bills until the money runs dry. They manage to get themselves named in wills, as beneficiaries, and powers of attorney. This will continue unless or until a judge intervenes and declares the individual incompetent, and/or assigning guardianship to someone else.

Swindles and Shams – The elderly are particularly vulnerable to a number of rackets out there that suck them in with false promises and prizes. Swindlers convince them to pay or donate money. The old folks are induced by gifts they will receive or prizes they have won; or they are coerced to give to a bogus charity through heartbreaking stories complete with wrenching visual graphics; or they are compelled to invest in a speculative or fraudulent investment with grandiose guarantees of giant windfalls. Once the money changes hands the perpetrator vanishes.

Healthcare Fraud – This seems the easiest scam to get away with, given that the government pays a lot of the bills and they basically do not have the resources to keep close tabs on providers. Commonplace practices include charging for services not rendered, overcharging, double billing, and charging for unnecessary services or medications. Of course, the patient is a poor source of information about these things and places considerable trust in their caregivers and healthcare providers. Thus, the abuser is seldom audited and may continue exploiting patients until they move on or get caught. Even then, the penalty seldom fits the crime; oftentimes it is a slap on the wrist. Worst case is they'll pay a fine or lose their license to practice, but they often find a way to resume in another state. The government, insurance companies, and patients get ripped off to the tune of tens of billions of dollars annually.

MORALITY

OBJECTIVE	Develop and maintain a solid moral foundation based upon the love of God and his mercy. The objective is to love God above all others and love your neighbor as yourself.
INTERVENTION	Define and discuss morality in terms of the higher power within us, and the inherent knowledge of right and wrong. Discuss the conscience which discerns the truth and what is good, and compels us to do the right thing.
PLAN	Establish your priorities in accordance with the will of God. Develop high standards of morality, responsibility, and ethical conduct. Display the love of God as an example to others.

In this book, holistic health has been a repeated theme: being healthy and whole body, mind, and spirit. That is, we exist physically, mentally, and spiritually; and all three need to be exercised for us to be completely healthy. This lesson focuses on our spiritual health. Morality exercises our spiritual component. Morality is exhibited in the Golden Rule: Do unto others as you would have them do unto you (LUK 6:31). This means we should treat others the way we would like to be treated: with love, respect, kindness, courtesy, humility, and patience. All of these attributes can be considered fruits of the Spirit (GAL 5:22-23; 2 PE 1:5-8)

Many people do not understand spirituality or deny that they possess a spiritual component. But even those who don't believe in God or don't engage in religious activities will often concede that they have a conscience. We all have heard the saying: Let your conscience be your guide. The conscience is a resource, a repository if you will for our knowledge of right and wrong. It does not lie, even when another part of us is compelled to do the wrong thing or not to do the right thing. When we sin the conscience kicks in and punishes us with guilt, making us feel ashamed. Don't you feel good when you do good things, and bad when you do bad things? Of course, we sometimes feel good after doing something bad, but the deed will not escape the conscience for long. Do your feelings get hurt when you hurt others? Guilt is a reminder to make it up to those we have wronged, and strive to discontinue the behavior. If we modify our errant behavior the guilt subsides. Hence, the Golden Rule: Most people feel better when they follow it.

"Right is right even if no one is doing it; wrong is wrong even if everyone is doing it." – St. Augustine

So then, one could argue that the conscience, or spirit, or heart (or whatever you want to call it) is the higher power within us. It is a wellspring of goodness and other spiritual gifts such as those identified above; it compels us to act in a virtuous manner. And all of these higher powers are a product of love. I have found that most people regard love as the greatest power of them all, whether they are religious or not. That statement must be true, seeing that God is love. He showed his great love by making the supreme sacrifice in order to save us. In response we should love God back; that is the greatest commandment. The second greatest commandment is to love all people, and that includes oneself.

- DEU 6:5 ~ You shall love the LORD your God with all your heart and with all your soul and with all your might.

- MAT 22:35-40 ~ And one of them, a lawyer, asked him a question to test him. "Teacher, which is the great commandment in the Law?" And he said to him, "You shall love the Lord your God with all your heart and with all your soul and with all your mind. This is the great and first commandment. And a second is like it: You shall love your neighbor as yourself. On these two commandments depend all the Law and the Prophets."

- 1 JO 4:7-8 ~ Beloved, let us love one another, for love is from God, and whoever loves has been born of God and knows God. Anyone who does not love does not know God, because God is love.

- 1 CO 13:13 ~ So faith, hope, and love abide, these three; but the greatest of these is love.

- COL 3:13-15 ~ And you, who were dead in your trespasses and the uncircumcision of your flesh, God made alive together with him, having forgiven us all our trespasses, by canceling the record of debt that stood against us with its legal demands. This he set aside, nailing it to the cross. He disarmed the rulers and authorities and put them to open shame, by triumphing over them in him.

- 1 PE 4:8 ~ Above all, keep loving one another earnestly, since love covers a multitude of sins.

Clearly, God's perfect love is the spiritual footing for morality. As God has showed us his unconditional love, so we are to show others that same love. We are to love others as much as we love ourselves; not love them more or love them less, but the same. We are all equal in the eyes of God and he loves each one of us the same; so should we. Jesus Christ is the human example of that love; he is the standard of morality to which we should aspire.

"All sects are different, because they come from men; morality is everywhere the same, because it comes from God." – Voltaire

The law of morality was written into each one of us by God himself. Everyone knows to do the right thing. If evil exists, there must be such a thing as goodness. This implies a moral law. For a moral law to be applied to all mankind there must be a supreme lawgiver. And that lawgiver, by definition, must be perfect; because only a perfect being could absolutely determine what is right or wrong. And God bestowed that knowledge upon everyone; it is another way in which we are created in his image (GEN 1:26-27; ROM 8:29).

- ROM 2:14-15 ~ When Gentiles, who do not have the law, by nature do what the law requires, they are a law to themselves, even though they do not have the law. They show that the work of the law is written on their hearts, while their conscience also bears witness, and their conflicting thoughts accuse or even excuse them.

- ROM 13:8-10 ~ If we live, we live to the Lord, and if we die, we die to the Lord. So then, whether we live or whether we die, we are the Lord's. For to this end Christ died and lived

365

again, that he might be Lord both of the dead and of the living. Why do you pass judgment on your brother? Or you, why do you despise your brother? For we will all stand before the judgment seat of God; for it is written, "As I live, says the Lord, every knee shall bow to me, and every tongue shall confess to God."

Those who deny knowledge of right and wrong, or contend that morality is relative are lying to themselves. Truth is not relative; something cannot be true for some and false for others. Truth by definition is absolute; facts are facts. If it is sunny right now in Tokyo, that fact is true for everyone, everywhere, at this time and forevermore. Morality is also absolute: everyone everywhere and at all times knows that cold blooded murder is wrong. There is nothing relative about it. Even the psychopathic killer knows that fact, though he probably doesn't care. But this is the key is it not: caring? And that requires love. We can choose right or we can choose wrong. Morality begins with the knowledge and ability to discern good from evil; but it is shown in words and actions. Unfortunately, all of us make the wrong choices way too often. But we can change that; we can do better. We can raise the standards for ourselves, though we cannot attain the perfection of Christ in this imperfect world.

"A system of morality which is based on relative emotional values is a mere illusion, a thoroughly vulgar conception which has nothing sound in it and nothing true." – Socrates

"Relativity applies to physics, not ethics." – Albert Einstein

"Virtue is a disposition, or habit, involving deliberate purpose or choice." – Aristotle

There are people who say that love is relative. Certainly, there are different types of love. In fact, the Greeks have several different words for love. The three that we are most familiar with are listed below.

> ➢ Eros – This is erotic or physical love. It is accurately described as sexual love or lust.
> ➢ Philia – This is brotherly love. It represents camaraderie; kind of a mental type of love. It is based on positive regard for fellow human beings. (Philadelphia is sometimes referred to as the city of brotherly love.)
> ➢ Agape – This is unconditional, perfect love. It represents the love of God. It is demanded in God's commandment to love him above all others. Agape love is of the spiritual realm. It is the most powerful type of love.

Obviously, spiritual love is what is needed. It is the greatest of the three mentioned above; the highest power if you will. Agape love is the foundation of morality. Such love is a gift from God. As God has given his love to us, we should give our love freely. It will not always be returned by those to whom you give it; but rest assured, it will come back to you.

- PSA 23:5-6 ~ You prepare a table before me in the presence of my enemies; you anoint my head with oil; my cup overflows. Surely goodness and mercy shall follow me all the days of my life, and I shall dwell in the house of the LORD forever.
- LUK 6:36-38 ~ Jesus said, "Be merciful, even as your Father is merciful. Judge not, and you will not be judged; condemn not, and you will not be condemned; forgive, and you will be forgiven; give, and it will be given to you. Good measure, pressed down, shaken together, running over, will be put into your lap. For with the measure you use it will be measured back to you."

It is resolved that unconditional love is the perfect standard, which is exhibited in the love of God towards all humankind. This is not unlike the love we have for our children: we love them unconditionally, whether they are good or bad. Loving others is not as easy sometimes, but it is the moral and ethical equivalent. So examine your standards and your priorities. Do you place God first and everyone else second (including yourself)? What exactly do you value? Values are reflected in your character, demeanor, and the way you treat others. The most understood among these values is the Golden Rule. Other common values that people of high moral character possess are as follows.

> Life is precious, especially if you believe in the sanctity of human life.
> All humans are worthy of being loved and forgiven as God commands.
> We should have positive regard and respect for everyone regardless of race, religion, age, gender, and socio-economic status.
> It is well to hope for peace and goodwill towards all people.
> Try earnestly to do the right thing; think about what Jesus would do before acting.
> When values conflict, choose the course of action that supports the greater good.

"Ethics, too, are nothing but reverence for life. This is what gives me the fundamental principle of morality: namely that good consists in maintaining, promoting, and enhancing life, and that destroying, injuring, and limiting life are evil." – Albert Schweitzer

"In law a man is guilty when he violates the rights of others. In ethics he is guilty if he only thinks of doing so." – Immanuel Kant

Our great nation was founded upon lofty ideals and morals: equality, liberty, and human rights bestowed by God. Our founding fathers revered these and other principles found in the Holy Bible. That's right: our republic was built upon the fundamentals of the Judeo-Christian faith system. The notions of unalienable rights endowed by our Creator and basic rights of an American citizen are provided in our founding documents. The Declaration of Independence, the Constitution, and the Bill of Rights provide a firm foundation for law and order. Morality is the basis of every legal system that ever existed. Morality represents obedience to the law: the laws of God, and the laws of men which are derived from them.

- ROM 13:1-7 ~ Let every person be subject to the governing authorities. For there is no authority except from God, and those that exist have been instituted by God. Therefore whoever resists the authorities resists what God has appointed, and those who resist will incur judgment. For rulers are not a terror to good conduct, but to bad. Would you have no fear of the one who is in authority? Then do what is good, and you will receive his approval, for he is God's servant for your good. But if you do wrong, be afraid, for he does not bear the sword in vain. For he is the servant of God, an avenger who carries out God's wrath on the wrongdoer. Therefore one must be in subjection, not only to avoid God's wrath but also for the sake of conscience. For because of this you also pay taxes, for the authorities are ministers of God, attending to this very thing. Pay to all what is owed to them: taxes to whom taxes are owed, revenue to whom revenue is owed, respect to whom respect is owed, honor to whom honor is owed.

"Let us with caution indulge the supposition that morality can be maintained without religion. Reason and experience both forbid us to expect that national morality can prevail in exclusion of religious principle." – George Washington

To reiterate, all laws are based on God's perfect Law, and Christ is the standard of perfect obedience to that Law. We are commanded by God to obey him and the laws of the land. Governments are established by God for our own good, to keep the peace, administer justice, and protect us. You are subject to the authorities and their laws, so if you violate the law you can expect consequences: not just from the justice of man but also of God. Doing no wrong to another and loving others equally will fulfill the laws of men and of God. But if there is conflict between the two, meaning that the requirements of society are in opposition to the requirements of God, then obviously God's Law trumps that of mankind.

The book of Daniel provides excellent examples of this sacred duty. Recall the story of Daniel in the lions' den. He was preferred over all the noblemen, advisors, and governors under King Darius because of his excellent spirit. Jealous rivals plotted against Daniel and tricked the king into issuing a decree that no god could be worshipped for thirty days but Darius. The evil schemers knew full well that Daniel would not obey this law, and made sure the king did not renege. Darius reassured Daniel that God would deliver him from the mouths of the lions, but the king still anguished about it all night. Daniel was spared for obeying God, while those who conspired against Daniel (and their families) became a feast for the hungry lions (DAN 6). Read also the story of Shadrach, Meshach, and Abednego who were spared from the fire for obeying God; but the fire became the fate of those that did not (DAN 3). Fire will be the fate of all who oppose God (REV 14:11; REV 19:20).

- ACT 5:28-29 ~ The high priests admonished the apostles for violating their command to cease and desist from teaching in the name of Jesus and blaming His death on them. Peter answered them by saying, "We must obey God rather than men."

- HEB 13:17 ~ Obey your leaders and submit to them, for they are keeping watch over your souls, as those who will have to give an account. Let them do this with joy and not with groaning, for that would be of no advantage to you.

Is morality of utmost importance? Well, yes and no. Civilized society cannot be maintained without it and our nation will perish if it dissipates. People suffer severely in its absence and others die needlessly. But nobody is capable of fulfilling the law alone, for all are guilty of disobedience and rebellion. Fortunately, God in his mercy allowed his Son to die in our place; otherwise, we could not be saved. Rebellion against tyranny which oppresses people is justified as it supports the greater good; but rebellion against God condemns us to death. Our response to God's love is our love; and our response to Christ's sacrifice is to give our lives as a living sacrifice (ROM 12:1-2). But remember this: In faith we are saved because of God's mercy and loving kindness, not by our obedience to the law (JOH 3:16; EPH 2:8-9).

- JOH 15:13 ~ Jesus said, "Greater love has no one than this, that someone lay down his life for his friends."

In group therapy, when I introduce the concept of morality, I often begin by making two columns on the board. Then I ask the participants to define morality in five words or less. Next I have them identify the source of our knowledge of morality, or the basis of right and wrong. The most common responses are listed in the table below. A lot of thoughtful discussion commences as we attempt to obtain a consensus about what morality is and where it comes from. Most people will agree that morality is a behavior or intention reserved only for Homo sapiens; it is not observed in any other species on the planet. Since we all possess the knowledge of good and evil, it is reasonable to assume that we are born with it, or otherwise are endowed with it. As our morality develops over time, we become more accountable for our behavior; and we establish personal standards, a moral compass, to which our conscience is compelled to obey. If we do not adhere to those standards, our conscience will let us know we have done wrong. We will feel guilty, even if we might not get caught. Thus, our knowledge of sin comes with an understanding of its consequences.

We are motivated to do right, not only because it is proper, but also because it yields positive results a lot more often than doing wrong. Further, doing wrong always seems to catch up with us, because there are natural as well as supernatural ramifications. And all the while, something inside us senses that someone is watching and knows, and judges. It is wise to maintain the moral high ground whenever facing a dilemma that has opposing costs and benefits, and aspects of good and evil; not just for our own benefit, but also for our family, society, and humankind. God will always be the standard for the greatest good.

Morality Definitions	Morality Sources
Beliefs	Upbringing
Norms	Laws
Values	Society
Doing the Right Thing	Religion
The Golden Rule	Spiritual Essence
Virtue	Conscience
Ethics	Discernment
Standards of Conduct	Higher Power
Caring	God, Jesus Christ
The Greater Good	Love

- JAM 2:10 ~ For whoever keeps the whole law but fails in one point has become accountable for all of it.

- JAM 4:17 ~ Whoever knows the right thing to do and fails to do it, for him it is sin.

- 1 JO 5:17 ~ All wrongdoing is sin, but there is sin that does not lead to death.

Activity

What is the source of morality and truth and how are these conveyed to us?

_____

_____

What are the first and second most important commandments of God?

_____

_____

See how many gifts or fruits of the spirit you can remember.

_____

_____

What are your **priorities**? Make a list and number them in order of importance.

_____   _____   _____

_____   _____   _____

_____   _____   _____

What are your **moral values**? Make a list and number them in order of importance.

_____   _____   _____

_____   _____   _____

_____   _____   _____

Compare your moral values to your priorities listed above. Do they match up? Do some of the things you value reflect the spiritual part of your being (spiritual fruit such as love, faith, hope, patience, joy, kindness)? What would you like to add to your list of values and priorities?

_____   _____   _____

_____   _____   _____

_____   _____   _____

The Four Pillars of Fate

The founding fathers of this great nation based their worldview and ideology on biblical principles and high ethical standards: equality, liberty, justice, godliness. They understood that the system of government being formed could only survive if these principles and standards were upheld from generation to generation. Our Constitution, Bill of Rights, and Declaration of Independence were the work of great thinkers: Washington, Adams, Jefferson, Hamilton, Franklin, Madison, Jay, Webster, Rush, Hancock, and others. God's Holy Word was central to the beliefs and philosophy of these men who knew that all virtues are fruits of the spirit. Collectively, the patriarchs comprised possibly the greatest think tank ever assembled, producing the framework which became the American Experiment.

The basis of our free society and democratic republic include three pillars suggested by Alexis de Tocqueville: "Liberty cannot be established without morality, nor morality without faith." They are etched in stone on our National Monument to the Forefathers (Plymouth Massachusetts, 1889): Faith, Liberty, Education, Law, Morality. Of course, law comes from morality and implies justice; education helps instill our knowledge of law and justice which is the fourth pillar. It is important to understand that all four pillars are essential; for without Morality, Faith, Liberty, or Justice the entire system collapses. A good analogy is a four-legged stool which will hold the weight of a grown man, unless any of the legs are fractured or wobbly in which case there comes a great fall. These American ideals originated from the Holy Bible, clearly evident in the following scripture.

- 2 PE 1:1-8 ~ Simon Peter, a servant and apostle of Jesus Christ, to those who have obtained a faith of equal standing with ours by the righteousness of our God and Savior Jesus Christ: May grace and peace be multiplied to you in the knowledge of God and of Jesus our Lord. His divine power has granted to us all things that pertain to life and godliness, through the knowledge of him who called us to his own glory and excellence by which he has granted to us his precious and very great promises, so that through them you may become partakers of the divine nature, having escaped from the corruption that is in the world because of sinful desire. For this very reason, make every effort to supplement your faith with virtue, and virtue with knowledge, and knowledge with self-control, and self-control with steadfastness, and steadfastness with godliness, and godliness with brotherly affection, and brotherly affection with love. For if these qualities are yours and are increasing, they keep you from being ineffective or unfruitful in the knowledge of our Lord Jesus Christ.

Morality is virtuosity: the idea of doing no wrong and/or doing the right thing. An entire lesson on morality was presented previously. To summarize, morality is governed by the conscience where God has placed that divine knowledge. It deteriorates in the minds of postmodernists and atheists who would shun their responsibility in favor of doing whatever they wish, and rationalize the behavior by claiming there is no absolute right or wrong. They maintain that such distinctions are a matter of opinion or preference rather than a collective rule, thereby diminishing unity among citizens and fidelity in relationships. There is nothing relative about goodness, notwithstanding the notion of acting in a manner that advances the greater good. While there may be a hierarchy in terms of how good or how evil, there is no mistaking good from evil. And the ultimate good is love.

Clearly, ethical behavior is not a result of unguided chemical processes in the brain; it is a conscious decision that requires forethought and sound judgment. That process is guided by the moral law, which is not so dissimilar to the laws of nature: for that which is immoral is often unnatural. However, it is only the physical laws to which the naturalists cling, disregarding that the laws of conscience, freedom, and logic cannot be observed in the physical realm but derive from the supernatural. Funny how those who deny absolute goodness, minimize evil, or downplay the importance of moral law fail to realize (or refuse to admit) that all legal systems and associated precepts are based upon a perfect standard which is God/Christ, and the Golden Rule conveyed in his command to love all people the same.

- GEN 4:6-7 ~ The LORD said to Cain, "Why are you angry, and why has your face fallen? If you do well, will you not be accepted? And if you do not do well, sin is crouching at the door. Its desire is for you, but you must rule over it."

- ISA 5:20 ~ Woe to those who call evil good and good evil, who put darkness for light and light for darkness, who put bitter for sweet and sweet for bitter!

- ISA 32:17-18 ~ The effect of righteousness will be peace, and the result of righteousness, quietness and trust forever. My people will abide in a peaceful habitation, in secure dwellings, and in quiet resting places.

- MAR 12:28-34 ~ One of the scribes came up and heard them disputing with one another, and seeing that he answered them well, asked him, "Which commandment is the most important of all?" Jesus answered, "The most important is, 'Hear, O Israel: The Lord our God, the Lord is one. And you shall love the Lord your God with all your heart and with all your soul and with all your mind and with all your strength.' The second is this: 'You shall love your neighbor as yourself.' There is no other commandment greater than these." And the scribe said to him, "You are right, Teacher. You have truly said that he is one, and there is no other besides him. And to love him with all the heart and with all the understanding and with all the strength, and to love one's neighbor as oneself, is much more than all whole burnt offerings and sacrifices." And when Jesus saw that he answered wisely, he said to him, "You are not far from the kingdom of God." And after that no one dared to ask him any more questions. (see also MAT 22:35-40; LUK 10:25-27)

Faith relates to trust. And who should you trust? God that's who, for only He can be trusted always and forever! To reiterate, virtue extends from morality, known absolutely only by God who is perfect in knowledge. If you are going to believe in something stick with the truth and seek moral superiority, because these are unequivocal. Absolutes are universal: a fact is true for all people and for all time; for example, that which is morally reprehensible is considered wrong in every advanced culture. Faith is not blind as the saying goes; but justice should be. Faith should be based on evidence, facts, truth.

That's why our faith and trust are placed in God alone who is the Lawgiver, and whose divine nature is revealed to us by the example of perfect obedience to the Law which is

Christ the Lord. Through Jesus, the imperfections of immorality are removed and the associated punishment for sin is covered in accordance with the atoning sacrifice of his lifeblood in our place. There is no other faith that matters or that can save or that can ensure total freedom, much less enable pure thinking and the expression of unconditional love – like the love of God which is the very foundation of morality and every order of laws developed by civilized societies throughout history. So most importantly, love God with all our heart, soul, strength, and mind; and secondly, love others as much as you love yourself; all moral laws hang on these two.

- ROM 3:27-31 ~ How can anyone boast then? It is excluded. By what law: works? No, by the law of faith.
- ROM 4:15-16; ROM 5:13 ~ The law brings wrath, but where there is no law there is no transgression. That is why it depends on faith, in order that the promise may rest on grace and be guaranteed to all his offspring – not only to the adherent of the law but also to the one who shares the faith of Abraham, who is the father of us all... For sin indeed was in the world before the law was given, but sin is not counted where there is no law.

Liberty provides the actual choice which is an unalienable right endowed by our Creator upon all human beings. Contrary to the position of secularists, liberty is the will to follow the way of righteousness not the freedom to reject it or simply to do our own thing. By rejecting righteousness they reject God and are therefore guilty of the unpardonable sin of disbelief. Of course, without liberty nobody could believe in God or choose him. But those who live for the world would rather place their faith in unproven theories and fanciful ideologies. Beware! Choices have consequences; and the relative costs and benefits will become readily apparent the second you act. We receive immediate knowledge of results by the reactions of people (like disgust or rejection), society (such as legal problems or incarceration), and our own conscience (disappointment, guilt).

If you choose wrong you violate the law and must suffer the consequences, which without faith you cannot bear. Though without faith you will not care for without it you have no basis for morality and therefore nothing to choose, but everything to lose. If we are unable to choose then we are mere automatons that act without discernment, awareness, or an intelligence of our own, and everything we do becomes pointless. God, who is in control of the entire creation, allows us to affect it by virtue of our free will. It is advisable to choose God, to do right, and to trust in his promises for in these we find true happiness and receive eternal life. Any other choice will yield temporary satisfaction or fleeting success at best, and that's it.

- DEU 11:26-28; DEU 30:19 ~ God said, "I am setting before you today a blessing and a curse: the blessing, if you obey the commandments of the LORD your God, which I command you today, and the curse, if you do not obey the commandments of the LORD your God, but turn aside from the way that I am commanding you today, to go after other gods that you have not known... I call heaven and earth to witness against you today, that I have set before you life and death, blessing and curse. Therefore choose life, that you and your offspring may live. "

- JAM 1:25 ~ But the one who looks into the perfect law, the law of liberty, and perseveres, being no hearer who forgets but a doer who acts, he will be blessed in his doing.

Justice is the fourth pillar; it depends on the other three, and they depend on it. It is written: Where there is no law there is no sin. If there is no sin and there is no law, then there is no morality. But as God gave us the Law, He likewise added discernment and free will. Defiance of any law brings the need for justice. There are natural and spiritual consequences for committing evil, as well as for doing good; these consequences are negative and positive, respectively. Everybody knows this whether they want to acknowledge it or not, whether they are theists or atheists, naturalists or creationists. Those who choose not to believe that there is a penalty for sin are lying to themselves. We are free to choose to obey the law; but when we violate the law we know full well that it is the wrong decision even before we chose it. Yes, we know when we have done wrong and we can be sure there will be repercussions; and that is a just reward. We also know there is no law against being good (GAL 5:22-23).

Our forefathers believed in equal representation under the law. That is, laws should be enforced equally regardless of social status, demographics, or accumulated wealth. Justice should be administered in accordance with the seriousness of the crime, the facts of the case, and extenuating circumstances affecting choice. Punishment or correction must be doled out accordingly to be fair; and there is nobody more fair or just than God. He gives us exactly what we ask for and deserve based on whether we choose him or not.

- EPH 6:7-8 ~ Render service with good will as to the Lord and not to man, knowing that whatever good anyone does, this he will receive back from the Lord, whether he is a bondservant or is free.

Once again, faith enters into the mix, because our faith in God justifies us and we are found not guilty. Believers are given a pardon which is undeserved thanks to God being merciful to anyone who believes on his promises, and therefore trusts in Christ for redemption and reconciliation. For those that do not believe, or reject his mercy, they will have to suffer the consequences, which is death. God offers all people his undeserved grace: an inheritance in heaven and payment for your sins. In fact, that grace is the motivation for our faith, given freely by the Holy Spirit to all who would receive it. Take it or leave it.

Such is the justice of the Lord whereby you can reject his offer and do it your way, and die; or accept it and do it his way, and live. Our founding fathers knew this and chose to do it God's way; and under God's guidance the nation has prospered. If we disregard God and the guidelines outlined herein there will be a great fall in this country (Guinness, 2012). Our fate is sealed in our choice to stand firm like the four pillars that uphold our nation, or sit idly by and watch it all come down.

- GEN 15:6 ~ Abram believed the LORD, and he counted it to him as righteousness.
- LUK 11:23 ~ Jesus said, "Whoever is not with me is against me, and whoever does not gather with me scatters."
- JOH 11:25-26 ~ Jesus said to Martha, "I am the resurrection and the life. Whoever believes in me, though he die, yet shall he live, and everyone who lives and believes in me shall never die. Do you believe this?"

- GAL 2:16 ~ We know that a person is not justified by works of the law but through faith in Jesus Christ, so we also have believed in Christ Jesus, in order to be justified by faith in Christ and not by works of the law, because by works of the law no one will be justified
- GAL 4:4-5; COL 1:19-22~ When the fullness of time had come, God sent forth his Son, born of woman, born under the law, to redeem those who were under the law, so that we might receive adoption as sons... For in him all the fullness of God was pleased to dwell, and through him to reconcile to himself all things, whether on earth or in heaven, making peace by the blood of his cross.
- TIT 3:4-6 ~ When the goodness and loving kindness of God our Savior appeared, he saved us, not because of works done by us in righteousness, but according to his own mercy, by the washing of regeneration and renewal of the Holy Spirit, whom he poured out on us richly through Jesus Christ our Savior.

Clearly, the pillars are gifts from the Almighty; they enable us to commune together, to grow and prosper, to realize our full potential, and to develop relationships with each other and with God himself who gave them. The pillars are as interdependent as our body, mind, and spirit are to life, and as the Holy Trinity to God. Without faith there is no virtue; without virtue there is no freedom; without free will there is no choice; without choice there is nothing to believe; without belief there is no justice; without justice there is no liberty; without liberty there is no morality; without morality there is no reason; without reason there is no meaning. Missing any one of the pillars renders life meaningless: with no control, purpose, direction, consequences, hope, joy, understanding, love, or future.

The degradation of integrity causes the entire structure to collapse into a world without faith, morality, liberty, and justice; resulting in the decay of society, the failure of the American Dream, and the fall of mankind. Other systems of government such as communism, socialism, totalitarianism, despotism, etc. do not depend on the pillars but deny that these gifts exist and are inalienable. Or, they endeavor to snatch them away as if they were given by governments and not God. So, without justice you are left with evil; without faith you are left with despair; without liberty you are left with slavery; and without morality you are left with chaos. Sounds like perdition... Or in the words of Patrick Henry, "Is life so dear or peace so sweet as to be purchased at the price of chains and slavery? Forbid it, Almighty God! I know not what course others may take, but as for me, give me liberty or give me death."

References

Guinness, Os (2012). *A Free People's Suicide: Sustainable Freedom and the American Future*. Downer's Grove, IL: IntraVarsity Press.

Suffering

Suffering is something everybody has to endure from time to time. It is generally associated with pain, which can be experienced physically and/or mentally (i.e., emotional pain). Emotional or mental pain can be caused by grief and loss, sadness and depression, worry and anxiety, anguish and distress, meanness and evil. Physical pain may be due to injury, illness, or extreme environmental or situational conditions. Suffering is most uncomfortable regardless of the source. But a broken spirit is perhaps the worst kind of pain, and the only cure is God's love (PSA 34:18; PSA 51:17).

Two primary explanations for suffering can be associated with the opposing forces of good and evil. God is good and this is displayed by his endless, unconditional, and powerful love. And because we know love, we also can be hurt when it's gone. For example, we feel pain when we lose someone we love, when our love is not reciprocated, or when someone we love is suffering; animals also exhibit emotional pain due to loss and suffering. Similarly, we suffer because of sin, which also causes others to suffer. Thus, suffering occurs when love is absent or evil is present. Love represents obedience and sin represents disobedience to God.

Suffering can be natural, unnatural, or supernatural any of which can result in mental or physical pain.

> Natural: Calamity brings hard times due to natural disaster, disease, hunger, degeneration of the body, and organic maladies; or due to injuries, mishaps, the elements, animal attack, or parasites. Thus, natural misfortune brings pain; continuous or severe physical pain often leads to psychological and emotional pain as well.

> Unnatural: The sin of mankind, reflected in the evil people do to others or themselves, is neither natural nor civilized. Antisocial, criminal, and maladaptive behaviors produce individual, social, and relational consequences and/or punishment. Of course, proper and upright behaviors generally yield positive outcomes. The cause-effect connection of behavior is based on our sense of morality and justice; this knowledge resides in the conscience of every human being. We know we have done wrong when we go against our moral standards or break the law.

> Supernatural: God himself tests us and judges us, and this can be painful in a spiritual sense (which is unlike mental and physical pain as it is troublesome to the soul). The guilt imposed by our conscience convicts us in order to correct us. The perfect example of spiritual pain can be seen in the suffering of Christ who took upon himself the sin of the world. Another example is the suffering of people who follow Christ but are rejected by secular society and often condemned, jailed, murdered, or tortured for their faith. Supernatural pain is quite evident in the suffering that will be the penalty for not following Christ, as represented in the eternal damnation of the unfaithful.

Suffering in general is a result of the fall of man; it is in our nature to sin because original sin is active in everyone (GEN 3). Therefore, most of our suffering is our own fault. Sin corrupts the thinking and perverts the mind. And because all have sinned, everyone will suffer the consequences, the principal consequence being death. But God has a plan to eliminate sin once and for all, thereby also eliminating death and suffering.

- JOB 3:20-26 ~ Why is light given to him who is in misery, and life to the bitter in soul, who long for death, but it comes not, and dig for it more than for hidden treasures, who rejoice exceedingly and are glad when they find the grave? Why is light given to a man whose way is hidden, whom God has hedged in? For my sighing comes instead of my bread, and my groanings are poured out like water. For the thing that I fear comes upon me, and what I dread befalls me. I am not at ease, nor am I quiet; I have no rest, but trouble comes.

- 1 PE 5:10 ~ After you have suffered a while, the God of all grace, who has called you to his eternal glory in Christ, will himself restore, confirm, strengthen, and establish you.

- REV 21:1,4 ~ I saw a new heaven and a new earth, for the first heaven and the first earth had passed away, and the sea was no more… God will wipe away every tear from their eyes, and death shall be no more, neither shall there be mourning, nor crying, nor pain anymore, for the former things have passed away.

"The greatest griefs are those we caused ourselves." – Sophocles

"Never to suffer would never to have been blessed." – Edgar Allan Poe

"To live is to suffer; to survive is to find some meaning in the suffering." – Friedrich Nietzsche

"The wound is the place where the Light enters you." – Rumi

It is ridiculous to blame God for sin and suffering, as he is the cure for it; he took the sin of the world and placed it on the shoulders of his only Son, Jesus Christ, to bear it for us (ISA 53). Thus, God suffers because we suffer; and instead of being outside of it as many skeptics suggest, he placed himself in the middle of it. He took the brunt of the sin of mankind from ages past to ages hence, and suffered to the extreme: more than any other human will suffer. So perish the thought that God doesn't care, or he is a bystander, or he won't intervene, or he can't feel suffering. Ponder the suffering and sacrifice of Jesus: how he took the burden of our sin upon himself and died a horrible death to make payment for sin. And ponder how he will eliminate sin and death at the resurrection, when he returns to take us home free of sin.

- PSA 34:19 ~ Many are the afflictions of the righteous, but the LORD delivers him out of them all.
- ROM 8:18-19 ~ I consider that the sufferings of this present time are not worth comparing with the glory that is to be revealed to us. For the creation waits with eager longing for the revealing of the sons of God.

Believe it or not, there can be positive aspects to pain and suffering; this is part of our education, our training if you will, for a greater purpose. Knowledge of suffering prepares us for future events and for our calling to be a disciple of Christ. Suffering is a personal experience, and provides wisdom unique to each person and different from all others. Your calling in life will be largely developed upon a foundation of such experience, making you uniquely qualified to fulfill a destiny meant only for you. Some of the things we can learn from suffering, setbacks, and tribulations are as follows.

Endurance and perseverance	Change of direction
Courage and patience	Acceptance and conviction
Caring and compassion	Strengthening of faith
Meaning, clarity, and purpose	Relationship and character building

"Although the world is full of suffering, it is full also of the overcoming of it. Character cannot be developed in ease and quiet. Only through experience of trial and suffering can the soul be strengthened, ambition inspired, and success achieved." – Helen Keller

"Whoever fights monsters should see to it that in the process he does not become a monster. And if you gaze long enough into an abyss, the abyss will gaze back into you." – Friedrich Nietzsche

"Meaninglessness does not come from being weary of pain; meaninglessness comes from being weary of pleasure." – G. K. Chesterton

Additionally, there are constructive responses to suffering that will not only mitigate the pain, but also will help others to cope with their suffering.

> ➤ Altruism: make it up to people or pay it forward; fix the past and build the future
> ➤ Forgiveness: of others and oneself
> ➤ Therapy: face the suffering, express it, deconstruct it, process it, and release it
> ➤ Calibrating the moral compass; raising your standards of ethics or performance
> ➤ Giving your burden to Christ
> ➤ Depending exclusively on God's Grace and not your own power
> ➤ Looking forward; reevaluating your journey and service to the Lord

There are destructive ways of dealing with suffering as well.

> ➤ Repression of feelings and thoughts
> ➤ Anger towards yourself, others, or God
> ➤ Fear of the past, present, or future versus trust in the promises of God
> ➤ Ignoring the reasons or causes of your suffering and that of others
> ➤ Converting suffering and pain into psychological problems

"Our fears are more numerous than our dangers, and we suffer more in our imagination than in reality." – Lucius Annaeus Seneca

Those who follow Christ will endure trials and tribulations because of their faith. This is because the secular world enables evil and promotes sin. Don't be dismayed when your faith is tested, for if you pass the test you will be greatly rewarded. Greater punishment is the reward for those who make no attempt to follow Christ or who persecute Christians.

- JOB 11:13-20 ~ If you prepare your heart, you will stretch out your hands toward God. If iniquity is in your hand, put it far away, and let not injustice dwell in your tents. Surely then you will lift up your face without blemish; you will be secure and will not fear. You will forget your misery; you will remember it as waters that have passed away. And your life will be brighter than the noonday; its darkness will be like the morning. And you will feel secure, because there is hope; you will look around and take your rest in security. You will lie down, and none will make you afraid; many will court your favor. But the eyes of the wicked will fail; all way of escape will be lost to them, and their hope is to breathe their last.

- 2 CO 12:7-10 ~ To keep me (Paul) from becoming conceited because of the surpassing greatness of the revelations, a thorn was given me in the flesh, a messenger of Satan to harass me, to keep me from becoming conceited. Three times I pleaded with the Lord about this, that it should leave me. But he said to me, "My grace is sufficient for you, for my power is made perfect in weakness." Therefore I will boast all the more gladly of my weaknesses, so that the power of Christ may rest upon me. For the sake of Christ, then, I am content with weaknesses, insults, hardships, persecutions, and calamities. For when I am weak, then I am strong.

- 2 TI 3:12 ~ Indeed, all who desire to live a godly life in Christ Jesus will be persecuted.

- 1 PE 3:17-18 ~ It is better to suffer for doing good, if that should be God's will, than for doing evil. For Christ also suffered once for sins, the righteous for the unrighteous, that he might bring us to God, being put to death in the flesh but made alive in the spirit.

- 1 PE 4:12-17 ~ Beloved, do not be surprised at the fiery trial when it comes to test you, as though something strange were happening to you. But rejoice insofar as you share Christ's sufferings, that you may also rejoice and be glad when his glory is revealed. If you are insulted for the name of Christ, you are blessed, because the Spirit of glory and of God rests upon you. But let none of you suffer as a murderer or a thief or an evildoer or as a meddler. Yet if anyone suffers as a Christian, let him not be ashamed, but let him glorify God in that name. For it is time for judgment to begin at the household of God; and if it begins with us, what will be the outcome for those who do not obey the gospel of God?

Many people believe that suffering is God's punishment, or that they are being chastised by God for their sins. But God forgives anyone who comes to him in sincere repentance and contrition. He took the punishment and the grief upon himself, and sets you free if you believe in him.

- LAM 3:31-33 ~ The Lord will not cast off forever, but, though he cause grief, he will have compassion according to the abundance of his steadfast love; for he does not afflict from his heart or grieve the children of men.

- JOH 16:33 ~ Jesus said, "I have said these things to you, that in me you may have peace. In the world you will have tribulation. But take heart; I have overcome the world."

- 2 CO 1:3-4 ~ Blessed be the God and Father of our Lord Jesus Christ, the Father of mercies and God of all comfort, who comforts us in all our affliction, so that we may be able to comfort those who are in any affliction, with the comfort with which we ourselves are comforted by God.

Everyone has problems; not to worry, it will pass soon enough. Don't let it bring you down, let God lift you up. Turn to the Lord in crisis and you will find solutions, peace, and comfort. And the Lord will use you to bring comfort to others, having overcome the trials and tribulations of life with that same comfort you received from Jesus Christ. Who better to serve than those who understand the pain of others (ROM 12:15)? You have the knowledge of sin, and of the agony Christ endured because of it; and you have the power of God's love to heal those experiencing pain and suffering whether physical, mental, or spiritual.

CARING AND DOING

OBJECTIVE	Understand that achieving goals depends on having a healthy desire and making sufficient effort to ensure success. Both of these attributes, desire and effort, work together to enhance performance.
INTERVENTION	Discuss caring and doing in the context of happiness, success, and growth. Identify how caring and doing interact with one another, such that obtaining positive results will rise and fall when your desire and/or effort go up and down, respectively.
PLAN	Put your heart into everything you do, however important it may seem. Do not get wrapped up in the worldly trend of caring about others or doing things for them only if they can do something that benefits you in return. Instead, freely give your time and love.

In a recent article by David Wong (pseudonym for writer and humorist Jason Pargin) the following proposition was posed: The world only cares about what it can get from you. This statement generates an interesting discussion about the state of this nation in general and morality in particular. In a way, the above assertion may be true of the world; but it is not the way God looks at the world. God's way is to care first and act upon that.

- JOH 3:16-17 ~ Jesus said, "God so loved the world, that he gave his only Son, that whoever believes in him should not perish but have eternal life. For God did not send his Son into the world to condemn the world, but in order that the world might be saved through him."

In this day and age people seem to care less and less; as a result, they end up doing less as well. While doing seems a more valued attribute than caring, a combination of the two yields the highest returns. I ask my patients what type of hospital staff members are appreciated the most, versus the least, etc. The following table illustrates the results that I obtain every time I conduct this workshop and ask that question.

	Patient Preferences	
	Caring	Doing
1.	√	√
2.	x	√
3.	√	x
4.	x	x

Obviously, everyone prefers practitioners on their treatment team that not only can get the job done, but also care about the patients, the job, and/or quality of services. But if only one of these two attributes are exhibited by the practitioner, people will select doing over caring every time. After all, if the helper cannot get the job done, or meet a person's needs, or help them with their goals, they have no business being there. It's one thing to have a great personality, a warm bedside manner, or an upbeat attitude; but if people are unable to perform, finish the job, or respond to a customer's needs, what good are they? Caring alone cannot make one successful, but being able to do something, provide a service, or meet a demand can.

Here is another example. Suppose a nice young lady is being escorted to dinner by a perfect gentleman. He opens the car door for her, holds her chair as she sits; he orders the wine, the dinner, and caters to her every need. He smiles a lot, and is very witty and polite. When the waiter delivers the bill the man reports to the young lady, "I seem to be a little short right now, do you mind covering the tab this time?" That would be an inglorious end to an otherwise perfect evening, would it not? Let's face it, if we are looking for a long term relationship, a soul mate, or whatever: it is one thing to be nice, chivalrous, friendly, and considerate, and yet another to put bread on the table, bring home the bacon, contribute to reducing one's burden, or help meet their needs.

Hence, Wong was right regarding the way of the world. However, we must not be so utterly concerned about what the world thinks, but what God thinks. God does everything with love, as should we. His love is the foundation of morality: the standard of perfection toward which Christians strive. Love enables us to value all human life, to do the right thing, and to obey our Heavenly Father. In fact, love is the answer to all our problems, shortcomings, and sins. The love of Christ is evidence that God's will be done. Thus, the best way of getting anything done is with love (e.g., caring): the way of God (MAT 22:36-40; JOH 14:6).

- LUK 6:31 (KJV) ~ Do unto others what you would have them do unto you.

If someone can get things done and does everything reasonably well, but does not care or stops caring, eventually their performance will fade. They will be content with doing the bare minimum to get by, or just enough to get what they want. On the other hand, if they truly care about their job and they endeavor to do the best they can, their performance will continuously improve. I sum up this point in the following equation: $D \times E = R^2$. Translated into English, it means Desire times Effort equals Results squared. I believe that results can grow exponentially when one has great desire (i.e., puts his or her heart into it), and when the effort expended matches or exceeds that required for the task at hand.

- ECC 9:10 (NIV) ~ Whatever your hand finds to do, do it with your might, for in the grave, where you are going, there is neither working nor planning nor knowledge nor wisdom.

"Is it not strange that desire should so many years outlive performance?" – William Shakespeare

"Everyone is made for some particular work, and the desire for that work has been put in every heart." – Rumi

"What the mind can conceive and believe, and the heart desire, you can achieve." – Norman Vincent Peale

Another suggestion Wong makes in his article is that the hippies got it wrong. I agree, but perhaps for a different reason. Their idyllic world of free love, flower power, and community of wealth stood in stark contrast with their philosophy of doing your own thing and if it feels good it must be okay to do it. It comes as no surprise that communism in general, and the hippie communes in particular, consistently failed. History has proven it. For such a system to work everyone must be equally productive and so should the payoffs be equitable; but there is no incentive for growth, no motivation to excel. Because: it only takes one person who does not pull their weight, or who does not want to share, or who freeloads on the community for the entire system to collapse. It seems that some of our leaders in government have been trying to impose a welfare state in this country. Their argument comes across as altruistic, appealing to the young, helpless, uninformed, or ignorant about what government can do for them. But there are hidden costs and a hidden agenda. It's about what they can get for themselves at the expense of others (to Wong's point). Politically induced socialism only serves to widen the distance between the oligarchs and the proletariat. The system is designed to make the citizenry dependent on the government creating a sort of learned helplessness. The ways in which such a situation is forced upon the citizenry is to take away liberty, destroy capitalism and free markets, impose taxation without representation, perpetuate mounting debt, and all the other things our forefathers fought against to create this great republic. Then why does capitalism fail? It is replaced by socialism, communism, or totalitarianism. And that's where we are headed if we cease to care about anything except what is in it for me.

"Ask not what your country can do for you; ask what you can do for your country." – John F. Kennedy

It is too easy to become complacent with the bare minimum, especially if a person doesn't have to do anything to receive it. Since they receive just enough to get by they end up doing as little as possible as well. Anyone who lives such a trite existence for very long also will cease to care in the end. Stop caring and stop doing; stop doing and stop caring. I have seen countless cases over decades of clinical practice where people have pursued with great vigor a life where everything is handed to them. For example, many wish to be declared disabled, receive a pension, and live in a medicated state (or sedated) indefinitely. After they succeed with that plan they begin to lose hope, purpose, and desire. Eventually they begin to hate their lives, often wishing it to end. They will rationalize that they cannot work or earn income as it will be discounted from their welfare check, food stamps, or whatever; thereby inhibiting them from achievement that would raise them above that level and beyond, not to mention lift them up.

"There has never yet been a man in our history who led a life of ease whose name is worth remembering." – Theodore Roosevelt

Can you see how desire and effort interact? In time, if caring drops so does performance; and when performance drops over time so does caring. But both can work in concert to produce great things. I have often stated that a person who thinks or feels negative will not obtain positive results. As a rule, they either will not do anything or they will do something negative, possibly regrettable. On the other hand, a person who is in a positive state of mind will be more likely to act, and will obtain positive results more often than not.

Have you observed persons who are enthusiastic about their jobs? They always try to do their best. They radiate positivity and it's contagious. Even a person who digs ditches for a living will be noticed and recognized if his attitude is optimistic and his performance is exemplary. He'll be the one that the foreman promotes to train others how to dig ditches the way he does.

"Enthusiasm is the mother of effort, and without it nothing great was ever achieved." – Ralph Waldo Emerson

Wong was not the first to observe that we are what we do. Doing is what defines us in the minds of others. The notion actually was advanced by Aristotle: We are what we repeatedly do; and Solomon: what you think you are (PRO 23:7). So if I consistently sell cars for a living I am known as a car salesman. If I sell a lot of cars I am viewed as a good car salesman. I have seen professional athletes who were at the peak of their success with everything they wanted and more, until they were caught in a scandal such as adultery, drugs, crime, or worse. After falling from grace so to speak, most people remembered the guy who used to play great basketball, golf, or football as the player that fooled around. Years later, after the abilities have faded and the player has left the game, which of these two ways was that person most remembered: for their athletic prowess or the way they destroyed their marriage, family, and career? He played a mean game but didn't care about his wife and kids. That's when his game began to falter; and he never did get it back, not like it was. He was more concerned with satisfying his libido than protecting his reputation. You see, there is not only the influence of doing but also of caring.

Priorities get out of whack when ethics goes out the window. If you are reviewing several applicants for the job or the team, with relatively equal abilities, who gets the position? I would submit: the one with the superior attitude, scruples, and caring. Other things being equal, ethics trumps. It is easier to teach a skill (doing) than a trait (caring). Certainly, you need to be able to provide goods or services that benefit people; but don't forget the importance of talent, education, and experience. Add to those humility and respect and you have a winning formula. If you cannot do any of these things you are not going to be a happy person. Self-esteem tends to drop the less you do or can do; and so does caring. All three go up and down together. This is why people who lose functioning through disease, injury, or age are the highest risk for suicide. They hate themselves because they are unable to do the things they used to be able to do, and then they lose the will to carry on.

In order to do something well, considerable work is required. This is where effort comes in. With sufficient effort a person can learn to do anything. With sufficient practice they can learn to do it well. It will take longer to master things that you have never tried, unless you have natural talent. But even then it still takes hard work and perseverance to excel. That's why a lot of people give up. It's too hard, or I can't get the hang of it; it's taking too long, or it's too late. We can come up with every excuse in the book as to why not to do something; but they will not outweigh the reasons for doing it. People are fascinated when others do something that impresses them; imagine the lift to one's self-esteem if he or she could do it as good or better.

"Satisfaction lies in the effort, not in the attainment; full effort is full victory." – Mahatma Gandhi

"Leaders are made, they are not born. They are made by hard effort, which is the price that all of us must pay to achieve any goal that is worthwhile." – Vince Lombardi

"The worst loneliness is to not be comfortable with yourself." – Mark Twain

Wong makes another good point here. He says that people waste a lot of time appreciating the creativity, talent, products, or services of others. Such people even take the time to critique how satisfactory or unsatisfactory were others' performances or products. Think of how much they could accomplish if they used all that time to develop, cultivate, and realize their own dreams, ideas, gifts, or interests. Allow your own brainstorms, inspirations, or beauty to motivate you to get busy, accomplish goals, or create a masterpiece. People get lazy. We want it done for us. We lose the desire long before making the effort. If you don't want to you probably won't. If you don't think you can you are unlikely to try. If it is very hard and time consuming you just might quit. It's the classic Approach-Avoidance conflict proposed by the late Kurt Lewin: the closer to the goal the greater becomes the resistance, at least for some people. Perseverance is definitely a virtue when backed by righteous motivation.

- PRO 13:4 ~ The soul of the sluggard craves and gets nothing, while the soul of the diligent is richly supplied.

Wong refers to the consequences of not doing something, based upon a quote from Christ: Every tree that does not bear good fruit will be cut down and thrown into the fire (MAT 7:19). Of course, Wong is applying the verse to works. It also is written: Faith without works is dead (JAM 2:17). Notice how faith comes before works; it is the motivation to act. And faith is one of the fruits of the spirit which generates production.

Our fruit is supposed to reflect our character. Certainly, if our actions are guided by the aforementioned spiritual gifts they will benefit others and will do no wrong to others. That's because our ethics or morality, that basic esteem we have for humanity, is founded upon God's love. This should be the motivation. Yes, we need to do things that benefit others; and we need to do things because it will help us meet our personal needs. But it should not be done out of selfishness or greed. Paul spoke when quoting Christ: It is more blessed to give than to receive (ACT 20:35). The world cares only about what it can get from you; such is the way of the world. I recommend that you follow the way of God and give freely.

Unfortunately, when you endeavor to do what is right and pursue the ways of the Lord, be prepared to be ridiculed, debased, and knocked down. Some persons do not appreciate others appearing to be above them or better at something, so they attempt to bring them down to their level. Others just put people down because it makes them look higher in their own eyes. They may be struggling with their own self-esteem issues; they are not getting anything done and are not too content with themselves because of it. So if you are excelling, succeeding, or obeying God, many will misconstrue such things as pious or arrogant and try to sabotage, criticize, or devalue your accomplishments. Just make sure you are not the one sabotaging your own achievement with negative thinking or self-deceit. That will really bring down your self-image; stop telling yourself you are worthless, unremarkable, or can't cut it. This is especially ridiculous given that God says you are precious, unique, and capable of anything as long as you acknowledge him as your coach, mentor, and creator.

- MAT 19:26 ~ Jesus looked at them and said, "With man this is impossible, but with God all things are possible."
- MAR 9:23 ~ Jesus said, "All things are possible for one who believes."
- PHP 4:13 ~ I can do all things through Christ who strengthens me.

In conclusion, to be successful in this world or in this society you must be able to meet a need; it's the law of supply and demand. The question you must ask yourself is, "What can I do?" People have expectations of us: our loved ones, society, government, and others that we meet. We place expectations upon ourselves as well. More importantly ask yourself, "What does God expect?" The mission of a child of God is to serve others; by doing so we serve God. And you will gain respect from others, confidence for yourself, and help from God. So evaluate your gifts: talent, expertise, character, experience. You might also consider additional skills and knowledge that you do not currently possess which are worth obtaining in order to be a better steward. When you attend to the needs of others, do so with a kind heart, with humility, and with love; and God will be pleased.

- ISA 6:8 ~ I heard the voice of the Lord saying, "Whom shall I send, and who will go for us?" Then I said, "Here I am! Send me."

- MAT 25:37-40 (paraphrased) ~ Jesus taught the people about the day of his return: The righteous will say, "Lord when did we ever feed you when you were hungry, or clothe you, or give you drink?" The King will reply, "I tell you the truth, whenever you did any of these things to help the lowliest of these your brothers and sisters, you did it for me."

- 1 PE 3:15 ~ In your hearts honor Christ the Lord as holy, always being prepared to make a defense to anyone who asks you for a reason for the hope that is in you; yet do it with gentleness and respect.

References

Wong, David (December 17, 2012). *Six harsh truths that will make you a better person.*
http://www.cracked.com

Final Activity

List several things that you know how to do reasonably well; these are things that you could make money doing and/or that would benefits others. In other words, these are things you can do now to get your momentum moving forward. So, what can you do right now?

_____ _____ _____ _____

_____ _____ _____ _____

_____ _____ _____ _____

_____ _____ _____ _____

Next list several things that you could be doing differently than you have in the past. These are changes that would yield better results in terms of efficiency and/or effectiveness. That is, these are things that you do all the time but could be doing better. So, what can you do differently?

_____ _____ _____ _____

_____ _____ _____ _____

_____ _____ _____ _____

_____ _____ _____ _____

Pick a few of the above items and explain what and how you would change to improve performance, achieve better results, or feel more satisfied (thereby raising your self-esteem).

_____

_____

_____

_____

_____

Now identify some things that you have never tried before, or that you never were very good at, which are worth trying or doing. See if you can widen your horizons and increase your potential by doing more. What can you master that you haven't done or excelled at before?

_____ _____ _____ _____

_____ _____ _____ _____

_____ _____ _____ _____

_____ _____ _____ _____

FRUIT OF THE SPIRIT

- Patience
- Love
- Beauty
- Faith
- Joy
- Peace
- Virtue
- Goodness
- Justice
- Purity
- Truth
- Hope
- Honesty
- Kindness
- Righteousness

- Temperance
- Humbleness
- Charity
- Gentleness
- Thoughtfulness
- Self-Control
- Mercy

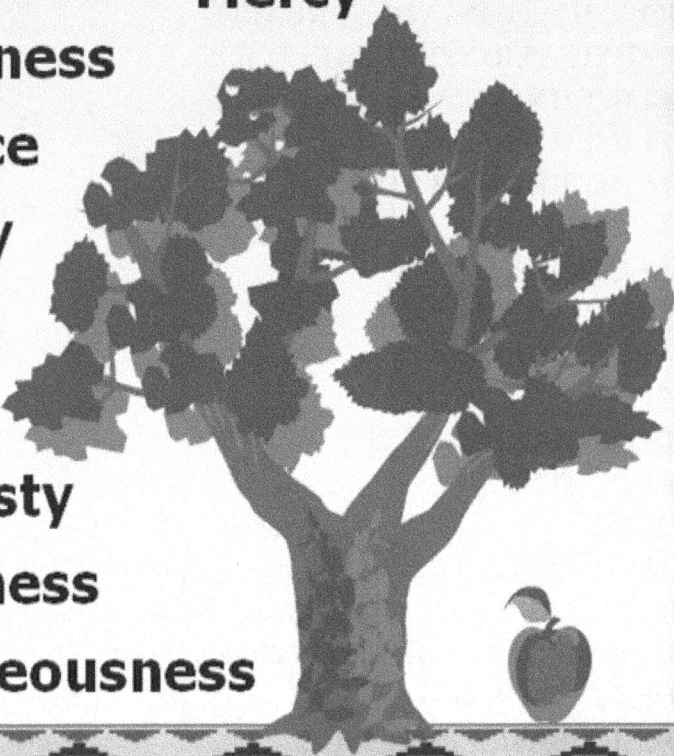

387

INDEX

ABUSE AND NEGLECT	356
ADDICTION	332
ARMOR OF GOD	204
ASSERTIVENESS TECHNIQUES	138
ASSERTIVENESS	131
ASSESSMENT TOOLS	34
ASSESSMENT	31
BAD HABITS	322
BEREAVEMENT	293
BIBLICAL PERSPECTIVES	12
CARING AND DOING	380
CASE STUDIES	4
CHANGE (CHRIST INSPIRED)	13
CHANGES	73
CHOICES	327
CHRISTIAN COUNSELING PHILOSOPHY	19
CLINICAL DIAGNOSIS	31
CLINICAL OVERVIEW	15
COMMUNICATION (NONVERBAL)	189
COMMUNICATION (VERBAL)	187
CONFLICT (INTERNAL)	269
CONFLICT (OTHERS)	271
CONFLICT RESOLUTION	269
CONNECTED	62
CONNECTIONS	152
CONQUERING SIN	200
CREATIVE THINKING	142
DECEIT	219
DECISION MAKING	174
DEVELOPMENT	40
DILEMMA	343
DREAMS AND VISIONS	150
DUMPING THE EMOTIONAL BAGGAGE	299
ENVIRONMENTAL MODIFICATIONS	70
ERRORS IN THINKING	165
EVIDENCE BASED PRACTICE	1
FORGIVENESS PROCESS	240
FOUR PILLARS OF FATE	371

INDEX

FRIENDSHIP	. . . .	247
GOALS DEVELOPMENT	. . . . .	40
GREED	. . . .	215
GRIEVING (STAGES)	. . . . . .	294
GUILT (HEALTHY)	. . . . . .	227
GUILT (RESPONSE TO)	. . . . .	229
GUILT (UNHEALTHY)	. . . . .	230
HELPING MODEL	. . . . . .	27
HELPING MODELS	. . . . . .	25
HIERARCHY OF NEEDS	. . . . .	118
HIGHER POWERS	. . . . . .	84
HOUSEHOLD OF SAINTS	. . . . .	259
IDOLATRY	. . . .	221
IRRATIONAL THINKING	. . . . .	164
LAZINESS	. . . .	220
LOSS	. . . .	293
LUST	. . . .	213
MANAGING ANGER	. . . . . .	98
MANAGING PAIN	. . . . . .	100
MANAGING STRESS	. . . . . .	92
MARRIAGE	. . . .	248
MORALITY	. . . .	364
MOTIVATION	. . . .	114
MULTICULTURAL FOUNDATIONS	. . . .	5
NEEDS (GOD HELPS)	. . . . . .	122
OBSTACLES TO SUCCESS	. . . . .	287
OUTLETS (MENTAL)	. . . . . .	306
OUTLETS (PHYSICAL)	. . . . .	305
OUTLETS (SPIRITUAL)	. . . . .	308
OVERCOMING ADVERSITY	. . . . .	198
OVERINDULGENCE	. . . . . .	322
PARENTHOOD	. . . .	253
PLANNING	. . . .	153
POTENTIAL	. . . .	149
PRIDE	. . . .	217
PURPOSEFUL LIVING	. . . . . .	86
REALITY TESTING	. . . . . .	181
RELATIONSHIP WITH GOD	. . . . .	257

INDEX

RELATIONSHIPS (BUILDING) 247

RELATIONSHIPS (IMPACT) 264

RELAXATION, BREATHING AND IMAGERY . . . 106

RESENTMENT AND FORGIVENESS 234

RESENTMENT PROCESS 234

RIGHTS 133

SELF- CONTROL MECHANISMS 92

SELF- ESTEEM 83

SELF-CONTROL 111

SPIRITUAL APPLICATION 28

SPIRITUAL ASSESSMENT 33

SPIRITUAL GROWTH IN COUNSELING 12

SPIRITUAL TOOLS 57

SUFFERING 375

SUICIDE PREVENTION 340

SUICIDE RISK ASSESSMENT 347

SUPPORT TEAMS 282

SYSTEMS MODEL 265

TEMPTATION 212

THEORETICAL AND EMPIRICAL FOUNDATIONS . . . 1

THEORETICAL FRAMEWORK 115

THERAPEUTIC INTERVENTIONS 342

TOOLS FOR CHANGE 57

TRAUMA TREATMENT 314

UPS AND DOWNS 83

VIOLENCE 351

VISION 157

www.ingramcontent.com/pod-product-compliance
Lightning Source LLC
Chambersburg PA
CBHW080243030426
42334CB00023BA/2678